The Global Diffusic

The diffusion of markets and democracy around the world was a defining feature of the late twentieth century. Many social scientists view this economic and political liberalization as the product of independent choices by national governments. This book argues that policy and political changes were influenced heavily by prior actions of external actors: not just other governments, but international organizations and communities of experts. Drawing together insights from economics, sociology, political science, and international relations, the contributors focus on four mechanisms by which markets and democracy have diffused through interdependent decision making: coercion and the impact of powerful countries and international actors; economic competition for markets and investment; learning from experiences of other countries; and emulation among countries. These mechanisms are tested empirically using sophisticated quantitative techniques in areas as diverse as capital account and investment policy, human rights and democratization, and government downsizing, privatization, and taxation.

BETH A. SIMMONS is Clarence Dillon Professor of International Affairs in the Department of Government and Director of the Weatherhead Center for International Affairs at Harvard University.

FRANK DOBBIN is Professor of Sociology at Harvard University.

GEOFFREY GARRETT is President of the Pacific Council on International Policy and Professor of International Relations at the University of Southern California.

The Global Diffusion of Markets and Democracy

Edited by

Beth A. Simmons,
Frank Dobbin, and
Geoffrey Garrett

CAMBRIDGE
UNIVERSITY PRESS

CAMBRIDGE UNIVERSITY PRESS
Cambridge, New York, Melbourne, Madrid, Cape Town, Singapore, São Paulo

Cambridge University Press
The Edinburgh Building, Cambridge CB2 8RU, UK

Published in the United States of America by Cambridge University Press, New York

www.cambridge.org
Information on this title: www.cambridge.org/9780521703925

First published 2008

Printed in the United Kingdom at the University Press, Cambridge

A catalogue record for this publication is available from the British Library

ISBN 978-0-521-87889-0 hardback
ISBN 978-0-521-70392-5 paperback

Contents

Appendixes

Figures

Tables

Contributors

FRANK DOBBIN is Professor of Sociology at Harvard Univesity. He is the editor of *The New Economic Sociology: A Reader* and *The Sociology of the Economy*. Dobbin's book *Forging Industrial Policy: The United States, Britain, and France in the Railway Age* was awarded the American Sociological Association's Max Weber Award.

ZACHARY ELKINS is Assistant Professor of Political Science at the University of Illinois, Champaign-Urbana. An expert on democracy, national identity, and institutional reform in Latin America, he is completing a book manuscript entitled *Designed by Diffusion: Constitutional Reform in Developing Democracies*.

GEOFFREY GARRETT is Professor of International Relations, Business Administration, Communication, and Law at the University of Southern California and President of the Pacific Council on International Policy. He is author of *Partisan Politics in the Global Economy*.

KRISTIAN SKREDE GLEDITSCH is Professor in Government at the University of Essex and Research Associate at the International Peace Research Institute, Oslo. An expert on conflict and cooperation and democratization, he is author of *All International Politics is Local: The Diffusion of Conflict, Integration, and Democratization*.

ANDREW T. GUZMAN is Professor of Law at the University of California, Berkeley where he is also director of the International Legal Studies Program. He was Commentaries Editor of the *Harvard Law Review* and also holds a Ph.D. in economics from Harvard University.

BRUCE KOGUT is the Bernstein Chair Professor at the Business School, Columbia University. He has previously held appointments at INSEAD and the Wharton School of the University of Pennsylvania. Kogut is a member of non-profit and profit boards in Europe, Russia, and India.

CHANG KIL LEE is Assistant Professor of Public Administration at Sejong University in Seoul, Republic of Korea. After receiving his Ph.D. degree on organizational behavior from Cornell University in 2001, he worked for the Korean government as a director of the OECD Asian Center for Public Governance. His research interests include public management reforms and governance networks.

J. MUIR MACPHERSON is an Assistant Professor of Strategy at the McDonough School of Business, Georgetown University. His research addresses the effects of international networks on the diffusion of management practices and the returns to cross-border mergers and acquisitions.

DENNIS P. QUINN is Professor in the Strategy, Economics, Ethics, and Public Policy group at the McDonough School of Business, Georgetown University. Quinn has spent more than a decade working on the causes and consequences of financial liberalization around the world.

FRANCISCO O. RAMIREZ is Professor of Education and Sociology (by courtesy) at Stanford University and a Faculty Affiliate at the Center for Democracy, Development, and the Rule of Law. During 2006–2007 he was a Fellow at the Center for the Advanced Study of the Behavioral Sciences.

BETH A. SIMMONS is Clarence Dillon Professor of International Affairs and Director of the Weatherhead Center for International Affairs at Harvard University. Her book *Who Adjusts? Domestic Sources of Foreign Economic Policy During the Interwar Years, 1924–1939* was recognized by the American Political Science Association as the best book published in 1994 in government, politics, or international relations.

DAVID STRANG is Professor of Sociology at Cornell University. His current research focuses on the diffusion of management practices within organizational communities such as management consulting, the Internet, and the post-9/11 spread of civil liberties resolutions across American cities.

DUANE SWANK is Professor of Political Science at Marquette University. An expert on comparative and international political economy, he has published widely in the world's leading political science journals and currently sits on the editorial boards of *American Journal of Political Science*, *Comparative Political Studies*, and *Journal of European Public Policy*.

A. MARIA TOYODA is Assistant Professor of Political Science at Villanova University. She was a Research Scholar at Stanford University's

Freeman Spogli Institute for International Studies and a Council on Foreign Relations International Affairs Fellow in Japan in 2006–2007.

MICHAEL D. WARD is Professor of Political Science at the University of Washington. He has previously held appointments at the University of Colorado, the Wissenschaftszentrum Berlin, and the Université Pierre Mendes France in Grenoble, France.

CHRISTINE MIN WOTIPKA is Assistant Professor of Education and (by courtesy) Sociology at Stanford University. She was previously Global Fellow at the University of California, Los Angeles International Institute. Her research interests include cross-national studies of gender and science, women in higher education, and international human rights.

Acknowledgements

We thank participants at conferences we organized on policy diffusion at Yale, UCLA, and Harvard for their insights and suggestions. In addition to the volume participants, we are grateful to Eduardo Castro, Barry Eichengreen, David Frank, Jeffrey Frieden, Richard Grossman, Alexandra Guisinger, Torben Iversen, Miles Kahler, Michael Mann, Peter Marsden, Lisa Martin, John Meyer, Helen Milner, Kathleen McNamara, Huw Pil, and Ronald Rogowski. We thank the Weatherhead Center for International Affairs at Harvard and the International Institute at UCLA and the Leitner Program in International Political Economy at Yale for support. Peter Gourevitch provided useful comments on an early draft of the Introduction. Simmons and Dobbin thank the Center for Advanced Studies in the Behavioral Sciences for fellowship support.

1 Introduction: the diffusion of liberalization

Beth A. Simmons, Frank Dobbin, and Geoffrey Garrett

The worldwide spread of economic and political liberalism was one of the defining features of the late twentieth century. Free-market oriented economic reforms – macroeconomic stabilization, liberalization of foreign economic policies, privatization, and deregulation – took root in many parts of the world. At more or less the same time, a "third wave" of democratization and liberal constitutionalism washed over much of the globe. Most economists believe the gains to developing countries from the liberalization of economic policies to be in the hundreds of billions of dollars. But they also acknowledge the instability and human insecurity sometimes left in liberalization's wake.[1] Political scientists argue that the rise of democracy has contributed to the betterment of both human rights and international security.[2] While the precise effects of these twin waves of liberalization are still debated, it is hard to deny that they have had a tremendous impact on the contemporary world. This book examines the forces that help account for the spread of political and economic liberalization. Why has much of the world come to accept markets and democracy?

Some commentators focus on the exercise of American power. According to this line of argument, the hegemonic United States – often acting through the Bretton Woods international economic institutions it helped create after the Second World War – has used a combination of carrots (political and military support as well as preferential access to American markets) and sticks (from strings attached to financial assistance to threats of military coercion) to impose its vision for political and economic liberalism on the rest of the world. Others see the decentralized process of technologically induced globalization at work. Sharp declines in the ability of governments to control cross-border movements of goods, services, and capital are thought to have forced countries to

[1] Dobson and Hufbauer 2001; Kaplinsky 2001; Prasad, Rogoff, Wei, and Kose 2003.
[2] Doyle 1986.

compete with each other for investment and market share by enacting political and economic reforms that reduce governmental constraints on finance and firms. Still another line of argument focuses more on the emergence of influential ideologies, from monetarism to glasnost to "rights talk," that may have little to do with political power or market dynamics.

This book puts these processes under the analytic microscope. The wave-like structure of liberalization's spread around the world suggests that these policy changes are hardly independent events. We are interested primarily in how a given country's policy choices are affected by the prior choices of other countries, sometimes mediated by international organizations and private transnational actors. There is considerable variation in the spread of liberal policies across time and space, which the contributors to this volume exploit to explore the processes underpinning liberalization. Our principal objective is to shed light on the causal mechanisms that explain the timing and geographic reach of liberal innovations. What has caused these new policies to diffuse across time and space? Conversely, what factors put the brakes on such diffusion, and why are some countries willing to take an apparently independent course?

The contending approaches to liberalization we outline share the assumption that national policy choices are at least to some extent interdependent – that governments adopt new policies not in isolation but in response to what their counterparts in other countries are doing. In this introduction, we review four distinct mechanisms through which interdependent decision making may take place – coercion, competition, learning, and emulation. We begin by describing the patterns of liberalization that we seek to explain. We then move on to distinguish *interdependent* decision making by national governments from the null hypothesis of *independent* decision making, which has been for decades the workhorse approach in comparative and international political economy. We then elaborate the four classes of diffusion hypotheses found in the literature, which are subsequently tested alongside one another and developed in the other chapters in this book. We end by previewing the findings of the coming chapters.

The spread of economic and political liberalism

We define liberalism conventionally. Economic liberalism, in the classic rather than the American sense, refers to policies that reduce government constraints on economic behavior and thereby promote economic exchange: "marketization." Political liberalism refers to policies that

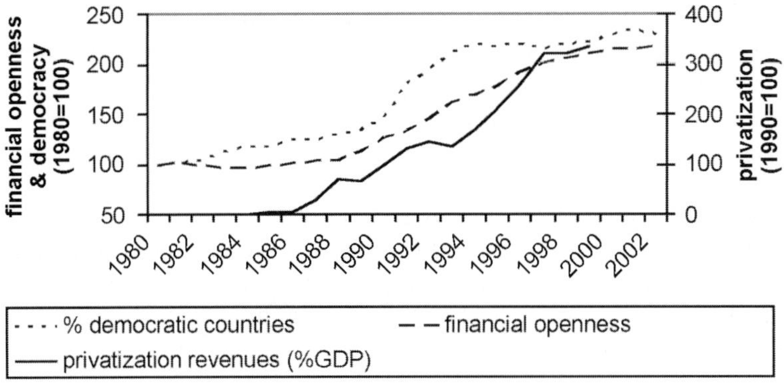

Figure 1.1 Political and economic liberalization around the world

reduce government constraints on political behavior, promote free political exchange, and establish rights to political participation: "democratization."

There is no doubt that both forces have been powerful facets of the global political economy in recent decades. Figure 1.1 documents this trend on three key indicators of liberalization in the 1980s and 1990s. The privatization of state-owned enterprises went from an iconoclastic policy idea in Margaret Thatcher's 1979 British election manifesto to a major element of economic policy in both developed and developing countries over the course of twenty years.[3] At more or less the same time, there was a dramatic opening of national economies to external forces – exemplified by substantial reductions in policy restrictions on cross-border capital flows.[4] But the scope of liberalization was not limited to economic policy. Perhaps the headline political statistic of the late twentieth century was that the proportion of democratic countries in the world more than doubled from under 30% in the early 1980s to almost 60% in the first years of the twenty-first century (while the number of sovereign states in the world also doubled to roughly 200).[5]

Moreover, all three curves in Figure 1.1 follow the classic S-shaped logistic curve associated with the diffusion of innovation, beginning with hesitant early moves to liberalize in only a few countries, followed by a rapid escalation in the trend, and finally a leveling off. In less than a

[3] Brune, Garrett, and Kogut 2004. [4] Simmons and Elkins 2004.
[5] Przeworski *et al.* 2000.

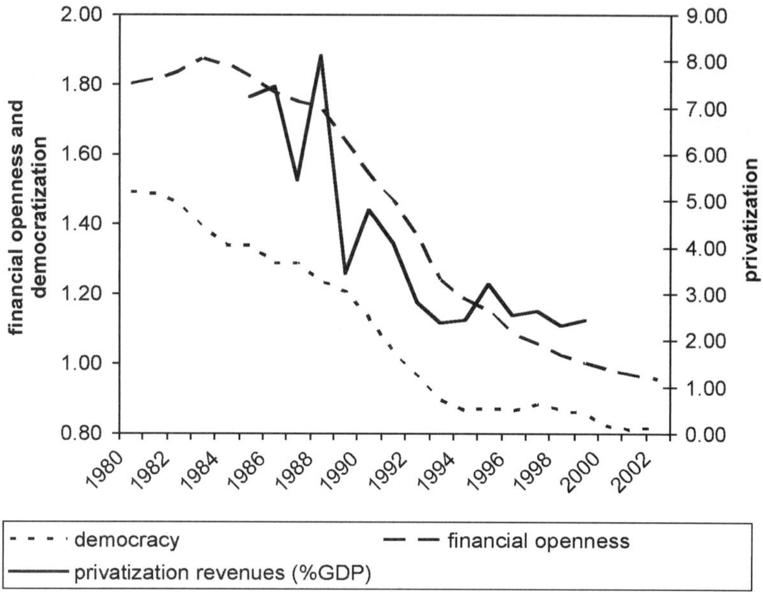

Figure 1.2 Variations in liberalization around the world (std. deviation/mean)

generation a new equilibrium level of much more liberalism appears to have been established in each realm.

Figure 1.2 demonstrates that in addition to this broad trend toward political and economic liberalism, there was considerable convergence in national trajectories.[6] Cross-national variation, defined in terms of coefficients of variation (the standard deviation of each distribution divided by its mean) declined substantially in each of the three areas of privatization (representing domestic economic liberalization), capital account openness (external economic liberalization), and democracy (political liberalization).

It is important to note, however, that these broad global trends toward liberalism belie substantial variations in the paths pursued by countries in different parts of the world. Figures 1.3 to 1.5 break down the global averages presented in Figure 1.1 by geographic region. As students of democracy know well, there have been three waves of democratization in recent decades (see Figure 1.3). Latin American countries began to

[6] For recent reviews of the "convergence" literature see Heichel, Pape, and Sommerer 2005; Knill 2005.

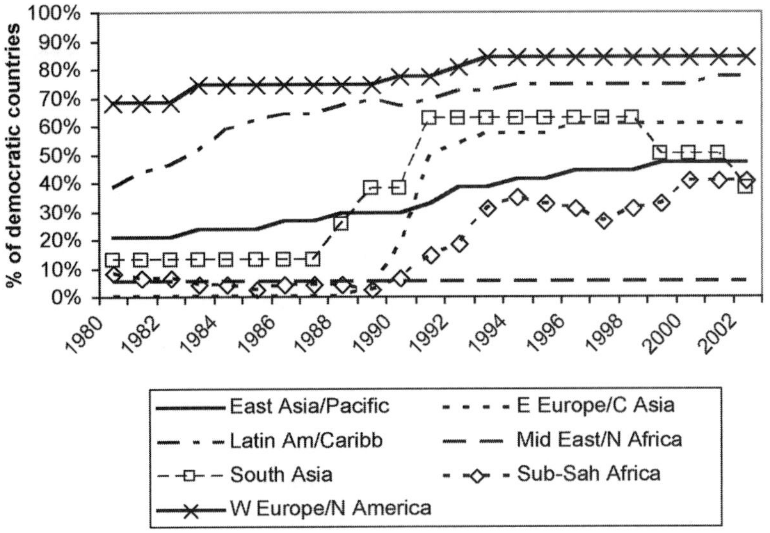

Figure 1.3 Regional variations in democracy

democratize in the 1970s, to the point where today the region is almost as democratic as North America and Western Europe. The same kind of pattern, though less pronounced, was apparent in East Asia and the Pacific. A second wave of democratization centered around the fall of the Berlin Wall and the subsequent velvet revolutions in the former Soviet bloc between 1989 and 1991 – but it should also be noted that the pace and extent of democratization was almost as great, and began just a few years earlier, in South Asia. The number of democracies in Sub-Saharan Africa also began to increase in 1989, though that region still lags behind Eastern Europe and Central Asia. Only the Middle East and North Africa saw no significant democratization in the 1980s and 1990s.

Figure 1.4 presents data on the openness of national economies to international financial flows with respect to: foreign direct investment (FDI); the buying and selling of stocks, bonds, and currencies across national borders; and international bank lending. The most dramatic feature of this figure is the rapid march among the countries of North America and Western Europe toward complete financial openness. The same general trend, though muted, obtained in Central Europe, East Asia, and Latin America. There were small moves toward capital mobility in Sub-Saharan Africa, but only in the mid and late 1990s. Financial policy remained relatively closed in the Middle East and in South Asia in the 1980s and 1990s.

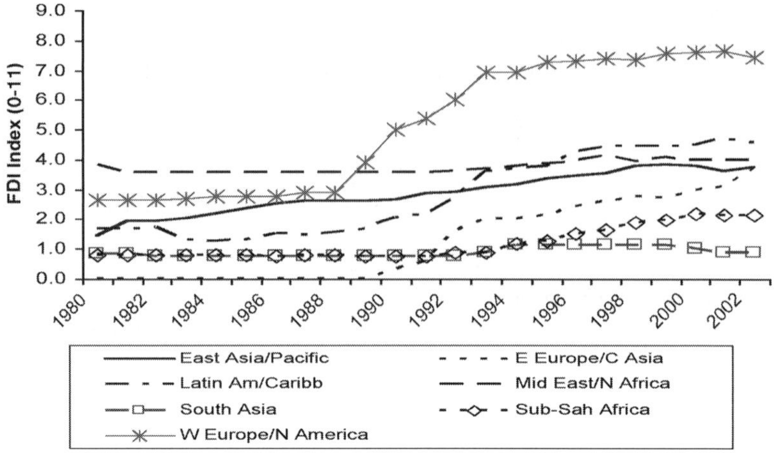

Figure 1.4 Regional variations in financial openness

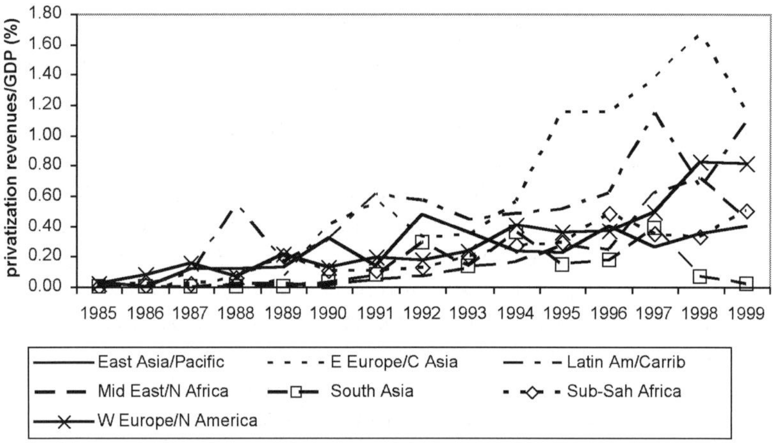

Figure 1.5 Regional variations in privatization

Finally, Figure 1.5 presents data on regional variations in privatization. Given that the data are measured in terms of the prices at which state-owned assets were sold (relative to GDP), it is not surprising that these curves are less smooth. Nonetheless, it is clear that privatization took off earlier and was more pronounced in Eastern Europe and Central Asia, Latin America and North America, and Western Europe than elsewhere. The radical and thoroughgoing nature of the velvet revolutions in the former Soviet countries is readily apparent in the case of privatization, no doubt in large measure because these countries had the most state-owned assets to sell in the 1990s.

Figures 1.3 to 1.5 demonstrate that despite the global trend toward liberalism, there were important differences in the trajectories of different parts of the world – differences across regions, over time, and among different dimensions of liberalization. The Middle East and North Africa did not liberalize much, if at all, in the 1980s and 1990s. Latin America democratized and marketized gradually over the whole period, whereas the shift from state socialism to capitalist democracy was much more abrupt in Eastern Europe.

Clearly, some countries and even entire regions seem exempt from the general liberalizing trends. How do we understand these variations? Growing literatures in political science and sociology point to different dynamic explanations for such policy clustering, which we dub "diffusion." Let us now define diffusion and distinguish it from alternative causal processes.

Policy diffusion – and its alternatives

International policy diffusion occurs when government policy decisions in a given country are systematically conditioned by prior policy choices made in other countries (sometimes mediated by the behavior of international organizations or private actors and organizations). Theories of diffusion have pointed to diverse mechanisms ranging from Bayesian learning to rational competition through hegemonic domination to unthinking emulation of leaders. Theories of diffusion encompass a wide array of assumptions about who the primary actors are, what motivates their behavior, the nature and extent of the information on which they base decisions, and their ultimate goals.

But what theorists of diffusion explicitly *reject* is the notion that processes of policy and political change can adequately be understood by conceiving of national governments as making decisions independently of each other. Policy independence is thus the null hypothesis that motivates our inquiry.[7] Most cross-national social science research focuses on variants of this null hypothesis, developing explanations based on the specific conditions governments encounter. For example, differences in economic development,[8] social cleavages,[9] national institutions,[10] and elite interactions[11] have all been argued to play important roles in democratization.

[7] Compare for example Lenschow, Liefferink, and Veenman 2005.
[8] Przeworski *et al.* 2000. [9] Collier 1999. [10] Linz and Stepan 1996.
[11] O'Donnell, Schmitter, and Whitehead 1986.

Students of the spread of democracy, and of market institutions, frequently presume that decisions to democratize are made in isolation.

A small literature has developed that takes seriously the international diffusion of democracy,[12] but theoretical development and empirical testing are still at a very early stage. Perhaps more surprisingly, the political economy literature is also dominated by research that assumes independent policy choice across countries. Political economists have analyzed restrictions on cross-border capital flows as tools of economic repression[13] or reasoned that such controls could be explained by partisanship, domestic cleavages, and governments' desires for seigniorage.[14] Recent work on the choice of monetary and exchange rate institutions also focuses on the null hypothesis, as amply demonstrated by a recent special issue of *International Organization*, which focused on domestic political pressures,[15] domestic veto players,[16] federalism,[17] coalition governments,[18] and domestic policy transparency[19] as determinants of national monetary institutions and policies.

In the past twenty years, an important strand of research in political economy has linked domestic policy choice with constraints, pressures, and opportunities generated by the international economy. Peter Gourevitch studied the impact of position in the international economy on domestic responses to economic crisis.[20] Ronald Rogowski analyzed trade policy coalitions in comparative advantage terms.[21] Jeffry Frieden hypothesized that the preferences of domestic groups vis-à-vis financial liberalization and exchange rate policy were the function of their specific endowments.[22] But these studies tend to reduce "external influences" to simple exogenous factors, notably changes in relative prices around the world.[23] None explicitly explores the possibility of interdependent decision making – the impact of policy choices in other countries on the behavior of governments at home.

Frieden and Rogowski posited the simplest possible argument to explain economic liberalization in recent decades. They contend that "exogenous easing," such as declining transport and communication costs, has greatly increased the opportunity costs of closure.[24] Over time, these costs have mounted on governments, increasing the incentive to open their economies. As Geoffrey Garrett and Peter Lange were quick

[12] See Huntington 1991; Markoff 1996; O'Loughlin, Ward, Lofdahl, Cohen, Brown, Reilly, Gleditsch, and Shin 1998; Starr 1991.
[13] Giovannini and De Melo 1993.
[14] Epstein and Schor 1992; Grilli and Milesi-Ferretti 1995; Quinn and Inclan 1997.
[15] Clark 2002. [16] Keefer and Stasavage 2002. [17] Hallerberg 2002.
[18] Bernhard and Leblang 2002. [19] Broz 2002. [20] Gourevitch 1986.
[21] Rogowski 1989. [22] Frieden 1991. [23] Keohane and Milner 1996.
[24] Frieden and Rogowski 1996.

to note, however, the pace and extent of liberalization have varied substantially across countries.[25] Garrett and Lange argued that it was critical to take seriously this variation, rather than dismissing it as "noise," as theorists of exogenous easing tended to do. They proposed a framework for analyzing how constellations of domestic interests and institutions mediate between lower costs of international movements and national policy liberalization. Their focus, however, was still squarely on domestic institutions, with no serious thought given to external policy influences.

Our intention is not to deny that relative prices and other factors exogenous to the decision-making environment in any one country affect policy choice. But from our perspective, the critical analytic point is that exogenous shocks – such as changing world prices – are a commonly experienced phenomenon to which governments must decide how to respond. Their responses are no doubt influenced in a "bottom-up" fashion by conditions and institutions within their own countries.[26] But they are surely also affected by the decisions and behavior of other countries. The challenge facing theorists of international policy diffusion is first to demonstrate that domestic political and economic factors cannot alone predict when governments adopt new policies, and then to develop and test hypotheses that distinguish among the several possible mechanisms of diffusion. We argue that government decision making in these critical areas has in fact been highly interdependent and that the mechanisms of diffusion can potentially be teased out in empirical analyses.

Mechanisms of global diffusion

There is an affinity between the recent "strategic turn" in the social sciences and attention to international policy diffusion.[27] But diffusion processes are characteristically uncoordinated[28] and cannot always easily be subsumed under the umbrella of fully informed, rational decision making. Indeed, diffusion is a much broader phenomenon whose study long predates the influence of game theory.

Anthropologists in the first half of the twentieth century "laid primary stress on diffusion, that is, the process of adopting or borrowing by one culture from another various devices, implements, institutions, and beliefs."[29] More recently, sociologists have argued that nations mimic

[25] Garrett and Lange 1995.
[26] See for example Gilardi's study of the diffusion of independent regulatory agencies; Gilardi 2005.
[27] Lake and Powell 1999. [28] Elkins and Simmons 2005. [29] Malinowski 1944: iii. 17.

their successful peers almost ritualistically.[30] Economists debate whether there is a rational/material base to international financial crises, or whether they result from "contagious" herd behavior.[31] Political scientists have incorporated the diffusion of ideas into their accounts of the choice of economic policies.[32] Students of organizational behavior model international networks among people and firms that are said to drive the diffusion of technology and management practices.[33]

But which of these processes is the most important, and under what circumstances does each operate? How can we distinguish among them, both theoretically and empirically? This introduction distinguishes among four causal mechanisms of international diffusion: *coercion*, *competition*, *learning*, and *emulation*. In practice, of course, the diffusion mechanisms we discuss are sometimes commingled and the lines between them are not always sharp. Nonetheless, we believe that clearly staking out the theoretical terrain is a precondition to social scientific progress on a critical dynamic in world politics that is all too often shrouded in imprecise thinking by scholars who talk past each other while preaching to the converted.

Coercion

One prominent explanation for the spread of economic and political liberalism involves a distinctly anti-liberal mechanism: coercive power. It can be exercised by a range of actors: governments, international organizations, and even non-governmental actors.[34] Coercion can be applied in various ways from the subtle to the overt: through the threat or use of physical force,[35] the manipulation of economic costs and benefits, and even through the monopolization of information or expertise. The underlying logic of coercion thus involves power asymmetries that strong actors exploit to impose their preferences for policy change on the weak. Coercion theorists suggest that policies diffuse from the "center" both actively through "conditionality" and passively through "unilateralism" by more powerful actors.[36] Essentially, coercion involves the (usually

[30] Thomas, Meyer, Ramirez, and Boli 1987. [31] Kaminsky and Reinhart 2000.
[32] Hall 1989; McNamara 1998.
[33] Goolsbee and Klenow 1999; Keller 2002; Powell 1990.
[34] Private banks, for example, in IMF conditionality. See Edwards 1997; Gould 2003.
[35] We would expect physical coercion to be rare in the diffusion of economic policy in the latter half of the twentieth century, but it has been used repeatedly historically and contemporaneously by powerful countries to influence domestic institutions in weaker countries. See Owen 2002.
[36] Essentially hierarchical in nature, coercion is a form of "vertical diffusion" discussed in much of the literature on federalism and European regionalism. See for example Daley and Garand 2005; Gilardi 2005.

conscious) manipulation of incentives by powerful actors to encourage others to implement policy change.

The diffusion of economic liberalization is thought by many to be the outcome largely of coercive pressures. The primary agents are powerful governments or the intergovernmental organizations they dominate. Using a strategy of conditionality, these actors link policy reform to political membership (e.g. in the European Union) or to economic resources (e.g. from the International Monetary Fund (IMF)) in a demonstrable quid pro quo fashion.[37] The logic is straightforward. Developing countries need financial assistance from the strong either to ward off crises or to make infrastructural investments that are hard to fund through private markets.[38] Lenders, however, then condition their financial support on domestic economic reforms they deem desirable – macroeconomic stabilization, free trade and cross-border capital movements, privatization and deregulation ("The Washington Consensus").[39]

Why should powerful actors care about the economic policies of other countries? Economists have provided a range of motives for conditionality: discouraging moral hazard problems that can lead to system-wide financial instability,[40] encouraging the repayment of sovereign debt,[41] and (to come full circle) protecting lenders' investments.[42] On the other side of the bargaining table, those who borrow from the IMF or World Bank, like those who line up to join the European Union[43] or to receive various forms of bilateral aid,[44] have little choice but to accept neoliberal economic policy prescriptions.

Can conditionality plausibly account for the spread of economic liberalization over the past few decades? Economists have noted that IMF conditionality suffers to the extent that it cannot be credibly

[37] See, for example, on the World Bank, Mosley, Harrigan, and Toye 1995.

[38] James Vreeland argues that the countries that go under IMF programs do so not only because of economic need, but also because they have the political will to undertake the kinds of reforms they know the IMF will impose on them; Vreeland 2003.

[39] Williamson 1993. For more recent reflections by Williamson on these policy recommendations see Williamson 1997, 2000.

[40] Guitian 1995; Mishkin 1999.

[41] Babai 1988; Fafchamps 1996; Hopkins, Powell, Roy, and Gilbert 1997.

[42] Guitian 1995; Khan and Sharma 2001.

[43] Schimmelfennig, Engert, and Knobel 2003.

[44] Some research even suggests that aid conditionality itself has diffused among potential donors, as minor donors have increasingly converged on the aid practices of major countries. Rob Kevlihan argues for example that Ireland's aid policies have moved beyond "first generation" economic policy conditionality and have converged toward the "second generation" political conditionality of the rest of Western Europe; Kevlihan 2001.

enforced.[45] A raft of studies has exposed non-compliance with IMF programs, implying that even the most stringent formal conditionality may not lead to the anticipated policy results – either because it is hard to monitor what the recipients of conditional assistance are actually doing[46] or because recipients lack the institutional capacity to effect policy change.[47] These problems may explain why the World Bank in particular has recently talked more about program "ownership" than conditionality.[48] Some even question the characterization of conditionality as coercive. James Vreeland argues that governments often accept IMF loans because they *want* "conditions" externally imposed on them, rather than the other way around.[49] In a similar vein, Alan Drazen argues that conditions encourage policies that are in a country's "self-interest" when the government faces "heterogeneous preferences" (political opposition) domestically.[50]

The debate about formal conditionality only applies to developing countries that receive support from the international financial institutions (IFIs). There is, however, a less formal face to conditionality that may be associated with the influence of powerful actors through bilateral aid and treaties or through organizations such as the World Trade Organization (WTO), the European Union (EU), and the North American Free Trade Alliance (NAFTA) – and with the demands that participation imposes on weaker members. In these cases, there is often no explicit quid pro quo. Rather, weaker parties simply expect that they will receive some benefits by making the policy change favored by the more powerful actor. In the cases of the EU and NAFTA, membership has its privileges, but also its costs in terms of policy latitude.

Implicit pressures for policy conformity with the preferences of the strong seem very common in international relations. Bilateral aid is often tied to policy liberalization.[51] Developing countries negotiating with the United States over the extension of various free trade areas (bilateral, regional, and multilateral) feel pressure to liberalize their telecommunications, insurance, and financial sectors.[52] Potential recipients

[45] Eichengreen and Ruehl 2000; Sachs, Huizinga, and Shoven 1987. A similar credibility problem applies to poverty-reduction programs. Donors that sincerely want to reduce poverty have a hard time tying such aid to political or economic reforms. See Svensson 2000. Several studies reveal how unsuccessful conditionality has been at securing broader goals, such as political liberalization, in developing countries. See Santiso 2003.

[46] Cordella and Dell'Ariccia 2002. [47] Martinez-Vazquez *et al.* 2001.

[48] This is more true of the World Bank than of the IMF, however. See Nelson 1996.

[49] Vreeland 2003. [50] Drazen 2002. [51] McPherson 1987.

[52] A clear example is that of the recent negotiations between the United States and five Central American countries for a Central American Free Trade Agreement with the United States; see the *Financial Times* of London, December 17, 2003, THE AMERICAS, page 2.

of US foreign direct investment find themselves pressured to liberalize their capital accounts.[53] Similarly, historical research suggests the French have actively campaigned for capital account openness.[54] More overtly, the European Union's negotiations with Latin American countries over free trade contained a contentious "democracy clause," the explicit purpose of which was to bolster political as well as economic reforms in Latin America (just as potential EU members must undertake democratic reforms before their admission to the club).[55] The European Commission and the United States have demanded sweeping privatization programs of developing countries as the price for further agricultural liberalization in the context of WTO discussions.[56] In a range of policy arenas, powerful external actors have become actively involved in domestic political processes with an eye to altering policy or institutional outcomes.[57]

In empirical investigations of conditionality, it is important to be precise about exactly how the outcome under investigation is linked to power asymmetries. At a minimum, it is necessary to identify the coercive actors, to show that they promote the policy in question, and to show evidence of formal conditionality or, in the case of informal conditionality, of especially noteworthy "persuasive opportunities" when policy liberalization was on the negotiating table. If the International Monetary Fund is the hypothesized source of dominant influence, for example, empirical tests should demonstrate that: (1) the IMF includes the specific policy change as part of its performance expectations during the period in question; and (2) the country in question made use of IMF resources, thus placing it under Fund conditionality. Similarly, studies linking policy diffusion to particular dominant actors will be persuasive to the extent that they can show that: (1) particular actors favor particular policy changes;[58] and

[53] Singapore is a recent and important case in point. *The Straits Times* (Singapore), November 22, 2002.
[54] Abdelal 2006.
[55] See for example Sanahuja 2000. Emilie Hafner-Burton's research on human rights conditionality links improvements in rights practices to highly conditioned preferential trade arrangements, which tie rights improvements directly to market benefits. See Hafner-Burton 2005.
[56] Katharine Ainger, "Comment & Analysis: A privatisers' hit list: European Commission demands to deregulate services spell disaster for the developing world," *The Guardian* (London), April 18, 2002.
[57] See for example Siegel and Weinberg 1977.
[58] It may be, for example, that the United States encourages particular governments to hold democratic elections when US security interests are served. It is less likely that the US pressures governments to sign human rights treaties, since the US itself has not signed these accords and regularly argues that this in no way undermines its commitment to human rights.

(2) those actors have plausible leverage over the target countries. To demonstrate conditionality, studies should show that countries subject to leverage (trade, aid, or security dependence) are more likely, ceteris paribus, to adopt reforms promoted by powerful actors. It may also be possible to show that the *timing* of liberalization is influenced by moments of vulnerability: preceding or during a multilateral trade round of negotiations, during periods of "candidacy" for admission to clubs such as the EU or the WTO, during periods in which bilateral trade agreements are being negotiated with the US or the EU, or in anticipation of the disbursement of a loan tranche from the IMF.

Conditionality is hardly the only way coercion can be applied. As Lloyd Gruber has argued, the powerful may influence the weak even if the former do not tie benefits to the behavior of the latter. He dubs this "go-it-alone power": the ability to unilaterally influence a government's policy choice by altering the nature of the "status quo" it faces. For instance, the United States' decision to liberalize trade with Canada had a profound effect on Mexico's own economic liberalization program.[59] Mexican leaders would have preferred, Gruber argues, to liberalize at a more leisurely pace, but the US–Canadian agreement created conditions that could have diverted trade and investment to the north – leaving Mexico worse off than the pre-agreement status quo. Go-it-alone power amounts to a fairly passive yet profound form of coercion among asymmetric players, in which the powerful government need not worry about enforcement and the credibility of threats.

Coercion of a sort may also be exercised by a country that seizes the policy initiative. A potential monopolist's decision about how much to produce affects whether other potential producers will enter the market, and if so, how much they will produce. "Stackelberg leaders" thus enjoy "first mover" advantages that shape the choice set of other governments. Unilateral action could also be "coercive" by virtue of its power as a focal point with the ability to solve coordination problems characterized by multiple equilibriums.[60] Where nations need to coordinate their policies, participants may follow the behavior of a powerful nation simply in virtue of its salience, as Geoffrey Garrett and Barry Weingast argue has often been the case with respect to the influence of German rules and practices

[59] Gruber 2000.

[60] Schelling 1960. In this section, we discuss the role of dominant powers in solving coordination problems among countries. We will discuss a looser definition of focal points below when we analyze the mechanisms underlying social emulation.

in the process of European integration.[61] The salience of German institutions as a model for Europe has probably played an important role in the development of these supranational innovations, even though few would argue that Germany has overtly sought to "coerce" Europe to follow its lead.

Can the coordinating power of liberal focal points account for the diffusion of markets and democracy? Quite clearly, if there is in fact no coordination problem to be solved, this model of diffusion misses the mark. The appropriateness of this approach will depend on the strategic structure of the specific issue area at stake.[62] Moreover, the policies of powerful countries are only one possible source of focal points; other social conventions, such as precedents, may prove equally influential.[63] Furthermore, experimental evidence suggests that the coordinating power of a dominant leader weakens when trust in the dominant actor erodes,[64] suggesting that the diffusion effects of coercive coordination could be self-limiting. Even the first move of a Stackelberg leader committed to liberalization, Pahre shows, may under some circumstances *undermine* the willingness of others to liberalize.[65] The conditions under which coercive coordination can account for diffusion of liberalization must be very carefully specified.

Finally social constructivists analyze "hegemonic ideas" that involve more subjective forms of power than traditional coercion or focal unilateralism. Hegemony in the Gramscian sense refers to the "control of social life by a group or a class through cultural as opposed to physical means."[66] Without exerting physical power or materially altering costs or benefits, dominant actors can have their influence felt through ideational channels. The thrust of this approach is that dominant ideas are rationalized, often with elegant theoretical justifications, and become part of the discourse influencing how policymakers conceptualize their problems and order potential solutions. Albert Hirschman, for example, argued that global Keynesianism owed much to the hegemonic position of the United States.[67]

[61] Garrett and Weingast 1993. For example, the European Central Bank looks very similar to the dominant pre-euro European central bank, the German Bundesbank. The European Union's political system – an "upper house," the Council of Ministers, directly representing the governments of states, and a "lower house," the European Parliament, representing the citizens of all member states – is very similar to Germany's Bundesrat and Bundestag; Tsebelis and Garrett 2001.

[62] For example, even though standard setting is often considered a class coordination game, Beth A. Simmons has argued that while accounting standards may primarily be a coordination problem, establishing rules to regulate money laundering is not; Simmons 2001.

[63] Crawford and Haller 1990. [64] Wilson and Rhodes 1997. [65] Pahre 1999.

[66] Femia 1983. [67] Hirschman 1989. See also Haas 1980.

But how do hegemonic ideas emerge and become politically ascendant? Most scholars believe that the fact they are endorsed by a powerful actor is not enough. For example, the roles of epistemic communities or policy entrepreneurs with the expertise to articulate and disseminate theories and policy prescriptions are often highlighted.[68] Sociologists use the phrase "normative" isomorphism to describe the process whereby professional groups theorize new policies and actively seek to sell them to corporations or nation-states.[69] Nonetheless, it is likely that because powerful countries have the research infrastructure, the critical intellectual mass, and well-developed connections between the policy world and various research nodes, they are likely to be influential, perhaps unduly, in the framing of policy discussions.[70]

To be useful as an explanation for policy diffusion, theories of hegemonic ideas must indicate plausible mechanisms for their transmission. Economists (typically those trained in the United States or a handful of Western European countries) are often viewed as the most important actors in the diffusion of liberal economic reforms around the world – independently of the power they may exercise through the conditionality of international financial institutions.[71] Sebastian Edwards has argued that the evidentiary contributions of the World Bank have altered the terms of the intellectual debate over economic policy.[72] Practically every international financial institution – from the Bank for International Settlements to the International Monetary Fund to the various regional development banks – has a research department engaged in the dissemination of economic models favored by economists in wealthy, core countries.[73] But the influence of economists' ideas does not require the support of international institutions. Western (especially US) economists have a long history of providing advice as consultants to various governments around the world, based on theories developed in their home institutions. Their impact seems nowhere more evident than in Latin America,[74]

[68] For a general discussion of the role that epistemic communities play in formulating theories and articulating solutions that eventually influence policy see Haas 1992. For a test of the proposition that policy entrepreneurs have a significant impact on the probability that a particular policy innovation (in this case school reform) will get on the political agenda and be approved see Mintrom 1997; Mintrom and Vergari 1998.

[69] DiMaggio and Powell 1983, 1991.

[70] Hira 1998. For a highly critical view of how economic theory gains policy adherents, see Krugman 1995.

[71] Kogut and McPherson 2005. [72] Edwards 1997: 47.

[73] On the importance of economists working in the IMF and the World Bank for the spread of economic ideas internationally see also de Vries 1997; Polak 1997.

[74] Drake 1994; Montecinos 1997; Murillo 2002. Harberger 1997 discusses his involvement in economic reform in Latin America over several decades.

although the independent causal influence of US economists' influence in developing regions is difficult to sort out empirically.[75] (Because "hegemonic ideas" may be better classified with processes of social construction and emulation than with diffusion by coercion, we revisit these issues at greater length below.)

On the whole, coercion models highlight the role of powerful actors in the diffusion of policy. They typically emphasize some combination of policy conditionality, political and economic power, and focal points – and these are often mutually reinforcing.[76] What unites this perspective is the necessary influence of an external source of pressure or ideas. Observers may differ in their assessment of the extent to which dominant actors actively, even aggressively, seek to influence policies elsewhere. One should also not dismiss the complementarity of interests (or indeed the complicity) of policy adopters around the world. But the notion of differences in power – and hence the asymmetrical flow of influence – is what distinguishes this approach from other perspectives on diffusion that tend to be less hierarchical and more decentralized.

Competition

Competition among governments for capital and market share for their domestic goods and services offers a far more decentralized explanation for the diffusion of liberal economic policies than power, hierarchy, and coercion. According to this perspective, governments have strong incentives to choose "market friendly" policies that make their jurisdiction an attractive place for global investment, and to remain competitive in product markets by minimizing costs. The central insight of those who espouse competitive models of liberal policy diffusion is that incentives to liberalize increase after key competitors open their markets. Simplifying regulatory requirements, ameliorating investment risks, and reducing tax burdens are often viewed as policy choices that can, quite quickly, make an investment locale more attractive and an economy more efficient and competitive, at least on the margins. Competition arguments are typically applied to economic policies, though there is some evidence that investors and even buyers in the global marketplace have preferences for certain political systems, sometimes for liberal democracy and sometimes for benevolent authoritarianism.[77] Thus a competitive dynamic is plausibly at work with respect to both market and political genres of liberalization.

75 But see Kogut and Macpherson's effort, this volume.
76 See for example the discussion in Ikenberry 1990.
77 Jensen 2003; Meyer 1998.

Competitive models of liberalization tend to assume that governments compete with each other for a fixed quantity of trade or investment, but that they would choose – were they left to their own wishes – to retain more extensive interventions in their economies for social or political purposes. Governments know who their competitors are, and are able to connect policy choices to competitive advantages. Liberalization may effectively increase global business activity as international transactions costs are reduced, but the central concern of policymakers is the potential redistributive nature of policies taken elsewhere. Certainly, there are policies that could make one's own jurisdiction attractive in the long term (better infrastructure, a more educated workforce), but these are not likely to influence investors' or traders' decisions in the short to medium term. Thus, competitive models focus on the strategic interdependence of relatively short-term policy responses, such as capital account liberalization, tax breaks, and labor rights.[78] Liberalization by a competitor is understood as an unwanted disturbance to a level of protection, taxation, or regulation that might have been preferred on domestic grounds alone.

That jurisdictions compete in their formulation of economic policies is hardly a new insight. This dynamic has been documented extensively at the subnational level. In the United States, for example, states engage in fierce competition to attract investment through the use of specific economic incentives.[79] The spread of competitive innovations ranging from welfare policies to lotteries has also been documented on the subnational level.[80] Competitive models are also increasingly employed in studies of regional integration and convergence, for example in the context of the European Union.[81]

Diffusion by competition explicitly or implicitly underlies much current thinking about policy adoption in the context of growing global economic integration. The argument is a mainstay of studies of globalization's effect on environmental protection. The expense of complying with environmental regulations has fueled a debate over whether, and to what extent, increasingly mobile firms' exit threats can reduce environmental regulations in wealthy jurisdictions and account for the "dumping" of dirty production activities in developing countries and emerging markets with lax regulations.[82] Some studies

[78] See Rodrik 1997; Mosley and Uno 2007; Simmons and Elkins 2004.
[79] Gray 1994. See also Cai and Treisman 2004.
[80] Berry and Berry 1990; Brueckner 2000; Peterson and Rom 1990.
[81] See for example Sinn and Ochel 2003.
[82] See for example Porter 1999; Tanguay 2001. However, for a study that finds no link between environmental pollution and various forms of globalization, see Wheeler 2001. In the popular literature, see Korten 1995.

on environmental protection show that regulatory races to the bottom can be intensified as the number of competing jurisdictions and exit options increase.[83]

The presumed effects of global competition for capital and trade have also fueled the debate over the future of the "Keynesian welfare state" since the early 1990s.[84] Studies in the 1970s and 1980s emphasized the incentives and ability governments had to buffer local economic actors from the vicissitudes of the global market through various forms of social protection and government spending.[85] After a generation of effective Keynesian management of the economy,[86] many believe, governments have now lost the ability to steer independent courses in the global economy. Business demands less, not more, government interference with market forces. In marked contrast with the post-Second World War period of Keynesianism and state expansion, scholars describe a competitive dynamic in which maintaining the domestic social bargain forged two generations ago is increasingly hard to do.[87]

Competition sparked by increasing market integration has spawned research on the empirical manifestations purportedly associated with such competition. The "convergence" literature developed in the 1990s to test the hypothesis that governments increasingly were constrained by capital mobility and the internationalization of production from pursuing independent fiscal, wage, and social policies. In the area of taxation, the convergence literature predicted a shift in the incidence of taxation from the more to the less internationally mobile factors of production.[88] Dani Rodrik purported to show that capital mobility was indeed associated with lower taxation of capital,[89] although subsequent studies questioned this finding.[90]

[83] Kunce and Shogren 2002; Massey 1999.

[84] For early statements of the argument see Helleiner 1994; Kurzer 1993; Pfaller, Gough, and Therborn 1991; Pierson 1991.

[85] Cameron 1978; Katzenstein 1985; Ruggie 1982. For more recent support see also Hicks and Swank 1992; Swank 1992; Huber, Ragin, and Stephens 1993. Rodrik has proposed that the positive trade–spending relationship holds for the rest of the world; Rodrik 1998.

[86] The seminal study of this period remains Shonfield 1965.

[87] See the essays in Kitschelt *et al.* 1999; Scharpf 1991; Schwartz 1994; Schwartz 1998.

[88] For a good review of the literature on tax harmonization see Oates 2001.

[89] Rodrik 1997. See also Genschel 2002.

[90] See for example Garrett and Mitchell 2001; Holzinger and Knill 2005; Swank 1992; Swank 1998. Duane Swank and Sven Steinmo tried to reconcile the mixed results in the literature, arguing that while marginal capital tax rates in the OECD have declined considerably since the mid-1980s in the face of increasing international financial integration, the base of capital taxation has been sufficiently broadened (by reducing depreciation allowances and other tax credits) that the overall tax take – and hence the ability of governments to fund spending by taxing capital – has been largely unaffected. Swank and Steinmo 2002. Richard Baldwin and Paul Krugman have recently argued against the

Competition for mobile capital and export markets has been hypothesized by some to be causally connected with downward pressures on government spending, social programs, and the overall size of the government sector. The causal mechanism in these studies relates to market pressures to reduce regulatory and social programs that raise the costs associated with investment, and the need to keep production costs competitive. Several studies have focused on competitive effects on government spending, but few clear results emerge. Geoffrey Garrett has found a global tendency for countries experiencing rapid trade integration to reduce government spending growth, though curiously capital mobility had no such effects.[91] Indeed, in the first systematic study of the correlates of capital mobility, Dennis Quinn found government spending to be higher in OECD countries that were more open to cross-border capital movements.[92] More evident have been the constraining effects of global markets on government programs in developing countries. Studies that have focused on the developing world have tended to argue that globalization has limited welfare states.[93] Perhaps this is due, as Layna Mosley suggests, to the much greater scrutiny international investors apply to the spending patterns of developing countries compared to the industrialized democracies.[94]

Competition has also been implicated in a number of institutional changes. Comparative legal scholars have discovered the effects competitive pressures may have on legal models, institutions, and practices. Governments are thought to compete in the global economy by moving their legal systems toward the American model. Pressure for openness and transparency, which American legal norms are thought to exemplify, underlie this analysis.[95]

Two critical points must be noted about the vast academic literature that has emerged to test the purported effects of heightened competition associated with more integrated global markets. First, most of this literature assumes competitive dynamics drive countries toward a market-friendly form of convergence, but this assumption is usually not tested directly. "Openness" is often viewed as sufficient to account for competitive pro-market outcomes.[96] As we will discuss in greater detail below, a more precise test of the competition hypothesis would involve linking liberalization in country A to the policies of A's *competitors* in the world

proposition that competition leads to convergence on tax policy, by pointing to the rents governments are able to collect under conditions of industrial agglomeration within their jurisdictions; Baldwin and Krugman 2004.

[91] Garrett 1998; Garrett and Mitchell 2001. [92] Quinn 1997.

[93] Kaufman and Segura-Ubiergo 2001; Rudra 2002. [94] Mosley 2003.

[95] Kelemen and Sibbitt 2004; Twining 2004.

[96] See for example Neumayer and de Soysa's test of liberalization's effect on labor standards and practices; Neumayer and de Soysa 2006.

economy. There is no particular reason to believe that A's level of exposure to world markets per se would result in policy liberalization, especially if few other countries with whom A competes have themselves liberalized. There is a marked disjuncture between the theory of the race to the bottom – in which liberalization by one government forces another to liberalize – and empirical tests – where the "openness" of a country's markets to the international economy is modeled as the stimulus for liberalization. More precise specifications of the sources of competitive pressures may help overcome the inconsistent empirical results typical of the globalization research program.[97]

It should also be noted that there is an important theoretical alternative to competitive convergence: competitive *divergence* based on the Tiebout model of the provision of local public goods.[98] The Tiebout model illustrates how under fiscal federalism residents can vote with their feet and migrate to jurisdictions with the level and type of local public goods provision that they prefer. The result is that all localities do not provide the same services to their residents; rather, local governments specialize – and people relocate to find the jurisdictions that fit their preferences (e.g. low taxes versus good schools).[99] Of course, as traditionally applied, Tiebout models assume readily available "exit" options, and thus assume a high degree of human mobility between jurisdictions. Whether such mobility can account for significant heterogeneity of preferences among countries and homogeneity within them is not at all obvious.[100] More realistically, perhaps, Ronald Rogowski uses a Tiebout-like model in which capital moves to friendly jurisdictions, while labor does not. Such sorting, he argues, reinforces liberalization in jurisdictions to which capital is initially attracted but, crucially, reinforces market intervention and closure in the jurisdictions from which capital has fled.[101] The result is that globalization simply reinforces existing *differences* in policy regimes among countries, all else being equal.

[97] See for example the results from specifications of competitive networks in Simmons and Elkins 2004.
[98] Tiebout 1962.
[99] For a critical review of Tiebout models to governmental entities, see Donahue 1997.
[100] Alberto Alesina and his colleagues, however, have applied Tiebout logic internationally, arguing that with the increased mobility of people as well as capital, states are becoming both smaller and more homogeneous – as people no longer have to accept government policies that they do not support. See Alesina and Spolaore 2003. See also Bolton and Roland for an application to regional autonomy and irredentist movements; Bolton and Roland 1997.
[101] Rogowski 2003.

Governments in a Tiebout framework are far more passive than those postulated in the competitive model we have in mind. They tend to reflect political demands, and respond to changes in the domestic polity as these evolve through the sorting process. It is equally (perhaps more) plausible that the policy choices of other governments are anticipated to affect payoffs in the home jurisdictions, creating strong incentives to match them without waiting passively for sorting to take place. Governments are expected to respond fairly urgently and in kind to incentives created by competitors' market-friendly innovations.[102] As a result, liberal policies are expected to spread in a specific way: along channels carved out among competitors.

To develop more precise tests of competitive pressures for policy diffusion, it is important to specify as precisely as possible the areas in which key economic constituencies of a government can be expected to be sensitive to the policies of governments in other countries. Exporters should be sensitive to policies that affect input costs, such as wages, and so a policy that reduces wage costs in a competitor country should lead domestic exporters to call for an "equal playing field." Foreign direct investors have to consider a range of transactions costs flowing from the political risks and contractual hazards inherent in operating a firm in a foreign jurisdiction.[103] Policies that reduce these transactions costs in nations that compete for foreign investments should stimulate similar innovations at home.[104]

Liberalization of the capital account is a prominent example: in the long term, investment flows can be encouraged by improvements in infrastructure and labor market quality, but in the short run governments seek strong policy signals that foreign capital is welcome.[105] They are therefore likely to respond in kind to capital market liberalization by their competitors.[106] In

[102] For case studies in the area of finance that examine the political processes by which such policy changes take place, see Encarnation and Mason 1990; Goodman and Pauly 1993. A further example is that of Australia and New Zealand in the 1980s. The two countries had similar economic profiles – profitable raw materials and agricultural sectors supporting protected manufacturing sectors, relatively loose macroeconomic policies, highly regulated economies, and large state-owned sectors. The United Kingdom, long the major export market for primary products, entered the European Community (as it then was) in 1973 and began consuming continental products, just as global mineral markets destabilized. These shocks led Australia to begin to liberalize in the early 1980s; New Zealand soon went further than Australia, with radical central bank reform and large-scale privatization, then Australia responded with a privatization campaign of its own. See Castles, Gerritsen, and Vowles 1996.

[103] Henisz 2000. [104] See Elkins, Guzman, and Simmons, this volume.

[105] Economists find that capital and trade flows respond positively to such signals of liberalization. See for example Bartolini and Drazen 1997.

[106] Simmons and Elkins 2004.

Latin America, this dynamic took over after Chile liberalized under Pinochet; other countries began to open their capital accounts as well for fear that capital flows would be diverted to Chile. Foreign direct investment is also sensitive to corporate tax rates, particularly in developing countries,[107] and reductions in competitors' rates could stimulate reductions at home. Governments also compete for international capital by floating their own sovereign bonds, and investors are notoriously concerned about fiscal recklessness that can spur inflation and limit their liquidity. Governments competing for portfolio capital may do so by curtailing government spending and may compete to liberalize the capital account.[108]

Models of diffusion that rely on economic competition may be useful in exposing the proximate explanation for policy liberalization – a specific policy move by a competitor. But they are typically silent about the deeper structure of ideas that presumably gives rise to the belief that the best way to respond to liberalization elsewhere is roughly in kind. Competition models imply mechanistic accounts of structural pressures that are tightly coupled with the policy innovations of competitor nations. Competition theorists assume that the pressure from a change in a competitor's policy so clearly indicates the range of plausible responses that whether and how governments learn about liberalization (discussed below) has no independent explanatory power.[109]

Competitive models of diffusion do not address deeper constitutive questions: how do governments come to believe in the first place that liberalization will contribute to economic growth and development? And if they believe a competitor's liberalization will attract valuable economic activity, why not liberalize unconditionally? The answer must lie in the disturbance that external competition implies to a locally determined equilibrium level of policy liberalization, explanations for which have traditionally been the bailiwick of "endogenous" theories of protection.[110] Competitive models of diffusion are useful only in that they model the external forces that disturb these domestic policy equilibriums.

Empirically, competitive interdependence in adoption is straightforward to examine. In the case of policies that affect local production costs, where the competition is between foreign and local producers serving the local market, the relevant competitors may be a country's trade partners. The best measure might be the prevalence of the target

[107] Gastanaga, Nugent, and Pashamova 1998.
[108] Simmons and Elkins 2003, 2004. [109] This point is made by Levy 1994.
[110] For but one example see the endogenous tariff literature: Nelson 1988.

policy among the home country's trade partners, weighted for trade flows. In most cases, however, theory suggests that countries adopt new policies to compete with their peers for market share in, or investment from, a third country or group of countries. In these cases, the policies of trade partners are not most relevant, for the competitive action is in global or third markets.[111]

The specific hypothesis might be that as barriers to trade are lifted in country A, country B will have incentives to reduce barriers because both want access to the market of country C. A good indicator for competition in third markets would be the average of policies taken in countries weighted with respect to the degree of similarity in their export market profiles. Structural equivalence in trade networks would measure the degree to which any given economy represents a competitive pressure.[112] Alternatively, the strength of sectoral competition between two countries might be most important. In each case, the solution would be to create a correlation matrix of countries' exports, and weight the policies of those whose profiles are most highly correlated accordingly. As this weighted group of competitors liberalizes, we would expect a country to do the same.

Competition for capital can be measured in an analogous way, but one has to think carefully about how to weight the relevant competitors. For policies that influence foreign direct investment, it might be most appropriate to group countries by their inherent attractiveness to investors. Competitive distance in this case could be a function of the degree of similarity in quality of the workforce (as measured by literacy, etc.) and infrastructure (electricity, communications, transportation). The more similar two countries are on these dimensions, the more competitive for FDI they will be and the greater the weight of country A's policy in predicting country B's.[113] For policies expected to affect non-equity portfolio investment, countries with similar credit ratings might be the most direct competitors.[114] For competition to be supported as a diffusion mechanism, policy innovation would have to be shown to be conditioned by the policies of competitors for the resources in play.

[111] Spatial models measuring the "distance" between two competitors are an especially promising way to proceed empirically. Such spatial models are explained in a recent article by Beck, Gleditsch, and Beardsley 2006.

[112] Burt develops applicable models of structural equivalence in markets; Burt 1987. See also Finger and Kreinin 1979.

[113] See for example Elkins, Guzman, and Simmons, this volume.

[114] Simmons and Elkins 2003, 2004.

Learning

In the policy literature, "learning" refers to a change in beliefs, or a change in the strength of one's confidence in existing beliefs, resulting either from observation and interpretation or from acquisition of new theories or behavioral repertoires.[115] Some researchers distinguish "simple learning," in which new information leads to changes in means but not ends, from more complex cognitive processes involving new beliefs about ends as well. In the realm of public policy, actors may be learning at both the simple tactical level (how to better achieve a particular goal) and at a deeper level (what goals they should pursue).[116] With respect to tactics, governments may always try to stimulate economic growth, but they may become convinced, for example, that export promotion rather than import substitution is the way to go. Or at a deeper level, political liberalization – the extension of the franchise, the guarantee of individual rights – likely involves new thinking about the desirability of these goals.

An essential insight is that one can learn not only directly from one's own experience, but also vicariously from the policy experiments of others. Policy diffusion takes place via learning when governments in one country draw lessons from the experiences of others, and apply these lessons in designing their own policies. Learning theories of policy diffusion can be applied at various levels of analysis. First, policymakers can alter their individual beliefs in ways that shape policy. In an institutionally thin environment, in which decision makers have the ability to act upon their own beliefs, individual cognitive change may be sufficient to explain policy change – as has often been suggested with respect to crisis decision making in foreign policy.[117] Second, more useful for understanding the diffusion of liberal policies among countries, Ernest Haas' work has drawn attention to the generation of social knowledge, or "the sum of technical information and of theories about that information which commands sufficient consensus at a given time among interested actors to serve as a guide to public policy designed to achieve some social goal."[118] In this approach, policy innovation spreads in the wake of the diffusion of a shared fund of (often technical) knowledge among elites

[115] See the very useful review of the learning literature, especially as it has been applied to foreign policy decision making, by Jack Levy 1994.

[116] Philip Tetlock, for example, argues that learning can be hierarchical, but that most foreign policy learning takes place at the tactical level: political decision makers reconsider their basic strategic assumptions and orientation only after repeated failures to generate a tactical solution. See Levy 1994: 286.

[117] Jervis 1976. [118] Haas 1980: 367–8.

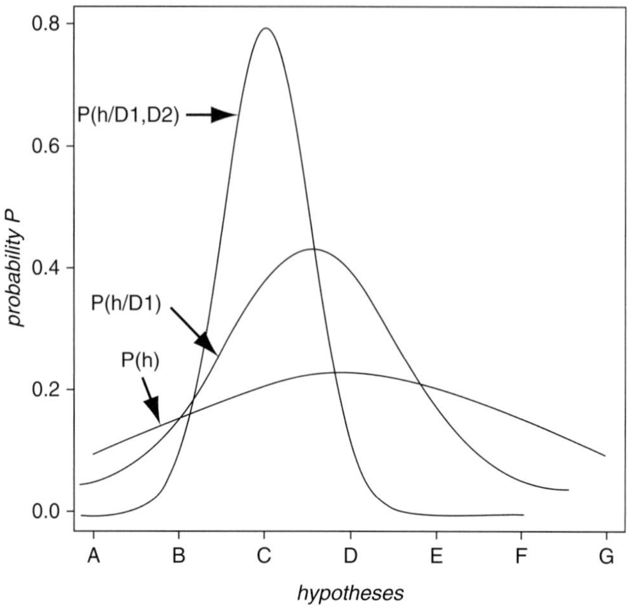

Figure 1.6 Bayesian updating

about what is effective. Of course, organizations themselves do not literally "learn"; only individuals do. As Jack Levy has noted, policy change is often a process of "encoding individually learned inferences from experience into organizational routines."[119]

Economists take a more objectivist and individualistic view. They focus on the process of Bayesian updating, in which individuals add new data to prior knowledge and beliefs to revise their behavior accordingly. With each new data point, the range of hypotheses that might explain all accumulated data may shift and narrow. The more consistent the new data, the more likely an actor's probability estimates of the truth of various hypotheses are to converge on a narrow range of possibilities – and ultimately policies.

Figure 1.6 illustrates the basic Bayesian mechanism. The flattest curve represents an actor's initial estimate of which of several possible relationships is true. The wide dispersion indicates a good deal of uncertainty, but hypothesis D is initially viewed as most likely. New data allow for a revision of the probability that D is true. In this case, the first round of new data causes the actor to believe that D and C are equally probable.

[119] Levy 1994. Generally, see Levy's discussion, 1994: 287–9.

Another round of observed data solidifies the belief in the probability of C. Bayesian learning has the effect of shifting both the *mean* and the *dispersion* of beliefs about the true nature of relationships in the world. In Figure 1.6, additional information shifted actors' beliefs in hypothesis D toward hypothesis C. At the same time certainty about this assessment solidified in the face of new information.

It is important to note, however, that nothing in the Bayesian learning mechanism guarantees that actors will converge on "the truth." The process merely describes the way in which new information affects actors' probability assessments. Just as an individual can "learn" a theory in physics that is later disproved, nations can take the wrong lessons from the policy experiences of others or can learn a wrong-headed theory. Exactly what actors learn will be influenced by a number of factors, including the source of new information and how it is processed. Of course, relevant data can come from a range of sources, including one's own past experiences[120] and dyadic interactions.[121] Most relevant to policy diffusion, however, may be the policy experiences of other countries. Governments draw conclusions based on the data generated by policy experiments elsewhere, thus narrowing the range of interpretations regarding the causal relationship between the policy and its hypothesized outcome.

In this way, the probability of liberal policy innovation in a given country can change as the result of "natural experiments" with liberal policies elsewhere. Consider the case of privatization. Prior to Margaret Thatcher's ascent to power in the United Kingdom, state-owned firms were widely accepted in both developed and developing countries. No government had ever engaged in a sustained program of selling off state-owned enterprises.[122] Britain's privatization drive provided a natural experiment to determine the consequences of denationalization of major public enterprises. The policy seemed to work – firms were sold at handsome profits while the labor problems associated with nationalized industries in Britain declined. Privatizations also generated very useful revenues for the government in its efforts to balance the budget. In the medium run, some British industries did better under private

[120] In the area of security relationships, for example, Reiter argues that governments are most likely to learn lessons from their own past experiences; Reiter 1996. See also Huth and Russett 1984; Leng 1983; Levite, Jentleson, and Berman 1994.

[121] Scholars of international relations have developed models in which bargaining leads to Bayesian updating regarding the nature of an adversary or its level of resolve. See for example Powell 1988; Wagner 1989.

[122] The exception to this rule was Pinochet's Chile.

management and some did worse. But there were few glaring disasters (at least until the rise in train fatalities following the privatization of British Rail – but this was at the very end of Britain's privatization program, not at the beginning).

The result of the British privatization program was that countries "learned" that economists' arguments about the desirability of private ownership were plausible. Economists quickly jumped on the bandwagon to argue that there were, in fact, very few natural monopolies, and hence most state-owned industries in most countries were inefficient and would benefit from being sold.[123] Governments in other countries updated their prior assumptions about the costs and benefits of state ownership. Privatization was now viewed as more attractive.[124]

Bayesian learning is a "rational" process in the sense that individual actors make optimal use of available information.[125] Some theorists note that policy choices elsewhere may be assumed to reveal private information that can help policymakers to make better-informed decisions. It is important to note, however, that in learning models the choices of others are important not because they affect the *payoffs* of a policy choice (as in the competition dynamic), but rather because others' choices generate new data that informs *beliefs* about causal relationships.

Sociologists tend to believe that the Bayesian approach is both too naive in terms of actual decision making and too demanding in terms of informational requirements to explain national policy choice. Information does not wash up in undifferentiated waves on the shores of a nation's decision-making machinery. Rather, sociologists suspect that information is likely to be "channeled," with some sources being more important than others. In his influential research on the spread of Keynesian ideas, for example, political scientist Peter Hall noted that "The process whereby one policy paradigm comes to replace another is likely to be more sociological than scientific."[126] How and why

[123] The evidence on the benefits of privatization, however, appears considerably shakier on closer inspection. For a discussion of the literature, see Brune, Garrett, and Kogut 2004.

[124] The privatization example also provides some evidence for negative learning in developing regions of the world. Success stories of privatization are rare in low-income countries, and the long-term promise of privatization in sectors posing regulatory complications remains to be established, making positive updating far less likely in Africa for example; Ramamurti 1999.

[125] But the aggregation of these individual choices may not be socially optimal. Economists recognize that sequential social learning can be responsible for "herd behavior," as evident in successive international financial crises in the 1990s. More generally, models in which actors learn from the decisions of a small number of leaders and suppress their own private information tend to lead to Pareto-inefficient outcomes. See Banerjee 1992; Bikchandani, Hirshleifer, and Welch 1992.

[126] Hall 1993: 280.

information becomes channeled in particular ways becomes crucial for understanding why particular countries and certain regions seem to have been swept up in liberalizing waves, while others have eschewed the innovations implemented elsewhere.

But policy information may be channeled by the salience of its apparent success. Policies that seem to "work" are much more likely to cause leaders to positively update their prior beliefs about their likelihood of success at home. To wit: although the Japanese "miracle" provided an economic model for Asia and beyond in the 1970s and 1980s, it fell on hard times during Japan's decade of stagnation in the 1990s. Chile explicitly cited the successes associated with US–Canadian experience with bilateral trade liberalization as an indicator of the possible benefits for Chile of a similar agreement.[127] Chile itself has often been cited as a relevant "success story" for liberalization in emerging market economies, from Latin America to Asia to Eastern Europe.[128] Because it is very hard to pin down causal relationships between policy and outcomes, policy-makers may use cognitive shortcuts which channel attention to highly successful countries or to highly successful outcomes – rather than assessing all available information as the Bayesian approach demands.

Channeled learning may be facilitated by communication networks among actors who already are connected in other ways. The exchange of information via existing networks is central to many sociological studies of policy diffusion.[129] In these models, the cognitive process is dominated by an "availability heuristic," in which actors unable to retrieve a full sample of information base their decisions on only those instances that are available to them – limiting the viable range of policy alternatives.[130]

Several important studies indicate the importance of learning within communications networks in the policy arena.[131] Virginia Gray's pioneering work on policy innovation among the states of the United States, for example, demonstrated that the intensity of contact among officials was associated with policy diffusion.[132] Recent research on how

[127] When asked what are the benefits and drawbacks of bilateral trade liberalization with the United States, Ricardo Lagos Escobar, President of Chile, answered, "Experience with a trade agreement with Canada indicates the positive effects, such as an increase in trade with Canada of more than 40 percent and an increase in our gross domestic product," *The San Diego Union-Tribune*, January 18, 2004, OPINION; page G-5.

[128] Biglaiser 2002; Edwards and Edwards 1992.

[129] Coleman, Katz, and Menzel 1966; Rogers 1995. See also Axelrod 1997.

[130] Kahneman, Slovic, and Tversky 1982; Gale and Kariv 2003; Weyland 2005.

[131] The international relations literature has recognized a role for channeled learning outside of the policy realm. For example, with respect to coup contagion see Li and Thompson 1975.

[132] Gray 1973. See also Lutz 1987.

developing countries formulate and implement policies – ranging from pension reform to exchange rate policies to privatization programs – similarly point to strong social learning from neighbors.[133] It is well documented in the international literature that the process of negotiating and maintaining institutional affiliations may create opportunities to learn and persuade.[134]

International institutions are another natural conduit for learning and, especially, for organized pedagogy. Joseph Nye found that international institutions reinforced learning with respect to nuclear policy through their use of rules and standard operating procedures.[135] Miles Kahler has noted that the international financial institutions shape learning to reinforce their policy preferences.[136] Indeed, the International Monetary Fund regards its research function as a way to disseminate the lessons of earlier liberalizers (usually developed countries) to the rest of the world (primarily the developing countries).[137] Rainer Eising attributes the spread of liberalization in the electricity sector in Europe to learning facilitated by the Council of the European Union.[138]

In all of these cases, international organizations, either as agents or as sets of rules that enhance transparency, appear to have had important effects on information flows and policy transmission. Such institutions shape and filter the policy relevant information upon which policymakers draw their conclusions. Nevertheless, the influence on policy may not be obvious and automatic. David Levi-Faur's account of policy liberalization and regulatory reform in Latin America and Europe for example demonstrates that despite much learning, very different institutional environments produce different outcomes.[139]

How might one devise tests for the influence of learning on policy diffusion? There are good reasons to suppose that learning is most likely when we see either *highly successful* or *clearly disastrous* policy changes in country A, followed by similar changes (or heightened resistance to change) in B and C. That is, measurable policy success should predict adoption elsewhere. In the case of privatization, for example, higher rates of investment and economic growth and lower deficits would suggest that the policy worked at the national level. Over time, the ratio of these measures among privatizers relative to non-privatizers should predict future privatization efforts.

[133] Brooks 2005; Khamfula 1998; Meseguer 2004. [134] Haas 1959. [135] Nye 1987.
[136] Kahler 1994.
[137] Many examples could be cited, but for an explicit effort to pass on the positive lessons of liberalization see Quirk 1994.
[138] Eising 2002. [139] Levi-Faur 2003.

It may be that learning happens at the global level, and it may be that it happens among groups of peers who share information and whose experiences are more relevant to each other. In the case of privatization, the policy spread first among European countries, then to Australia and New Zealand and only later to the developing world. Different peers might matter in different cases. As a result, one could measure the success of a policy among states in the same region or cultural group, or among states at the same level of development. Like firms that have sunk investments in particular technologies,[140] in the absence of spectacular success, governments may be reluctant to change course if the adjustment cost appears high and the payoff uncertain.[141] Thus, one might expect that governments will change only in the face of strong and compelling evidence.

The bottom line on the learning approach to diffusion is clear. Information about success or failure of policy change in other countries is expected to influence the probability of policy change in the country under analysis. The information may be acquired rationally, dispassionately, and completely, as in strict Bayesian models. It might be mediated through existing communication networks. Information might flow more quickly among peer groups of countries whose experiences are deemed most relevant to each other. In all cases, however, evidence of success should be expected to increase the likelihood of adoption elsewhere, while spectacular failure should put the brakes on foreign policy adoptions. As we shall see, this connection to some reasonable measure of "success" becomes more tenuous as we move away from learning and toward diffusion processes based on emulation.[142]

Emulation

Diffusion studies have a venerable history in sociology, where the focus had been on individual, organizational, and social-movement adoption of innovations.[143] Sociologists have studied public policy diffusion through the lens of "social construction" since the late 1970s.[144] John Meyer's

140 See for example Atkeson and Kehoe 2001.

141 On the likelihood of incremental change in the absence of a dramatically successful model, see Schneider and Ingram 1988.

142 Many researchers find that learning and emulation are not necessarily mutually exclusive. See for example Meseguer 2005.

143 For reviews see Strang and Meyer 1993; Dobbin 1994; Rogers 1995; Strang and Soule 1998. Classic studies include Coleman *et al.* 1966; Hägerstrand 1967.

144 The first sustained analysis appeared in Meyer and Hannan 1979. For reviews of the literature, see Dobbin 1994; Strang and Meyer 1993; Strang and Soule 1998.

influential "world polity" approach draws on the Weberian view of an increasingly global culture comprising broad consensus on what is "appropriate": the set of appropriate social actors (individuals, organizations, and nation-states have replaced clans, city-states, and fiefdoms), appropriate societal goals (economic growth and social justice have replaced territorial conquest and eternal salvation), and means for achieving those goals (tariff reduction and interest rate manipulation have replaced plunder and incantation). It is this logic of appropriateness that diffuses around the globe, first in the West and then elsewhere, to create the world polity.[145] Eleanor Westney pointed out that this process is best described not as imitation but as emulation.[146]

This constructivism is distinguished from materialist and individualist theories by its focus on the inter-subjectivity of meaning. Both legitimate ends and appropriate means are shared social constructs.[147] According to this view, we are not born into the world with ready-made understandings of what tariffs on trade, for example, do and mean. Nor do we each derive our own understanding *de novo*. Moreover, understandings of cause and effect can vary over time. Tariffs were thought to do very different things in 1880, 1947, and 1995. Constructivism is rooted in Max Weber's insight that to understand social action we must grasp its meaning to the actors themselves, and that that meaning is an empirically traceable product of social context.[148]

The causal imagery of the world polity approach to international policy diffusion is classically sociological. The conventions of nation-states and of organizations are socially generated, much like the conventions of families, social movements, or religions. While policymakers see themselves as collectively trying to divine the "best practice" in each policy area, and see policy as evolving toward more and more effective forms, in fact policymakers are seldom able to judge whether a popular new policy improves upon the status quo. They operate under teleological assumptions about the trajectory of public policy, but policy evolution is messier than these assumptions imply. The effects of particular policies are often complex and uncertain, and so even the most rational of decision makers can rarely find incontrovertible evidence of the efficacy of a prospective policy. Theory and rhetoric often serve as the bases of decision making, and theory and rhetoric change over time.

145 Boli-Bennett and Meyer 1978; Strang 1991. 146 Westney 1987.
147 Berger and Luckmann 1966; Hirschman 1977; Meyer, Boli, Thomas, and Ramirez 1997.
148 Weber 1978: 4.

Early constructivist studies traced the diffusion of educational and human rights policies from first-world nations to third-world nations, showing that most countries adopted these policies not when they were developmentally ready but when the "fad" became irresistible.[149] Meyer and colleagues showed that between 1950 and 1970 all countries expanded mass schooling, which had been defined as key to achieving both growth and democracy, regardless of political ideology or level of development.[150] Developing countries signed human rights treaties early and often to signal their commitment to global norms, even when Amnesty International was chiding them for rights abuses.[151] Any two countries ratifying constitutions in 1980 specified virtually the same set of rights, as did any two countries ratifying in 1850.[152]

In international relations theory, the constructivist paradigm made inroads via the early contributions of Hedley Bull and others of the British School who theorized the role of "international society" in maintaining order in an anarchical international setting.[153] In the United States, the constructivist paradigm began to make its mark in the late 1980s as political scientists sought to parse the shared beliefs underlying the foreign policies of different countries.[154] By the late 1990s, a spate of studies highlighted how international agencies and governments actively construct theories of action and corresponding models of behavior.[155] Defining the nation-state as the appropriate collective actor had been the first major project of social construction of the modern world.[156] International relations theorists have focused on the creation of shared norms. For instance, Peter Katzenstein's collection of constructivist studies of national security explores how cultural meaning shaped the reconfiguration of national security theory and practice after the fall of Soviet Communism.[157]

The sociological approach has also gained currency not only in analyses of business strategy,[158] but also in comparative politics. Peter Hall argued

[149] Boli-Bennett and Meyer 1978.

[150] Meyer, Ramirez, Rubinson, and Boli-Bennett 1977. See also Meyer, Ramirez, and Soysal 1992.

[151] Boli and Thomas 1999; Boyle and Preves 2000; Forsythe 1991; Ramirez and McEneaney 1997. In a recent study, Wade Cole shows that newly established states are more likely to sign international human rights covenants, symbolizing their commitment, but not more likely to sign the optional protocols that ensure enforcement; Cole 2005.

[152] Boli 1987. [153] Bull 1977. See also Buzan 1993; Herrell 1993.

[154] Katzenstein 1978. For an interesting discussion of the movement, see Keohane 1988.

[155] Finnemore and Sikkink 2001; Ruggie 1998; Wendt 1999.

[156] Thomas and Meyer 1984; Ruggie 1993; Krasner 1993. [157] Katzenstein 1996.

[158] Edelman studies organizational rights, whereas Davis, Diekmann, and Tinsley and Dobbin and Dowd explore the social construction of corporate strategy; Davis, Diekmann, and Tinsley 1994; Dobbin and Dowd 2000; Edelman 1992.

that the ideas of John Maynard Keynes led to a new approach to economic management of the economy that ultimately spread widely throughout the world. Peter Gourevitch charted the global policy response to three major economic crises, finding that political coalitions shaped country response but also that during each crisis, the macroeconomic strategy favored by one group of economists came to dominate. Frank Dobbin showed that a new macroeconomic orthodoxy spread following the Great Depression, but that national industrial policy strategies resisted change. In these studies, professional economists were the main purveyors of new macroeconomic conventions.[159]

For constructivists, understanding how public policies become socially accepted is the key to understanding why they diffuse. Social acceptance of a policy approach can happen in at least four ways: (1) leading countries serve as exemplars ("follow the leader"); (2) expert groups theorize the effects of a new policy, and thereby give policymakers rationales for adopting it; (3) specialists make contingent arguments about a policy's appropriateness, defining it as right under certain circumstances; and (4) policies go through different stages of institutionalization, typically spreading beyond the countries for which they were invented in a second phase of diffusion.

In marked contrast with the coercion approach to diffusion, constructivists emphasize the voluntary adoption of new policies, embraced by policymakers seeking to do their best. Leading nations and IFIs may play roles, but followers are typically willing. As compared to learning theorists, constructivists describe policymakers as seeking to learn from the experiences of others but as rarely able to establish the efficacy of a given policy. Policymakers are constrained by bounded rationality, meaning that they are unable to envision the full range of policy alternatives and unable to assess the costs and benefits of each.[160] In consequence it is often the rhetorical power of a new policy approach, rather than hard evidence that the policy has reduced deficits, or increased female enrollments, that matters.

First, policymakers often play "follow the leader."[161] When the US is on top, others translate its happenstance policy shifts into demonstration projects. America's securities laws, antitrust regulations, and central bank structure are copied in Indonesia, Namibia, and Uruguay. Uruguay's innovative banking laws don't spread in the other direction, not because there is anything wrong with them but because it is hard to tell a story about their efficacy so long as Uruguay is struggling to pave its roads.

[159] Hall 1989; Gourevitch 1986; Dobbin 1993. [160] March and Simon 1993.
[161] Haveman 1993a, 1993b.

Because causal processes are difficult to isolate empirically, followers may copy almost anything. For a time in the 1980s, American firms copied Japan's quality circles, but also her factory jumpsuits. They may copy policies almost ritualistically, as when twenty American states copied California's fair trade policy so nearly verbatim that half copied two serious typographical errors.[162] Conversely, there are models that fail to catch on despite their apparent efficacy. While they have been lauded as promoting development, East Asian trade policies have not caught on, perhaps because they do not jibe with current economic thinking.[163]

Constructivists expect that policymakers will emulate the policies of leaders even in the absence of evidence of the efficacy of those policies.[164] To give rational learning theory its due, we assume that when followers embrace a policy in the presence of plausible evidence of its efficacy – when a policy has performed as advertised in early adopters – learning has occurred. Where they adopt absent such evidence, we assume that construction has taken place. What makes a country a "leading" country? Britain had been the model for economic policies late in the nineteenth century, followed by the US for much of the twentieth century, but France made a showing after strong postwar growth, and Germany and Japan were emulated in the 1980s, before the US became the economy to follow again in the 1990s.[165] One way to operationalize the theory is simply by the presence of the target policy in the leader *du jour*. Another strategy, employed by organizational sociologists, is to measure the proportion of the largest, richest, or fastest-growing units – in this case nation-states – with the policy in place.[166]

Second, "expert theorization" happens when policy professionals, academics, intergovernmental organizations (INGOs), and non-governmental organizations (NGOs) theorize a new policy solution.[167] Such "epistemic communities" help to define new solutions to existing problems, and new paradigms for thinking about problems and solutions.[168] A policy may spread even without a particular exemplar, although experts frequently

[162] Jack Walker documents this, working with a database showing interstate copying of leaders to be common. See Walker 1969.
[163] Gruen 1999. [164] See the discussion in Strang and Macy 2001.
[165] See Shonfield 1965 on France, Johnson 1982 on Japan, and McNamara 1998 on Germany.
[166] Haveman 1993.
[167] Strang and Meyer 1993 contend that the first step is the theorization of similarities across countries, of salient identity dimensions that make up groups of countries. Enrione, Mazza, and Zerboni show that new corporate governance regimes are spread by international actors, but also by local experts who help to theorize their importance; Enrione, Mazza, and Zerboni 2006.
[168] Haas 1989 was one of the early scholars to link epistemic communities to policymaking.

riff on the experience of a leader. After the US adopted antitrust laws to protect consumers from price-fixing in 1890, economists retheorized the policy as a way to promote competitive markets and other countries adopted it in the hope of replicating America's growth.[169] DiMaggio and Powell[170] call this "normative isomorphism," for experts advocate new policy norms that lead to isomorphism.

Students of organizational policy find that it is usually specific groups of professionals – finance or personnel experts – who sell particular policies. Students of human rights policies have generally identified NGOs or INGOs as defining policy norms.[171] Empirically, national membership in, or presence of, an NGO or INGO that supports a certain policy should increase the likelihood of adopting that policy. Ramirez, Soysal, and Shanahan[172] found that the extension of suffrage to women hinged before 1930 on the number of national organizations promoting suffrage, and after 1930 on a nation's participation in a pro-suffrage international alliance.

The finding that policies thought to come with development, such as welfare programs and environmental protections, spread to nation-states at *all* levels of development suggests that NGOs have succeeded in defining global, non-contingent, norms about how nation-states should behave. But research shows that countries that support new rights but lack the resources to provide them may decouple formal policy from practice.[173] Strang and Chang find that ratification of International Labor Organization treaties guaranteeing welfare rights leads to increases in welfare expenditures in developed countries, but not in developing countries. This may not represent bad faith so much as the power of new international norms even in countries that are not developmentally ready to implement them.[174] To give coercion theory its due, in the analyses in this volume participation in World Bank and IMF programs are typically taken to measure coercion, but participation in human rights INGOs and NGOs (which do not hold purse strings) are more typically taken to indicate social construction.

While professionals and experts have generally been found to be the agents of diffusion in organizational studies, studies of public policy diffusion often neglect the role of agency. What kinds of individuals and

[169] Wilson 1980. [170] DiMaggio and Powell 1983; Edelman 1992; Fligstein 1990.
[171] Berkovitch 1999; Berkovitch and Bradley 1999; Boli and Thomas 1997; McNeely 1995; True and Mintrom 2001.
[172] Frank, Hironaka, and Schofer 2000; Ramirez, Soysal, and Shanahan 1997.
[173] The idea that policy can be decoupled from day-to-day activities is sketched in the organizational literature, in Weick 1976, and Meyer and Rowan 1977.
[174] Strang and Chang 1993.

groups matter? A study of the spread of professional licensing for thirty different occupational groups found that the groups themselves promoted adoption among the American states.[175] Studies in this volume address agency. In the chapter by Kogut and Macpherson, privatization is argued to have flourished where its main professional proponents, US-trained economists, were dominant. More generally, if we see an effect of local Chicago-trained economists on economic policies, net of all else, we would be inclined to chalk one up for "expert theorization." But sometimes it can be difficult to distinguish expert theorization from coercion, for the tail can wag the dog – as we noted, governments may participate in World Bank programs so that they can justify fiscal austerity programs (championed by economists) to their constituents. Kogut and Macpherson rule this out in their empirical analysis.

Third, policymakers and expert groups often construct certain policies as appropriate for countries with given characteristics – we term this the contingency hypothesis. Thus, for instance, the five-year industrial plan was embraced outside of the Communist world by countries ideologically oriented to government leadership in industry, such as France and Korea.[176] Women's rights conventions have a global character, but Islamic countries developed a distinct version.[177] Empirically, constructivists suggest that when a country fits the prescription, it will follow others that fit the prescription. When trade liberalization was prescribed for developed countries but not for middle-range countries that were trying to substitute local production for imports,[178] constructivists would expect to see developed countries behaving like their peers and developing countries behaving like *their* peers. The strongest test of the contingency hypothesis combines qualitative evidence of expert theorization of the particular contingency with quantitative evidence that countries sharing the relevant characteristics have adopted.

A weaker version of the contingency hypothesis comes from reference group theory in social psychology, which suggests that individuals emulate the behavior of peers because they surmise that the policies of peers will "work" for them as well. Socio-cultural linkages may contribute to "psychological proximity"[179] among nations: for example, Britain looks to North America[180] for policy solutions, whereas Syria looks to Saudi Arabia.[181] The reference group hypothesis is based on the idea that policymakers engage in a kind of inductive reasoning based on

175 Zhou 1993. 176 Cohen 1977. 177 Berkovitch and Bradley 1999.
178 O'Donnell 1973. 179 Rose 1993.
180 Examples include Waltman 1980, and Lester and Bindman 1972: Ch. 3.
181 Stone 1999.

observation. It is also possible that reference groups produce the kinds of weak-tie networks that Mark Granovetter has shown to be conduits of information.[182]

In organizational studies, firms learn of new practices even through weak ties to other firms; the poison pill strategy spread through corporate board networks and became ubiquitous in no time.[183] In research on policy diffusion, "region" often stands in for reference group, or for contagion by proximity. For instance, Ramirez, Soysal, and Shanahan find that women's suffrage spread regionally – between 1930 and 1990, the prevalence of suffrage rights in regional neighbors influenced hold-outs.[184] The contributors to this volume have striven to specify what it is about regional proximity that causes bandwagoning. For instance, among nearby countries, is it physical proximity and information flows, trade flows as a source of commercial contact, or heightened contact among religious groups that predicts the influence of one country on another?[185] This can be tested by looking at whether a country's likelihood of adopting an innovation is best predicted by its prevalence among neighbors, trade partners, or religious community members.

Countries also look to structural equivalents to evaluate policy options. Ronald Burt has shown, in a reanalysis of data from the classical study of the spread of tetracycline among physicians in the mid-1950s, that physicians defined themselves as like others on the basis of shared structural positions.[186] They followed others who were structurally similar, rather than those they had direct contact with (the contagion hypothesis). The most detailed international measure is trade equivalence, but trade equivalence may capture competition. For policy choices that may be driven by competition, i.e. capital account openness, we assume that when structural equivalence predicts adoption we are observing competition at work. Otherwise, when structural equivalence predicts adoption we would look for qualitative evidence that countries draw inductive conclusions based on the policies of their equivalents.

Fourth, a policy that experts or NGOs initially prescribe for a certain group of countries often becomes generally accepted practice, through a sort of sequential combination of "expert theorization" and "follow the leader." Policies adopted to address a particular problem thus spread to countries without the problem as part of standard operating procedure.

[182] Granovetter 1995. [183] Davis 1991. [184] Ramirez, Soysal, and Shanahan 1997.
[185] For example, Simmons and Elkins 2004 present evidence that cultural peers – indicated by common religious orientation – are significant in explaining external financial and monetary liberalization.
[186] Burt 1987.

The studies of mass schooling mentioned above show this pattern, for after the Second World War what was defined as a necessary component of industrialization by European nation-states needing skilled workers came to be a necessary component of nation-building for third-world nations.[187] This is known as the "stages-of-institutionalization" thesis following Tolbert and Zucker's finding that civil service reforms spread first to the big cities they were prescribed for and then became standard operating procedure, spreading to towns too small to make use of them.[188] Once a new policy reaches a certain threshold, policymakers take it for granted as necessary. Empirically, countries that should not adopt a policy following a stages-of-industrialization logic, adopt it anyway. As in the case of policies with positive network externalities, the prevalence of a policy predicts its adoption. But the stages-of-institutionalization process can be recognized in two ways. On the one hand, it suggests that policies will first diffuse to countries for which they are prescribed and will only later diffuse elsewhere. On the other hand, for policies that carry no clear network externalities – women's rights – qualitative evidence may help us to confirm that social construction is at work.

An important component of our research agenda is to distinguish rational learning from emulation through social construction. Where policymakers have knowledge of the efficacy of a new policy, rational learning may be taking place. Some contagion studies have isolated the processes. Holden shows that airline hijackings stimulate new hijackings, but that successful hijackings (where a ransom is paid) are more likely to be copied. Conell and Cohn find that French coal-mining strikes ignite other strikes, but that successful strikes were more likely to ignite others.[189] These studies suggest that when they have hard evidence that a strategy works, people are more likely to copy it. Both studies also find that people emulate strategies even in the absence of evidence.

The researchers whose work is collected in this volume look for an effect of social construction and emulation – net of the effect of learning, and of competition as well. Constructivist studies of human rights typically suggest that learning and competition are not plausible diffusion mechanisms, but studies of economic liberalization present the opportunity to isolate social construction from learning and competition, and that is one of the advances of this volume.

Sociology's constructivist studies of international diffusion via social emulation have been rightfully criticized for operating at a high level of

187 Meyer *et al.* 1977; Ramirez and Boli 1987; Meyer, Ramirez, and Soysal 1992.
188 Tolbert and Zucker 1983. 189 Holden 1986; Conell and Cohn 1995.

abstraction, both theoretically and empirically. Theoretically, practitioners describe a sweeping global trend rather than focusing on the variable regional and national environments it faces. Empirically, they use quantitative analysis to model the global diffusion of policies across over 100 countries, but often fail to document the local processes involved in policy diffusion.[190]

World polity theorists describe a fundamentally sociological process underlying the diffusion of national policies that mirrors the processes underlying the diffusion of organizational practices and individual behaviors. Policymakers in the modern world operate under norms of political justice and economic rationality, but they derive ideas about how to bring about justice and economic growth from the world around them. Given changing definitions of human rights and of economic efficiency, and given uncertainty about whether policies designed to increase educational levels of women or expand high-technology exports will have the intended effects, policymakers copy the policies they see experts promoting and leading countries embracing. Policy decisions are only loosely based on competition or learning, strictly defined, although policymakers may describe their behavior as competitive and evidence-based.

Varieties of liberalism: contributions to this volume

The chapters in this book explore these four diffusion mechanisms with respect to three distinct clusters of economic and political liberalization. Three chapters examine the liberalization of domestic economic policies – reductions in corporate tax rates, government workforce downsizing, and privatization. Two chapters study the liberalization of foreign economic policies – bilateral investment treaties (BITs) and capital account openness. Finally, two chapters focus on political liberalization; democratization and the ratification of women's rights treaties. In the conclusion we consider the implications of all these chapters for the relative explanatory power of coercion, competition, learning, and emulation as mechanisms of the international diffusion of liberalism. Here we provide a brief policy-by-policy preview.

Domestic economic liberalization

Why have governments increasingly implemented domestic policies that seem to favor marketization over governmental intervention? Duane

190 Finnemore 1996. Some very good case studies do explore international diffusion processes at the local level. See for example Jacoby 2000.

Swank examines the diffusion of new "market-conforming" corporate tax structures in the OECD following the adoption of a new tax regime in the United States in 1986.[191] Swank argues that competition was the major driver of diffusion because the US tax changes were most closely followed in other developed economies with similar political economic structures to those in America – that is, the institutions of liberal (uncoordinated) market institutions. According to Swank, competition with the US for investment was the driving force of policy change among these countries, but not among the coordinated market economies of northern Europe. These countries came to adopt reforms similar to those enacted by Reagan because the US is the dominant host and supplier of capital investment throughout the developed world. The market for FDI in coordinated market economies, in contrast, operates more independently from the US and is driven by other considerations.

Bruce Kogut and Muir Macpherson argue that patterns of privatization around the world have been significantly influenced by the impact of the new economic orthodoxy associated with the University of Chicago. While coercion (through IMF conditionality) and competition (for FDI and trade) matter at the margins, they find no learning effects. Rather, they argue for the social construction of the idea of privatization. When the idea appeared in the United States there was much debate, with some arguing that it was nonsense. Even as it spread abroad, there was debate in the countries that embraced privatization. The construction of this solution within nations depended on its proponents winning, and often tailoring privatization to local conditions.[192] Yet for Kogut and Macpherson, American economists have been the principal purveyors of the neoliberal model of economic policymaking. This may have affected the diffusion of privatization in two ways. Governments that favored privatization (and other neoliberal economic policies) may have been more likely to send young economists to the US, and to Chicago in particular, for further training. Alternatively, individuals who went to Chicago, for whatever reason, may have brought back home pro-privatization convictions. Either way, Kogut and Macpherson have shown how the process of the construction of a new orthodoxy came about.

Chang Kil Lee and David Strang examine public sector downsizing in the 1980s and 1990s in the OECD.[193] As in the case of "market

[191] Original version published in *International Organization*; see Swank 2006.

[192] See also Starr 1989 on the diversity of how privatization was implemented within nations.

[193] Original version published in *International Organization*; see Lee and Strang 2006.

conforming" tax policies, there is no evidence of coercion. But unlike Swank, Lee and Strang do not believe that competition was the main driver of reductions in public sector employment. Instead, they focus on an interesting learning process. In the context of the dominance of neoliberal thinking about the efficacy of downsizing, countries took strong signals from evidence that downsizing worked to improve economic performance but heavily discounted evidence showing that bigger public sectors were good for growth (by providing collective goods such as education and infrastructure under-supplied by markets). Lee and Chang thus propose a hybrid emulation and learning dynamic in which an influential epistemic community defined downsizing as a solution to the problem of poor economic performance, which in turn catalyzed only one type of learning – countries ignored evidence that was inconsistent with the new received wisdom but acted upon evidence that was consistent with it.

Foreign economic liberalization

The second cluster of chapters focuses on policies that open up the national economy to the rest of the world, and particularly to international capital markets and investment. Zachary Elkins, Andrew Guzman, and Beth A. Simmons explore the diffusion of bilateral investment treaties (BITs) that seek to improve foreign investors' legal redress in countries where local regulatory and legal practices may appear to put foreign investment at risk.[194] The chapter finds considerable evidence for diffusion through competition. Developing countries are much more likely to sign a bilateral investment treaty (usually with a developed country) when their prime competitors for trade and investment have done so. Other mechanisms may also be at play. Coercion is not ruled out: countries that draw on the resources of the IMF tend to be much more likely to sign a BIT, which may reflect a degree of pressure to do so. Elkins, Guzman, and Simmons also find no evidence of learning from others' success in attracting capital through committing to BITs, but no evidence of emulation through region, common language, or colonial history. This chapter demonstrates that in this case, it is very likely that two rational mechanisms – competition and learning – mutually reinforce one another and go a long way to explain the explosion of bilateral investment treaties in the mid-1990s.

Dennis Quinn and Maria Toyoda examine the history of capital account openness around the world in the last half of the twentieth

[194] Original version published in *International Organization*; see Elkins, Guzman, and Simmons 2006.

century. Their principal finding is that global anti-capitalist sentiments (as measured by vote shares for Communist parties in stable democracies) had a strong and significant negative effect on capital account openness in all countries, including non-democracies and democracies without Communist parties. This can be understood as a form of emulation, though a very different form from that identified by Meyer's world polity approach. Though they find some evidence for learning and competition, the main thrust of Quinn and Toyoda's chapter is that a strong, grassroots anti-capitalist movement led developing countries to balk at paying the price of capital account openness for several decades, before global sentiment against markets declined precipitously from the mid-1980s forward. Those countries bucked the first-world trend.

Political liberalization

Finally, we turn to two chapters that deal with two very different forms of political liberalization. Kristian Gleditsch and Michael Ward examine the diffusion of democracy, and begin with the observation that the process of democratization has been geographically clustered. Given that most of the domestic correlates of democracy (levels of income, education, etc.) tend to change slowly, there is a strong prima facie case to be made that democracy spreads by some sort of regional diffusion. What is the nature of the diffusion? Gleditsch and Ward contend that coercion is the most important driver of this dynamic, though in a way that is quite different from the core–periphery archetype.[195] In the case of democratization, powerful pro-democracy groups in neighboring countries apparently represent a very effective power resource for would-be democratizers. Conversely, civil conflict in neighboring countries reduces the capacity of democratizers elsewhere in the region. Power operates here, but it is localized power resources available to pro- and anti-democracy groups within nations that matter.

Christine Min Wotipka and Francisco Ramirez also find evidence of the diffusion of human rights, specifically the rights of women. They examine a rather more symbolic form of liberalization, ratification of the Convention on the Elimination of All Forms of Discrimination against Women (CEDAW). They find that countries emulate others when they are part of a global political order promoted by non-governmental and intergovernmental agencies and groups of professionals seeking to define an expanding set of inalienable human rights

[195] Original version published in *International Organization*; see Gleditsch and Ward 2006.

and seeking to ensure that countries at all levels of development guarantee those rights. The United Nations drafted CEDAW, and each of three UN-sponsored conferences on the status of women stimulated a round of new ratifications, even in developing countries with poor human rights track records. The more countries around the world, and the more in the region, that had ratified, the more likely ego was to ratify. Network connections with international rights organizations increased the likelihood of ratification. By contrast, level of development was a poor predictor – underdeveloped countries were *more* likely to ratify – and conditionality appeared to play no role – countries dependent on foreign aid were no more likely to ratify.

Conclusion

Liberalization of both polities and markets has been one of the most significant developments of the second half of the twentieth century. The wave-like nature of these developments provides important clues that liberalization across countries might very well be a consequence of interdependent decision making. It would be surprising indeed if unique features of each domestic polity could explain the tripling of democratic governments over this time, the nearly universal adoption of women's rights treaties, the exponential explosion of treaties to liberalize and protect foreign investments, the wave of privatizations, the apparent spreading preference among elites for smaller government, and the liberalization of capital markets that have characterized the past few decades. Far from assuming that these developments are in any way inevitable or reversible, these trends demand explanation. Theories of diffusion help us to think systematically about the mechanisms that may underlie the waves of individual policy choices that collectively contribute to the globalization of the second half of the century.

The spread of economic and political liberalism is far from the first global wave of policy and political change. The signing of the Treaty of Westphalia in 1648 heralded the spread of the territorially bounded nation-state.[196] Participatory democracy became increasingly prevalent in the nineteenth century following the earlier French and American revolutions.[197] Mercantilism, orthodox macroeconomic policies, and Keynesianism all enjoyed extended periods in the sun as global models for economic policy.[198] What is more distinctive about the late-twentieth-century

[196] Krasner 1993;Thomas and Meyer 1984. [197] Boli 1987. [198] Gourevitch 1986.

wave of liberalization has been its rapidity, its wide geographic reach, and its conjoining of political and economic reform – as we saw in broad relief at the outset of this chapter.

Liberalization is a complex process that could be analyzed in terms of the underlying conditions as well as the proximate causes that seem to ignite its spread. This volume focuses primarily on the latter, but we recognize the important role of the former. The spread of liberalism in the latter part of the twentieth century was no doubt in part the product of a long build-up of historical forces such as the "American Century" of economic expansion, the victory of the Allies in the Second World War, and the failure of Communist states to realize their promise of political inclusion. Later, the waning of the German and Japanese interventionist economic models, the unraveling of Communism as an alternative to liberal democracy, and unprecedented growth during the 1990s in the paradigmatic liberal state, the United States, all played powerful triggering roles. These conditions alone, however, cannot explain why particular policies that often look remarkably similar across countries cluster in time and space. It is clear that countries often end up with policies that look very much like those in other countries, but it is not clear why.

Three social sciences disciplines – economics, political science, and sociology – have devoted much attention to this question, but they have done so in very different ways that tend to look inward rather than to reach out to engage insights from other perspectives. One consequence of the isolation of different camps is that analysts have rarely spelled out the broad theoretical assumptions underlying their arguments; they have generally only addressed internecine disputes among like-minded scholars who share a core set of assumptions. Conversely, when scholars from different disciplines reach the same conclusions they tend to be unaware of this cross-disciplinary consensus. As a result, the wheel has been reinvented more than once. Moreover, when it comes to empirical tests, analysts have often failed to adequately test competing hypotheses.

The goal of this volume is to remedy each of these weaknesses. The four clusters of theories we have reviewed in this introduction imply different processes behind the diffusion of liberal policies.

Coercion theorists depict a world in which the actions of a few powerful players – through carrots and sticks, go-it-alone power, or as focal points – have a disproportionate influence on the behavior of other countries. The United States and the International Monetary Fund and the World Bank promote liberal economic reforms either because they further American interests or simply because Americans believe them to be efficient, depending on whom you listen to. The clear implication is that countries adopt policies that may or may not be effective for them, or in their own interest.[199]

Competition theorists describe a very different mechanism, whereby a policy that gives one country a competitive edge leads others to follow suit, even if those countries would have preferred, ex ante and in a world of independence rather than interdependence, not to adopt them. Brazilian policymakers may favor high import tariffs that shield domestic industries, but competition for export markets and foreign capital with Argentina, Chile, and Mexico may lead them to lower tariffs. Following this logic, the preferences of global business for free trade and low tax rates trump the preferences of domestic groups for protection and redistribution. Power thus plays a role in these models as well, but it is the power of the market as a decentralized economic force, rather than national power as conventionally understood.

Rational learning theory implies a kind of cost-benefit analysis, but one with very different foundations than the competition approach. The roots of the theory are psychological, and the driving question is how individuals and policymaking groups draw lessons from the experiences of other countries. They may draw lessons by observing the effects of policies other countries adopt, and they may engage in Bayesian updating, in which they constantly add new bits of evidence to the existing knowledge base. Policymakers can draw the wrong lessons from observation, but the overarching theme here is that countries have "learned" to pursue liberal policies because those policies are most effective. Like competition theorists but unlike coercion theorists and constructivists, learning theorists tend to attribute the success of liberalism to its efficacy in promoting growth and political stability.

Constructivists depict yet another causal imagery based on social emulation. They see the diffusion of liberal policies as a matter of ideology, broadly understood. A global polity has emerged over the past several hundred years, under which there has been a shifting consensus about the optimal means to achieving economic growth and political stability. Experts and international organizations promote formal theories to account for the success of certain policies, and in the end it is the rhetorical power of these policies and theories that carries them around the world. Moreover, countries that see themselves as members of some sub-global groupings, based on history, culture, language, and geography, may come to select similar sets of policies more or less as a result of their belonging to these self-identified communities of nations.

[199] See for example Henisz, Zelner, and Guillen 2005.

While the four approaches to international diffusion have some common intuitions about process, they nonetheless focus on different core propositions.[200] They also have different implications for the future course of global liberalization. It is not the case that each and every theory is applicable to each and every policy domain. But many theories have not been tested even in venues for which they are appropriate. What is most exciting about this cornucopia of theories is that while they do point to some overlapping predictions, they also point to a number of quite distinct causal mechanisms that can be differentiated in empirical tests. The promise of diffusion analyses that take the plausible alternative mechanisms into account is that they can begin to sort out which of the various mechanisms have played roles in the diffusion of which liberal policies. Knowing which mechanisms are most likely at work will help us to refine our theories, and also to better understand where policy may move in the future. The remainder of this volume is devoted to this crucial empirical agenda.

The pattern of findings across the studies presented here is striking, and it suggests the promise of integrative theoretical approaches as well as important new avenues of study.

Taken together, these studies suggest that simple coercion is seldom the main process underlying policy diffusion. There is little evidence, among developed or underdeveloped countries, that the IMF or World Bank, the American government or the European Union, has significantly influenced policies by threatening governments. The studies do show significant effects of competition and learning from first movers, however. In the realm of foreign trade, countries sign bilateral trade agreements when their direct competitors have done so. In domestic policy, countries learn from the successful public sector downsizings of their peers. It is perhaps not surprising that competition drives nations' behavior in trade, and that learning drives their behavior in domestic policy.

What is more surprising is that learning is conditioned by belief patterns. While there is evidence that countries learn from successful public sector downsizings that are consistent with current economic beliefs, countries ignore evidence that conflicts with those beliefs. And so the prevailing wisdom shapes the kinds of learning that can occur. Similarly, purveyors of the prevailing neoliberal wisdom about the privatization of public enterprises shape the adoption of privatization programs. In economic policy, it appears, what is fashionable in economic theory plays a

[200] For a recent argument that these (and possibly other) diffusion mechanisms can in fact all be subsumed within a single theoretical framework, see Braun and Gilardi 2006.

big role in what is implemented. This suggests that straightforward learning models, in which policymakers assess the cold, hard evidence and base policy decisions on it, may not depict the process accurately. When countries view the policy experiments through rose-colored lenses, they are more likely to replicate those experiments. When countries have vocal proponents for fashionable new policies around, they are more likely to follow them.

When it comes to the diffusion of new political norms, these studies show that resources can be as important as global political norms. Women's rights spread to countries that have formal connections to international organizations, suggesting that concrete connections matter. Democracy spreads through sets of neighboring countries, evidently because neighbors provide concrete resources for building democratization movements.

What these studies have shown, above all, is that the compartmentalization of different theories focusing on different issue areas has impoverished both theory and research. We see evidence that power resources influence the diffusion of democracy. We see evidence that ideological trends shape the spread of capital account liberalization. We see evidence that academic movements shape the diffusion of government downsizing and privatization. Scholars from each of these issue areas have much to learn from the work of others. In the future, researchers in each camp should take insights from other camps to heart, and build them into research programs.

References

Abdelal, Raui. 2006. Writing the Rules of Global Finance: France, Europe, and Capital Liberalization. *Review of International Political Economy* 13 (1):1–27.

Alesina, Alberto and Enrico Spolaore. 2003. *The Size of Nations*. Cambridge, MA.: MIT Press.

Atkeson, Andrew and Patrick J. Kehoe. 2001. The Transition to a New Economy after the Second Industrial Revolution. Unpublished manuscript, NBER Working Paper No. 8676.

Axelrod, Robert. 1997. The Dissemination of Culture – a Model with Local Convergence and Global Polarization. *Journal of Conflict Resolution* 41: 203–26.

Babai, Don. 1988. The World Bank and the IMF: Backing the State Versus Rolling It Back. In *The Promise of Privatization: A Challenge for U.S. Policy*, edited by Raymond Vernon, 254–85. New York, NY: Council on Foreign Relations.

Baldwin, Richard E. and Paul Krugman. 2004. Agglomeration, Integration and Tax Harmonisation. *European Economic Review* 48 (1):1–23.

Banerjee, A. 1992. A Simple Model of Herd Behavior. *Quarterly Journal of Economics* 65: 595–621.

Bartolini, Leonardo and Allan Drazen. 1997. Capital-Account Liberalization as a Signal. *American Economic Review* 87 (1):138–54.

Beck, Nathaniel, Kristian S. Gleditsch, and Kyle Beardsley. 2006. Space Is More Than Geography: Using Spatial Econometrics in the Study of Political Economy. *International Studies Quarterly* 50 (1):27–44.

Berger, Peter L. and Thomas Luckmann. 1966. *The Social Construction of Reality: A Treatise in the Sociology of Knowledge*. Garden City, NY: Doubleday.

Berkovitch, Nitza. 1999. *From Motherhood to Citizenship: Women's Rights and International Organizations*. Baltimore: Johns Hopkins University Press.

Berkovitch, Nitza and Karen Bradley. 1999. The Globalization of Women's Status: Consensus/Dissensus in the World Polity. *Sociological Perspectives* 42 (3):481–98.

Bernhard, William and David Leblang. 2002. Political Parties and Monetary Commitments. *International Organization* 56 (4):803–30.

Berry, Frances Stokes and William D. Berry. 1990. State Lottery Adoptions as Policy Innovations: An Event History Analysis. *The American Political Science Review* 84: 322–9.

Biglaiser, Glen. 2002. *Guardians of the Nation?: Economists, Generals, and Economic Reform in Latin America*. Notre Dame, IN: University of Notre Dame Press.

Bikchandani, S., D. Hirshleifer, and I. Welch. 1992. A Theory of Fads, Fashion, Custom, and Cultural Change as Informational Cascade. *Journal of Political Economy* 100: 992–1026.

Boli, John. 1987. Human Rights or State Expansion? Cross-National Definitions of Constitutional Rights. In *Institutional Structure: Constituting State, Society, and the Individual*, edited by George M. Thomas, John W. Meyer, Francisco O. Ramirez, and John Boli, 133–49. Beverly Hills, CA: Sage Publishing.

Boli, John and George M. Thomas. 1997. World Culture in the World Polity: A Century of International Non-Governmental Organization. *American Sociological Review* 62 (2):171–90.

Boli, John and George M. Thomas, eds. 1999. *Constructing World Culture: Internationl Nongovernmental Organizations since 1975*. Stanford: Stanford University Press.

Boli-Bennett, John and John W. Meyer. 1978. The Ideology of Childhood and the State. *American Sociological Review* 43: 797–812.

Bolton, Patrick and Gerard Roland. 1997. The Breakup of Nations: A Political Economy Analysis. *Quarterly Journal of Economics* 112 (4):1057–90.

Boyle, Elizabeth Heger and Sharon Preves. 2000. National Legislating as an International Process: The Case of Anti-Female-Genital-Cutting. *Law & Society Review* 34: 401–35.

Braun, Dietmar and Fabrizio Gilardi. 2006. Taking "Galton's Problem" Seriously: Towards a Theory of Policy Diffusion. *Journal of Theoretical Politics* 18 (3):298–322.

Brooks, Sarah M. 2005. Interdependent and Domestic Foundations of Policy Change: The Diffusion of Pension Privatization around the World. *International Studies Quarterly* 49 (2):273–94.

Broz, J. Lawrence. 2002. Political System Transparency and Monetary Commitment Regimes. *International Organization* 56 (4):861–87.

Brueckner, Jan K. 2000. Welfare Reform and the Race to the Bottom: Theory and Evidence. *Southern Economic Journal* 66 (2):505–25.

Brune, Nancy, Geoffrey Garrett, and Bruce Kogut. 2004. The International Monetary Fund and the Global Spread of Privatization. *IMF Staff Papers* 51.

Bull, Hedley. 1977. *The Anarchical Society: A Study of Order in World Politics.* New York: Columbia University Press.

Burt, Ronald S. 1987. Social Contagion and Innovation: Cohesion Versus Structural Equivalence. *The American Journal of Sociology* 96 (6):1287–335.

Buzan, Barry. 1993. From International System to International Society – Structural Realism and Regime Theory Meet the English School. *International Organization* 47 (3):327–52.

Cai, Hongbin and Daniel Treisman. 2004. State Corroding Federalism. *Journal of Public Economics* 88 (3–4):819–43.

Cameron, David R. 1978. The Expansion of the Public Economy: A Comparative Analysis. *The American Political Science Review* 72 (4):1243–61.

Castles, Francis Geoffrey, Rolf Gerritsen, and Jack Vowles, eds. 1996. *The Great Experiment: Labour Parties and Public Policy Transformation in Australia and New Zealand.* St. Leonards, NSW, Australia: Allen & Unwin.

Clark, William R. 2002. Partisan and Electoral Motivations and the Choice of Monetary Institutions under Fully Mobile Capital. *International Organization* 56 (4):725–49.

Cohen, Stephen S. 1977. *Modern Capitalist Planning: The French Model.* Berkeley: University of California Press.

Cole, Wade M. 2005. Sovereignty Relinquished? Explaining Commitment to the International Human Rights Covenants, 1966–1999. *American Sociological Review* 70 (3):472–96.

Coleman, James Samuel, Elihu Katz, and Herbert Menzel. 1966. *Medical Innovation; a Diffusion Study*. Indianapolis: Bobbs-Merrill Co.

Collier, Ruth Berins. 1999. *Paths toward Democracy: The Working Class and Elites in Western Europe and South America.* Cambridge; New York: Cambridge University Press.

Conell, Carol and Samuel Cohn. 1995. Learning from Other People's Actions: Environmental Variation and Diffusion in French Coal Mining Strikes, 1890–1935. *American Journal of Sociology* 101 (2):366–403.

Cordella, Tito and Giovanni. Dell'Ariccia. 2002. Limits of Conditionality in Poverty Reduction Programs. *IMF Staff Papers* 49: 68–86.

Crawford, Vincent P. and Hans Haller. 1990. Learning How to Cooperate: Optimal Play in Repeated Coordination Games. *Econometrica* 58 (3): 571–95.

Daley, Dorothy M. and James C. Garand. 2005. Horizontal Diffusion, Vertical Diffusion, and Internal Pressure in State Environmental Policymaking, 1989–1998. *American Politics Research* 33: 615–44.

Davis, Gerald. 1991. Agents without Principles: The Spread of the Poison Pill through the Intercorporate Network. *Administrative Science Quarterly* 36: 583–613.

Davis, Gerald F., Kristina A. Diekmann, and Catherine H. Tinsley. 1994. The Decline and Fall of the Conglomerate Firm in the 1980s: The Deinstitutionalization of an Organizational Form. *American Sociological Review* 59: 547–70.

de Vries, Barend A. 1997. The World Bank as an International Player in Economic Analysis. In *The Post-1945 Internationalization of Economics*, edited by A. W. Coats, 225–44. Durham, NC: Duke University Press.

DiMaggio, P. J. and W. W. Powell. 1983. The Iron Cage Revisited – Institutional Isomorphism and Collective Rationality in Organizational Fields. *American Sociological Review* 48 (2):147–60.

DiMaggio, Paul and Walter W. Powell. 1991. *The New Institutionalism in Organizational Analysis*. Chicago: University of Chicago Press.

Dobbin, Frank. 1993. The Social Construction of the Great Depression: Industrial Policy During the 1930s in the United States, Britain, and France. *Theory and Society* 22: 1–56.

Dobbin, Frank. 1994. Cultural Models of Organization: The Social Construction of Rational Organizing Principles. In *Sociology of Culture: Emerging Theoretical Perspectives*, edited by Diana Crane, 117–41. Oxford: Basil Blackwell.

Dobbin, Frank and Timothy Dowd. 2000. The Market That Antitrust Built: Public Policy, Private Coercion, and Railroad Acquisitions, 1825–1922. *American Sociological Review* 65: 635–57.

Dobson, Wendy and Gary Hufbauer. 2001. *World Capital Markets: Challenge to the G-10*. Washington, DC: Institute for International Economics.

Donahue, John D. 1997. Tiebout? Or Not Tiebout? The Market Metaphor and America's Devolution Debate. *Journal of Economic Perspectives* 11 (4): 73–81.

Doyle, Michael. 1986. Liberalism and World Politics. *The American Political Science Review* 80: 1151–69.

Drake, Paul W. 1994. *Money Doctors, Foreign Debts, and Economic Reforms in Latin America from the 1890s to the Present*. Wilmington, DE: SR Books.

Drazen, Allan. 2002. Conditionality and Ownership in IMF Lending: A Political Economy Approach. *IMF Staff Papers* 49: 36–67.

Edelman, Lauren N. 1992. Legal Ambiguity and Symbolic Structures: Organizational Mediation of Civil Rights Law. *The American Journal of Sociology* 97 (6):1531–976.

Edwards, A. C. and S. Edwards. 1992. Markets and Democracy – Lessons from Chile. *World Economy* 15 (2):203–19.

Edwards, Sebastian. 1997. Trade Liberalization Reforms and the World Bank. *American Economic Review* 87 (2):43–8.

Eichengreen, Barry and Christof Ruehl. 2000. The Bail-in Problem: Systemic Goals, Ad Hoc Means. Unpublished manuscript, NBER Working Paper No. 7653, Cambridge, MA.

Eising, Rainer. 2002. Policy Learning in Embedded Negotiations: Explaining EU Electricity Liberalization. *International Organization* 56 (1):85–120.

Elkins, Zachary, Andrew Guzman, and Beth A. Simmons. 2006. Competing for Capital: The Diffusion of Bilateral Investment Treaties, 1960–2000. *International Organization* 60 (4):811–46.

Elkins, Zachary and Beth A. Simmons. 2005. On Waves, Clusters, and Diffusion: A Conceptual Framework. *The Annals of the American Academy of Political and Social Science* 598 (1):33–51.

Encarnation, Dennis J. and Mark Mason. 1990. Neither Miti nor America: The Political Economy of Capital Liberalization in Japan. *International Organization* 44 (1):25–54.

Enrione, Alfredo, Carmelo Mazza, and Fernando Zerboni. 2006. Institutionalizing Codes of Governance. *American Behavioral Scientist* 49 (7):961–73.

Epstein, Gerald and Juliet Schor. 1992. Structural Determinants and Economic Effects of Capital Controls in OECD Countries. In *Financial Openness and National Autonomy: Opportunities and Constraints*, edited by Tariq Banuri and Juliet Schor, 136–61. Oxford: Clarendon Press.

Fafchamps, Marcel. 1996. Sovereign Debt, Structural Adjustment, and Conditionality. *Journal of Development Economics* 50 (2):313–35.

Femia, Joseph V. 1983. Gramsci's Patrimony. *British Journal of Political Science* 13 (3):327–64.

Finger, J. M. and M. E. Kreinin. 1979. Measure of Export Similarity and Its Possible Uses. *Economic Journal* 89 (356):905–12.

Finnemore, Martha. 1996. *National Interests in International Society, Cornell Studies in Political Economy*. Ithaca, NY: Cornell University Press.

Finnemore, Martha and Kathryn Sikkink. 2001. Taking Stock: The Constructivist Research Program in International Relations and Comparative Politics. *Annual Review of Political Science* 4: 391–416.

Fligstein, Neil. 1990. *The Transformation of Corporate Control*. Cambridge, MA: Harvard University Press.

Forsythe, David P. 1991. *The Internationalization of Human Rights*. Lexington, MA: Lexington Books.

Frank, David John, Ann Hironaka, and Evan Schofer. 2000. The Nation-State and the Natural Environment over the Twentieth Century. *American Sociological Review* 65: 96–116.

Frieden, Jeffry A. 1991. Invested Interests – the Politics of National Economic-Policies in a World of Global Finance. *International Organization* 45 (4):425–51.

Frieden, Jeffry A. and Ronald Rogowski. 1996. The Impact of the International Economy on National Policies: An Analytical Overview. In *Internationalization and Domestic Politics*, edited by Robert O. Keohane and Helen V. Milner, 25–47. Cambridge; New York: Cambridge University Press.

Gale, Douglas and Shachar Kariv. 2003. Bayesian Learning in Social Networks. Unpublished manuscript, New York University, New York.

Garrett, Geoffrey. 1998. Global Markets and National Politics: Collision Course or Virtuous Circle? *International Organization* 52 (4):787–824.

Garrett, Geoffrey and Peter Lange. 1995. Internationalization, Institutions, and Political Change. *International Organization* 49 (4):627–55.

Garrett, Geoffrey and Deborah Mitchell. 2001. Globalization, Government Spending, and Taxation in the OECD. *European Journal of Political Research* 39 (2):145–77.

Garrett, Geoffrey and Barry Weingast. 1993. Ideas, Interests, and Institutions: Constructing the EC's Internal Market. In *Ideas and Foreign Policy*, edited by Judith Goldstein and Robert Keohane, 173–206. Ithaca, NY: Cornell University Press.

Gastanaga, Victor M., Jeffrey B. Nugent, and Bistra Pashamova. 1998. Host Country Reforms and FDI Inflows: How Much Difference Do They Make? *World Development* 26 (7):1299–314.

Genschel, P. 2002. Globalization, Tax Competition, and the Welfare State. *Politics and Society* 30 (2):245–75.

Gilardi, Fabrizio. 2005. The Institutional Foundations of Regulatory Capitalism: The Diffusion of Independent Regulatory Agencies in Western Europe. *The Annals of the American Academy of Political and Social Science* 598 (1):84–101.

Giovannini, Alberto and Martha De Melo. 1993. Government Revenue from Financial Repression. *American Economic Review* 83 (4):953–63.

Gleditsch, Kristian Skrede and Michael D. Ward. 2006. Diffusion and the Spread of Democratic Institutions. *International Organization* 60 (4):911–33.

Goodman, John and Louis Pauly. 1993. The Obsolescence of Capital Controls? Economic Management in an Age of Global Markets. *World Politics* 46: 50–82.

Goolsbee, Austan and Peter J. Klenow. 1999. Evidence on Learning ND Network Externalities in the Diffusion of Home Computers. Unpublished manuscript, NBER Working Paper No. 7329.

Gould, Erica R. 2003. Money Talks: Supplementary Financiers and International Monetary Fund Conditionality. *International Organization* 57 (3):551–86.

Gourevitch, Peter Alexis. 1986. *Politics in Hard Times: Comparative Responses to International Economic Crises*. Ithaca: Cornell University Press.

Granovetter, Mark S. 1995. *Getting a Job: A Study of Contacts and Careers*. Chicago: University of Chicago Press.

Gray, Virginia. 1973. Innovation in the States: A Diffusion Study. *American Political Science Review* 67: 1174–85.

Gray, Virginia. 1994. Competition, Emulation, and Policy Innovation. In *New Perspectives on American Politics*, edited by Lawrence C. Dodd and Calvin C. Jillson, 230–48. Washington, DC: CQ Press.

Grilli, Vittorio and Gian Marie Milesi-Ferretti. 1995. Economic-Effects and Structural Determinants of Capital Controls. *International Monetary Fund Staff Papers* 42 (3):517–51.

Gruber, Lloyd. 2000. *Ruling the World: Power Politics and the Rise of Supranational Institutions*. Princeton: Princeton University Press.

Gruen, Nicholas. 1999. Toward a More General Approach to Trade Liberalization. *Economic Record* 75 (231):385–96.

Guitian, Manuel. 1995. Conditionality: Past, Present and Future. *Staff Papers* 42 (4):792–825.

Haas, Ernst B. 1959. *The Future of West European Political and Economic Unity*. Santa Barbara: Technical Military Planning Operation, General Electric Company.

Haas, Ernst B. 1980. Why Collaborate? Issue-Linkage and International Regimes. *World Politics* 32 (3):357–405.

Haas, Peter M. 1989. Do Regimes Matter: Epistemic Communities and Mediterranean Pollution Control. *International Organization* 43: 377–404.

Haas, Peter M. 1992. Epistemic Communities and International Policy Coordination – Introduction. *International Organization* 46 (1):1–35.

Hafner-Burton, Emilie M. 2005. Trading Human Rights: How Preferential Trade Agreements Influence Government Repression. *International Organization* 59 (3):593–629.

Hägerstrand, Torsten. 1967. *Innovation Diffusion as a Spatial Process*. Chicago: University of Chicago Press.

Hall, Peter A. 1989. *The Political Power of Economic Ideas: Keynesianism across Nations*. Princeton, NJ: Princeton University Press.

Hall, Peter A. 1993. Policy Paradigms, Social Learning, and the State: The Case of Economic Policy Making in Britain. *Comparative Politics* 25 (3):275–96.

Hallerberg, Mark. 2002. Veto Players and the Choice of Monetary Institutions. *International Organization* 56 (4):775–802.

Harberger, Arnold C. 1997. Good Economics Comes to Latin America, 1955–1995. In *The Post-1945 Internationalization of Economics*, edited by A. W. Coats, 301–11. Durham, NC: Duke University Press.

Haveman, Heather A. 1993a. Follow the Leader: Mimetic Isomorphism and Entry into New Markets. *Administrative Science Quarterly* 38: 593–627.

Haveman, Heather A. 1993b. Organizational Size and Change – Diversification in the Savings and Loan Industry after Deregulation. *Administrative Science Quarterly* 38 (1):20–50.

Heichel, Stephan, Jessica Pape, and Thomas Sommerer. 2005. Is There Convergence in Convergence Research? An Overview of Empirical Studies on Policy Convergence. *Journal of European Public Policy* 12 (5):817–40.

Helleiner, Eric. 1994. *States and the Reemergence of Global Finance: From Bretton Woods to the 1990s*. Ithaca: Cornell University Press.

Henisz, Witold J. 2000. The Institutional Environment for Multinational Investment. *Journal of Law, Economics, and Organization* 16 (2):334–64.

Henisz, Witold J., Bennet A. Zelner, and Mauro F. Guillen. 2005. The Worldwide Diffusion of Market Oriented Infrastructure Reform, 1977–1999. *American Sociological Review* 70 (6):871–97.

Herrell, A. 1993. International Society and the Study of Regimes: A Reflective Approach. Unpublished manuscript, Regime Theory and International Relations, Oxford.

Hicks, Alexander M. and Duane H. Swank. 1992. Politics, Institutions, and Welfare Spending in Industrialized Democracies, 1960–82. *The American Political Science Review* 86 (3):658–74.

Hira, Anil. 1998. *Ideas and Economic Policy in Latin America: Regional, National, and Organizational Case Studies*. Westport, CT: Praeger.

Hirschman, Albert O. 1977. *The Passions and the Interests: Political Arguments for Capitalism before Its Triumph*. Princeton, NJ: Princeton University Press.

Hirschman, Albert O. 1989. How the Keynesian Revolution Was Exported from the United States, and Other Comments. In *The Political Power of Economic Ideas: Keynesianism across Nations*, edited by Peter A. Hall, 347–60. Princeton, NJ: Princeton University Press.

Holden, Robert T. 1986. The Contagiousness of Aircraft Hijacking. *American Journal of Sociology* 91 (4):874–904.

Holzinger, Katharina and Christoph Knill. 2005. Causes and Conditions of Cross-National Policy Convergence. *Journal of European Public Policy* 12 (5): 775–96.

Hopkins, Raul, Andrew Powell, Amlan Roy, and Christopher L. Gilbert. 1997. The World Bank and Conditionality. *Journal of International Development* 9 (4):507–16.

Huber, Evelyne, Charles Ragin, and John D. Stephens. 1993. Social Democracy, Christian Democracy, Constitutional Structure, and the Welfare State. *American Journal of Sociology* 99 (3):711–49.

Huntington, Samuel P. 1991. *The Third Wave: Democratization in the Late Twentieth Century*. Norman: University of Oklahoma Press.

Huth, Paul K. and Bruce Russett. 1984. What Makes Deterrence Work? Cases from 1900 to 1980. *World Politics* 36 (4):496–526.

Ikenberry, G. John. 1990. The International Spread of Privatization Policies: Inducements, Learning, and Policy Bandwagoning. In *The Political Economy of Public Sector Reform and Privatization*, edited by Ezra N. Suleiman and John Waterbury, 88–109. Boulder: Westview Press.

Jacoby, Wade. 2000. *Imitation and Politics: Redesigning Modern Germany*. Ithaca, NY: Cornell University Press.

Jensen, Nathan M. 2003. Democratic Governance and Multinational Corporations: Political Regimes and Inflows of Foreign Direct Investment. *International Organization* 57 (3):587–616.

Jervis, Robert. 1976. *Perception and Misperception in International Politics*. Princeton, NJ: Princeton University Press.

Johnson, Chalmers A. 1982. *MITI and the Japanese Miracle: The Growth of Industrial Policy, 1925–1975*. Stanford, CA: Stanford University Press.

Kahler, Miles. 1994. External Influence, Conditionality, and the Politics of Adjustment. In *Voting for Reform: Democracy, Political Liberalization, and Economic Adjustment*, edited by Stephan Haggard and Steven Benjamin Webb, 89–136. New York: Oxford University Press.

Kahneman, Daniel, Paul Slovic, and Amos Tversky. 1982. *Judgment under Uncertainty: Heuristics and Biases*. Cambridge; New York: Cambridge University Press.

Kaminsky, Graciela L. and Carmen M. Reinhart. 2000. On Crises, Contagion, and Confusion. *Journal of International Economics* 51 (1):145–68.

Kaplinsky, Raphael. 2001. Globalisation and Economic Security. *IDS Bulletin* 49 (6):13–24.

Katzenstein, Peter J., ed. 1978. *Between Power and Plenty: Foreign Economic Policies of Advanced Industrial States*. Madison: University of Wisconsin Press.

Katzenstein, Peter J. 1985. *Small States in World Markets: Industrial Policy in Europe*. Ithaca, NY: Cornell University Press.

Katzenstein, Peter J. 1996. *The Culture of National Security: Norms and Identity in World Politics*. New York: Columbia University Press.

Kaufman, Robert R. and Alex Segura-Ubiergo. 2001. Globalization, Domestic Politics, and Social Spending in Latin America: A Time-Series Cross-Section Analysis, 1973–1997. *World Politics* 53 (4):553–87.

Keefer, Philip and David Stasavage. 2002. Checks and Balances, Private Information, and the Credibility of Monetary Commitments. *International Organization* 56 (4):751–74.

Kelemen, R. Daniel and Eric C. Sibbitt. 2004. The Globalization of American Law. *International Organization* 58 (1):103–36.

Keller, Wolfgang. 2002. Geographic Localization of International Technology Diffusion. *American Economic Review* 92 (1):120–42.

Keohane, Robert O. 1988. International Institutions: Two Approaches. *International Studies Quarterly* 32: 379–96.

Keohane, Robert O. and Helen V. Milner, eds. 1996. *Internationalization and Domestic Politics*. Cambridge; New York: Cambridge University Press.

Kevlihan, Rob. 2001. Becoming a 'Player': Ireland and Aid Conditionality with Reference to Sudan. *European Journal of Development Research* 13 (1):70–86.

Khamfula, Yohane. 1998. Influence of Social Learning on Exchange Rate Policy in Developing Countries: A Preliminary Finding. *Applied Economics* 30 (5):697–704.

Khan, Mohsin S. and Sunil Sharma. 2001. IMF Conditionality and Country Ownership of Programs. Unpublished manuscript, International Monetary Fund Working Paper WP/01/142, Washington DC.

Kitschelt, Herbert, Peter Lange, Gary Marks, and John Stephens, eds. 1999. *Continuity and Change in Contemporary Capitalism*. Cambridge, UK; New York: Cambridge University Press.

Knill, Christoph. 2005. Introduction: Cross-National Policy Convergence: Concepts, Approaches and Explanatory Factors. *Journal of European Public Policy* 12 (5):764–74.

Kogut, Bruce and J. Muir McPherson. 2005. The Decision to Privatize as an Economic Policy Idea: Economists, Palace Wars, and Diffusion. Unpublished manuscript, INSEAD, Fontainebleau, France.

Korten, David C. 1995. *When Corporations Rule the World*. London: Earthscan.

Krasner, Stephen D. 1993. Westphalia. In *Ideas and Foreign Policy*, edited by Judith Goldstein and Robert O. Keohane, 235–64. Ithaca: Cornell University Press.

Krugman, Paul. 1995. Cycles of Conventional Wisdom on Economic Development. *International Affairs* 71 (4):717–32.

Kunce, Mitch and Jason F. Shogren. 2002. On Environmental Federalism and Direct Emission Control. *Journal of Urban Economics* 51 (2):238–45.

Kurzer, Paulette. 1993. *Business and Banking: Political Change and Economic Integration in Western Europe*. Ithaca: Cornell University Press.

Lake, David A. and Robert Powell. 1999. *Strategic Choice and International Relations*. Princeton, NJ: Princeton University Press.

Lee, Chang Kil and David Strang. 2006. The International Diffusion of Public Sector Downsizing. *International Organization* 60 (4):883–909.

Leng, Russell J. 1983. When Will They Ever Learn? Coercive Bargaining in Recurrent Crises. *Journal of Conflict Resolution* 27 (3):379–419.

Lenschow, Andrea, Duncan Liefferink, and Sietske Veenman. 2005. When the Birds Sing. A Framework for Analysing Domestic Factors Behind Policy Convergence. *Journal of European Public Policy* 12 (5):797–816.

Lester, Anthony and Geoffrey Bindman. 1972. *Race and Law*. London: Longman.
Levi-Faur, David. 2003. The Politics of Liberalisation: Privatisation and Regulation-for-Competition in Europe's and Latin America's Telecoms and Electricity Industries. *European Journal of Political Research* 42 (5):705–40.
Levite, Ariel, Bruce W. Jentleson, and Larry Berman, eds. 1994. *Foreign Military Intervention: The Dynamics of Protracted Conflict*. New York: Columbia University Press.
Levy, Jack S. 1994. Learning and Foreign Policy: Sweeping a Conceptual Minefield. *International Organization* 48 (2):279–312.
Li, Richard and William Thompson. 1975. The 'Coup Contagion' Hypothesis. *Journal of Conflict Resolution* 19 (1):63–88.
Linz, Juan J. and Alfred C. Stepan. 1996. *Problems of Democratic Transition and Consolidation: Southern Europe, South America, and Post-Communist Europe*. Baltimore: Johns Hopkins University Press.
Lutz, James M. 1987. Regional Leadership Patterns in the Diffusion of Public Policies. *American Politics Quarterly* 15: 387–98.
Malinowski, Bronislaw. 1944. *A Scientific Theory of Culture*. Chapel Hill: The University of North Carolina Press.
March, James G. and Herbert Alexander Simon. 1993. *Organizations*. Cambridge, MA: Blackwell Business.
Markoff, John. 1996. *Waves of Democracy: Social Movements and Political Change*. Thousand Oaks, CA: Pine Forge Press.
Martinez-Vazquez, Jorge, Felix Rioja, Samuel Skogstad, and Neven Valev. 2001. IMF Conditionality and Objections: The Russian Case. *American Journal of Economics & Sociology* 60 (2):501–17.
Massey, Rachel I. 1999. The Credibility of Exit Threats: Refining The "Race to the Bottom" Debate. *Journal of Public & International Affairs* 10: 47–62.
McNamara, Kathleen R. 1998. *The Currency of Ideas: Monetary Politics in the European Union*. Ithaca, NY: Cornell University Press.
McNeely, Connie L. 1995. *Constructing the Nation-State: International Organization and Prescriptive Action*. Westport, CT: Greenwood Press.
McPherson, M. 1987. The Promise of Privatization. In *Privatization and Development*, edited by Steve H. Hanke, 17–21. San Francisco, CA: International Center for Economic Growth ICS Press.
Meseguer, Covadonga. 2004. What Role for Learning? The Diffusion of Privatisation in OECD and Latin American Countries. *Journal of Public Policy* 24 (3):299–325.
Meseguer, Covadonga 2005. Policy Learning, Policy Diffusion, and the Making of a New Order *The Annals of the American Academy of Political and Social Science* 598 (1):67–82.
Meyer, John W., John Boli, George M. Thomas, and Francisco O. Ramirez. 1997. World Society and the Nation-State. *American Journal of Sociology* 103 (1):144–81.
Meyer, John W. and Michael T. Hannan. 1979. *National Development and the World System: Educational, Economic, and Political Change, 1950–1970*. Chicago: University of Chicago Press.

Meyer, John W., Francisco O. Ramirez, Richard Rubinson, and John Boli-Bennett. 1977. The World Educational Revolution, 1950–1970. *Sociology of Education* 50 (4):242–58.

Meyer, John W., Francisco O. Ramirez, and Yasmine N. Soysal. 1992. World Expansion of Mass Education, 1870–1980. *Sociology of Education* 65 (2):128–49.

Meyer, John W. and Brian Rowan. 1977. Institutionalized Organizations: Formal Structure as Myth and Ceremony. *American Journal of Sociology* 83: 340–63.

Meyer, William H. 1998. *Human Rights and International Political Economy in Third World Nations :Multinational Corporations, Foreign Aid, and Repression.* Westport, CT: Praeger.

Mintrom, Michael. 1997. Policy Entrepreneurs and the Diffusion of Innovation. *American Journal of Political Science* 41 (3):738–70.

Mintrom, Michael and Sandra Vergari. 1998. Policy Networks and Innovation Diffusion: The Case of State Education Reforms. *The Journal of Politics* 60 (1):126–48.

Mishkin, Frederic S. 1999. Lessons from the Asian Crisis. *Journal of International Money and Finance* 18 (4):709–23.

Montecinos, Veronica. 1997. Policy Elites in Latin America. In *The Post-1945 Internationalization of Economics*, edited by A. W. Coats, 279–300. Durham, NC: Duke University Press.

Mosley, Layna. 2003. *Global Capital and National Governments*. Cambridge, UK; New York: Cambridge University Press.

Mosley, Layna and Saiko Uno. 2007. Racing to the Bottom or Climbing to the Top? Economic Globalization and Collective Labor Rights. *Comparative Political Studies* 40: 923–48.

Mosley, Paul, Jane Harrigan, and J. F. J. Toye. 1995. *Aid and Power: The World Bank and Policy-Based Lending*. London; New York: Routledge.

Murillo, Maria Victoria. 2002. Political Bias in Policy Convergence: Privatization Choices in Latin America. *World Politics* 54 (4):462–93.

Nelson, D. 1988. Endogenous Tariff Theory – a Critical Survey. *American Journal of Political Science* 32 (3):796–837.

Nelson, Joan M. 1996. Promoting Policy Reforms: The Twilight of Conditionality? *World Development* 24 (9):1551–9.

Neumayer, Eric and Indra de Soysa. 2006. Globalization and the Right to Free Association and Collective Bargaining: An Empirical Analysis. *World Development* 34 (1):31–49.

Nye, Joseph S. 1987. Nuclear Learning and U.S.-Soviet Nuclear Regimes. *International Organization* 41 (3):371–402.

O'Donnell, Guillermo A. 1973. *Modernization and Bureaucratic-Authoritarianism; Studies in South American Politics, Politics of Modernization Series, no. 9.* Berkeley: Institute of International Studies University of California.

O'Donnell, Guillermo A., Philippe C. Schmitter, and Laurence Whitehead. 1986. *Transitions from Authoritarian Rule*. Baltimore: Johns Hopkins University Press.

O'Loughlin, J., M. D. Ward, C. L. Lofdahl, J. S. Cohen, D. S. Brown, D. Reilly, K. S. Gleditsch, and M. Shin. 1998. The Diffusion of Democracy, 1946–1994. *Annals of the Association of American Geographers* 88 (4):545–74.

Oates, Wallace E. 2001. Fiscal Competition or Harmonization? Some Reflections. *National Tax Journal* 54 (3):507–12.

Owen, John M. Jr. 2002. The Foreign Imposition of Domestic Institutions. *International Organization* 56 (2):375–409.

Pahre, Robert. 1999. *Leading Questions: How Hegemony Affects the International Political Economy*. Ann Arbor: University of Michigan Press.

Peterson, Paul E. and Mark C. Rom. 1990. *Welfare Magnets: A New Case for a National Standard*. Washington, DC: Brookings Institution.

Pfaller, Alfred, Ian Gough, and Göran Therborn. 1991. *Can the Welfare State Compete? A Comparative Study of Five Advanced Capitalist Countries*. London: Macmillan.

Pierson, Christopher. 1991. *Beyond the Welfare State? The New Political Economy of Welfare*. University Park, PA: Pennsylvania State University Press.

Polak, Jacques J. 1997. The Contribution of the International Monetary Fund. In *The Post-1945 Internationalization of Economics*, edited by A. W. Coats, 211–24. Durham, NC: Duke University Press.

Porter, Gareth. 1999. Trade Competition and Pollution Standards: "Race to the Bottom" or "Stuck at the Bottom"? *Journal of Environment & Development* 8 (2):133–51.

Powell, Robert. 1988. Nuclear Brinksmanship with Two-Sided Incomplete Information. *American Political Science Review* 81: 717–35.

Powell, Walter W. 1990. Neither Market nor Hierarchy: Network Forms of Organization. In *Research in Organizational Behavior*, edited by L. L. Cummings and B. Shaw, 295–336. Greenwich, CT: JAI Press.

Prasad, Eswar, Kenneth Rogoff, Shang-jin Wei, and M.Ayhan Kose. 2003. Effects of Financial Globalization on Developing Countries: Some Empirical Evidence. www.imf.org/external/np/res/docs/2003/031703.pdf.

Przeworski, Adam, Michael E. Alvarez, Jose Antonio Cheibub, and Fernando Limongi. 2000. *Democracy and Development: Political Institutions and Material Well-being in the World, 1950–1990, Cambridge Studies in the Theory of Democracy*. Cambridge: Cambridge University Press.

Quinn, Dennis P. 1997. The Correlates of Change in International Financial Regulation. *American Political Science Review* 91 (2):531–52.

Quinn, Dennis P. and Carla Inclan. 1997. The Origins of Financial Openness: A Study of Current and Capital Account Liberalization. *American Journal of Political Science* 41 (3):771–813.

Quirk, Peter J. 1994. *Adopting Currency Convertibility: Experiences and Monetary Policy Considerations for Advanced Developing Countries*. Washington, DC: International Monetary Fund.

Ramamurti, Ravi. 1999. Why Haven't Developing Countries Privatized Deeper and Faster? *World Development* 27 (1):137–55.

Ramirez, Francisco O. and John Boli. 1987. The Political Construction of Mass Schooling: European Origins and Worldwide Institutionalization. *Sociology of Education* 60: 2–17.

Ramirez, Francisco O. and Elizabeth H. McEneaney. 1997. From Women's Suffrage to Reproduction Rights? Cross-National Comparisons. *International Journal of Comparative Sociology* 66: 6–24.

Ramirez, F. O., Y. Soysal, and S. Shanahan. 1997. The Changing Logic of Political Citizenship: Cross-National Acquisition of Women's Suffrage Rights, 1890 to 1990. *American Sociological Review* 62 (5):735–45.

Reiter, Dan. 1996. *Crucible of Beliefs: Learning, Alliances, and World Wars*. Ithaca, NY: Cornell University Press.

Rodrik, Dani. 1997. *Has Globalization Gone Too Far?* Washington, DC: Institute for International Economics.

Rodrik, Dani. 1998. Why Do More Open Economies Have Bigger Governments? *Journal of Political Economy* 106 (5):997–1032.

Rogers, Everett M. 1995. *Diffusion of Innovations*. New York: Free Press.

Rogowski, Ronald. 1989. *Commerce and Coalitions: How Trade Affects Domestic Political Alignments*. Princeton, NJ: Princeton University Press.

Rogowski, Ronald. 2003. International Capital Mobility and National Policy Divergence. In *Governance in a Global Economy: Political Authority in Transition*, edited by Miles Kahler and David A. Lake, 255–74. Princeton, NJ: Princeton University Press.

Rose, Richard. 1993. *Lesson-Drawing in Public Policy: A Guide to Learning across Time and Space*. Chatham, NJ: Chatham House Publishers.

Rudra, Nita. 2002. Globalization and the Decline of the Welfare State in Less-Developed Countries. *International Organization* 56 (2):411–45.

Ruggie, John Gerard. 1982. International Regimes, Transactions, and Change: Embedded Liberalism in the Postwar Economic Order. *International Organization* 36 (2):379–415.

Ruggie, John Gerard. 1993. Territoriality and Beyond: Problematizing Modernity in International Relations. *International Organization* 47(1): 139–74.

Ruggie, John Gerard. 1998. What Makes the World Hang Together? Neo-Utilitarianism and the Social Constructivist Challenge. *International Organization* 52 (4):855–86.

Sachs, Jeffrey, Harry Huizinga, and John B. Shoven. 1987. U.S. Commercial Banks and the Developing-Country Debt Crisis. *Brookings Papers on Economic Activity* 18 (2):555–606.

Sanahuja, Jose Antonio. 2000. Trade, Politics, and Democratization: The 1997 Global Agreement between the European Union and Mexico. *Journal of Interamerican Studies and World Affairs* 42 (2):35–62.

Santiso, Carlos. 2003. Sisyphus in the Castle: Improving European Union Strategies for Democracy Promotion and Governance Conditionality. *European Journal of Development Research* 15 (1):1–28.

Scharpf, Fritz Wilhelm. 1991. *Crisis and Choice in European Social Democracy*. Ithaca, NY: Cornell University Press.

Schelling, Thomas C. 1960. *The Strategy of Conflict*. Cambridge: Harvard University Press.

Schimmelfennig, Frank, Stefan Engert, and Heiko Knobel. 2003. Costs, Commitment and Compliance: The Impact of EU Democratic Conditionality on Latvia, Slovakia and Turkey. *Journal of Common Market Studies* 41 (3):495–518.

Schneider, Anne and Helen Ingram. 1988. Systematically Pinching Ideas: A Comparative Approach to Policy Design. *Journal of Public Policy* 8 (1):61–80.

Schwartz, Herman. 1994. Small States in Big Trouble: State Reorganization in Australia, Denmark, New Zealand, and Sweden in the 1980s. *World Politics* 46 (4):527–55.

Schwartz, Herman. 1998. Social Democracy Going Down or Down Under: Institutions, Internationalized Capital, and Indebted States. *Comparative Politics* 30 (3):253–72.

Shonfield, Andrew. 1965. *Modern Capitalism: The Changing Balance of Public and Private Power*. London; New York: Oxford University Press.

Siegel, Richard L. and Leonard Weinberg. 1977. *Comparing Public Policies: United States, Soviet Union, and Europe*. Homewood, IL: Dorsey Press.

Simmons, Beth A. 2001. The International Politics of Harmonization: The Case of Capital Market Regulation. *International Organization* 55 (3):589–620.

Simmons, Beth A. and Zachary Elkins. 2003. Globalization and Policy Diffusion: Explaining Three Decades of Liberalization. In *Governance in a Global Economy: Political Authority in Transition*, edited by Miles Kahler and David A. Lake, 275–304. Princeton, NJ: Princeton University Press.

Simmons, Beth A. and Zachary Elkins. 2004. The Globalization of Liberalization: Policy Diffusion in the International Political Economy. *American Political Science Review* 98 (1):171–89.

Sinn, Hans-Werner and Wolfgang Ochel. 2003. Social Union, Convergence and Migration. *Journal of Common Market Studies* 41 (5):869–96.

Starr, Harvey. 1991. Democratic Dominoes – Diffusion Approaches to the Spread of Democracy in the International System. *Journal of Conflict Resolution* 35 (2):356–81.

Starr, Paul. 1989. The Meaning of Privatization. In *Privatization and the Welfare State*, edited by Sheila Kamerman and Alfred Kahn. Princeton, NJ: Princeton University Press.

Stone, Diane. 1999. Learning Lessons and Transferring Policy across Time, Space, and Disciplines. *Politics* 19 (1):51–9.

Strang, David. 1991. Global Patterns of Decolonization, 1500–1987. *International Studies Quarterly* 35 (4):429–54.

Strang, David and Patricia M. Y. Chang. 1993. The International-Labor-Organization and the Welfare-State – Institutional Effects on National Welfare Spending, 1960–80. *International Organization* 47 (2):235–62.

Strang, David and Michael W. Macy. 2001. In Search of Excellence: Fads, Success Stories, and Adaptive Emulation. *American Journal of Sociology* 107 (1):147–82.

Strang, David and John W. Meyer. 1993. Institutional Conditions for Diffusion. *Theory and Society* 22: 487–511.

Strang, David and Sarah A. Soule. 1998. Diffusion in Organizations and Social Movements: From Hybrid Corn to Poison Pills. *Annual Review of Sociology* 24: 265–90.

Svensson, Jakob. 2000. When Is Foreign Aid Policy Credible? Aid Dependence and Conditionality. *Journal of Development Economics* 61 (1):61–84.

Swank, Duane. 1992. Politics and the Structural Dependence of the State in Democratic Capitalist Nations. *American Political Science Review* 86 (1):38–54.

Swank, Duane. 1998. Funding the Welfare State: Globalization and the Taxation of Business in Advanced Market Economies. *Political Studies* 46 (4):671–92.

Swank, Duane. 2006. Tax Policy in an Era of Internationalization: An Assessment of a Conditional Diffusion Model of the Spread of Neoliberalism. *International Organization* 60 (4):847–82.

Swank, Duane and Sven Steinmo. 2002. The New Political Economy of Taxation in Advanced Capitalist Democracies. *American Journal of Political Science* 46 (3):642–55.

Tanguay, Georges A. 2001. Bidding for Polluting Firms: The Race for the Bottom. *Pennsylvania Economic Review* 10 (1):14–24.

Thomas, George M. and John W. Meyer. 1984. The Expansion of the State. *Annual Review of Sociology* 10: 461–82.

Thomas, George M., John W. Meyer, Francisco O. Ramirez, and John Boli. 1987. *Institutional Structure: Constituting State, Society, and the Individual.* Newbury Park, CA: Sage Publications.

Tiebout, Charles Mills. 1962. *The Community Economic Base Study.* New York: Committee for Economic Development.

Tolbert, Pamela S. and Lynne G. Zucker. 1983. Institutional Sources of Change in the Formal-Structure of Organizations – the Diffusion of Civil-Service Reform, 1880–1935. *Administrative Science Quarterly* 28 (1):22–39.

True, Jacqui and Michael Mintrom. 2001. Transnational Networks and Policy Diffusion: The Case of Gender Mainstreaming. *International Studies Quarterly* 45 (1):27–57.

Tsebelis, George and Geoffrey Garrett. 2001. The Institutional Foundations of Intergovernmentalism and Supranationalism in the European Union. *International Organization* 55 (2):357–90.

Twining, William. 2004. Social Science and Diffusion of Law. *Journal of Law and Society* 32: 203–40.

Vreeland, James Raymond. 2003. *The IMF and Economic Development.* New York: Cambridge University Press.

Wagner, R. Harrison. 1989. Uncertainty, Rational Learning, and Bargaining in the Cuban Missile Crisis. In *Models of Strategic Choice in Politics*, edited by Peter Ordeshook, 177–205. Ann Arbor: University of Michigan Press.

Walker, Jack. 1969. The Diffusion of Innovation among the American States. *American Political Science Review* 63: 880–99.

Waltman, Jerold L. 1980. *Copying Other Nations' Policies: Two American Case Studies.* Cambridge, MA: Schenkman.

Weber, Max. 1978. Basic Sociological Terms. In *Economy and Society*, edited by M. Weber, 3–62. Berkeley: University of California Press.

Weick, Karl. 1976. Educational Organizations as Loosely Coupled Systems. *Administrative Science Quarterly* 21 (1):1–19.

Wendt, Alexander. 1999. *Social Theory of International Politics.* Cambridge, UK; New York: Cambridge University Press.

Westney, Eleanor. 1987. *Imitation and Innovation: The Transfer of Western Organizational Patterns to Meiji Japan.* Cambridge, MA: Harvard University Press.

Weyland, Kurt Gerhard. 2005. Theories of Policy Diffusion: Lessons from Latin American Pension Reform. *World Politics* 57 (2):262–95.

Wheeler, David. 2001. Racing to the Bottom? Foreign Investment and Air Pollution in Developing Countries. *Journal of Environment & Development* 10 (3):225–45.

Williamson, John. 1993. Democracy and the Washington Consensus. *World Development* 21 (8):1329–36.

Williamson, John. 1997. The Washington Consensus Revisited. In *Economic and Social Development into the XXI Century*, edited by Louis Emmerij, 48–61. Washington, DC: Inter-American Development Bank.

Williamson, John. 2000. What Should the World Bank Think About the Washington Consensus? *World Bank Research Observer* 15 (2):251–64.

Wilson, James Q., ed. 1980. *The Politics of Regulation*. New York: Basic.

Wilson, Rick K. and Carl M. Rhodes. 1997. Leadership and Credibility in N-Person Coordination Games. *Journal of Conflict Resolution* 41 (6):767–91.

Zhou, Xueguang. 1993. Occupational Power, State Capacities, and the Diffusion of Licensing in the American States: 1980–1950. *American Sociological Review* 58 (4):536–52.

2 Tax policy in an era of internationalization: an assessment of a conditional diffusion model of the spread of neoliberalism*

Duane Swank

Neoliberal reforms in public policies and economic institutions proliferated across the developed democracies and the globe in the latter decades of the twentieth century.[1] National structures of taxation have not been immune to neoliberalism. Beginning in the early 1980s, policymakers throughout the Organization for Economic Cooperation and Development (OECD) significantly altered the content of tax policies. The relative priority accorded equity and growth goals, the use of investment and behavioral incentives, and the level of tax rates were all notably changed: marginal income and corporate profits tax rates were scaled back, the number of brackets were cut and inflation-indexed, and tax-based investment incentives were eliminated or reduced to broaden the tax base. Why have nearly all developed nations enacted this set of market-conforming tax policies?[2]

To answer this question, I build on my recent work on the determinants of change in tax policy in the developed democracies and explore

* This chapter is a slightly modified version of an article that appeared in *International Organization*, November, 2006. Earlier drafts of the article were presented at the Center for European Studies and Weatherhead Center for International Affairs, Harvard University; Center for International Studies, UCLA; and Yale University as well as the 2002 Annual Meetings of the American Political Science Association. An earlier version was published as Minda de Gunzburg Center for European Studies, Harvard University, Working Paper #120. I thank Alex Hicks, Rob Franzese, Torben Iversen, Andy Martin, Cathie Jo Martin; participants in the Yale, UCLA, and Harvard conferences, especially Geoffrey Garrett, Helen Milner, Dennis Quinn, and Beth A. Simmons; two anonymous referees and the editors of *International Organization*; and reviewers for Cambridge University Press for helpful comments. I also gratefully acknowledge the contribution of Sven Steinmo that comes by way of our past collaborative work on tax policy.

1 See, among others, Campbell and Pedersen 2001; and the Introduction to this volume.

2 The present analysis is limited to the developed democracies for two reasons. First, a central theoretical motivation of the chapter is to explore how domestic politics and political economic institutions of democratic market economies shape policy diffusion. Second, the large majority of international investment moves between the developed economies. Given that the current chapter focuses on the influence on policy of tax competition for mobile assets, a sample of developed nations is particularly appropriate.

the dynamics of diffusion of the neoliberal tax policy paradigm in the area of capital taxation.[3] While I assess general competition, policy learning, and social emulation models of tax policy diffusion, I argue that the highly visible 1986 market-conforming tax reform in the United States should be especially important in promoting diffusion. Specifically, I argue that (asymmetric) competition for mobile assets associated with US reforms significantly influences national policy choices in other polities. My central argument is, however, that while the competitive incentives to adopt US tax policy are substantial, the relative weight assigned the benefits of neoliberal reform as well as economic and political costs of policy change is fundamentally dependent on features of the domestic political economy. Domestic politics should be important: the degrees to which the median voter has shifted right and right-of-center parties have governed in recent years should be consequential for the pace and depth of tax policy change. The character of a nation's production regime is also crucially important: the extent to which the domestic political economy is composed of coordinated or uncoordinated market institutions should shape the assessment by national policymakers of the benefits and costs of adoption and non-adoption of the new tax policy regime.

I organize my analysis as follows. First, I briefly discuss recent trends in taxation and review theories about contemporary tax policy change. Next, I elaborate my arguments about policy diffusion. I then develop empirical models of statutory and effective tax rates on capital and assess these with 1981 to 1998 data from sixteen nations. I conclude with a summary of what is known about the forces driving tax policy change and the diffusion of neoliberal policies in an era of globalization.

Tax policy change in the developed democracies

Beginning in the early 1980s, incumbent governments significantly altered national policies on the taxation of corporate profits and capital income. The near universal system of relatively high marginal statutory tax rates and extensive use of tax instruments to target investment (and otherwise shape the behavior of economic agents in accord with national policy goals) was significantly reformed in nearly all nations. Table 2.1

[3] Swank 1998; Swank and Steinmo 2002. Regarding the focus on capital taxation, it is important to note that while the shift to neoliberal tax policy affects both labor and capital income taxation, the combination of rate reductions and base broadening has been especially pronounced in corporate tax policy; Ganghof 2004. Moreover, many of the central questions surrounding the mechanisms of diffusion (e.g. pressures from tax competition) are more relevant to the capital tax side.

Table 2.1. *The taxation of corporate and capital income, 1981–1998*

	Top marginal rate corporate income[1]			Rates of general investment incentives[2]		Effective rate of tax on capital[3]		
Nation	1981	1989	1998	1980	1992	1981	1989	1996
Australia	46	39	36	18	0	47	48	47
Austria	na	na	34	na	na	23	21	26
Belgium	48	43	40	5	0	39	34	36
Canada	48	39	38	7	0	39	43	51
Denmark	40	50	34	0	0	43	46	52
Finland	na	na	28	na	na	34	41	38
France	50	39	42	10	0	28	26	29
Germany	56	56	48	0	0	32	29	24
Ireland	45	43	32	0	0	na	na	na
Italy	36	46	41	0	0	23	28	33
Japan	42	40	34	0	0	37	51	43
Netherlands	48	35	35	12	0	32	29	31
New Zealand	42	33	33	0	0	36	40	35
Norway	51	51	28	0	0	44	30	29
Sweden	58	52	28	10	0	54	64	53
Switzerland	10	10	8	0	0	na	na	na
United Kingdom	52	35	31	0	0	63	61	47
United States	46	34	35	10	0	45	43	37
Mean	45	40	34	5	0	39	40	38
Coefficient of variation	.126	.177	.154	—	—	.314	.357	.249

[1]Highest statutory corporate tax rate. Source: for 1981–1992, Cummins, Hassett, and Hubbard 1995; for 1993–1998, Coopers and Lybrand International Tax Network, selected years.
[2]Rate for general statutory investment incentives. Investment incentives for specific regions and industries, certain forms of fixed business investment, and special investment programs (e.g. Denmark and Sweden's investment reserve fund) are not included. Source: Cummins, Hassett, and Hubbard 1995.
[3]The total tax burden on capital income equals taxes on property income and immovable property plus taxes on unincorporated and corporate enterprise profits plus taxes on capital and financial transactions, all as a percentage of operating surplus. Mendoza, Razin, and Tesar 1994. Also see Appendix 2.2 Data sources.

summarizes the most significant features of changes in corporate and capital taxation. Policymakers reduced statutory corporate tax rates on average from 45 percent in 1981 to 34 percent in 1998. They also commonly eliminated or reduced various investment credits, exemptions, and grants that had significantly lowered effective corporate tax rates on reinvested profits. As Table 2.1 illustrates, the general investment tax credit was eliminated by 1992 in all nations that had employed it.[4]

These notable changes in the substantive content of tax policy reflect, in part, a long-term shift in economist and policymaker thinking about optimal tax structure. While the system of high marginal statutory rates, targeted investment incentives, and other tax expenditures was once viewed as a means to foster both equity and growth, the extant structure of taxation had by the early 1980s become emblematic of unfairness, undue complexity, and inefficiency. By the mid-1980s, significant numbers of OECD finance ministers and their economic advisers had come to view the existing tax structure as the source of inefficient allocation of productive investment and lost tax collections; tax rate cuts and base broadening were commonly seen as mechanisms to bolster both economic efficiency and maintain government revenues.[5] Generally, statutory rate cuts coupled with base-broadening elimination of tax expenditures have become part and parcel of neoliberal economic orthodoxy (e.g. the "Washington Consensus").

Two departures from the trend toward market-oriented taxation, however, stand out. First, the pace and depth of the near-universal course of policy reform varies across nations. As the Table 2.1 data illustrate, some nations (e.g. the Anglo democracies, France, and the Netherlands) cut statutory rates relatively quickly (and concomitantly reduced or eliminated tax-based investment incentives). On the other hand, tax rates remained constant or increased in several other political economies; significant market-oriented tax reforms did not occur until the late 1990s in Italy and statutory rates in some nations (e.g. Germany) remained moderately high in 1998. Second, despite notable and widespread cuts in statutory income tax rates, the effective capital tax rate in the typical developed democracy has actually remained relatively stable: governments collected on average 39 percent of capital income in revenue in 1981 and 38 percent in 1996. This tendency toward stability largely reflects the joint effects of rate cuts and substantial base

[4] See, among others, Boskin and McClure 1990; Ganghof 2000; Genschel 1999; and Pechman 1988. In addition, two points need to the clarified. First, depreciation for investments in equipment and plant has been everywhere maintained. Moreover, some countries have maintained non-trivial tax-based investment incentives. Second, personal income tax structure, which determines the tax burden on unincorporated enterprise and household capital income, has been similarly changed. For instance, top marginal central government rates declined from 63 to 42 percent between 1976 and 1997 in the typical OECD economy; Steinmo 2002: Table 3.

[5] See Steinmo 2002; Swank 1998.

broadening as well as moderate to strong general capital income growth from the mid-1980s.[6]

With these central features of corporate and capital tax reform in mind, central questions for analysis are as follows. What political economic forces have promoted the general shift to market-conforming tax policy? Is the process of tax policy change an interdependent one where reforms in other nations affect the probability of reform in each specific political economy? And, if diffusion occurs, what form does it take and do domestic factors shape the actual pace and depth of adoption of neoliberal tax policy reforms across countries and time?

Theories of tax policy change

In a recent paper, Steinmo and I assessed the widely debated "globalization thesis"of tax policy change.[7] As an alternative to the conventional thesis, we argued that domestic economic changes as well as internationalization of markets have promoted the shift in the content of tax policy toward the market-oriented model. To elaborate, the common globalization thesis of tax policy reform suggests that the capacity of mobile asset holders to move investment across national borders forces incumbent governments (regardless of ideology or constituency) to compete for investment. Taxes on capital (and generally mobile, high-income earners) are progressively lowered while tax burdens on relatively immobile factors and activities (i.e. most labor and consumption) are increased. The empirical record of tax policy change discussed above, however, does not match globalization theory very well.[8] Indeed, the story is more complex. Steinmo and I argued that, as the globalization thesis suggests, economic pressures on governments from international capital mobility contribute to the reduction of tax rates on mobile asset holders. Policymakers must, however, maintain revenues in the context of rising

[6] Two additional points deserve mention. First, the coefficient of variation (the standard deviation divided by the mean) for corporate tax rates reveals continued divergence around the new statutory corporate tax structure; in the case of the stable effective capital tax burden, the coefficient of variation suggests some moderate convergence by the late 1990s. Second, recent efforts to measure effective capital tax rates through 2000 by the OECD and European Union show a modest increase of roughly two points in effective capital tax burdens from 1996 to 2000; Carey and Rabesona 2002; European Commission 2004.

[7] Swank and Steinmo 2002.

[8] Extant research suggests, on balance, that internationalization has not generated a "run to the bottom" in effective capital tax burdens or a shift of taxation to labor and consumption. See Garrett 1998a, 1998b; Garrett and Mitchell 2001; Hayes 2003; Quinn 1997; Swank 1998. Some have found support for the conventional thesis; Rodrik 1997.

needs, the downward stickiness of public expenditure, and substantial public debt (see below for elaboration). A practical solution to these contradictory pressures is simultaneously to cut statutory tax rates and significantly broaden tax bases. Reduced rates retain taxable income that might be shifted through transfer pricing to low-tax nations while cuts in investment credits and allowances might also sustain revenue collections: governments can retain foreign investment and collect taxes from it if the investment comes from nations that provide credits for foreign tax payments and that tax reinvested profits themselves.[9] In addition, reductions in statutory marginal tax rates send important signals about domestic investment environments to transnationally mobile capital (see below for details).[10]

Steinmo and I argued that domestic economic stress and budgetary dynamics also shape tax policy reform. Post-1970 declines in investment rates as well as the secular rise in general and structural unemployment are likely to prompt efficiency-enhancing reforms in tax policy (i.e. statutory and effective capital tax rate cuts). Cuts in effective tax burdens on capital are, however, circumscribed by budget dynamics: increases in needs and demands for income maintenance, political limits on retrenchment in social spending, and the consequent specter or reality of rises in public debt constrain the reductions in capital tax burdens and even prompt tax increases. Reductions in effective tax rates on capital are also constrained by difficulties in shifting tax burdens to labor. Capital mobility, itself, pressures policymakers to lower non-wage labor costs. Moreover, since the mid-1980s, policymakers have increasingly focused on reductions in labor taxes that create "tax-wedge" effects on employment.[11]

Tax policy reform as an interdependent process: diffusion processes

Internationalization, adverse domestic economic change, and budgetary dynamics exert varying levels of direct pressure on incumbent governments. There is little question that post-1980 tax policy reforms across the developed democracies were shaped to some extent by responses of national policymakers to these common forces. As Simmons, Dobbin, and Garrett (hereafter SDG) note in the Introduction to this volume, there are theoretical and substantive reasons to believe, however, that neoliberal policies also diffused across regions, types of political

[9] Slemrod 1990. [10] Ganghof 2000.
[11] See, among others, the OECD *Jobs Study*; OECD 1994.

economies, and, in some cases, the globe. As SDG point out, four sets of mechanisms are likely conduits for the diffusion of neoliberal policies and institutions: coercion, the competitive pressures of markets, policy learning, and social emulation.

In the present chapter, I focus most centrally on the competitive pressures of markets as the potential source of the diffusion of capital tax policy. In addition, I elaborate and test policy learning and social emulation models of policy diffusion where learning and emulation are assessed as alternatives or supplements to core models. In a final stage of analysis, I also explore the possibility of contagion effects and the temporal dynamics of diffusion and policy change. Coercive pressures for tax policy diffusion, on the other hand, where coercion is defined as "the manipulation of economic costs and benefits, and even the monopolization of information and expertise – all with the aim of influencing policy adoption elsewhere," should be of marginal importance to the present study.[12] This is so largely because of the nature of the sample and the policy area being studied. That is, while right-of-center governments in the dominant political economies have ideological and economic interests in aggressively promoting neoliberal economic orthodoxy around the globe, it is largely irrational for dominant actors such as the United States to systematically use coercion to promote the adoption of specific neoliberal tax reforms (in the other rich democracies) that purportedly give the target nation an edge over the United States (or others) in competition for mobile assets.

General and asymmetric competition Previous work referenced above on the determination of contemporary tax policy highlights and tests variations of the globalization thesis: in order to attract and retain mobile assets, national policymakers lower tax burdens on capital and otherwise move policy in a market-conforming direction. Recent work on tax policy and the arguments advanced by authors of this volume make clear, however, incumbent governments not only respond to pressures emanating from increased levels of international openness, they are also likely to take leads from policy change in other nations.[13]

As a number of contributors to the present volume argue, national policymakers may monitor and respond to policy change among all member nations of a particular set (homogenous diffusion). Thus, Britain, Germany, and Sweden, for instance, might survey and react to

[12] Simmons, Dobbin, and Garrett this volume.

[13] See, among others, Ganghof and Eccleston 2004; Hayes 2003; Basinger and Hallerberg 2004.

tax policy change across the OECD. On the other hand, a developed democracy may monitor and respond to policy change in those polities with which it most extensively competes. Thus, British or Swedish policymakers may closely follow tax policy in nations with which they share ample flows of foreign investment and those nations that possess a similar cross-national distribution of investment (i.e. those countries with which they compete in global markets). Thus, I develop and test models of homogenous and competitive diffusion of capital tax policy below. There are good theoretical and evidentiary reasons to believe, however, that an equally if not more plausible competition model is one that brings the seminal mid-1980s US tax policy reform center stage. Moreover, I argue that because the shift to the neoliberal tax structure entails the potential for significant economic and political costs, one must also incorporate domestic political and institutional factors into the model of capital tax policy diffusion.[14]

The linchpin of contemporary tax policy reform is arguably the US 1986 Tax Reform Act. The act embodied the fundamentals of the new tax policy paradigm: top statutory corporate rates were reduced over multiple years from 46 to 34 percent, the investment tax credit was abolished, and accelerated depreciation and a variety of other allowances were significantly scaled back. (Top marginal personal rates were reduced from 50 to 28 percent, the number of brackets cut from 15 to 2, and a variety of tax expenditures limited and eliminated.)

The cross-national implications of the 1986 Act were immediately clear. Vito Tanzi notes that the 1986 reforms, enacted in the context of substantial cross-national convergence in academic and policymaker thinking about tax policy and motivated by common concerns over slow economic growth and rising unemployment, "sent shock waves to other countries."[15] As Tanzi suggests, US policy change offers other nations "a challenge and an opportunity" to reform tax policy. Specifically, Tanzi cites a variety of OECD, International Monetary Fund (IMF), and country-specific sources to illustrate that in the wake of the US reforms, policymakers in most advanced industrial democracies became intensely interested in the new US tax structure. The general interest among

[14] In the analysis to follow, I assume that all policymakers seek to maximize – subject to political, economic, and institution constraints and thus common situational tradeoffs – economic performance and political support. In the short term, incumbent governments will also strive to maintain revenue levels to fund favorite and politically popular programs as well as limit public deficits and debt. Left and Christian Democratic governments, however, have different intermediate and long-term targets for the level and distribution of taxes than center and right parties.

[15] Tanzi 1987: 335.

OECD policymakers stemmed from the fear that lower marginal rates may result in a "capital drain" of mobile investment and a "brain drain" of mobile high-income earners to the United States. Ultimately, Tanzi argues that the US tax reform did not initiate the process of cross-national adoption of the market-conforming tax model: common economic challenges and the increasing acceptance of the new market-oriented tax policy structure had generated moderate reforms in some nations.[16] Mid-1980s tax policy reform in the United States did, however, significantly accelerate the process: policymakers in other nations not only faced significant economic problems and growing dissatisfaction with extant tax structure, but they perceived that the United States significantly improved its position in competition for mobile assets.

Other general and country-specific analyses echo Tanzi's cross-national survey of the impact of the 1986 US tax reforms.[17] As these observers explain, policymakers in other polities quickly realized the importance of US reforms. Notable reductions in the statutory corporate rate attracts and retains profitable foreign direct investment, retains investment income in the low-tax jurisdiction by reducing the incentive to cross-nationally shift earnings through transfer pricing, and provides the opportunity for multinational enterprises to claim credits for taxes paid in the low-tax jurisdictions. As most analysts also emphasize, the effects of corporate tax rate reduction should be especially pronounced internationally if initiated by countries such as the US whose domestic markets and supply of foreign investment is very important for a large number of countries.[18] Indeed, the United States accounted in the late 1990s for 39 percent of all foreign direct investment inflows and 49 percent of all portfolio capital investment inflows in the developed democracies; in terms of bilateral capital flows it was the most important host and source country for capital flows in the large majority of developed democracies; it was near the top of the list of capital-partner

[16] Britain reduced marginal personal income tax rates in 1979 and corporate rates in 1984; several other nations had enacted modest reforms in the direction of lower marginal rates and a larger tax base. See Tanzi 1987; Boskin and McClure 1990; Pechman 1988. However, the large majority of nations had yet to execute significant reforms in 1986.

[17] See contributions to Boskin and McClure 1990; Pechman 1988; Ganghof and Eccelston 2004.

[18] Two technical points are in order. First as tax credits, allowances, and deductions modify the statutory rate – that is produce a lower effective tax rate – on marginally profitable investment, the statutory rate becomes particularly important in attracting and retaining clearly profitable foreign investment. As governments of source countries do not give tax refunds for taxes paid in relatively high-tax jurisdictions, there is a strong incentive to reduce rates below those in source countries that supply ample capital investment; Ganghof and Eccelston 2004.

countries for all developed democracies.[19] Thus, as Ganghof and Eccelston point out in their synoptic review of the literature on these points: "These ... mechanisms go a long way in explaining the strong downward trend in CT [corporate tax] rates after the US tax reform."[20]

In addition, leading international tax specialists such as Roger Gordon and Joel Slemrod have pointed out that the impact of US tax policy change must also be examined in historical perspective.[21] As these scholars argue, before the tax reforms of the mid-1980s, the United States acted as a Stackelberg leader, namely, a dominant economy with a positive net foreign investment flow to the rest of the world. As such, the United States could keep corporate rates high and other nations had an interest in following suit. (As multinational enterprises can generally get credits for taxes paid in host jurisdictions, other nations had strong incentives to keep rates close to the US rates. In doing so, they could simultaneously preserve investment while accomplishing redistributive and revenue goals.) With the decline of the position of the United States as net lender of capital, Slemrod, Gordon, and others have pointed out that the Stackelberg equilibrium became a non-cooperative Nash equilibrium where tax competition through rate reductions was increasingly likely. Yet, as discussed above, the formidable role of the United States as dominant host and supplier of capital relative to other developed democracies is likely to sustain the "leading" role for the US in tax policy in an era of tax competition.

Conditional diffusion of neoliberal reforms In addition to the perceived competitive benefits accorded those nations who follow the US lead, national policymakers face the risks of economic and political costs by adopting the market-conforming tax regime. The post-Second World War tax structure of significant marginal statutory rates on capital and high-income earners, coupled with substantial investment and related incentives, served as a central mechanism for achieving growth and equity in contemporary democratic capitalism.[22] As I detail below, the active use of tax policy in the form of general and targeted investment credits also complemented other elements of macro- and microeconomic management in many political economies. Significant and rapid reform of the

[19] On shares of developed country inflows (1997 is the sample year), see IMF 1998. For extensive data on bilaterial capital flows, see recent editions of the OECD's *International Direct Investment Statistics Yearbook*.

[20] Ganghof and Eccelston 2004: 523. [21] Gordon 1992; Slemrod 2004.

[22] See, among others, Steinmo 1993; Swank 1992.

postwar tax structure thus generates economic uncertainty and raises the specter of economic performance problems.

Second, rapid and deep policy change toward the neoliberal tax structure may entail substantial political costs. Not only are those economic interests who benefit from the current structure of taxation likely to mobilize to resist policy change, those who support the redistributive character of extant corporate and personal income taxation are likely to act to thwart policy reform. In this context, it is important to keep in mind that although the majority of income redistribution comes through the mechanism of cash and in-kind social transfers, personal and capital income taxation contributed roughly 28 percent of income redistribution in the typical developed democracy during the period 1980–2000.[23] Moreover, as discussed below, the redistributive character of the corporate and personal income tax system has significantly contributed to the socioeconomic and political integration of labor in industrial capitalism over the last century. As a result of these real and perceived redistributive functions of tax policy, as well as basic preferences of median voters for at least modest income redistribution, trade union movements, social democratic parties, progressive center parties and groups, and influential portions of mass electorates are likely to resist rapid and deep neoliberal policy change. As noted international tax economist Joel Slemrod has recently pointed out: "Although to economists the link between the corporate tax and tax progressivity is not straightforward, and in part depends on incidence assumptions, to many voters the corporate tax is the linchpin of any progressive tax system."[24]

Ultimately, the likelihood of adoption of US neoliberal tax policy by other nations should be a function of the relative weights assigned by policymakers to the expected benefits and political and economic costs associated with neoliberal tax structure. By "relative weights," I mean the assessment of the benefits and costs associated with the shift to neoliberal tax structure in light of basic policy priorities (i.e. economic performance and political support) and of the probability that the benefits and costs will materialize.[25] These assessments, and the ultimate decision to adopt or not adopt neoliberal reforms, should be, in turn, fundamentally determined by domestic politics and political economic institutions.

[23] These estimates of the role of taxation in total fiscal redistribution (the change between pre- and post-fisc income inequality as measured by the GINI index) are made on the basis of 1980–2000 data from the twelve principal nations of the Luxembourg Income Study; Mahler and Jesuit 2004.

[24] Slemrod 2004: 1172. [25] See footnote 14 on assumptions on general policy priorities.

First, domestic political forces should influence the pace and depth of a nation's tax policy response to US tax reform. Recent levels of success by right-of-center political parties should matter. Specifically, frequent government control by right-of-center parties in years preceding the proposal of market-conforming tax policy reforms should facilitate adoption of those reforms. Extended right-party government will bolster mass and elite support for liberalization and market-oriented policies generally, and produce incremental (if not dramatic) enactments of a variety of neoliberal economic and social policy reforms that lay the groundwork for a shift in the tax policy paradigm. Second, from the perspective of a substantial body of political economy theory, the position of the median voter ultimately determines policy: electoral support for notable reductions in marginal capital tax rates is requisite for adoption of focal reforms. As suggested above, substantial reductions in marginal tax rates on capital imply potential diminution of the commitment to redistribution and economic gains for upper-income strata as well as raise the specter of reductions in social protection and public goods provision. Thus, a recent and general shift to the right by the median voter suggests increased demands for less government intervention and generally augurs well for the success of significant neoliberal reforms. Overall, a shift to the right at the mass and elite level should significantly increase the weight assigned potential benefits and diminish the costs associated with adoption of the US model.[26]

In addition, the character of domestic political economy should matter. Specifically, the nature of the production regime should be fundamentally important to the pace and depth of adoption of the neoliberal tax policy model. As Soskice has argued, countries may be classified by the extent of national coordination through economy-wide collective bargaining among relatively centralized national employer and union associations.[27] Second, nations will vary according to the degree of sector (or business group) coordination of the economy, or the level of cooperation by enterprises in organizing product, financial, and labor markets. With regard to national coordination, supply-side oriented economic policies place a strong emphasis on employment. Active labor market policies generously fund training, placement, relocation, and general employment services (and the income maintenance system contains relatively

[26] An additional argument is that the pace and depth of tax policy change is conditioned by the extent of "veto points" in the focal political system. See Hallerberg and Basinger 1998. Multiparty legislatures and cabinets and horizontally and vertically fragmented political authority create opportunities for opponents of policy change to slow or block reform. I report results of tests of this argument below.

[27] Soskice 1999; Hall and Soskice 2001; contributions to Kitschelt *et al.* 1999.

strong work incentives). Macroeconomic and supply-side policies have sought full or near-full employment, and extensive public control of banking and credit has allowed governments to channel resources to employment-enhancing investments. Corporatist institutions, where labor has regularly exchanged wage restraint for full employment commitments and improvements in social protection, undergird macroeconomic and supply-side policies. In the 1970s and 1980s, wage restraint and currency devaluations further promoted growth and employment in core export-oriented industries in nationally coordinated economies.[28] The role of tax policy in the model is important: high marginal rates on uninvested profits coupled with general investment reserves, investment tax credits, and other incentives for saving complement other supply-side policies in promoting long-run economic growth and employment.

Sector-coordinated market economies typically exhibit moderate to high levels of centralization of collective bargaining; relatively centralized wage bargaining is supported by works councils and other cooperative arrangements between business and labor at the firm level. In addition, as Soskice and collaborators have demonstrated, the sector-coordinated economy is structured by high levels of organization of economic activity within industrial sectors oriented to the long-term development and production of high-quality, diversified consumer and industrial goods.[29] Trade associations, holding companies, industry-financial networks, and informal cooperative business groups typically organize research and development and technology transfer, export and marketing strategy, vocational training, some aspects of competition and pricing, and other activities. Coordination of economic activity by business is supported by stable long-run labor–business relations and by state regulatory frameworks. Traditionally interventionist tax policy has played two key roles in sector-coordinated economies. First, it has generally facilitated state promotion of long-run growth (e.g. regional and sector targeting of investment during periods of economic modernization and restructuring). Second, tax policies of high marginal capital tax rates (and high employer social insurance contributions) have been instrumental to the maintenance of social solidarity and long-term stability in labor and industrial relations.[30]

The significance to tax policy change of national or sector coordination should be clear. As Hall and Soskice have argued, elements of national economic models are functionally interdependent.[31] Fundamental

[28] Katzenstein 1985; Huber and Stephens 1998.
[29] Soskice 1999; Hall and Soskice 2001.
[30] See Swank 2002: Ch. 5 and the literature cited therein.
[31] Hall and Soskice 2001.

reforms in one area have significant implications for the performance of other aspects of the model. More concretely, business, labor, and the state have interests in the preservation of the basic elements of the extant model.[32] For instance, as Thelen demonstrates for the case of Germany, employers in sector-coordinated market economies may not embrace (or they may even oppose) significant neoliberal reforms when faced with the uncertainty those reforms generate.[33] In fact, German employer support for maintenance of basic features of the generous welfare state (and its funding arrangements) was arguably rooted in the interests of business in promoting long-term stability in the labor and industrial relations system.[34] Generally, the greater the national or sector coordination of the economy, the higher the costs (e.g. economic uncertainty, political resistence) to policymakers from adoption of market-conforming tax policy reforms.

Policy learning and social emulation Two alternative diffusion processes may be relevant for understanding the shift to the market-oriented tax structure: policy learning and social emulation. As to policy learning, two central claims of proponents of the neoliberal tax structure are that it enhances efficiency by removing distortions to the market allocation of capital and that it maintains (or even increases) revenue collection from capital income while lowering capital tax rates. That is, the treasury is protected and government intervention in markets is reduced (and thereby efficiency presumably increased) by simultaneously cutting rates and broadening the tax base through the elimination of incentives that were designed primarily to channel investment in accord with policy goals.

The mid-1980s US tax reform, the archetype of the shift to the neoliberal tax paradigm, may have served as a natural experiment (as did early, extensive privatization in Britain) to test the claims of proponents about efficiency and revenues. As such, the US tax reform may have generated "information externalities" for countries throughout the OECD on the veracity of proponents' claims. As Tanzi notes, the US reforms drew intense interest throughout the democratic market economies. There is also clear evidence that while concerns about tax competition were predominant, policymakers were also interested in efficiency and revenue potential. In fact, at a January 1987 meeting, OECD heads of government, finance ministers, and international business elites suggested that the investment and revenue performance of the US in the

[32] Soskice 1999. [33] Thelen 1999. [34] Swank 2002: Ch. 5.

years immediately following the reform would serve as a test for the soundness of the new policy regime.[35] Thus, one can plausibly hypothesize that a policy learning mechanism, where adoption of the US tax reforms will be contingent on the relative performance of the US economy (e.g. in relative investment and revenue growth) in the years immediately following the reforms, supplemented competitive forces in pressing the spread of neoliberal tax policy. I test such a hypothesis below.

Finally, it may be likely that nations that share common political histories and institutions, cultures, and, to a lesser extent, geographic boundaries emulate recent policy innovations in peer countries. That is, similar policy orientations and legacies (e.g. shared traditions in the level and form of state interventions), framed within shared histories of political development, institutional patterns, and cultures, undergird this process. Indeed, in influential work on "families of nations," Francis Castles and collaborators have suggested that policies often diffuse most readily within culturally and politically similar groups of nations.[36] In the democratic capitalist world, these families include the English-speaking countries that are linked by language and common legal and political traditions, the Nordic countries who share culture, legal traditions, and centuries of interdependent political development, and the continental European nations that are united by religion and other cultural attributes as well as shared political history. Thus, one might hypothesize that as in other policy areas, a focal nation would monitor and respond to recent policy changes in taxation within its family of nations more readily than past changes in other families or across the developed democracies as a whole.

Empirical models of tax policy reform

I evaluate hypotheses about the diffusion of neoliberal tax policy reforms by using the linear models of corporate and capital taxation developed in Swank and Steinmo as a base.[37] In that paper, the authors modeled marginal corporate and effective average capital tax rates as functions of internationalization (international capital mobility and trade openness), domestic economic pressures (the rise of long-term unemployment), and domestic budgetary dynamics (need and public sector debt effects on spending). The general model included controls for economic growth,

[35] This meeting, held on January 12 and 13 in France, focused on the merits of recent and planned personal and corporate tax policy change in the developed democracies; OECD 1987.

[36] Castles 1993, 1998. [37] Swank and Steinmo 2002.

profits, and investment – themselves measures of important aspects of domestic economic performance – as well as partisan control of government and prior levels of tax rates. Swank and Steinmo estimated the models with 1981–1995 data for fourteen developed democracies.

In the present chapter, I extend the sample to 1981–1998 data from sixteen advanced nations.[38] With minor exceptions, I utilize the same general models as Swank and Steinmo as a basic framework to assess the various diffusion processes highlighted above. (See Appendix 2.1 and 2.2 on specific operationalizations and data sources for all measures.) The basic linear model of corporate and capital tax rates is given by:

$$\begin{aligned} \text{Tax Rate}_{i,t} = \alpha &+ \phi(\text{Tax Rate})_{i,t-1} \\ &+ \beta_1(\text{International Capital Mobility})_{i,t-1} \\ &+ \beta_2(\text{Trade Openness})_{i,t-1} \\ &+ \beta_3(\text{Structural Unemployment})_{i,t-1} \\ &+ \beta_4(\text{Needs})_{i,t-1} + \beta_5(\text{Public Debt})_{i,t} + \beta_6(\text{Growth})_{i,t-1} \\ &+ \beta_7(\text{Profits})_{i,t-1} + \beta_8(\text{Investment})_{i,t-1} \\ &+ \beta_9(\text{Right Party Government})_{i,t-1} + \epsilon_{i,t}, \qquad (1) \end{aligned}$$

Again, this model assumes independence in national responses, or that the shift to a market-conforming tax model is a function of varying national responses to common domestic and international political economic forces.

The central hypotheses on diffusion are modeled in three ways. First, I use general spatial lags. I test the proposition that policymakers monitored and responded to tax policy change in all other developed nations by including an unweighted spatial lag:

$$\begin{aligned} \text{Tax Rate}_{i,t} = \alpha + \phi(\text{Tax Rate})_{i,t-1} &+ \phi_s(\text{Tax Rate}_{\text{mean } j-n})_{i,t-1} \\ &+ \beta_1(\text{International Capital Mobility})_{i,t-1} + \cdots\cdots\cdot \\ &\beta_9(\text{Right Party Government})_{i,t-1} + \epsilon_{i,t}, \qquad (2) \end{aligned}$$

[38] Models of corporate taxes are generally estimated with 1982 to 1998 data for fourteen nations while those for capital tax burdens are estimated with 1981 to 1996 data from sixteen countries. Models of diffusion of US reforms exclude the United States. The sixteen nations are: Australia, Austria, Belgium, Canada, Denmark, Finland, France, Germany, Italy, Japan, the Netherlands, New Zealand, Norway, Sweden, the UK, and the US; Austria and Finland are excluded from the corporate rate models because of data unavailability.

where ϕ_s is the coefficient for the spatial lag, (Tax Rate $_{\text{mean j–n}}$). (Tax Rate $_{\text{mean j–n}}$) is the average change in tax rates in *j* to *n* countries (nations other than *i*) at time *t–1*.[39] To assess the proposition that the impact of past tax change in other countries is conditional on their competitive relationship in capital markets with country *i*, I weighted tax rate change in each *j* to *n* nation at time *t–1* by three measures: total trade flows between *i* and *j*, total foreign direct investment flows between *i* and *j*, and the correlation between the cross-national distribution of direct investment flows of countries *i* and *j*, a measure of the similarity of two countries' capital market orientations.

$$\begin{aligned}\text{Tax Rate}_{i,t} = {} & \alpha + \phi(\text{Tax Rate})_{i,t-1} + \phi_{ws}(\text{Tax Rate}_{\text{mean weighted } j-n})_{i,t-1} \\ & + \beta_1(\text{International Capital Mobility})_{i,t-1} + \dots\dots\dots \\ & \beta_9(\text{Right Party Government})_{i,t-1} + \epsilon_{i,t}, \qquad (3)\end{aligned}$$

Total trade for country *i* with some other country *j* is highly correlated with country *i*'s capital stock position with *j* (i.e. inward direct investment in *i* by *j* and outward direct investment in *j* by *i*).[40] This latter capital stock measure is preferred for measuring the relative immediate importance of changes in tax policy in *j* on tax policy in *i*; however, consistent bilateral data on capital stock are only available for most of the sample from the late 1980s or early 1990s. Inward and outward direct investment flow-based measures are notably volatile from period to period and only partially capture the likely relative importance of tax policy changes in *j* on *i*. In any case, results from each of these measures are very similar. The trade-based measure is slightly stronger and more consistent in magnitude and significance. I report that result below.

Finally, for each country *i*, I weight past tax policy changes in other countries by a dummy variable that measures whether they are of the same "family of nations" as country *i*. Thus, tax policy change in country *i*

[39] See Beck 2001. Change measures of other-country (or US) tax reforms are particularly appropriate for our models as the control for the lagged tax rate effectively makes the dependent variable a change variable, or equivalent to $\text{Tax Rate}_{i,t} - \text{Tax Rate}_{i,t-1}$ in Eq. 1. When we substitute, $\text{Tax Rate}_{i,t} - \text{Tax Rate}_{i,t-1}$, for $\text{Tax Rate}_{i,t}$, only the coefficient for the lagged tax rate, ϕ, changes; it is equal to $\phi - 1$ when the dependent variable is a change measure. Effects of causal variables are mathematically equivalent across the two equations. I estimate effects of levels and changes in other-country and US tax rates in the context of error correction models; these are presented below.

[40] For instance, the simple cross-national correlation between trade with the US and capital stock position with the United States (1989–1991 means) is .689 ($p < .01$) for OECD nations. As is well known, this relationship stems from the fact that a significant portion of all trade is intra-firm trade; Bonturi and Fukasaku 1993.

is modeled as a function of the mean of past policy change in country *i*'s main reference political systems. This provides a straightforward test of one basic form of social emulation.

Second, I test the direct impacts of reforms in US corporate and capital tax rates on other nations' tax policies by adding lagged changes in US statutory corporate and effective average capital tax rates to the models; the competition-weighted measure of past policy change in non-US cases is left in the equation as a control. To provide specific quantitative evidence on the competition-driven diffusion of US tax reforms, I interact lagged US tax rates with lagged US trade flows in the focal non-US cases. Trade with the United States, as in the case of the general bilateral trade weights for competition, is used as a proxy for the extent of market integration for foreign direct investment. To echo the point above on measuring capital competition, the correlation for trade between the United States and some country *i*, and the inward and outward capital stock position of country *i* with the United States, is strong and highly significant ($r = 689, p < .01$). I also use a similar interaction-based test for the policy learning hypothesis in which I interact lagged changes in US rates with (one- through three-year) lagged measures of the relative (post-tax change) performance of the United States on the dimensions of domestic investment and income tax revenues. Specifically, I compute a variety of measures of the difference in US investment (or revenue) growth and investment (or revenue) growth in the focal country and use this to effectively weight lagged change in US tax rates. I report these tests below.

Third, tests of the conditional effects of US tax reforms (and general and weighted past policies in other nations) on tax policy change in other democracies are made through interaction analysis.[41] Following the theoretical predictions of preceding sections, changes in US corporate and capital tax rates are interacted with cross-nationally and temporally varying measures of two sets of variables: (1) measures of the ideological position of the median voter and average levels of government control by right parties over the last ten years; and (2) indices of nationally and

[41] Interaction analysis is well suited for examining the conditional effects of external forces on domestic political or policy outcomes. In short, the interaction of, for example, X_1 (the level of sector coordination of the economy, for instance) and X_2 (lagged US tax policy change), when the dependent variable is Y (current tax rates in other developed democracies), will tell us whether the effect of X_2 on Y varies with levels of X_1. The significance test for the interaction term indicates whether differences in the effect of X_2 at different levels of X_1 are significantly different from zero. The interaction term itself, when multiplied by a value of X_1 and added to the coefficient of X_2, becomes the slope for the effect of X_2 at that level of X_1. Standard errors for computing the significance of the effects of X_2 at some level of X_1 are easily calculated; Friedrich, 1982.

sector-coordinated market economies. A full discussion of the development of the indices for coordination of market economies is given in Appendix 2.3.[42]

The models are estimated by OLS (Ordinary Least Squares) regression analysis with panel correct standard errors.[43] A lagged dependent variable is included to explicitly model temporal dynamics and to minimize serial correlation of errors. Overall, this estimator will typically address common problems of contemporaneously correlated, cross-nationally heteroskedastic, and serially correlated errors present in pooled time series, cross-sectional data.[44] I also estimate and discuss two alternative estimators: fixed effects OLS with a lagged dependent variable and panel correct standard errors and with error correction models. Generally, coefficients in dynamic panel models (i.e. those with a lagged dependent variable) will tend to be inconsistent in the presence of fixed effects.[45] Given the widespread use of fixed effect estimators and their salutary effect on unmodeled unit (and time) effects, I note results from this alternative below.

I also estimate final empirical models of statutory corporate rates with a generalized error correction method. The estimating equation is:

$$\begin{aligned}\text{Tax Rate}_{i,t} - \text{Tax Rate}_{i,t-1} = \alpha &+ \phi(\text{Tax Rate})_{i,t-1} + \beta_1(\text{US Tax Rate})_{t-1} \\ &+ \beta_2(\Delta\text{US Tax Rate})_{t-1} \\ &+ \phi_{ws}(\text{Tax Rate}_{\text{mean weighted } j-n})_{i,t-1} \\ &+ \phi_{ws}/(\Delta\text{Tax Rate}_{\text{mean weighted } j-n})_{i,t-1} \\ &+ \beta_j(X)_{i,t-1} + \beta_k(\Delta X)_{i,t-1} + \epsilon_{i,t}, \qquad (4)\end{aligned}$$

where X is a vector of variables that consists of exogenous factors from Equation 1. This estimator, for instance, allows one to assess both the dynamic short-term responsiveness of tax rates in the developed

[42] Finally, I follow leads in Blanchard and Wolfers' analysis of the determinants of unemployment and estimate the tax policy effects of a variety of exogenous shocks (e.g. energy prices and real interest rates) and assess their impact on the results of diffusion models; Blanchard and Wolfers 1999. Results are noted below.

[43] An alternative approach is event history analysis. However, the occurrence of multiple points of reform in some nations, no clear single reform event during the sample period in a few others, and the presence of several common problems of event history analysis in the current modeling context suggest OLS regression is a more tractable strategy. New event history estimators such as Cox hazard models for multiple events offer promise for future work; Box-Steffensmeier and Zorn 2002.

[44] Beck and Katz 1996. [45] For example Kvist 1995.

democracies to changes in US tax rates (β_2) and the long-term structural relationship between US rates and tax policies in other nations (β_1).[46]

Findings

Results of the estimation of Equations 2 and 3 for corporate tax rates are presented in the first two columns of Table 2.2; comparable results for effective capital tax rates are presented in the fourth and fifth columns. The findings on the tax effects of common international and domestic forces are as follows. With regard to direct impacts of internationalization of markets, liberalization of international capital controls in prior years is associated with reductions in statutory corporate rates (but not with actual capital tax burdens).[47] Trade openness, while correctly signed is not systematically related to corporate and capital tax rate cuts. In terms of the general model, the most notable findings are as follows: low growth of per capita gross domestic product (GDP), profits, and domestic investment as well as high structural unemployment are associated with cuts in capital tax burdens. High public sector debt (but not needs for public spending) is positively and significantly related to effective capital tax rates.

As to general diffusion processes, unweighted past policy changes in other countries are not significantly related to current tax policy change in a focal nation (for either corporate and effective capital tax rates). Net of other factors in the model, national policymakers are not systematically influenced by the general course of recent policy change across the developed democracies.[48] Past policy change in countries that are more integrated with a particular nation's capital markets (recall the magnitude of inward and outward position of capital stock is proxied by trade) is

[46] See Beck and Katz 1996; Beck 2001. I extend the error correction models only to statutory rates to simplify analysis and to explore the relatively rich findings on the mediation of the impact of US policy change on statutory tax rates in other nations. I do not adopt the general error correction method as the principal estimation technique because of the greater flexibility of OLS regression of simple dynamic models. Error correction models serve as a check on the robustness of the simple dynamic models.

[47] Liberalization is associated with tax reform at lags of one through four years (but not contemporaneously related to tax policy). In Swank and Steinmo, we argued that liberalization and consequent growth in actual capital flows pressured policymakers, for reasons discussed above, to initiate tax policy reform; Swank and Steinmo 2002. Increases in formal–legal and actual capital mobility also reinforce calls from center-right partisans and business for general neoliberal reforms of social and economic policies. We documented these mechanisms with evidence from the case study literature and our own interviews with policymakers.

[48] In the case of these tests (and all others presented below), I examined longer-term lags for core variables. In no instance did a longer time lag change reported results.

Table 2.2. *The impact of international factors and policy diffusion on statutory marginal corporate tax rates and effective average tax rates on capital, 1981–1998*

	Statutory rate I	Statutory rate II	Statutory rate III	Effective rate I	Effective rate II	Effective rate III
International factors						
Liberalization of capital controls $_{t-1}$	−.9004**	−.9082**	−.9547**	−.0655	−.0777	.0581
	(.3758)	(.3790)	(.4591)	(.4319)	(.4326)	(.5453)
Trade $_{t-1}$	−.0022	−.0055	−.0067	−.0065	−.0060	−.0099*
	(.0092)	(.0093)	(.0096)	(.0063)	(.0064)	(.0071)
Average statutory tax rates in other countries $_{t-1}$	.1249	—	—	—	—	—
	(.2206)					
Weighted statutory tax rates in other countries $_{t-1}$	—	.1438*	.0493	—	—	—
		(.1053)	(.1038)			
Change in US top statutory corporate tax rate $_{t-1}$	—	—	.0876	—	—	—
			(.1295)			
US trade $_{t-1}$	—	—	.0086	—	—	.0138
			(.0215)			(.0307)
US corporate tax rate $_{t-1}$ × US trade $_{t-1}$	—	—	.0167**	—	—	—
			(.0076)			
Average effective tax rates in other countries $_{t-1}$	—	—	—	.1149	—	—
				(.1528)		
Weighted effective tax rates in other countries $_{t-1}$	—	—	—	—	.0014	—
					(.1108)	
Change in US effective tax rate on capital $_{t-1}$	—	—	—	—	—	−.0678
						(.1332)
Effective US tax rate $_{t-1}$ × US trade $_{t-1}$	—	—	—	—	—	.0119*
						(.0087)

General model						
Structural unemployment	.1090	.0985	.1190	−.2206**	−.2221**	−.2365**
	(.1114)	(.1118)	(.1245)	(.1099)	(.1098)	(.1300)
Public sector $debt_t$	.0104	.0104	.0089	.0182**	.0176**	.0186**
	(.0092)	(.0092)	(.0112)	(.0095)	(.0094)	(.0111)
Needs – elderly population	−.0600	−.0572	−.0505	−.0097	−.0143	−.0077
	(.1402)	(.1364)	(.1519)	(.1426)	(.1429)	(.1583)
Tax rate $_{t-1}$	.8922**	.8960**	.9005**	.9490**	.9497**	.9487**
	(.0355)	(.0353)	(.0361)	(.0291)	(.0268)	(.0274)
$Growth_{t-1}$	−.0165	−.0166	.0342	.2348**	.2210**	.2516**
	(.1394)	(.1393)	(.1423)	(.1338)	(.1332)	(.1356)
Percent change real $profits_{t-1}$	−.0281	−.0244	−.0340	.1670**	.1709**	.1744**
	(.0662)	(.0658)	(.0676)	(.0662)	(.0617)	(.0665)
Domestic $investment_{t-1}$	.0286	.0342	.0388	.0523	.0606	.0632*
	(.0476)	(.0483)	(.0495)	(.0499)	(.0481)	(.0489)
Right government	−.0050	−.0039	−.0051	−.0042	−.0044	−.0049
	(.0059)	(.0061)	(.0065)	(.0085)	(.0086)	(.0085)
Constant	7.6267	7.3412	7.2765	1.1701	1.2845	.9242
Observations	238	238	238	256	256	256
R^2	.8466	.8474	.8466	.9062	.9060	.9090

Statutory corporate tax models are estimated with 1982–1998 data by OLS; effective capital tax rate models are estimated with 1981–1996 data. The table reports OLS unstandardized regression coefficients and panel correct standard errors; Beck and Katz 1996.

*indicates significance at the .10 level or below.

**indicates significance at the .05 level or below.

modestly influential in the case of corporate tax rates but not for effective capital tax rates. Recent corporate tax policy change in these "partner countries" is significantly ($p < .10$) related to contemporary corporate tax reform in focal countries.

Tests for the effects of changes in statutory corporate and effective capital tax rates in the United States are presented in the third and sixth columns of Table 2.2. While I estimated the tax impacts of past change in US rates as well as past US tax policy change interacted with a country's US trade in both sets of analyses, I report only the US tax rate × US trade interaction equation here (for the sake of parsimony). The direct linear effect of past changes in US corporate rates on current corporate tax rates elsewhere is .1917 ($p < .05$); the direct linear impact of US effective capital rates on capital taxes elsewhere falls just short of statistical significance. As the table indicates (and I will focus on corporate tax structure), a one point change in US rates is associated with a .1711 ($p < .10$) point change in corporate rates elsewhere when US trade is low (US trade at 5 percent of GDP). At moderate and high levels of US market integration (for example, US trade at 10 percent of GDP), however, the effect of a one point change in US rates is .25 points elsewhere ($.0876 + .0167 \times 10$; $p < .05$). For theoretical and substantive reasons discussed above, we would expect the general linear impact of US tax rate change to be important. We would also expect that this substantial and significant effect would increase with rises in market integration with the US; this is in fact the pattern of results that obtain.

I also re-estimated Table 2.2 models with longer lags of US tax policy change, British statutory and effective tax rates (recall the 1984 British reforms), and an average of British and US tax rates. Analysis of lags suggests that the change between t–2 and $t-1$ is in fact the optimal lag specification. Lagged British tax policy change (at lags of t–1 through t–4) were not significantly related to tax policy change across the developed democracies (at or below the .05 level); average UK/US rate measures were marginally but, in substantive magnitude and significance, not as strongly and robustly related to subsequent tax policy change in other nations as were US tax policy changes alone.[49]

Tax policy diffusion and domestic politics Assessments of the hypotheses that cross-national effects of US tax reforms are conditioned

[49] Results reported in Table 2.2 are near perfectly reproduced when moving to the fixed effects estimator discussed above. All core findings on the direct and conditional impacts of US tax policy presented in Tables 2.2 through 2.5 are reproduced in the presence of fixed effects.

by the extent of government control by right parties and the ideological position of the median voter are presented in Table 2.3. As the table illustrates, only one of four possible interactions between US tax reforms and domestic political conditions in the responding countries is significant. This occurs for the case of the interaction between US corporate tax rates and right party government. Where right-of-center parties have governed extensively in recent years, tax policy responsiveness to US tax reforms is significantly greater than elsewhere. A one point cut in US rates is associated with a decline of .22 percentage points in rates where right-of-center parties have held 75 percent of the cabinet portfolios over the last ten years. There is no support, however, for the notion that adoption of US tax policy change is stronger in polities where, net of other forces, the median voter is more ideologically supportive of neoliberal reforms.[50]

Tax policy change and production regimes Table 2.4 presents tests of the hypotheses that general effects of US tax policy change will be conditional on the organizational structure of the domestic political economy. As displayed in the first and fourth columns of Table 2.4, analyses indicate that where national coordination is strong (1.00 on the index), US corporate tax rate cuts have a trivial effect on policy reform in other polities ($b = .2119 + [-.3752 \times 1.00]$); where national coordination is weak (−1.00 on the index), as in the typical liberal market economy, US corporate tax change has a large effect on tax reform in the focal nation ($b = .2119 + [-.3752 \times -1.00]$). There is no significant mediation of the impact of US effective capital rate cuts by national coordination.

The role of sector coordination in mediating the effect of US tax reforms is stronger. In the case of both US corporate and effective capital tax rate change, the degree of sector coordination conditions the impact of US reform on tax policy change in other nations. To highlight the role of uncoordinated market economies, one can compute the impact of US corporate and effective capital tax rate cuts when sector coordination is very low (−1.00). In the case of corporate taxation, a one point cut in US statutory rates will be associated with a .3 point cut in the focal liberal market economy ($b = .1484 + [-.4707 \times -1.00]$). For effective capital tax rates, a cut of one point would be associated on average with roughly

50 I also assessed whether or not the responsiveness to past policy change in the United States was slower in nations with substantial veto points. Using the measure of total veto points developed by Huber, Ragin, and Stephens, I found no evidence for the veto point hypothesis; Huber, Ragin, and Stephens 1993.

Table 2.3. *The conditional diffusion of US tax policy change: the role of party governments and median voters, 1981–1998*

	Statutory rate I	Statutory rate II	Effective rate I	Effective rate II
Weighted statutory tax rates in other countries $_{t-1}$	.0508 (.1026)	.0512 (.1027)	—	—
Change in US top statutory corporate tax rate $_{t-1}$	−.1184 (.2099)	.1113 (.1284)	—	—
US trade $_{t-1}$	.0063 (.0213)	.0016 (.0244)	.0110 (.0304)	.0114 (.0805)
US corporate tax rate $_{t-1}$ × US trade $_{t-1}$	.0160** (.0076)	.0167** (.0078)	—	—
Weighted effective tax rates in other countries $_{t-1}$	—	—	.0222 (.1282)	.0196 (.1269)
Change in US effective tax rate on capital $_{t-1}$	—	—	−.2211 (.1920)	−.0003 (.1362)
Effective US tax rate $_{t-1}$ × US trade $_{t-1}$	—	—	.0125* (.0086)	.0096 (.0089)
Right party government (10-year average party control)	−.0035 (.0068)	—	−.0049 (.0055)	—
US corporate rate × right party government	.0045** (.0025)	—	—	—
US effective capital rate × right party government	—	—	.0042 (.0035)	—
Ideological position of the median voter $_{t-1}$	—	−.0089 (.0256)	—	−.0067 (.0270)
US corporate rate × median voter $_{t-1}$	—	.0038 (.0131)	—	—
US effective capital rate × median voter $_{t-1}$	—	—	—	.0145 (.0141)

Corporate tax models are estimated with 1982–1998 data by OLS; capital tax models are estimated with 1981–1996 data. The table reports OLS unstandardized regression coefficients and panel correct standard errors; Beck and Katz 1996. All estimates presented in the table are obtained by adding interactions between US corporate and capital tax rates and mediating factors to the full models presented in Table 2.2. Estimates for variables in general model are not reported to conserve space (and complete results are available from the author).

*indicates significance at the .10 level or below.

**indicates significance at the .05 level or below.

Table 2.4. *The conditional diffusion of US tax policy change: the role of nationally and sector-coordinated capitalism, 1981–1998*

	Statutory rate I	Statutory rate II	Statutory rate III	Effective rate I	Effective rate II	Effective rate III
Weighted statutory tax rates in other nations $_{t-1}$	.0462 (.1022)	.0370 (.1020)	.0336 (.1014)	—	—	—
Change in US statutory corporate tax rate $_{t-1}$	.2119** (.1119)	.1484 (.1286)	.2352** (.1113)	—	—	—
US trade $_{t-1}$	.0049 (.0234)	.0100 (.0291)	.0131 (.0319)	.0224 (.0428)	.0108 (.0347)	.0202 (.0448)
US corporate tax rate $_{t-1}$ × US trade $_{t-1}$	.0010 (.0097)	−.0023 (.0064)	−.1201 (.0086)	—	—	—
Weighted effective tax rates in other nations $_{t-1}$	—	—	—	.0288 (.1268)	.0160 (.1278)	.0272 (.1269)
Change in US effective tax rate on capital $_{t-1}$	—	—	—	.0666 (.1495)	−.0222 (.1372)	.0586 (.1477)
Effective US tax rate $_{t-1}$ × US trade $_{t-1}$	—	—	—	.0002 (.0133)	.0025 (.0097)	−.0032 (.0134)
National coordination $_{t-1}$	−.1091 (.5144)	—	−.0380 (.5148)	.2520 (.6417)	—	.2854 (.6384)
US corporate rate × national coordination $_{t-1}$	−.3752** (.1756)	—	−.2869* (.1864)	—	—	—
US capital rate × national coordination $_{t-1}$	—	—	—	−.2604 (.2597)	—	−.1750 (.2718)
Sector coordination $_{t-1}$	—	.1017 (.5050)	.1998 (.5111)	—	−.0758 (.4183)	−.1128 (.4119)
US corporate rate × sector coordination $_{t-1}$	—	−.4707** (.1597)	−.3609** (.1665)	—	—	—
US capital rate × sector coordination $_{t-1}$	—	—	—	—	−.2144** (.1173)	−.1642* (.1155)

Corporate tax models are estimated with 1982–1998 data by OLS; capital tax models are estimated with 1981–1996 data. The table reports OLS unstandardized regression coefficients and panel correct standard errors; Beck and Katz 1996. All estimates presented in the table are obtained by adding interactions between US corporate and capital tax rates and mediating factors to the full models presented in Table 2.2. Estimates for variables in general model are not reported to conserve space (and complete results are available from the author).

*indicates significance at the .10 level or below.

**indicates significance at the .05 level or below.

a .2 point reduction in the other liberal market economies ($b = -.0222 + [-.2144 \times -1.00]$).[51]

I also assessed the joint impacts of mediation of US tax policy change by national and sector coordination of the economy; the results of this analysis are displayed in the third and sixth columns of Table 2.4. As indicated in the table, sector coordination appears to be the most salient feature of the organization of the economy: in the presence of both sets of interactions, the US tax rate × national coordination interaction becomes significant at only the .10 level for statutory corporate taxes and it falls to insignificance in the effective capital tax rate models. As sector coordination and national coordination share core features (e.g. labor organization) and are significantly correlated across countries, I will subsequently report results from models with sector coordination only.[52]

Finally, it is interesting to note that in the models estimating the interaction of past US tax policy change and the degree of coordination of markets, the interaction between past US tax rates and a country's US trade becomes insignificant. Upon closer inspection, this finding is not surprising. The simple cross-national correlation between integration with US markets and sector coordination is very strong ($r = .776$, $p < .01$). The levels of multicollinearity when both US tax × US trade and US tax × sector coordination interactions are in the equation is also very high. Generally, this pattern of findings suggests that at a specific level of coordination of markets (coordination itself being highly correlated with US market integration), additional increases in US trade do not intensify the impact of past tax policy change in the United States.

As a concluding stage of the analysis, I assess the possibility that systematic policy learning and social emulation undergirds the diffusion of neoliberal tax policy as well as assess the temporal dynamics of diffusion. For parsimony, I focus on the corporate tax structure models (although the same patterns as reported below hold for capital taxation

[51] Effects of US rate cuts in uncoordinated market economies are in each case statistically significant; coefficients for the effects of US rate cuts in coordinated market economies are systematically insignificant. In addition, I explore whether unweighted and trade-weighted measures of tax policy change in non-US nations affected current policy changes differentially across uncoordinated and coordinated market economies. I found no evidence that this was the case.

[52] The same considerations apply to the interaction between US tax rate change and right governments. In the presence of the US tax rate × sector coordination interaction, the interaction between US rates and right governments falls to significance at the .10 level. For the sake of parsimony and protection against excessive multicollinearity, I report only the US tax rate × sector coordination interaction in the final models (and continue to acknowledge the prospect of a role for party governments in US-driven diffusion of tax policy).

albeit at weaker substantive and significance levels). I use the equation that includes the mediation of the impact of US tax policy by market coordination and controls for weighted past policy change in non-US cases as well as common international and domestic forces as a "final" baseline model. I employ the tests outlined above: for policy learning I explore the impacts of the interaction of past US policy change and past investment or revenue performance differentials between the US and focal nations (at lags of t–1 to t–3 years).[53] I also report the results of a straightforward test of social emulation where past policy change in other nations within the focal country's "family" (e.g. Anglo, Nordic, European continental) is the driving force behind diffusion of the neoliberal tax structure. Finally, I report results of the error correction model and discuss the information it provides about temporal dynamics.

The first column of Table 2.5 reports the complete baseline model while the second column displays the results for a representative policy learning model. As in the case of other specifications (e.g. longer lag lengths or revenue performance differentials), there is no evidence that responsiveness to US tax policy varies by the degree of relative superior US economic performance over performance in a particular country. The same null findings are produced if one weights past policy change in all nations by relative policy performance with the focal nation (results not reported). In addition, there is little evidence of social emulation. Past tax policy reforms in a nation's peer group are not related to contemporary policy change. This result holds with or without the extent specification of the US-centered, conditional diffusion mechanism.[54] On the other hand, these tests for policy learning and social emulation dynamics involve assessments of only one type of policy learning and one type of social emulation mechanism. For instance, learning may occur through assessment of theoretical and practical arguments for a new and innovative policy approach and not a comprehensive evaluation of relative economic performances. Social emulation of peers may occur through more complex linkages than those examined in this chapter. Yet, on balance, it would

[53] Thus, for the lag of one year, the interaction is US policy change from t–2 to t–1 and the investment rate or revenue growth difference between the US and the focal country in t–1.

[54] I also tested for the role of exogenous shocks that should effect capital accumulation and, in turn, policymakers' efforts to encourage it. Specifically, I added year dummies to the column III equation to account for general, unspecified common shocks that may affect tax policy reforms. I also estimated the direct and institutionally mediated effects of specific common shocks that should influence capital investment and policies designed to influence it: energy prices, inflation rates, and real interest rates; Blanchard and Wolfers 1999. Time dummies and estimates of specific shocks were consistently insignificant at the .05 level.

Table 2.5. *Final models for statutory corporate tax rates, 1982–1998: alternative diffusion processes and temporal dynamics*

	Final model		Policy learning model		Social emulation model		Error correction temporal dynamics	
Weighted statutory tax rates in other countries $_{t-1}$		—		—		—	−.0158	(.0147)
Δ Weighted statutory tax rates in other countries $_{t-1}$	.0370	(.1020)	.0486	(.0984)	.0484	(.1093)	.0728	(.1015)
US top statutory corporate tax rate $_{t-1}$		—		—		—	.1390**	(.0702)
Δ US top statutory corporate tax rate $_{t-1}$	.1484	(.1286)	.1601*	(.1120)	.1403	(.1211)	.0232	(.1263)
Sector coordination $_{t-1}$	.1017	(.5050)	.0111	(.4094)	.0405	(.4114)	−1.7608	(2.6660)
US corporate rate × sector coordination $_{t-1}$		—		—		—	.0519	(.0594)
Δ US corporate rate × sector coordination $_{t-1}$	−.4207**	(.1597)	−.4540**	(.1526)	−.4170**	(.1550)	−.4528**	(.1403)
US versus other country investment rates $_{t-1}$		—	.2909	(.2934)		—		—
Δ US corporate rate × investment difference $_{t-1}$		—	−.0180	(.0145)		—		—
Average tax rates in family of nations $_{t-1}$		—		—	−.0134	(.1306)		—
Liberalization of capital controls $_{t-1}$	−.7920**	(.4568)	−.8405**	(.4505)	−.7477**	(.4503)	−.5620	(.5237)
Trade $_{t-1}$	−.0048	(.0104)	−.0051	(.0100)	−.0050	(.0100)	.0152	(.0272)
Structural unemployment $_{t-1}$	.1380	(.1453)	.1351	(.1108)	.1120	(.1139)	.1475	(.1227)
Public sector debt$_{t}$	.0048	(.0160)	.0067	(.0110)	.0070	(.0109)	.0021	(.0150)
Elderly population $_{t-1}$	−.1147	(.1340)	−.1278	(.1362)	−.1254	(.1346)	−.0066	(.1426)
Growth$_{t-1}$	−.0170	(.1406)	−.0265	(.1375)	−.0104	(.1292)	−.0247	(.2091)
% Change profits$_{t-1}$	−.0208	(.0673)	−.0214	(.0661)	−.0222	(.0673)	−.0780	(.0717)

Domestic investment$_{t-1}$	.0219	(.0486)	.0491	(.0553)	.0278	(.0488)	−.0171	(.0585)
Right government$_{t-1..10}$	−.0048	(.0060)	−.0053	(.0059)	−.0053	(.0059)	−.0066	(.0056)
Δ Liberalization		—		—		—	.3949	(1.0030)
Δ Trade		—		—		—	−.0356	(.0527)
Δ Structural unemploy		—		—		—	−.5877	(.4161)
Δ Public sector debt		—		—		—	.0391	(.0532)
Δ Elderly population		—		—		—	−.4527	(1.2010)
Δ Growth		—		—		—	−.0533	(.1459)
Δ % Change profits		—		—		—	.0825	(.0820)
Δ Domestic investment		—		—		—	.0517	(.0665)
Δ Right government		—		—		—	.0652	(.0400)
Tax rate $_{t-1}$	.8917**	(.0367)	.8974**	(.0352)	.8938**	(.0354)	−.1558**	(.0448)
Constant	8.1427		7.9511		8.0336		3.5315	
Observations	221		221		221		221	
R^2	.8521		.8544		.8520		.2164	

Corporate tax models are estimated with 1982–1998 data by OLS. The dependent variable is Tax rate$_t$ in columns I to III equations and Tax rate$_t$ − Tax rate$_{t-1}$ in the fourth column. The table reports OLS unstandardized regression coefficients and panel correct standard errors for estimates of direct and conditional effects of US tax rates; to conserve space, only regression coefficients (and significance levels) are reported for other exogenous variables.

*indicates significance at the .10 level or below.

**indicates significance at the .05 level or below.

seem that theory and evidence on diffusion of neoliberal tax policy heavily favors an asymmetric competition model that highlights US policy reform.

Finally, I examined temporal dynamics by estimating a general error correction model of tax policy change. As noted above, this model (fourth column, Table 2.5) allows one to estimate long-term and short-term components of factors' influences on the shift to neoliberal tax structure. The results are instructive. First, while the interaction of the change in US rates and sector coordination is significant, the interaction between levels of US tax rates and sector coordination is not. This tells us explicitly that while policymakers in coordinated market economies were less responsive in the short term, the long-term relationship between US tax structure and tax policy in other nations did not vary by political institutional context.

Second, and related, the results of Table 2.5 allow us to compare the actual impact of levels of US tax rates and levels of (weighted) tax structure in non-US nations on tax policies in a focal nation. The latter measure captures the secular changes in policy that accumulate across nations and, in turn, allows one to look for any contagion effects that occur, net of effects of tax policy in the US and of common international and domestic forces. As the table reveals, the coefficient for past levels of US rates and current tax policy in a focal nation – that is the long-term structural relationship between the two – is indeed significant. For every one point drop in US rates in the long term, rates in other nations fall by .89 points (the long-term effect is given by dividing the coefficient of the causal variable by the coefficient of the lagged dependent variable). The coefficient of the (weighted) level of past tax rates in non-US cases is, however, insignificant. This tells us that there is no evidence for a "general contagion toward neoliberalism" net of US rate cut effects.

Conclusions

During the past two decades, the tax treatment of corporate and capital income has changed rather dramatically across the capitalist democracies. While the pace and depth of change varies, corporate and personal rates have been reduced and the tax base broadened through significant shifts away from significant investment credits and allowances in virtually all countries. In fact, not only have instruments and the settings of those instruments been altered, but the basic goals of tax policy have seemingly shifted from redistribution and interventionism toward efficiency.[55] How can one explain this significant move to neoliberal tax policy?

[55] See Swank 1998; Swank and Steinmo 2002. I use the language of Peter Hall's conceptualization of policy paradigm shift; Hall 1993.

The analyses presented in this chapter offer some clear answers to this question. To an extent, national policymakers responded to common international and domestic pressures. Internationalization, in some areas of tax policy, militated toward significant policy change; as Steinmo and I have argued elsewhere, the room for maneuver by policymakers, however, was constrained by domestic economic change (e.g. deindustrialization and economic performance problems) and domestic budgetary politics.[56] Yet, the shift to neoliberal tax structure was by no means solely a response by national policymakers to these common forces. Neoliberal tax policy diffused. Most centrally, past changes in US tax policy significantly shaped tax policy change in other nations. This was most clearly evident in more liberal market economies where the perceived relative benefits – largely an improvement in a nation's competitive position for mobile assets – offset the costs of economic uncertainty and political resistance that were more pronounced in coordinated market economies. In addition, it is important to reiterate that past policy change in nations outside the United States, regardless of the relationship to the nation in question, did not seem to influence appreciably tax policy reform. The diffusion of the neoliberal tax regime was driven by tax policy changes in the United States.

What do the above results reveal about the mechanisms of diffusion and about the future of neoliberal reforms? On the question of diffusion, substantial theory, an abundance of qualitative evidence about the perceptions of national policymakers, and the results presented above indicate that competitive pressures undergirded the diffusion of US reform. Policymakers in other nations say they were quite concerned with the tax competition for mobile assets with the US that was implied by the structural change in tax policy; economic theory tells us they were largely correct in being concerned about this despite the clear political (and plausible economic) costs of reform faced by policymakers in many nations. Moreover, quantitative analyses presented above reinforce this account. On the other hand, the results presented in previous sections of this chapter do not support policy learning or social emulation mechanisms of diffusion. Policymakers certainly recognized potential efficiency gains and revenue benefits of a shift to a neoliberal tax regime; they did not, however, systematically adopt the reforms on the basis of a comprehensive assessment of relative US performance in these areas. Second, a general test for diffusion through emulation of historically and socioculturally defined peer nations results in null findings. Overall, the results

[56] Swank and Steinmo 2002.

of systematic empirical analysis and the great weight of theory indicate competitive pressures – as mediated by domestic political economic institutions – drove diffusion.[57]

As to the generalizability of the results of this chapter's analysis, the large majority of findings presented above are premised on the assumptions that the political economies in question are relatively developed capitalist systems and stable democracies. That is, the results cannot be generalized much beyond the contemporary OECD world. Elsewhere, the role of coercive pressures for tax policy diffusion, for instance, may be much more relevant. On the other hand, the diffusion of markets and democracy itself, as well as the central competitive dynamics that surround capital taxation in a world of increasingly integrated capital markets, suggest that the conclusions of the present chapter may in fact become more generalizable as time passes.

Finally, on the long-term prospects of neoliberal reform in a relatively developed democratic capitalist world, the final set of analyses suggests that policymakers in coordinated market economies – political economic systems with notable traditions of (private) coordination of markets coupled with substantial public sector intervention and redistributive social and fiscal policies – ultimately moved toward neoliberal tax structure as the twentieth century drew to a close. This is certainly the proper interpretation of the quantitative findings and of the empirical record of tax reform. On the other hand, it is important to note that effective tax rates on capital, or the revenue actually raised by taxing capital, has on average actually been maintained if not increased.[58] While there is little question that tax policy has experienced structural change, including the shift in explicit goals from redistribution toward efficiency, the substantial capacity of governments to fund social protection and public goods provision in the capitalist democracies has not been diminished appreciably by the US-driven diffusion of neoliberalism.

Appendix 2.1 Operationalization of core variables (all variables lagged one year unless noted otherwise in text)

Statutory marginal corporate and effective average capital tax rates: see notes to Table 2.1.

[57] As such, my results are completely consistent with – indeed support – some chapters in this volume such as Elkins, Guzman, and Simmons. My findings are less consistent with others (Lee and Strang). Part of this inconsistency, however, may be explained by the difference in relevance of competition for mobile assets across policy areas (consider bilateral investment treaties and capital taxation versus general public sector size).

[58] See Table 2.1 and footnote 6 above.

International capital mobility: index of the liberalization of capital controls developed by Quinn (1997) where liberalization is a 0.0 to 4.0 scale of the removal of capital controls.
Trade openness: exports and imports as percentages of GDP.
Structural unemployment: the percentage of the civilian labor force unemployed for one year or more.
Profits: percentage change in real operating surplus.
Investment: percentage change in real machinery and equipment outlays.
Growth: percentage change in real per capita GDP
Public sector debt: gross public debt as a percent of GDP.
Needs/Old: percent of the population 65 and older.
Right government: percentage of cabinet portfolios held by right parties (one-year lags; ten-year means).
US trade: merchandise imports and exports as a percent of GDP.
Nationally coordinated and sector-coordinated economy: see Appendix 2.3 for the derivation of these two indices.
Median voter: ideological position of median voters as developed by HeeMin Kim (see Appendix 2.2), where median voter position is computed from vote shares for ideologically ranked parties (26-item index of parties' positions on traditional left–right continuum) through the application of the formula for the median in grouped data.

Appendix 2.2 Data sources

Data for internationalization variables

Exports and imports to and from the US: International Monetary Fund (hereafter IMF), *Direction of Trade Statistics*. Washington, DC: IMF, selected years.
Indexes of restrictions on capital and financial flows: Dennis Quinn, School of Business, Georgetown University. See Quinn 1997.
Exports and imports of goods and services in national currency units: OECD, *National Accounts of OECD Member Countries*. Paris: OECD, various years.
Gross domestic product in current US dollars: OECD, *National Accounts*. Paris: OECD, selected years.

Policy/Government/Politics (and see below on socioeconomic data for some data on standardizations)

Data for top statutory corporate tax rate: see notes to Table 2.1.
General government debt as a percentage of GDP: OECD, *Economic Outlook*, *National Accounts*. Both Paris: OECD, selected years.

Total and categorical tax revenues for computation of capital taxation (national currency units): OECD, *Revenue Statistics of Member Countries*. Paris: OECD, various years.

Right party cabinet portfolios as a percent of all cabinet portfolios. Sources for party portfolios: Eric Browne and John Dreijmanis, *Government Coalitions in Western Democracies*, Longman, 1982; *Keesings Contemporary Archives* (selected years). Sources for classification of parties: (1) Francis Castles and Peter Mair, "Left-Right Political Scales: Some 'Expert' Judgments," *European Journal of Political Research* 12: 73–88; (2) *Political Handbook of the World*. NY: Simon and Schuster, selected years; (3) country sources.

Political economic institutions: *Union membership*: Jelle Visser, Trade Union Membership Database, Unionization Trends Revisited, Typescripts, Department of Sociology, University of Amsterdam, 1992 and 1996; and unpublished data from Bernhard Ebbinghaus. *Confederal power, level of wage bargaining, and related union and employer measures*: Miriam Golden, Michael Wallerstein, and Peter Lange, Union Centralization Among Advanced Industrial Societies: Update, Department of Political Science, UCLA, 2002. *Political institutions data*: Huber, Ragin, and Stephens 1993; and country-specific sources. *Components of sector-coordinated economic model*: Hicks and Kenworthy database; Hicks and Kenworthy 1998. Values of the components from the Hicks-Kenworthy database for 1995 to 1997 have been extrapolated from 1960–1994 time series for those dimensions of the organization of capitalist economies.

Median voter: data supplied by HeeMin Kim, Department of Political Science, Florida State University, and published with CD version of the Parties Manifestos Data Set. See Ian Budge *et al.*, *Mapping Party Preferences: Estimated for Parties, Electors, and Governments, 1945–1998.*

Socioeconomic data

Consumer price index: IMF, *International Financial Statistics*. Washington, DC: IMF, various years.

Percent of the civilian labor force unemployed, wage and salary employees, civilian labor force, population, population 65 and older: OECD, *Labor Force Statistics*. Paris: OECD, various years.

Percent of civilian labor force unemployed one year or more (based on percent of unemployed out of work one year or more): OECD, *Employment Outlook*. Paris: OECD, various numbers.

Gross fixed capital formation, investment deflator, GDP deflator, gross domestic product, net operating surplus of domestic producers, national income, machinery and equipment expenditures (including transport equipment), compensation of employees by resident producers, private consumption expenditure, compensation of producers of government services, operating surplus of unincorporated enterprises, household property and entrepreneurial income, wages and salaries paid, and operating surplus for non-financial and financial corporate and quasi-corporate enterprises where national account aggregates other than deflators are in national currency: OECD, *National Accounts*. Paris: OECD, various years.

Table 2.6. *National political economic institutions, 1979–1997: principal components analysis*

	I	II
Level of collective bargaining	.7883	.1476
Union organization	.9410	−.0477
Employer organization	.6774	.3644
Labor–Management cooperation	.5697	.6620
Investor–Production enterprise linkages	.4558	.7336
Purchaser–Supplier relationships	.0314	.9081
Cooperative arrangements – Competitive firms	.0608	.9246

Note: Principal components is executed with varimax rotation. The exact measurement of the seven dimensions are (and see Appendix 2.2 on data sources and Appendix Table 2.7 on country scores on the two factors):

Level of collective bargaining: scale of the level of collective bargaining where 1 is plant level, 2 is industry level without constraints, 3 is industry level with constraints, 4 is sectoral level without sanctions, and 5 is sectoral level with sanctions.

Union organization: index (standard score) of union density (i.e. the percentage of employed wage and salary workers who are members of unions) and centralization of union confederation power, or power of appointment, veto over wage agreements, veto over strikes, and maintenance of strike of funds by the largest union confederation.

Employer organization: Index (standard score) of the presence of a national association of employers and powers of that association (i.e. power of appointment, power over industrial actions and collective bargains, and industrial conflict funds).

Labor–Management cooperation: Hicks-Kenworthy measure of management and labor cooperation on issues of employment security.

Investor–Production enterprise linkages: Hicks-Kenworthy measure of the strength of long-term cooperative relations between financial institutions and the enterprises they lend to.

Purchaser–Supplier relationships: Hicks-Kenworthy measure of the strength of long-term supplier–purchaser relationships.

Cooperative arrangements – Competitive firms: Hicks-Kenworthy measure of cooperation between competitive firms in research and development and technology sharing, export promotion, standard setting, training, and related firm cooperative activities.

Table 2.7. *Nation scores on nationally and sector-coordinated capitalism*

Nation	Nationally coordinated	Sector-coordinated	Nation	Nationally coordinated	Sector-coordinated
Australia	.14	−.82	Italy	.22	.74
Austria	.48	.41	Japan	−.37	1.19
Belgium	.36	.20	Netherlands	−.05	−.47
Canada	−.94	−.82	New Zealand	−.27	−.82
Denmark	.90	.20	Norway	1.12	.32
Finland	.82	.69	Sweden	1.38	.34
France	−.74	−.27	Switzerland	−.36	.20
Germany	.09	.53	United Kingdom	−.50	−.72
Ireland	.24	−.82	United States	−1.26	−.69

Appendix 2.3 National political economic institutions

To measure the degree to which a nation's economy is nationally and sector-coordinated, I replicated factor analysis in my earlier work of dimensions of economic coordination for the expanded sample of nation years used in the present study; Swank 2003. Specifically, I factor analyzed measures of seven dimensions of economic coordination of market economies for the years 1979 to 1997 using new and updated temporally and cross-nationally varying measures of coordination. The seven dimensions are discussed in this earlier work and listed in Table 2.6 along with the results of the factor analysis.

The results of the factor analysis are used to generate two variables – factor-score weighted, standard score indices of national coordination and sector coordination. The country values on these two variables are given in Table 2.7.

References

Basinger, Scott and Mark Hallerberg. 2004. Remodeling the Competition for Capital: How Domestic Politics Erases the Race to the Bottom. *American Political Science Review* 98 (2):261–76.

Beck, Nathaniel. 2001. Time-Series – Cross-Section Data: What We Have Learned in the Past Few Years. *American Review of Political Science* 4: 271–93.

Beck, Nathaniel and Jonathan Katz. 1996. Nuisance versus Substance: Specifying and Estimating Time-Series-Cross-Section Models. *Political Analysis* 6: 1–36.

Blanchard, Oliver and Justin Wolfers. 1999. The Role of Shocks and Institutions in the Rise of European Unemployment: The Aggregate Evidence. Unpublished manuscript, Department of Economics, MIT.

Bonturi, Marcos and Kiichiro Fukasaku. 1993. Global and Intra-firm Trade: An Empirical Note. *OECD Economic Studies* No. 20.

Boskin, Michael and Charles McLure Jr., eds. 1990. *World Tax Reform: Case Studies of Developed and Developing Countries*. San Francisco: ICS Press.

Box-Steffensmeier, Janet and Christopher Zorn. 2002. Duration Models for Repeated Events. *Journal of Politics* 64 (4):1069–94.

Campbell, John L. and Ove K. Pedersen. 2001. *The Rise of Neoliberalism and Institutional Analysis*. Princeton, NJ: Princeton University Press.

Carey, David and Josette Rabesona. 2002. Tax Ratios on Labour and Capital Income and on Consumption. *OECD Economic Studies* No. 35.

Castles, Francis. 1998. *Comparative Public Policy: Patterns of Post-war Transformation*. Northhampton, MA: Edward Elgar.

Castles, Francis G., ed. 1993. *Families of Nations: Patterns of Public Policy in Western Democracies*. Brookfield, VT: Dartmouth.

Coopers and Lybrand International Tax Network. Selected years. *International Tax Summaries*. New York: Wiley.

Cummins, Jason G., Kevin A. Hassett, and R. Glenn Hubbard. 1995. Tax Reforms and Investment: A Cross-Country Comparison. NBER Working Paper 5232. Cambridge, MA: National Bureau of Economic Research.

European Commission. 2004. *Structures of the Taxation Systems in the European Union: Data 1995–2002*. Luxembourg: Office of the Official Publications of the European Commission.

Friedrich, Robert. 1982. In Defense of Multiplicative Terms in Multiple Regression Equations. *American Journal of Political Science* 26 (4):797–833.

Ganghof, Steffen. 2000. Adjusting National Tax Policy to Economic Internationalization: Strategies and Outcomes. In *Welfare and Work in the Open Economy Volume II: Diverse Responses to Common Challenges*, edited by Fritz Scharpf and Vivien Schmidt, 597–645. Oxford: Oxford University Press.

Ganghof, Steffen. 2004. Progressive Income Taxation in Advanced OECD Countries: Revisiting the Structural Dependence of the State on Capital. Paper presented at the 100th Annual Meeting of the American Political Science Association, September, Chicago.

Ganghof, Steffen and Richard Eccelston. 2004. Globalization and the Dilemma of Income Taxation in Australia. *Australian Journal of Political Science* 39 (3):519–34.

Garrett, Geoffrey. 1998a. *Partisan Politics in the Global Economy*. New York: Cambridge University Press.

Garrett, Geoffrey. 1998b. Global Markets and National Policies: Collision Course or Virtuous Circle? *International Organization* 52 (4):787–824.

Garrett, Geoffrey and Deborah Mitchell. 2001. Globalization, Government Spending, and Taxation in the OECD. *European Journal of Political Research* 39 (2):145–77.

Genschel, Philipp. 1999. Tax Competition and the Welfare State. Typescript, Max Planck Institute for the Study of Societies, Cologne, Germany.

Gordon, Roger H. 1992. Can Capital Income Taxation Survive in Open Economies. *Journal of Finance* 47 (3):1159–80.

Hall, Peter A. 1993. Policy Paradigms, Social Learning, and the State: The Case of Economic Policy Making in Britain. *Comparative Politics* 25 (3):275–96.

Hall, Peter and David Soskice, eds. 2001. *Varieties of Capitalism: The Institutional Foundations of Comparative Advantage*. New York: Oxford University Press.

Hallerberg, Mark and Scott Basinger. 1998. Internationalization and Changes in Tax Policy in OECD Countries: The Importance of Domestic Veto Players. *Comparative Political Studies* 31 (3):321–53.

Hayes, Jude. 2003. Globalization and Capital Taxation in Consensus and Majoritarian Democracies. *World Politics* 56 (1):79–113.

Hicks, Alexander and Lane Kenworthy. 1998. Cooperation and Political Economic Performance in Affluent Democratic Capitalism. *American Journal of Sociology* 103 (6):1631–72.

Huber, Evelyne, Charles Ragin, and John D. Stephens. 1993. Social Democracy, Christian Democracy, Constitutional Structure, and the Welfare State. *American Journal of Sociology* 99 (3):711–49.

Huber, Evelyne and John D. Stephens. 1998. Internationalization and the Social Democratic Welfare Model: Crises and Future Prospects. *Comparative Political Studies* 33 (3):353–97.

International Monetary Fund. 1998. *Balance of Trade Statistics, 1998*. Washington, DC: IMF.

Katzenstein, Peter. 1985. *Small States in World Markets: Industrial Policy in Europe*. Ithaca, NY: Cornell University Press.

Kitschelt, Herbert, Peter Lange, Gary Marks and John Stephens, eds. 1999. *Continuity and Change in Contemporary Capitalism*. New York: Cambridge University Press.

Kvist, Jan F. 1995. On Bias, Inconsistency, and Efficiency of Various Estimators in Dynamic Panel Models. *Journal of Econometrics* 68 (1):53–78.

Mahler, Vincent and David Jesuit. 2004. State Redistribution in Comparative Perspective: A Cross-National Analysis of the Developed Democracies. Paper presented at the 100th Annual Meeting of the American Political Science Association, September, Chicago.

Mendoza, E. G., A. Razin, and L. L. Tesar. 1994. Effective Tax Rates in Macroeconomics: Cross-country Estimates of Tax Rates in Factor Incomes and Consumption. *Journal of Monetary Economics* 34 (3):297–323.

Organization for Economic Cooperation and Development. 1987. *Taxation in Developed Countries* Paris: OECD.

Organization for Economic Cooperation and Development. 1994. *The Jobs Study*, Volumes I and II. Paris: OECD.

Organization for Economic Cooperation and Development. Selected years. *International Direct Investment Statistical Yearbook*. Paris: OECD.

Pechman, Joseph A., ed. 1988. *World Tax Reform: A Progress Report*. Washington, DC: The Brookings Institution.

Quinn, Dennis. 1997. The Correlates of Change in International Financial Regulation. *American Political Science Review* 91 (2):531–52.

Rodrik, Dani. 1997. *Has Globalization Gone Too Far?* Washington, DC: Institute for International Economics.

Slemrod, Joel. 1990. Tax Principles in an International Economy. In *World Tax Reform: Case Studies of Developed and Developing Countries*, edited by Michael Boskin and Charles McClure, Jr., 11–24. San Francisco: ICS Press.

Slemrod, Joel. 2004. Are Corporate Tax Rates, or Countries, Converging? *Journal of Public Economics* 88 (6):1169–86.

Soskice, David, 1999. Divergent Production Regimes: Coordinated and Uncoordinated Market Economies in the 1980s and 1990s. In *Continuity and Change in Contemporary Capitalism*, edited by Herbert Kitschelt, Peter Lange, Gary Marks, and John Stephens, 101–34. New York: Cambridge University Press.

Steinmo, Sven. 1993. *Taxation and Democracy: Swedish, British and American Approaches to Financing the Modern State*. New Haven: Yale University Press.

Steinmo, Sven. 2002. A Political Economy of Economic Ideas: Tax Policy in the 20th Century. Unpublished manuscript, Department of Political Science, University of Colorado, Boulder.

Swank, Duane. 1992. Politics and the Structural Dependence of the State in Democratic Capitalist Nations. *American Political Science Review* 86 (1):38–54.

Swank, Duane. 1998. Funding the Welfare State: Globalization and the Taxation of Business in Advanced Market Economies. *Political Studies* 46 (4):671–92.

Swank, Duane. 2002. *Global Capital, Political Institutions, and Policy Change in Developed Welfare States*. New York: Cambridge University Press.

Swank, Duane. 2003. Withering Welfare? Globalisation, Political Economic Institutions, and Contemporary Welfare States. In *States in the Global Economy: Bringing Domestic Institutions Back In*, edited by Linda Weiss, 58–82. Cambridge: Cambridge University Press.

Swank, Duane and Sven Steinmo. 2002. The New Political Economy of Taxation in Advanced Capitalist Democracies. *American Journal of Political Science* 46 (3):642–55.

Tanzi, Vito. 1987. The Response of Other Industrial Countries to the U.S. Tax Reform Act. *National Tax Journal* 40 (3):339–55.

Thelen, Kathleen. 1999. Why German Employers Cannot Bring Themselves to Dismantle the German Model. In *Unions, Employers, and Central Banks*, edited by Torben Iversen, Jonas Pontusson, and Davod Soskice, 138–72. New York: Cambridge University Press.

3 The decision to privatize: economists and the construction of ideas and policies*

Bruce Kogut and J. Muir Macpherson

Introduction

Privatization is the distribution of state-owned assets to private owners. This distribution can happen by permitting spontaneous privatization, as frequently witnessed in Central and Eastern Europe; by giving or selling vouchers to the population to be redeemed for shares; or by sales through stock markets, private placements, or managerial buyouts. Privatization witnessed a global explosion in the 1980s and 1990s. Brune (2006) estimates that privatization revenues amounted to $1.3 trillion between 1985 and 2001, not including the mass privatization programs of the transition economies. Bortolotti, Fantini, and Siniscalco (2001) report that the global share of value added by state-owned enterprises fell from 9 percent to 6 percent in the 1978–1991 period. Privatization has been, in summary, of historic economic importance, reflecting a changed view of the state and its role in national economies.

Why do countries decide to implement privatization programs at a given time? The orientation of political parties in power (Bortolotti, Fantini, and Siniscalco 2001), the legal orientation of an economy (La Porta *et al.* 1998), the speed of privatization (Lopez-de-Silanes *et al.* 1997), and concerns over budgetary control and international financial institutions (Brune, Garrett, and Kogut 2004) have been found to be consequential for the volume and value of privatization. This line of inquiry points to a more fundamental question: why should these factors matter now? Countries were in debt and had right-wing governments in previous decades without privatizing. These factors have fluctuated repeatedly over time. They may add to the explanation of individual country adoption but they do not explain why privatization as a policy boomed in the 1980s and especially in the 1990s.

* We would like to acknowledge financial support of INSEAD and Georgetown University and the comments of Frank Dobbin and Barry Eichengreen. Andrew Spicer has been an important inspiration for many of the ideas in this chapter.

What has changed over time is the underlying diffusion of this economic policy as an idea among similar ideas. The very term of privatization was an obscure invention of Peter Drucker until adopted by the Thatcher government in the late 1970s (Yergin and Stanislaw 1998:114ff); previously, it was called "denationalization," a term that is defined by its opposite, the expropriation of property by the state. It makes sense that countries that have obvious incentives to privatize or that have an ideological predisposition to less government would adopt this new idea and privatize earlier than others. These are national explanations that influence the overall propensity of a country to privatize but cannot explain why privatization was so suddenly adopted in so many places in such a short period of time. This coterminous adoption implies that privatization was an idea embedded in a broad and global change in ideology.

We propose that for an economic idea to be implemented across many countries, the existence of a pre-existing epistemic community is vital for the articulation of the policy as well as for the command of the practical knowledge of "how to do it." As analyzed in the studies by Babb (2001) for Mexico and Valdes (1995) for Chile, the advocacy of American-trained economists was an important element in the adoption of privatization programs. These individual cases are surely expressions of the globalization of the economics profession, described by Marion Fourcade-Gourinchas (forthcoming). We argue, and find evidence below, that the epistemic community of American-trained economists had a significant and sizeable influence on the adoption of a privatization program.

The theoretical implications of this argument can be usefully highlighted at the outset. There is no doubt that the current age is marked by a high and rapid diffusion of institutions and ideas. It is reasonable to posit, as do Meyer, Boli, Thomas, and Ramirez (1997) that this diffusion is driven by a "world culture" which, like the Brownian motion of gas molecules in a sealed chamber, comes to homogenize all nation-states with an ergodic finality.[1] The process of this diffusion can be well described by the embracing typology of DiMaggio and Powell (1983) as competitive, mimetic, or normative.

There is another lens by which to understand these phenomena and that is to anchor the understanding of the diffusion in the situated knowledge of the relevant actors and the communities to which they belong. Through this lens, the study of nuclear bomb technology by MacKenzie and Spinardi (1995) is pertinent in posing a fundamental question: can

[1] Empirical evidence is given in Frank, Hironaka, and Schofer 2000; a review of this approach, among others, for explaining the impact of ideas is given in Campbell 2002.

we have diffusion of incompletely understood knowledge in the absence of social relationships (e.g. the mobility of scientists) embedded in communities of practice? These communities of practice – atomic physicists in the case of the nuclear bomb and economists in the case of privatization – consist of members who share a common language, identity, and problem orientation stored in partly explicit and partly tacit coded knowledge.[2] As in Knorr-Cetina's apt phrase of "epistemic cultures," such communities consist of shared understanding of what is warranted knowledge (Knorr-Cetina 1999).

The expression for members of policy communities of practice is "technocrats," a term that is so widely diffused in many developing countries as to have a clear ontological status in the popular language. It is not that "knowledge" is simply situated, it is that "practitioners" are also situated in positions of cultural, if not political, influence. To explain action, an epistemology must have an ontology. A technocrat is a person situated in an ideational field and in a field of practice. These fields may or may not be correlated. Hence, the empirical question of whether they are joined in the enactment of economic and social policies.

While a technocrat could be trained in many fields, we focus upon one professional community of economics. We propose that an adequate account of diffusion should address the microfoundations by which ideas are communicated and legitimated as economic policies within epistemic communities.[3] Ideas are *constructed* within social networks and they diffuse within given social and national structures, as Strang (1991) has forcefully argued. Institutions are not poured into nations like water into a vessel, as Buttel (2000) has also noted in his criticism of world culture theory. The debates within an epistemic community drive the collective learning, reducing heterogeneity to a more consensual view, at least until the next debate begins.

It is important then to take seriously the construction of ideas in order to identify the relationship of the knowledge of a community to the diffusion of a policy and its implementation. We can surely see variation in ideas within the social sciences and economics. The fascinating study of Dezalay and Garth (2002) on the transformation of Latin American elites, for example, notes that there was no global consensus; the variations in diffusion reflected "palace wars" in the United States epistemic communities of economics and human rights lawyers. This ambiguity

[2] See Lave and Wenger 1991 and Brown and Duguid 1991 for now classic statements.

[3] Haas 1992 provides the canonical explanation of the concept of an "epistemic community" in policy. For social networks and such communities, see Keck and Sikkink 1998; see also the volume by Goldstein and Keohane 1993 on the influence of ideas on policy.

provided national elites the ideological room to find local solutions to the challenge of modernization.

To analyze the influence of the economics community on privatization, the chapter below has the following order. We explain briefly the historical background to the idea of privatization and the innovation of the Thatcher government in transforming this policy into a coherent ideology. Using the context of privatization, we then discuss world cultural theory, and the associated ideas of coercive adoption, and compare this approach to the construction of ideas and policies. In particular, we emphasize that the transmission of ideas occurs through a global network of experts whose efficacy is nevertheless dependent upon local political conditions and the control over the exercise of state power.[4] Because it is important to understand why a hazard model specification is critical to our analysis, we explain briefly how a global diffusion can be sorted out statistically from the effect of the diffusion of the "diffusers," namely American-trained economists. Using self-collected data on 13,422 economists, we find in particular an important impact of American-trained, and especially University of Chicago-trained, economists on adoption. To provide a richer account of adoption (including what a statistical treatment cannot easily capture), we conclude by discussing briefly several country cases where privatization was adopted or not. The conclusions stress the importance of taking seriously the discourse of ideas on the content of political action.

Cycles in economic ideas

Privatization presupposes that the state owns assets. The ownership of enterprises by the state historically dates to ancient history; the ownership of lands and mines by the state is a common feature to most feudal histories. However, as an ideology in industrial countries, state ownership dates most prominently to the growth of socialism and state planning in Western Europe after the Second World War, to say nothing of the socialization of ownership that swept Central and Eastern Europe, China, and other socialist countries. In the UK, it coincides with the coming to power of a Fabian influenced elite, whereas in France, the motivation was the technocratic and St. Simonian orientation of planners, led by Jean Monnet, to rebuild the economy from "commanding heights." To Schumpeter, state ownership appeared to be inevitable, a view echoed by the influential study in 1965 by Schonfeld (Schumpeter 1943; Shonfeld 1965).

[4] See, for example, the insightful studies of Wade 2000 and Ziegler 1997.

State ownership of enterprises spread rapidly in developing countries as movements of national liberation led to independence. Ironically, due to an explicit concern that the World Bank should avoid making loans to compete with the private sector, it did not participate in, or grant any loans for the purpose of, private sector development until 1983 (Miller 1999:38). All its prior lending was to governments for financing state-led development projects and, hence, to state-owned enterprises. Data on expropriation (which often led to state ownership) clearly show one-time spikes following nationalization of colonial assets (e.g. tea plantations in Sri Lanka). In some industries, nationalization was triggered by demonstration effects, such as in the oil industry (Kobrin 1985). The "taken-for-granted" assumption of private multinational ownership rapidly dissolved before the imitative nationalizations of other states.

Consequently, the degree of state ownership in an economy varied dramatically across countries. In many countries that successfully modernized, state-owned enterprises played central roles. In Korea, the banking sector was state owned; in Taiwan, the policy was similar to the French whereby the state owned the "commanding heights"; and the Singapore government, especially through its state-owned holding company, Temasek, controls the most important companies in communication, transportation, and harbours.[5]

It is not surprising, then, that there was no consensual view on the economic implications of state ownership in developing or developed countries. Even by the late 1980s there were few studies on relative efficiency of state-owned enterprises and the private sector or on privatized companies. Some of the most influential economists, such as Jean-Jacques Laffont and Jean Tirole (1991) and David Sappington and Joseph Stiglitz (1987), provided formal models showing important cases in which state-owned enterprises should outperform the private sector due to informational properties. A landmark study of the early British privatization by Vickers and Yarrow showed mixed results.[6] There was, in fact, a poverty of evidence on the economic merits of privatization through the 1990s, as admitted in the many later studies that have sought to establish a consensual view.[7] The dearth of "science" regarding the

[5] See Amsden 1992 on Korea, Hamilton 1998 on Taiwan, and Low 1998 on Singapore.

[6] Vickers and Yarrow 1988.

[7] For *recent* positive appraisals of privatization, see Megginson and Netter 2001; Shirley articulated the Bank's position in *Bureaucrats in Business* 1995; Ramamurthi 1999 provides a penetrating critique of the Development report; see Shirley and Walsh 2001 for again a positive assessment. On the failure of privatization policies in Russia, see Nellis 1999.

benefits of privatization means that the early policy recommendations even within economics were *contested* by the core members of this community.

Adoption without social networks

The turning point in diffusion was the revolution in economic political thought during the 1980s. Prior to the Thatcher economic revolution, the number of acts of privatization was small. In the 1960s, Germany privatized part of its shares in Volkswagen, among other companies, though overall, the state (Federal, Land, and municipality) continued to hold large shares in industry; some of the largest banks in Germany are state owned. The Chilean government also started to privatize in the late 1970s the properties nationalized by Allende. The policy led to such difficulties that many firms (especially banks) were quickly renationalized before the privatization program commenced again in the early 1980s, leading to the quip of the "Chicago way to socialism."[8]

Privatization as an ideology dates from the conservative revolution of Margaret Thatcher in the United Kingdom. Thatcher was closely affiliated with the Institute of Economic Affairs – a policy think-tank influenced by two University of Chicago economists, Milton Friedman and Friedrich Hayek, and headed by Keith Joseph, later her Minister of Industry in charge of privatization. The term "privatization" only comes to replace the term "denationalization" during her tenure. She wrote in her memoirs:

> Privatization ... was fundamental to improving Britain's economic performance. But for me it was also far more than that: it was one of the central means of reversing the corrosive and corrupting effects of socialism ... Just as nationalization was at the heart of the collectivist programme by which Labour Governments sought to remodel British society, so privatization is at the centre of any programme of reclaiming territory for freedom (Thatcher 1993:676).

While heeding the caveat that correlation is not causality, privatizations clearly accelerate shortly after her (and Reagan's) election.

As a benchline model, it is useful to keep in mind that the performance of state-owned enterprises may have deteriorated in many countries, causing budgetary deficits and hence causing the search for solutions. World liquidity constraints stemming from financial crises might lead governments simultaneously to sell state assets. The correlation of privatization is, in this view, a solution discovered independently in many

[8] The European experience is briefly summarized in Boix 1997; for Chile, see Valdes 1995.

countries that face a common economic problem. Charts that show a diffusion of a policy cannot separate out directly "common stimuli, common response" explanations from other alternative explanations.

The diffusion of privatization policies began with British and Chilean privatizations of the late 1970s and early 1980s that demonstrated the feasibility of large-scale privatization. Hence, it is reasonable to think that one source of a common stimuli are their initial adoptions. With a common demonstration effect, nations may evidence obvious differences in the decision to adopt. If the subsequent country variation in adoption of privatization was purely the result of country-level differences, then the subsequent diffusion would be a case merely of the "common stimuli, varying response" models. This type of model treats the commonly observed example of Britain and Chile as a stimulus but looks at additional *independent* processes that govern the adoption of privatization in each country. Potential adopters would be completely uninfluenced by the subsequent decisions of other countries and variation in adoption would occur only through differences in relevant characteristics of each country. It is likely that the examples of Britain and Chile would matter, but those of other countries that followed them would not.

In short, diffusion can occur in the absence of social networks and dependent processes. Let's consider now the impact of information that spills across borders. This externality is an example of imitation. In the messy world of policy and its causal effects, imitation is often indistinguishable from "learning."[9] It is consistent with Kobrin's study of expropriation of oil fields that the Thatcher policies provided simply a demonstration effect that serves as an ideological "common stimuli," provoking a "common response." The Thatcher revolution was hardly a secret kept from other countries, as was the nuclear bomb technology studied by MacKenzie and Spinardi (1995). Yet, both the "bomb" and the "revolution" signal loudly once the act is done. There is a very important "marketing" externality in public decisions to adopt a new practice, as noted first by Kenneth Arrow (1962): the first case establishes the information in the form of a public good that such an innovation is feasible. This information need not be embedded in social networks, but could be accessible through public media, such as newspapers or television. Indeed, Benedict Anderson's thesis on the diffusion of nationalism points to the primary role played by the printing press in defining national identities (Anderson 1991).

Cross-sectional analysis often has difficulty in sorting out information from influence. Consider the classic study by Coleman, Katz, and Menzel

[9] See Lee and Strang 2006 for an innovative investigation into learning.

(1966) on the analysis of the adoption of medical innovations. This analysis was challenged by Ronald Burt, who argued that adoption was determined by critical actors in social networks (Burt 1987). More recently, Christophe van den Bulte and Gary Lilien (2001) reviewed the evidence, finding that networks did not matter at all; adoption was the outcome of marketing. This interesting debate over time has a simple message: any explanation for the adoption of privatization confronts the difficult analysis of separating a process of general diffusion from a specific channel. A control for time itself is usually inadequate to capture this broader diffusion effect.

Coercive diffusion of privatization

One specific channel that may have influenced some countries, and not others, to privatize is the coercive power of international financial institutions. Brune, Garrett, and Kogut (2004) find that privatization measured by its monetary value can be explained by the policies of international financial organizations (i.e. the World Bank and International Monetary Fund (IMF)) that imposed privatization as a condition for lending; they did not find this result for a count of privatization. In some regards, this explanation points to "coercion," even if national governments are occasionally complicit in order to avoid the political blame or to attract foreign capital. Indeed, by the late 1980s, both institutions had established conditionality (and often privatization) as a requirement to most structural adjustment loans.[10] However, as Brune *et al.* (2004) note, the effect of the IMF loans increased the market value, but not the count, of privatization. This subtle distinction reinforces the view that the IMF policies, even if directly non-consequential, can have a positive influence in signaling to markets a country's commitment to "reforms." Critically, the IMF effect changes over time periods in ways consistent with changes in the institution's commitment to privatization. Henisz, Zelner, and Guillen (2005) replicate the finding of Brune *et al.* (2004) and Kogut and Macpherson (2002) for the impact of IMF lending on privatization and neoliberal policy diffusion. These findings echo the earlier results of Strang and Chang (1993) that ratification of International Labour Organization (ILO) conventions subsequently influenced labor policy.

At the same time, the coercive influence of the IMF and World Bank (or any international convention) only takes the analysis one step

[10] Nellis 1999. Interestingly, the IMF conditions were found to influence privatization values, whereas the World Bank conditions did not; see Brune *et al.* 2004.

further. Why did these institutions come to believe that privatization should be made a condition to lending? One reason, for which there is sound documentation, is that these institutions moved ideologically toward the position of emphasizing private sector development, partly in response to the growing conservatism of host governments (Kapur, Lewis, and Webb 1997; Williamson 1990). In this view, the international organizations reflected the growing success of the Thatcher revolution – later reinforced by the ascendance of the Reagan administration – to reverse radically the policy of state intervention and state ownership of enterprises (Yergin and Stanislaw 1998). The policies of the IMF and World Bank followed the wishes of powerful donor countries, though not passively. The sea change was accompanied by a considerable discussion within the economics community on why privatization should be good.

This history does not fully account for some features of interest. Among the developed countries, only the UK fell under an IMF program until the Asian crisis at the end of our period of observation, yet developed countries were among the earliest adopters of privatization. Moreover, many medium- and lower-income countries adopted privatization policies without IMF or World Bank loans. We have, in other words, a broader global diffusion of a policy than can be explained by coercion from international financial institutions.

An alternative explanation is to regard diffusion as the result of a cultural process, of which the international institutions are one among many agents of exposure. Meyer *et al.* (1997) posit the creation of a world society that establishes a universal normative pressure. This thesis of "world society" contradicts the theories that view nations as defined cultural entities, with policies reflecting national "logics" (Dobbin 1994) or "institutional complementarities" that display path-dependent rigidities (Boyer and Drache 1996). World society theory embraces Galton's thesis made in the nineteenth century that nation-states are not independent since their cultures are products of a broad diffusion.[11] But its thesis is more radical, for in this view, national variations are anomalies unless justified in terms of general cultural principles (Meyer *et al.* 1997:170). Nations, though varying in their social structures, are "receptors" of the "blueprints" of global cultural models (Frank, Hironaka, and Schofer 2000).

The world society account is impressive insofar that the data regarding the joint diffusion of indicators of "blueprints" are compelling: national

[11] Galton 1889.

economic accounting, educational institutions, and environmental standards. In this view, diffusion has an implication of equifinality. The evidence points to considerable heterogeneity in the timing of adoption, suggesting that the content of ideas and practices is contested and spatially sensitive. As Buttel (2000) has noted, globalization is often equivalent to Americanization and its adoption is strongly conditioned on local national political structures which re-interpret these policies. In other words, there is disagreement not only over whether time correlations are sufficient evidence to establish the thesis, but also over the significance that the local experts, the technocrats, do not agree: it is a disarmingly strong structural thesis that world society occurs independent of the many histories of local dissent (Campbell 2002).

American economics and constructionist theory of adoption

To recapture the importance of agency within epistemic communities, it is important to take seriously the "diffusion of the diffusers" and the knowledge within this globalizing community as a prior condition of adoption. Economists are, of course, educated in institutions throughout the world, however nowhere in such numbers as in the United States and Anglo-Saxon countries. In reviewing the role of economists in Latin America, Dezalay and Garth conclude that "economics is American economics." However, the subtitle of their thesis is the effect of this community varied dramatically across countries, even within the South American region alone. As Fourcade-Gourinchas (forthcoming) documents, while the field of economics was itself in a process of global expansion during this period of time, the dynamics varied considerably by country.

There is surely good reason to believe that American economics and economists were consequential. It is of some irony that many of the conflicting views on diffusion are well illustrated in the debates of a particular social network of importance to the spread of privatization, namely, the economics community. The term "epistemic community" should not be taken lightly to mean that such communities have a monopoly on policy truth no matter their technical expertise. They are normative communities, specialized in a body of knowledge whose progress is contested but within boundaries of legitimated discourse and method. In this regard, the ideas within a community are learned in reference to particular identities. Lave and Wenger (1991) note that individual learning proceeds on the basis of identities acquired through participation in communities, such as through apprenticeship or professional programs.[12] This learning is not of the nature of "information" such as marketing as we discussed earlier, but rather of the acquisition of ontological categories and their relationships that anchor strong professional identities and epistemological stances.

In fact, there is considerable evidence that economics training is a transformative experience for doctoral students that creates strong professional identities. The study by Colander and Klamer (1987) was based on surveys of 212 graduate students at top economics departments. They found that in 1987, the students arrived largely liberal in their politics and interested in policy. In the course of their study, their concerns shifted toward mathematics and problem-solving abilities. They ranked knowledge of economic literature, history, or the economy as unimportant.

It is of interest for our later results indicating a differential influence of Chicago economists to note that the Colander and Klamer study found different schools of thought in regard to *some* issues. In particular, the University of Chicago presented a distinctive profile regarding a strong belief in rational expectations and market solutions. The idea of a "Chicago School" was coined by Miller in a 1962 article published in the *Journal of Political Economy* (belonging to the University of Chicago) to identify a group of economists centered around Milton Friedman, Marvin Reder, and George Stigler. To Miller, this school was marked by the belief in neo-classical economics and an identification of ideal and actual markets. In a memorable phrase, he notes a Chicago economist "applies economics to every nook and cranny of life." Stigler strongly denied this characterization in a response and went on to a number of studies to test the proposition. In a study of citations in Ph.D. doctorates in economics, Stigler and Friedland (1975) found no doctrinal differences, though they noted certain fields, such as monetary and fiscal policy, were marked by more strident debate. They did find, however, traces of acrimony in acknowledgement of influence. Analyzing citations for being favorable or unfavorable, they found Chicago theses cite unfavorably Harvard, and MIT theses cited unfavorably Chicago. It could well be that the notoriety of Chicago was due more to debates in a particular area (i.e. monetary policy). However, in their later study, Colander and Klamer (1987) found that in 1987, Ph.D. students at the University of Chicago had far stronger beliefs in rational expectations and market solutions than students at peer institutions.

12 Lave and Wenger 1991. See Brown and Duguid 1991.

The interesting implication of the debates in the American economic community for international diffusion is the observation by Dezalay and Garth that "palace wars" among economists and American social scientists spilled into Latin America and, presumably, the rest of the world. The role of the University of Chicago in the Chilean economic policies, including privatization, is especially well known.[13] Partly out of concern over the dominant influence of the Keynesian economist Raul Prebisch, the University of Chicago signed in 1956 an exchange agreement with the Universidad Catolica in Chile. This exchange created a cadre of pro-market technocrats who under Pinochet in the period between 1975 and 1983, held 78 percent of the economic policymaking positions (Biglaiser 2002; Silva 1991, citing Delano and Traslavina 1989; Harberger 1997). Even in Cold War-era Eastern Europe, Chicago economists engaged colleagues from socialist countries in joint conferences that served to spread their own ideology and use the reformist impulses of the Eastern economists to discredit Keynesianism along with socialism (Bockman and Eyal 2001). Thus, these struggles within the epistemic community of economists not only influenced policy abroad, but also discredited their intellectual opponents at home.

In other countries, the top advisers came from other universities. For example, the liberal minister of finance in Argentina, Domingo Cavallo, was trained at Harvard; Pedro Aspe who led privatization in Mexico did his Ph.D. at MIT; both knew each other from Cambridge. (See Sara Babb 2001, for a study of economists in Mexico.) The casual evidence does not obviously reflect palace wars by the 1990s. However, it should also be recalled that the surveys indicate a general convergence toward common beliefs in market solutions among economics graduates from most doctoral programs over the last two decades; our results below confirm this convergence.

It is important to note that the presence of US-trained economists in influential government positions is itself the outcome of a deeper process. When leaders appoint American-trained economists to top policymaking posts, they do so knowing full well that these economists are likely to enact liberal policies. These appointments are made only after leaders have become convinced that liberalization (including privatization) has become desirable or necessary. The presence of American-trained economists in government, academia, business, finance, and elsewhere serves to broker ideas from the wider epistemic community. This domestic economic community serves to legitimize as well as to adapt ideas of

[13] See the study by Valdes 1995.

privatization (Bockman and Eyal 2001). As a consequence, a reasonable measure for the influence of American economics on policy decisions is simply the presence of American-trained economists in a country.

The channel of influence of American economics is not limited to the local careers of foreign-born graduates of American economic programs. As we saw earlier, the IMF and World Bank were heavily dominated by economics graduates. The evidence is strongest for the IMF, where every administrative department has traditionally been held by an economist. Economists also make up the plurality of positions in the World Bank as well, even if their influence is more moderated by administrative professionals than in the IMF (de Vries 1986). The observation that the international financial institutions consisted of economists belonging to a defined epistemic community provides an alternative interpretation to coercion, namely, that these institutions could easily enter into the local discourse to construct new economic policies where there were resident economists. Our results will speak to this interpretation.

Testing for a global diffusion process

The ambition of this chapter is to test whether the decision to launch a privatization program is merely an independent response to a common stimulus, to coercive and imitative influences, or to the diffusion of the "diffusers" and their constructed consensus around policy. Our methodological approach to this analysis is the following. First, we code whether a country privatizes at all. Our goal is to find signs that a country has adopted privatization as a policy; the details of how it implements that idea are not important for our purposes. Second, we utilize a hazard model specification to test for diffusion processes not at the population, but the individual country level. Third, we test for both the cross-sectional effects of our diffusion variables and their changing impact over time. This allows us to better distinguish between a "common stimuli, varying response" interpretation and genuine processes of diffusion.

Our privatization data are drawn from the Global Privatization Database (2006) compiled by Nancy Brune.[14] We aggregate privatization transactions for each country and code two alternate events, the country's first privatization and the country's third privatization. While

[14] It is important to note that we are only interested in privatization outside of the former Communist countries. The timing of diffusion of privatization in these countries had less to do with Thatcher than with Gorbachev. For this reason, we exclude the former Communist countries from our analysis so as not to confuse these two distinct diffusion processes.

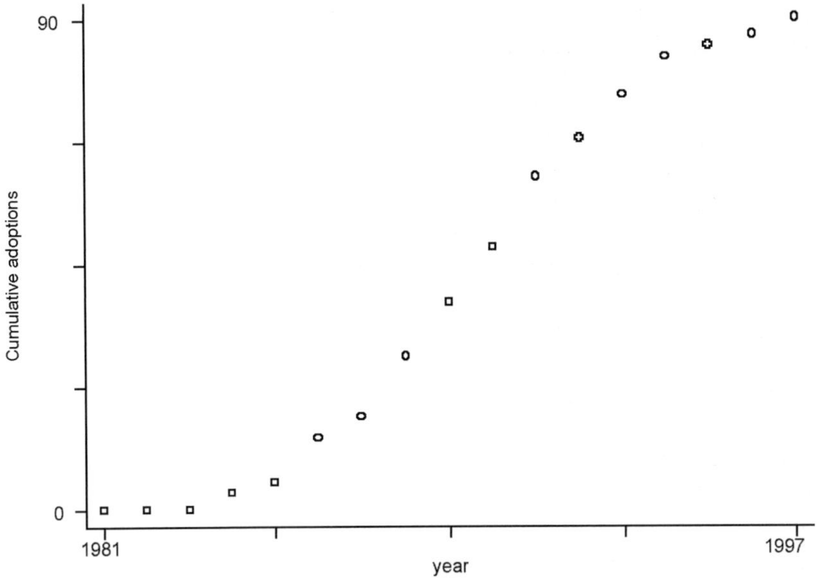

Figure 3.1 Cumulative number of privatization events

the very first privatization is desirable as the earliest possible observation of the event, it is not necessarily as clear a signal of the acceptance of and commitment to privatization. In the results presented below we use the third privatization as our indicator of privatization adoption; the results – as might be expected – are not fundamentally sensitive to this choice. Once a country is considered to have adopted privatization, it is dropped from the data set and no repeated events are possible.

We start the process in 1981 shortly after the election of Margaret Thatcher, widely viewed as an ideological watershed. The first UK privatizations take place immediately, as do the Chilean privatizations. As policy innovators, the UK and Chile are excluded from our sample since we are concerned with the process of policy diffusion and adoption, rather than policy innovation. Figure 3.1 shows the cumulative number of events. It has the familiar S-shaped curve seen in diffusion studies, usually attributed to differences in intrinsic propensities (of countries in this case) and differential access to information. As can been seen, the number of events flattens as the pool of non-adopters becomes depleted.

Our control variables are the log transform of each country's population and gross domestic product (GDP), and government consumption as a share of GDP. (Unless otherwise stated, all data for the variables in this study are drawn from the World Bank's *World Development Indicators* (WDI) CD-ROM. These are simply intended to control for the size of the country and its public sector. We also control for the extent to which a country has already adopted liberal economic policies by using the country's openness to trade and foreign investment. Trade openness is measured as the ratio of the sum of exports and imports over the country's GDP. Direct investment openness is measured as the ratio of the stock of foreign direct investment in the country over its GDP. Finally, it could be that some countries simply have fewer state-owned enterprises (SOEs) that could be privatized and therefore are less likely to even have use for the policy; we add a control for the size of the state sector, using a simple ordinal indicator (0–10) taken from *Economic Freedom of the World* (Gwartney *et al.* 1996; see also Brune *et al.* 2004). We use this variable for the size of the state-owned sector only as a measure of the initial conditions in the country as of 1981. We then include a set of variables intended to capture the country-specific factors that may influence a country's likelihood of adoption, as identified by prior work. We use the size of each country's budget surplus (deficit) to test the possibility that governments privatize in order to improve their fiscal balance. Governments might privatize in order to shed loss-making state-owned enterprises and raise capital at the same time.

To test the hypothesis that the wave of privatization resulted from the actions of right-wing governments, we include indicator variables for the presence of left-wing and right-wing governments in control of the executive branch. The omitted category includes centrist governments, governments controlled by parties not clearly identified by the right–left spectrum (e.g. Iran), and unelected governments. Data are drawn from the World Bank's "Database of Political Institutions" (DPI; Beck *et al.* 2001).

To capture the mechanisms of diffusion, we use three independent variables: competition in export markets, IMF coercion, and social learning through the epistemic community of US-trained economists. The diffusion of privatization via competition in export markets can be thought of as akin to the contagion of competitive currency devaluations. As one country allows its exchange rates to decline, its immediate competitors in overseas markets feel pressured to likewise allow their own currency to decline in order to stay competitive. Whatever the distributional effects or social costs of privatizing SOEs, if privatization enhances competitiveness (or governments believe it does), then they will feel pressured to privatize if their country's main competitors for export markets have privatized. Those state-owned assets put up for sale do not have to be in export industries themselves. For example, if privatization can improve the reliability of electricity to industrial customers or cut the waiting time to add an additional phone line, this can have an important impact on the competitiveness of exporters in a global marketplace.

Sociologists studying international diffusion via competition in trade networks have used the extent to which countries engage in international trade in the same commodities as a predictor of whether they will adopt the same practices (Guler, Guillen, and Macpherson 2002). This has been operationalized as a simple correlation of trade vectors which is then weighted by adoption. This measure has been very successful, but it has some weaknesses. For example, in 1985 the trade vectors of both Sweden and Paraguay are correlated with the United States at approximately 0.78. Despite the fact that Sweden's total trade is more than fifty times that of Paraguay, the correlational measure would give each equal influence over the US via the trade network. Furthermore, since the correlational measure is symmetric, Paraguay would be predicted to have just as much competitive influence over the US as the US would over Paraguay. We utilize a more sophisticated measure that better accounts for the relative magnitude of the competitive influences between country pairs transmitted via the trade network.

Our measure of competition in trade accounts for the relative influence of each country on each of 1,250 traded commodities and the influence in turn of those global commodity markets on each country. The effect of competition in export markets on the diffusion of privatization is measured by each country's exports in a given industry as a share of its GDP, weighted by the share of total global exports in this industry accounted for by countries that have already begun privatizing, and summing across all other countries and industries. More specifically,

$$Comp_i = \sum_j \sum_k \frac{Exports_{ik}}{GDP_i} * \frac{Exports_{jk}}{\sum_j Exports_k} * Privat_j \tag{1}$$

where $Comp_i$ is the competitive pressure to privatize experienced by country *i*; $Exports_{ik}$ is the value of exports by country *i* in industry *k*; $Exports_{jk}$ is the value of exports by country *j* in industry *k*; GDP_i is the GDP of country *i*; and $Privat_j$ is an indicator variable that is 1 when country *j* has privatized and is 0 otherwise. This measure was then logged and z-transformed for each year in order to eliminate time trends and overdispersion. Industry is classified at the 4-digit Standard International Trade Classification (SITC) level and trade data are taken from the *World Trade Flows* CD-ROM (Feenstra 2000).

IMF conditionality is operationalized as an indicator variable equal to 1 if a country received new loans from the IMF in a given year. An alternate specification using the value of the new loans as a fraction of the borrowing country's GDP was also used, but this variable was not significant. We interpret this to mean that the structural adjustment conditions on lending that encouraged privatization did not depend heavily on the size of the loans being sought by borrower countries (see Vreeland 2002).

For measures of the influence of epistemic communities, we wish to capture the influence of the epistemic community of American-trained economists in each country. (Unquestionably, it would be interesting to include graduates in economics programs located in other countries.) The American Economic Association (AEA) surveys its members every four years to create a membership directory. The survey asks respondents about their educational background, including the degrees they have received and the institutions that granted them. Respondents are also asked for their current institutional affiliation and address. These data are used to construct two measures.

First, we measure the influence of the American economics profession by counting the number of economists in each country with degrees granted by American universities. Second, we are also interested in the debates within this epistemic community and measure the influence of its most strongly pro-liberalization members by counting the number of economists in each country with degrees granted by the University of Chicago.

These counts are taken starting in 1981 and every four years thereafter when a new AEA membership directory is released. Responding to the survey is optional and response rates are not reported by the AEA. In addition, not all respondents choose to answer all items on the survey. Those that chose not to report on their educational background could not be properly classified for our measures and were dropped.

This exercise resulted in collecting data on 13,442 economists living outside the US, of which 6,493 had US degrees and 430 had degrees from the University of Chicago (of which 192 resided in Canada). There is a high correlation among the two measures of American degrees (.92). Some countries have low rates of membership, such as Switzerland, which indeed may reflect the strength of national or regional economics programs. From the detailed country histories, it is obvious, though, that the members of the AEA who chose to appear in the membership directory are a minority of the total number of foreign graduates in some countries. Some of the most important ministers in charge of privatization are not in the database. Thus, these counts are proxies for the influence of American economics and cannot be analyzed at the level of individuals.

The total count of economists with non-US, US, and Chicago degrees grows synchronously from survey to survey. It is therefore statistically vital to normalize the count, since the increase in the number of economists would reflect the time trend.[15] The increases appear to be both a function of increasing membership and improved survey collection methods on the part of the AEA. Using the survey as a longitudinal indicator of changing levels of economists in different countries is therefore questionable, but we can use the data as an indicator of each country's *share* of each type of economist so long as we assume that the changes in response rates will tend to affect all foreign countries equally. We do this by standardizing the number of each type of economist in each country by the total number of US economists reported to be living outside the US. The final measures are the log transformed percentage of all US economists (Chicago economists) in each country. One is added to this number to account for observations with zeros.

$$US\_Economists_i = Log\left(\frac{US\_Count_i}{\sum_j US\_Count_j} + 1\right) \quad (2)$$

Where $US\_Economists_i$ is one of our measures of the contagion effect of economists' epistemic community computed for country i; US_Count_i is the number of American-trained economists living in country i; and US_Count_j is the number of American-trained economists living in country j. The measure of the impact of Chicago economists is the same, only counts of Chicago economists are used as the numerator. Despite their limitations, the empirical question is whether these measures signal a microlevel diffusion of the diffusers. This question is best addressed in the hazard regression format developed below.

Methods

Of the possible methodologies by which to examine this question, a hazard model has conceptual and statistical advantages that have been rightly stressed in particular by studies in the organizational ecology literature. (See, for example, Tuma and Hannan 1984.) The advantage of a hazard model is to correct the estimates for censored observations (due in our case to previous adoption) as well as to control for, or

[15] On the request of a referee, we used the raw count; the results are the same and available on request.

estimate, the effects of a baseline hazard. This baseline hazard is very useful in a study such as ours that wishes to sort out diffusion as a general trend or as generalized contagion. A "contagion" spreads due to the adoption decisions of other countries. In this sense, diffusion is a population-driven phenomenon of innovators and imitators that has been used to understand the adoption of innovations, spread of disease, or medical services.[16] This idea of contagion has been picked up in the studies on the economics of financial crises among emerging markets that focus on channels of diffusion.[17]

Population-level studies, however, are impaired in identifying the spatial and individual characteristics of diffusion at the level of the adopting agent. The diffusion of privatization as a policy idea occurred in a changing historical context of a wider process of globalization in which individuals play substantial roles. This line of inquiry challenges the assumption of the nation as independent units of analysis not only by positing the presence of transnational channels of contagion, but also by identifying the microprocesses of global integration that are embedded in transnational policy communities.

Conceptually, it treats privatization as the adoption of a discrete economic policy. In this regard, the initial decision to privatize is distinctive from subsequent privatization acts, for it represents the adoption of an economic policy as a point in time when political viability was achieved and exercised. Statistically, it has the advantage of identifying the parameters of the underlying diffusion rate, as well as identifying the covariates that explain the hazard of adoption. We take advantage of this property to test not only the cross-sectional (proportional) impact of our variables on privatization, but also how that impact changes over time. If our diffusion variables can be shown to having an increasing impact over time, we believe this strengthens our argument that we are capturing the diffusion process and not just unobserved country heterogeneity.

We utilize the Weibull hazard function because of its flexibility in handling time-varying hazard rates and because when the shape parameter ρ is equal to 1 the Weibull reduces to the constant hazard exponential model. In reporting the results, we call this shape parameter "time" as its sign provides information as to whether baseline adoption increases or

[16] Stimulus–response models are often referred to as SIR models in epidemiology: susceptible, infected, removed. Population diffusion processes are proposed by Bass 1969 and Coleman, Katz, and Menzel 1966.

[17] See the seminal paper by Eichengreen, Rose, and Wyplosz 1996.

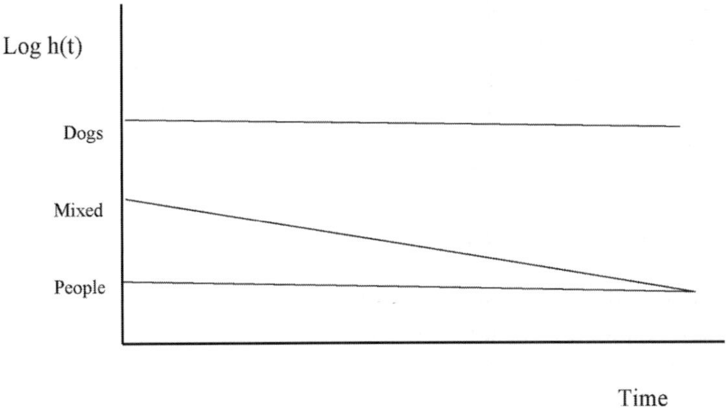

Figure 3.2 Constant hazard rates and yet a falling rate for the mixed populations

slows during the observed period. A declining hazard can represent a statistical bias arising from unobserved heterogeneity. In the case of declining hazards, it can often be the case that high-hazard individuals will adopt quickly and leave behind a core of low-hazard individuals, giving the appearance that the overall hazard has declined with time. In our case, we are testing for increasing hazard rates that run counter to this heterogeneity bias; hence a finding of an increasing parameter is a strong result.

As this claim is important to understand, let's consider what it means. The easiest way to think of the bias of heterogeneity is to consider two populations with exponential survival distributions, that is, with a constant rate of death at all moments in time; one population (say humans) has a lower hazard than another (say dogs), that is, dogs simply die at a higher fixed rate for every observed time period. At time 1, the observed hazard is simply the mixture of the two hazards weighted by their contribution to total population. But since dogs have a high hazard rate, they will die proportionately more at each period; hence they will contribute numerically less and less to the total population since fewer dogs survive than people. This heterogeneity caused by mixing two different populations (people and dogs) alone will cause the (mixed) hazard rate to fall, asymptotically, toward the lower rate of the human population. We illustrate this effect in Figure 3.2 which shows the two exponential hazards (one lower than the other because one has a lower fixed rate of dying). As the dogs that have the higher hazard rate die, the mixed hazard rate falls asymptotically to the lower rate of humans. For this reason, the test of a liability of newness by finding a *negative* sign to the baseline hazard rate is weak because a negative sign is in the direction of the bias caused by heterogeneity. Here is the strong point of the test of the baseline hypothesis that we propose: we expect to find a *positive* sign to the baseline hazard. Thus, the finding of a positively increasing hazard rate is counter to the bias and is a strong result.

This estimated parameter is important because we want to show that the baseline hazard is increasing over the period of our study (1980–1997). If the story of privatization's diffusion was merely a common response to a common stimulus, with those countries most predisposed to liberal policies adopting first, then the baseline hazard would *decline* as the liberal "dogs" were censored. If instead an ongoing diffusion process is propelling the adoption of privatization, we should see the baseline hazard *increase* as all countries experience this rising influence. The shape parameter is then a proxy for "information contagion" or "learning" in the global system (which might occur through demonstration effects or the accumulated know-how captured by consultants, bankers, lawyers, etc.). Technically, the Weibull specification allows for the estimation of a parameter labeled conventionally rho, (ρ). We first test the hypothesis the hazard rate for our overall sample is increasing with time, that is if $\rho > 1$. Then we allow the ρ parameter to vary across countries and use our explanatory variables to predict ρ.

We also used a "shared frailty" specification to try to sort out unobserved heterogeneity. Recall that the first estimates simply say, let's estimate the general diffusion directly and let's add in more of our central explanatory variables. Of course, the baseline hazard will change as we add in *observed* variables. But of course, as always, there are some influences on the likelihood of privatization that are not observed, at least not in our regression. So we will make the conjecture that we can capture these influences by specifying the distribution of their interaction with the other effects. Frailty marries a distribution, in our case, the gamma (often called the "happy conjugate" as the mixed distribution simplifies usually rather easily to an exponential family), to the Weibull and corrects for some of the error attributed to the scale parameter. The shared frailty model estimates an unobserved parameter that modifies a country's base hazard rate and is common across all observations of a given country. This specification constitutes an additional robustness check on the possibility of unobserved heterogeneity across countries in a hazard model. However, with technical sophistication often come new problems, so we offer these tests in the spirit of care and caution.

Results

We present three separate sets of regression results in Tables 3.1 to 3.3. Results are reported as hazard ratios, so a coefficient greater (less) than 1 indicates that an increase in the variable of one unit increases (decreases) the hazard of privatization by the indicated amount.

Table 3.1 shows the results estimating the standard Weibull models. Of our control variables, trade openness is at least marginally significant in all models that also include trade competition. We interpret this to mean that more open economies are somewhat less likely to privatize because they are already fairly open to and successful in international markets. This effect is balanced by their greater vulnerability to competitive pressures from other countries that compete for the same export markets, and for this reason each of these effects is seen only when controlling for the other. It is interesting to note that the size of the government sector, whether measured as government spending as a share of GDP or as the size of the state-owned sector, has no apparent impact on privatization.

Of the variables intended to capture the country-specific reasons to privatize, right-wing executive, left-wing executive, and budget balance, none are significant in any model. The political variables are not only lacking significance relative to the omitted category but are not significantly different from each other, either. What we observe is that both right and left governments privatize and do so in roughly equal proportions. This result is at odds with previous research. It should be noted that we have traded a larger sample for a poorer measure of political orientation, so the results are not directly comparable; in addition, we are looking at time to privatize as opposed to the amount of privatization.

We estimate the structural parameter ρ which measures the change in the baseline hazard of privatization over time. The large, positive coefficient shows that the hazard is increasing during the period of our sample, even after controlling for the other covariates. This increasing rate, which runs counter to the statistical bias discussed earlier, indicates that the likelihood of privatization increased over the observed period after controlling for economic variables. *A significantly increasing propensity to adopt privatization contradicts the argument of purely independent national decision making.* In other words, the increasing hazard points to a world diffusion of policy ideas, including privatization.

Our diffusion variables are supported and in the predicted directions. Trade competition, the use of IMF funds, and the presence of US-trained and University of Chicago-trained economists all increase the hazard of privatization. The effect of the use of IMF funds is only marginally

Table 3.1. *Weibull hazard model of privatization*

	Model 1	Model 2	Model 3	Model 4	Model 5	Model 6
Log population	1.237	1.334*	1.239	1.117	1.080	1.126
	(1.34)	(1.67)	(1.07)	(0.52)	(0.35)	(0.55)
Log GDP	1.218*	1.150	1.216	1.370*	1.159	1.311*
	(1.75)	(1.17)	(1.38)	(1.93)	(0.89)	(1.68)
Gov't consumption	1.036	1.029	1.027	1.035	1.037	1.036
	(1.31)	(1.06)	(0.99)	(1.23)	(1.29)	(1.30)
Budget balance	0.990	0.984	0.987	0.988	1.001	0.996
	(0.36)	(0.54)	(0.45)	(0.42)	(0.04)	(0.13)
Trade openness	0.992	0.985**	0.985**	0.987*	0.986*	0.988*
	(1.32)	(2.23)	(2.23)	(1.82)	(1.95)	(1.76)
Inward FDI stock	0.996	0.992	0.992	0.988	0.978	0.984
	(0.32)	(0.68)	(0.65)	(0.98)	(1.63)	(1.24)
Right gov't	1.909	1.548	1.672	1.570	1.701	1.669
	(1.62)	(1.04)	(1.18)	(1.04)	(1.20)	(1.17)
Left gov't	1.579	1.344	1.358	1.389	1.356	1.469
	(1.21)	(0.76)	(0.77)	(0.84)	(0.75)	(0.97)
Trade competition		1.863**	1.852**	1.723**	1.856**	1.766**
		(2.36)	(2.31)	(2.02)	(2.23)	(2.08)
Size of state sector			1.070	1.049	1.120	1.067
			(0.74)	(0.51)	(1.19)	(0.69)
IMF funds				1.906	2.106*	1.874
				(1.57)	(1.83)	(1.55)
US economists					2.879***	
					(3.27)	
Chicago economists						5.745**
						(2.29)
Time (ρ)	4.445***	4.768***	4.722***	4.792***	5.309***	4.998***
	(14.27)	(14.71)	(14.46)	(14.51)	(15.17)	(14.77)
No. of countries	92	92	92	92	92	92
Log likelihood	−17.62	−14.39	−14.11	−12.79	−8.58	−11.02

Absolute value of z statistics in parentheses.
*significant at 10%;
**significant at 5%;
***significant at 1%

significant and only when controlling for the presence of US-trained economists. This may indicate that the IMF's influence is limited by the local availability of technocrats capable of implementing structural adjustment policies such as privatization. The qualitative evidence discussed later reveals the IMF's occasional frustration by this constraint. All else equal, the hazard ratio on the IMF variable indicates that receiving loan money from the IMF in a given year approximately doubles the likelihood of privatizing in that year. Likewise, we can interpret the hazard ratio on the US economist variable to show that a one unit increase in the log of a country's share of the total US economists living abroad (i.e. nearly a three-fold increase in the economists in that country) would nearly triple its hazard of privatization. The Chicago variable tells us that a similar increase in the number of Chicago economists would cause an over five-fold increase in that country's hazard of privatization.

Through these channels the epistemic community of American-trained economists makes its influence felt. Both its direct influence within the country through resident members and its substantial control over policy at the IMF give it a dramatic impact on privatization. We can also observe evidence of how the ideological divides *within* the economics profession influence the "palace wars" in countries around the world. By comparing the hazard ratios on the US and Chicago variables, we can see that an equal number of Chicago economists has essentially twice the impact on privatization that other economists do. Their greater ideological commitment to liberal policies makes Chicago economists a more potent force for influencing the adoption of privatization.

Table 3.2 shows the results of the Weibull model with the gamma-distributed shared frailty parameter. We estimate two structural parameters in this model, the *time* parameter ρ and the *frailty* parameter θ. We find the time parameter ρ to be highly significant and indicative of a strong increase over time in the baseline hazard of privatization, as shown by its magnitude much greater than one. On the other hand, the frailty parameter θ is not significant in any model. Consistent with the insignificance of frailty, these results are qualitatively similar to those models, listed in Table 3.1, that do not include the frailty parameter. In fact, the point estimates are nearly identical for most coefficients. Since the frailty parameter is designed to capture the effect of unobserved heterogeneity, this consistency gives us a good deal of confidence that the Weibull model is well specified.

In Table 3.3, we show the results that test for these time-varying effects of our diffusion variables. Unfortunately, we cannot simultaneously estimate both the frailty parameter θ and the impact of our explanatory variables on the time parameter ρ. Since θ has already proved to be insignificant in the results from Table 3.2, we drop it from our estimation. In these models, we include covariates to estimate ρ in addition to testing their time-invariant, or cross-sectional, impact.

This procedure also provides an important test of the possibility that our diffusion measures are simply capturing otherwise unobserved differences in countries' underlying propensity to adopt privatization. For

Table 3.2. *Weibull hazard model of privatization with shared frailty*

	Model 1	Model 2	Model 3	Model 4	Model 5	Model 6
Log population	1.358	1.397	1.308	1.117	1.080	1.126
	(1.33)	(1.40)	(1.08)	(0.52)	(0.35)	(0.55)
Log GDP	1.247*	1.157	1.242	1.370*	1.159	1.311*
	(1.66)	(1.13)	(1.30)	(1.93)	(0.89)	(1.68)
Gov't consumption	1.052	1.039	1.040	1.035	1.037	1.036
	(1.40)	(0.91)	(0.99)	(1.23)	(1.29)	(1.30)
Budget balance	1.004	0.993	0.999	0.988	1.001	0.996
	(0.12)	(0.18)	(0.03)	(0.42)	(0.04)	(0.13)
Trade openness	0.991	0.984**	0.984**	0.987*	0.986*	0.988*
	(1.28)	(2.14)	(2.13)	(1.82)	(1.95)	(1.76)
Inward FDI stock	0.997	0.992	0.992	0.988	0.978	0.984
	(0.23)	(0.60)	(0.56)	(0.98)	(1.63)	(1.24)
Right gov't	1.851	1.564	1.683	1.570	1.701	1.669
	(1.37)	(1.02)	(1.13)	(1.04)	(1.20)	(1.17)
Left gov't	1.444	1.298	1.280	1.389	1.356	1.469
	(0.84)	(0.61)	(0.56)	(0.84)	(0.75)	(0.97)
Trade competition		1.880**	1.879**	1.723**	1.856**	1.766**
		(2.32)	(2.26)	(2.02)	(2.23)	(2.08)
Size of state sector			1.082	1.049	1.120	1.067
			(0.75)	(0.51)	(1.19)	(0.69)
IMF funds				1.906	2.106*	1.874
				(1.57)	(1.83)	(1.55)
US economists					2.880***	
					(3.27)	
Chicago economists						5.745**
						(2.29)
Time (ρ)	5.158***	5.128***	5.247***	4.792***	5.309***	4.998***
	(8.11)	(6.64)	(6.73)	(14.51)	(15.17)	(14.77)
Frailty (θ)	0.349	0.167	0.243	0.000	0.000	0.000
	(0.79)	(0.56)	(0.62)	(0.01)	(.)	(0.01)
No. of countries	92	92	92	92	92	92
Log likelihood	−17.30	−14.35	−14.04	−12.79	−8.58	−11.02

Absolute value of z statistics in parentheses.
*significant at 10%;
**significant at 5%;
***significant at 1%

example, if US economists are simply an indicator for countries more ideologically disposed to adopt privatization, then the effect of this heterogeneity should be stable over time. On the other hand, if, as we argue, American-trained economists become convinced of the value of privatization during the period under study and increasingly use their

Table 3.3. *Weibull hazard model with time coefficients*

	Model 1	Model 2	Model 3	Model 4
Cross-sectional effects				
Log population	1.125	1.141	0.858	0.883
	(0.53)	(0.61)	(0.60)	(0.49)
Log GDP	1.111	1.284	1.413*	1.718**
	(0.62)	(1.50)	(1.67)	(2.50)
Gov't consumption	1.033	1.031	1.018	1.026
	(1.16)	(1.11)	(0.50)	(0.75)
Budget balance	0.997	0.988	1.003	0.995
	(0.11)	(0.43)	(0.09)	(0.16)
Trade openness	0.987*	0.988	0.989	0.992
	(1.81)	(1.63)	(1.53)	(1.06)
Inward FDI stock	0.976*	0.982	0.979	0.981
	(1.76)	(1.38)	(1.41)	(1.27)
Right gov't	1.656	1.675	1.415	1.536
	(1.13)	(1.16)	(0.65)	(0.82)
Left gov't	1.364	1.516	0.958	1.146
	(0.76)	(1.03)	(0.09)	(0.29)
Trade competition	1.821**	1.683*	1.513	1.386
	(2.17)	(1.91)	(1.40)	(1.11)
Size of state sector	1.103	1.060	1.274*	1.227
	(1.03)	(0.61)	(1.89)	(1.64)
IMF funds	0.014	0.054	0.001**	0.014
	(1.50)	(1.09)	(2.24)	(1.43)
US economists	0.249		0.242	
	(1.08)		(1.17)	
Chicago economists		0.008		0.003
		(0.79)		(0.70)
Time-varying effects				
IMF funds	1.431*	1.304	1.711***	1.405*
	(1.80)	(1.37)	(2.60)	(1.71)
US economists	1.207**		1.218***	
	(2.31)		(2.63)	
Chicago economists		1.662		1.758
		(1.42)		(1.32)
Time (ρ)	4.151***	4.350***	4.055***	4.470***
	(8.87)	(9.91)	(8.60)	(10.16)
Regional dummies?	No	No	Yes	Yes
No. of countries	92	92	92	92
Log likelihood	−5.94	−9.14	−1.31	−4.71

Absolute value of z statistics in parentheses.
*significant at 10%;
**significant at 5%;
***significant at 1%

influence to push for its adoption, then the impact of US economists should rise over time.

As discussed at length above, the intellectual history of contemporary economics suggests a growing convergence around the ideas of the primacy of the market and hence a lessening distinction among Chicago economists and other economists. We can capture this history with the changing effects of the diffusion variables for economists over time. We showed in the cross-sectional models in Tables 3.1 and 3.2 that the impact of a given number of Chicago economists was higher than an equal number of US economists from other institutions. In Table 3.3 we relax the assumption that these relationships are stable over time. If the rest of the epistemic community of economists is being won over to the Chicago point of view on privatization, then we should see their impact catching up to Chicago's over this time period. If the Chicago School is itself ideologically stationary, then its effect should be stable over time. Similarly, if the epistemic community of economists that influence IMF policies is becoming increasingly pro-privatization, then we should observe the IMF's effect to increase with time.

Model 1 of Table 3.3 shows that both IMF lending and the presence of US economists in a foreign country had an increasing effect on the diffusion of privatization; this eliminates the cross-sectional effect. A likelihood ratio test comparing Model 1 to a model without the time-varying components shows that the time-varying model provides a significantly better fit to the data. The impact of both IMF lending and the presence of US economists has increased markedly over time but their direct cross-sectional effects are actually very small. These results are consistent with the view that these factors had little effect at the beginning of the time period but became very important by the end of the period. Such an interpretation would support our view that the IMF and US-trained economists served as vectors of contagion for the new ideas about liberalization and privatization that were spreading internationally during our time period. Model 2 retains the IMF effect but shows no effect of Chicago economists; given the strength of the earlier results, the implication is that there is no time-varying effect and hence the two Chicago variables lose significance. This finding accords well with the belief that Chicago economists were as committed to privatization at the beginning of the period as at the end, and hence an insignificant time-varying effect is found. In other words, the results indicate that Chicago won the palace war.

As an additional robustness check, we also include regional dummy variables in the second two models presented to control for any unobserved regional diffusion processes that might be correlated with the

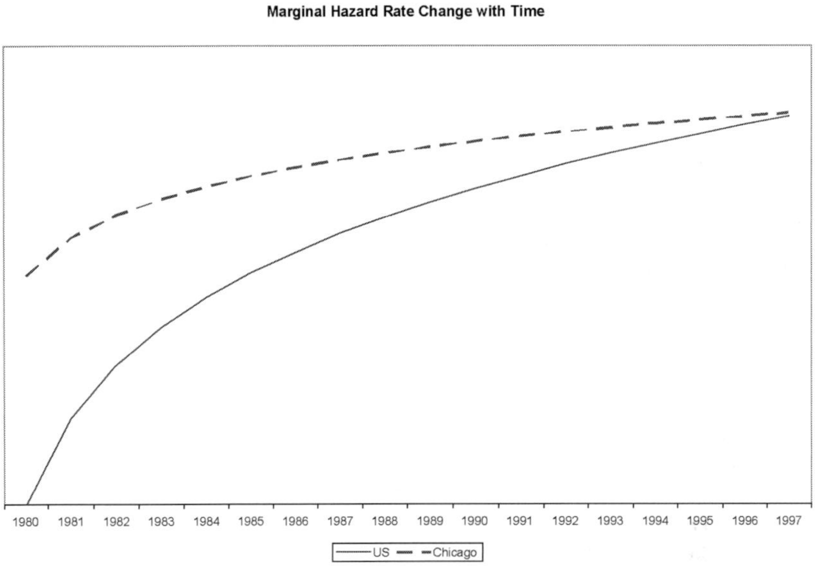

Figure 3.3 Convergence of US and Chicago economists

geographical distribution of economists. Eyeballing the data reveals that the spread of economists is itself regional, and hence once we control for regions, we might more accurately recover the over-time effect of the growing disapora of economists. Model 3 and Model 4 confirm our previous findings. While individual regional effects are significant, likelihood ratio tests indicate that as a group they do not significantly improve the fit of the model.[18]

One interesting way to visualize the consequences of the growing convergence of US economists toward the Chicago position is to graph their over-time marginal effects. Figure 3.3 graphically depicts this change in the marginal hazard rate due to both US-trained and Chicago-trained economists over our time period. While US economists have a much smaller impact on privatization in 1981, at the beginning of our study, by the end, in 1997, they cause nearly as large an increase in the hazard of privatization as Chicago economists. This graph succinctly summarizes the statistical evidence of the convergence in world views

18 In this case, the likelihood ratio test can be thought of as comparing the adjusted R-squared figures on an OLS regression. The dummy variables improve the fit of the model, but not significantly.

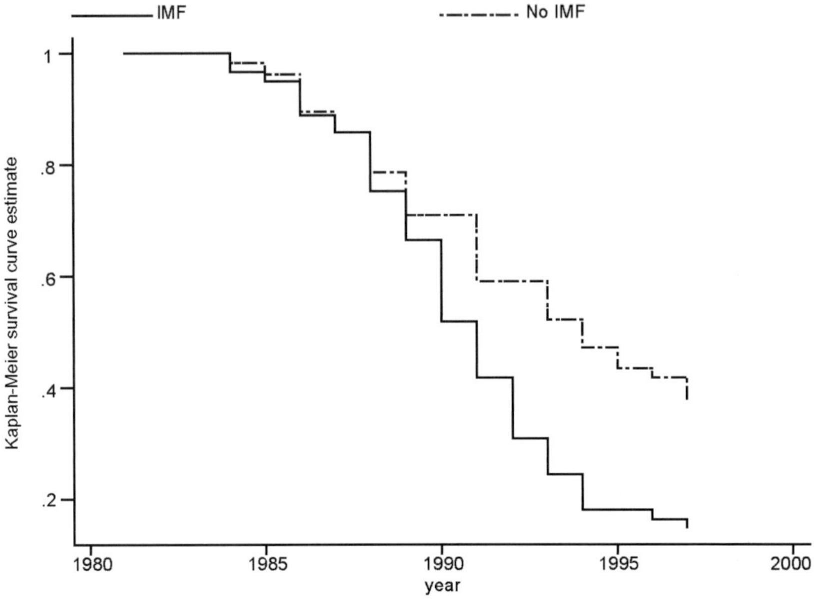

Figure 3.4 The effect of IMF conditionality on privatization (Kaplan-Meier non-parametric survival estimate)

between these two branches of the epistemic community of economists and the impact on adoption of a privatization policy.

The IMF was undergoing a similar shift toward more market-oriented and pro-privatization ideas, as shown by the IMF's significantly positive time-varying effects in Table 3.3. As discussed below, the IMF and World Bank only made loans conditional on privatization a widespread policy in the 1990s. In Figure 3.4, we plot the Kaplan-Meier survival estimates for those countries with and without IMF loans. We can see that there is a divergence only around the period of 1990 when the IMF began enforcing demands for liberalization as a condition of many of its loans. This result is consistent with the findings of Brune, Garrett, and Kogut (2004) regarding the effects of the IMF on privatization values. The IMF, once having adopted privatization as a condition, becomes salient to countries. The implication is the dynamic of the diffuser of the diffusers discussed earlier. There was an independent effect of the American economists on privatization adoption, which then became amplified through IMF policies. By the 1990s, there was broad economic consensus on the wisdom of privatization as a policy.

Qualitative evidence

The statistical evidence supports the claim that American-trained economists were proxy for a local community that promoted privatization. There nevertheless is considerable country variation that deserves attention. For purposes of comparison, we chose a few countries in each region that differ in their privatization dates. These cases indicate quite strikingly the importance of foreign-trained economists, while bringing to the fore a condition that was missing in the statistical work, namely, the importance of privatizations for leaders to forge important domestic alliances. Technocrats are a common agent in the adoption of privatization across countries, but they are surprisingly diverse in their political affiliations. This adaptability might well explain why variables that measure "left" or "right" governments generally do not predict the decision to privatize.

Technocrats are very potent agent for economic policy in Latin America. Latin America is of interest given the early privatization of Chile. Both Mexico and Argentina privatized substantially later. The Mexican discussion of privatization started immediately after the economic crisis in the early 1980s just after the "sexenio" (the six-year reign) of the new president de la Madrid. De la Madrid quickly nationalized the banks which were in crisis. Due to the fiscal and current account crisis, de la Madrid chose the MIT-trained economist Pedro Aspe as minister of treasury and the Yale-trained economist Jesus Silva Herzog for the Central Bank, both of whom clashed with the Cambridge-trained economists (Fourcade-Gourinchas and Babb 2002). Aspe promoted the idea of privatization, which de la Madrid thought might be a way to reforge his ties with the Mexican business community (Schamis 2002). It was however only during the sexenio of Salinas – himself a technocrat – and his American-trained economist minister for privatization, Jacques Rogozinski, that large-scale privatizations took place. However, the logic of the politics of patronage was oddly consistent, as privatizations often empowered the Mexican business community. Labor was far less appeased, as witnessed in the use of troops to enforce the privatization of the national railways. Centeno (1994) notes that the Mexican case shows how liberal policies can be chosen without international interference. And yet the close technocratic ties among economists in the US and in international financial institutions clearly indicate an active channel of discourse (Fourcade-Gourinchas and Babb 2002; Babb 2001).

The Argentine case begins as in Mexico, with a reluctant administration and president, Raul Alfonsin, forced by fiscal crisis to undertake minor privatizations. It was only after the increasing fiscal crisis that privatization picked up, especially when President Menem took office and chose Domingo Cavallo, a Harvard-educated economist, as minister of the economy. Cavallo implemented a broad liberal agenda, including a privatization program. Menem supported this program as a way to weaken the strong Peronist labor and to strengthen his domestic allies. In reviewing the experiences of privatization in Argentina (and in other Latin American countries), Manzetti (1999) writes, "the greatest supporters for privatization were some government technocrats who had reached the conclusion that privatization was necessary to alleviate unnecessary state responsibility while at the same time, enabling the executive to cut the budget deficit thus devoting funds to more urgent needs." Yet, this standard conclusion fails to note that many countries met these conditions. The key difference for these countries was the facility by which the American-trained technocrats generated sufficient local political legitimacy for liberalization that privatization policies could be used to build domestic alliances.

As an exercise in exploring a quasi-experimental design, we consider the country cases marked by the *absence* of technocrats. Privatization in this environment comes on the back of international programs following an economic or political crisis. Thus, even though Pakistan had inaugurated a privatization policy by 1990 according to our criteria, the World Bank criticized Pakistan for its pace and the quality of the program. An exasperated witness, Mirza (1995:12), thus complained that "a majority of bureaucrats in Pakistan civil services are trained for writing notes and summaries and do not possess specialized knowledge of financial and legal subjects … Their function at the Privatisation Commission has been confined to implementing plans and methods chalked for them by World Bank's technical staff."

Yet a principal story for many countries (e.g. India, South Africa, and Peru) is the combination of a demonstration effect plus a Western-trained elite. In his study of privatization in reference to Jordan, for example, Abu Shair (1997) concludes that "another reason is the imitation of the western idea of privatization, particularly that of the new conservatives in the USA and Britain. Since most of the government is composed of professionals educated in those two countries, any new academic or western image has been emulated to give the country a modern face. The preference for foreign experts, foreign models, and foreign stands is a consequence of Jordan's imitative modernism."

In unreported regressions, we rejected the hypothesis that ethnic diversity explains the pace of diffusion. A rapid review of a few countries suggests that these null findings are consistent with the political instability caused by ethnic rivalries that results in a sequence of stop–go policy initiatives. With a small presence of American-trained economists,

Malaysia, under Prime Minister Mahathir Mohamad, was an early privatizer. The privatization program was captured by powerful political interests and the tendering favored the ruling United Malay National Organisation; this meant also a bias away from nationals of Chinese origin (Jomo and Gomez 1997). Indonesia proceeded more slowly in its privatization. One of the leading economists in Indonesia, Pangestu, claims that the decline in oil receipts in the 1980s led to the replacement of an engineering class of technocrats by economists who came from the University of Indonesia and who were also close to the army (Pangestu, 1966:126ff.). However, privatization was seriously delayed, again partly due to fears over the Chinese community's commercial power. Ethnic rivalry is also claimed to have slowed privatization in Kenya (over the economic dominance of the Kikuyu), while in Ghana the fear concerned foreign and Asian (Indian) domination (Tangri 1999).

This rapid qualitative account underlines one important claim of this study, namely, that privatization does not arrive as a "blueprint" to be implemented, but as body of ideas that are heavily conditioned by domestic conditions. This account is similar to Fourcade-Gourinchas' (forthcoming) argument of the diverse country histories behind a globalizing professional community of economists. The growing consensus around private sector development and privatization in specific epistemic communities confronted differences in national elite structures and ideological heritages. In analyzing the adoption of Keynesianism, Hall (1989) for example noted that the revolving door of public service in the United States made government policy more open to current theories than the public servant institution in the United Kingdom. For a policy as filled with distributional consequences as privatization, the political context of a country is surely an important factor in understanding the adoption of privatization policies, even one that has little to do with notions of right and left. In his early study of the diffusion of privatization, Ikenberry (1990:107) noted that these policies were adopted around the world "because domestic groups and state officials found their own reasons to pursue them." Globalization oddly enough is always about local politics and, as we have indicated, the context of discourse.

Conclusions

Privatization has resulted in one of the most massive transformations of ownership in modern economic history. No matter how one views its economic benefits, the stunning aspect of its adoption is the rapidity of its diffusion as a *policy*. By the end of our observed period, almost all nations had launched a privatization policy to some extent.

The most interesting, perhaps even sensational, result is the effect of the number of US-trained economists in a country on adoption. This relationship is not surprising given the existing studies on the American economics profession and the University of Chicago economics department. It is nevertheless surely enchanting to observe the convergence in academic opinion reflected over time in the pattern of diffusion of privatization policies. The impact of academic epistemic communities is a formative effect on the ideational development of a technocratic elite.

There is an important implication for understanding the theoretical and empirical claims surrounding the meaning of broad phenomenological constructs, such as coercion. The implementation of policies may always have the semblance of coercion, but the act of coercion is preceded by the shared construction of an ontology of knowledge. The oft-heard claim that the International Monetary Fund "made a country do it" ignores that the IMF itself consists of technocrats engaged in the broad construction and assimilation of ideas and policies. It is misleading reification to label institutions as coercive without understanding that within their confines is to be found the struggle of ideas and their advocates for influence.

Ideas leave their historical markers. In the case of privatization, ideas matter to the tune of nearly $2 trillion in the valuation of sold shares, leaving aside the mass privatizations of transition economies. This demonstration of the power of the construction of ideas gives rise to a humbling or emboldening thought, depending on one's belief in the truth of an idea.

References

Abu Shair, Osama J. A. R. 1997. *Privatization and Development*, London: Macmillan.

Amsden, Alice. 1992. *Asia's Next Giant: South Korea and Late Industrialization*. New York: Oxford University Press.

Anderson, Benedict. 1991. *Imagined Communities: Reflections on the Origin and Spread of Nationalism*. London and New York: Verso.

Arrow, Kenneth J. 1962. Economic Welfare and the Allocation of Resources for Invention. In *The Rate and Direction of Inventive Activity: Economic and Social Factors*, National Bureau of Economic Research, Conference Series, edited by Richard R. Nelson. Princeton: Princeton University Press.

Babb, Sarah. 2001. *Managing Mexico: Economists from Nationalism to Neoliberalism*. Princeton: Princeton University Press.

Bass, Frank M. 1969. A New Product Growth Model for Consumer Durables. *Management Science* 13: 215–27.

Beck, Thorsten, George Clarke, Alberto Groff, Philip Keefer, and Patrick Walsh. 2001. New Tools in Comparative Political Economy: The Database of Political Institutions. *World Bank Economic Review* 15 (1):165–76.

Biglaiser, Glen. 2002. The Internationalization of Chicago's Economics in Latin America. *Economic Development and Cultural Change* 50: 269–86.

Bockman, Johanna and Gil Eyal. 2001. Eastern Europe as a Laboratory for Economic Knowledge: The Transnational Roots of Neoliberalism. *American Journal of Sociology* 108: 310–52.

Boix, Carles. 1997. Privatizing the Public Business Sector in the Eighties. *British Journal of Political Science* 27: 473–96.

Bortolotti, Bernardo, Marcella Fantini, and Domenico Siniscalco. 2001. Privatization: Politics, Institutions and Financial Markets. FEEM discussion paper.

Boyer, Robert and Daniel Drache, eds. 1996. *States Against Markets. The Limits of Globalization*. London and New York: Routledge.

Brown, John and Paul Duguid. 1991. Organizational Learning and Communities-of-Practice: Toward a Unified View of Working, Learning, and Innovation. *Organization Science* 2: 40–57.

Brune, Nancy. 2006. Explaining Financial Liberalization Around the World. Ph.D. thesis, Department of Political Science, Yale University.

Brune, Nancy, Geoff Garrett, and Bruce Kogut. 2004. Privatizations by Shares in the World Economy: Credible Ideologies and International Financial Institutions. *IMF Staff Papers* 54: 195–219.

Burt, Ron. 1987. Social Contagion and Innovation: Cohesion versus Structural Equivalence. *American Journal of Sociology* 92: 1287–335.

Buttel, Frederick. 2000. World Society, the Nation-State and Environmental Protection: Comment on Frank, Hironaka and Schofer. *American Sociological Review* 65: 117–21.

Campbell, John L. 2002. Ideas, Politics and Public Policy. *Annual Review of Sociology* 28: 21–38.

Centeno, M. A. 1994. Between Rocky Democracies and Hard Markets: Dilemmas of the Double Transition. *Annual Review of Sociology* 20: 125–247.

Colander, David and Arjo Klamer. 1987. The Making of an Economist. *Journal of Economic Perspectives* 1: 95–111.

Coleman, James S., Elihu Katz, and Herbert Menzel. 1966. *Medical Innovation: A Diffusion Study*. Indianapolis, IN: The Bobbs-Merrill Company.

Delano, Manuel and Hugo Traslavina. 1989. *La Herencia de los Chicago Boys*. Santiago, Chile: Ornitorrinco.

de Vries, Margaret Garritsen. 1986. The International Monetary Fund: Economists in Key Roles. In *Economists in International Agencies*, edited by A. W. Coats. New York: Praeger.

Dezalay, Yves and Bryant Garth. 2002. *The Internationalization of Palace Wars. Lawyers, Economists, and the Contest to Transform Latin-American States*. Chicago, IL: University of Chicago Press.

DiMaggio, Paul and Walter Powell. 1983. The Iron Cage Revisited: Institutional Isomorphism and Collective Rationality in Organizational Fields. *American Sociological Review* 48: 147–60.

Dobbin, Frank. 1994. *Forging Industrial Policy: The United States, Britain, and France in the Railway Age*. Cambridge: Cambridge University Press.

Eichengreen, Barry, Andrew Rose, and Charles Wyplosz. 1996. Contagious Currency Crises: First Tests. *Scandinavian Journal of Economics* 98: 463–84.

Feenstra, Robert C. *World Trade Flows, 1980–1997* (CD-ROM). 2000. Davis, CA: Institute of Governmental Affairs, University of California.

Fourcade-Gourinchas, Marion. Forthcoming. The Construction of a Global Profession: The Transnationalization of Economics. *American Journal of Sociology*.

Fourcade-Gourinchas, Marion and Sarah L. Babb. 2002. The Rebirth of the Liberal Creed: Paths to Neoliberalism in Four Countries. *American Journal of Sociology* 108: 533–79.

Frank, David, Ann Hironaka and Evan Schofer. 2000. The National State and the Natural Environment over the Twentieth Century. *American Sociological Review* 65: 96–116.

Galton, Francis. 1889. Comment on Edward B. Tylor's "On a Method of Investigating the Development of Institutions: Applied to Laws of Marriage and Descent." *Journal of the Royal Anthropological Institute* 18: 245–69.

Goldstein, Judy and Robert Keohane. 1993. Ideas and Foreign Policy: An Analytical Framework. In *Ideas and Foreign Policy*, edited by J. Goldstein and R. Keohane, 3–30. Ithaca: Cornell University.

Guler, Isin, Mauro Guillen, and Muir Macpherson. 2002. Global Competition, Institutions, and the Diffusion of Organizational Practices: The International Spread of the ISO 9000 Quality Certificates. *Administrative Science Quarterly* 47: 207–32.

Gwartney, James, Robert Lawson, and Walter Block. 1996. *Economic Freedom of the World: 1975–1995*. Toronto: Fraser Institute.

Haas, Peter M. 1992. Introduction: Epistemic Communities and International Policy Coordination. *International Organization* 46: 1–35.

Hall, Peter. 1989. *The Political Power of Economic Ideas. Keynesianism Across Nations*. Cambridge, MA: Harvard University Press.

Hamilton, Gary. 1998. Patterns of Asian Network Capitalism: The Cases of Taiwan and South Korea. In *Networks, Markets, and the Pacific Rim: Studies in Strategy*, edited by Mark Fruin, 181–99. New York: Oxford University Press.

Harberger, Arnold. 1997. *Good Economics Comes to Latin America, 1955–1995*. Durham, NC: Duke University Press.

Henisz, Witold J., Bennet A. Zelner and Mauro F. Guillen. 2005. The Worldwide Diffusion of Market-Oriented Infrastructure Reform, 1977–1999. *American Sociological Review* 70 (6):871–97.

Ikenberry, G. John. 1990. The International Spread of Privatization Policies: Inducements, Learning, and Policy Bandwagoning. In *The Political Economy of Public Sector Reform and Privatization*, edited by Ezra N. Suleiman and John Waterbury, 88–109. Boulder: Westview Press.

Jomo, K. S. and E. T. Gomez. 1997. Rents and Development in Multiethnic Malaysia. In *The Role of Government in East Asian Economic Development*, edited by M. Aoki, H.-K. Kim, and M. Okuno-Fujiwara, 342–72. Oxford: Clarendon Press.

Kapur, Devish, John P. Lewis, and Richard Webb. 1997. *The World Bank. Its First Half Century*, Volume 1. Washington, DC: Brookings Institute.

Keck, Margaret and Kathryn Sikkink. 1998. *Activists Beyond Borders*. Ithaca: Cornell University Press.
Knorr-Cetina, Karin. 1999. *Epistemic Cultures*. Cambridge, MA: Harvard University Press.
Kobrin, Steven. 1985. Diffusion as an Explanation of Oil Expropriation. *Journal of Conflict Resolution* 29: 3–32.
Kogut, Bruce and Muir Macpherson. 2002. The Decision to Privatize as an Economic Policy Idea: Trade Networks and Globalization. Paper presented at the Yale University conference on the Diffusion of Political and Economic Liberalism, organized by Geoffrey Garrett and Beth A. Simmons.
Laffont, Jean-Jacques and Jean Tirole. 1991. Privatization and Incentives. *Journal of Law, Economics and Organization* 7: 84–105.
LaPorta, Rafael, Florencio Lopez-de-Silanes, Andrei Shleifer, and Robert Vishny. 1998. Law and Finance. *Journal of Political Economy* 106: 1113–55.
Lave, Jean and Etienne Wenger. 1991. *Situated Learning: Legitimate Peripheral Participation*. Cambridge: Cambridge University Press.
Lee, Chang Kil and David Strang. 2006. The International Diffusion of Public Sector Downsizing. *International Organization* 60 (4):883–909.
Lopez-de-Silanes, Florencio, Andrei Shleifer, and Robert Vishny. 1997. Privatization in the United States. *Rand Journal of Economics* 28 (3).
Low, Linda. 1998. *Political Economy of a City-State: Government-Made Singapore*. Singapore: Oxford University Press.
MacKenzie, Donald and Graham Spinardi. 1995. Tacit Knowledge, Weapons Design, and the Uninvention of Nuclear Weapons. *American Journal of Sociology*. 101: 44–99.
Manzetti, Luigi. 1999. *Privatization South American Style*. Oxford: Oxford University Press.
Megginson, William and Jeffry Netter. 2001. From State to Market: A Survey of Empirical Studies on Privatization. *Journal of Economic Literature* 39: 321–89.
Meyer, John, John Boli, George Thomas, and Francisco Ramirez. 1997. World Society and the Nation-state. *American Journal of Sociology* 103: 144–81.
Miller, H. Laurence, Jr. 1962. On the 'Chicago School of Economics'. *Journal of Political Economy* 70 (1):64–9.
Miller, Michelle. 1999. *The World Bank. New Agendas in a Changing World*. London: Routledge.
Mirza, S. A. 1995. *Privatization in Pakistan*. Lahore: Ferozsons Ltd.
Nellis, John. 1999. Time to Rethink Privatization in Transition Economies? Discussion Paper No. 38, Washington, DC: International Finance Corporation.
Pangestu, Mari. 1966. *Economic Reform, Deregulation, and Privatization: The Indonesian Experience*. Jakarta: Centre for Strategic and International Studies.
Ramamurthi, Ravi. 1999. Why Haven't Developing Countries Privatised Deeper and Faster? *World Development* 27 (1):137–55.
Sappington, David E. and Joesph E. Stiglitz. 1987. Privatization, Information and Incentives. *Journal of Policy Analysis and Management* 6: 567–82.
Schamis, Hector. 2002. *Re-forming the State. The Politics of Privatization in Latin America and Europe*. Ann Arbor: University of Michigan Press.

Schumpeter, Joseph Alois. 1943. *Capitalism, Socialism, and Democracy*. London: G. Allen & Unwin, Ltd.
Shirley, Mary and Patrick Walsh. 2001. Public versus Private Ownership: The Current State of the Debate. World Bank Policy Research Working Paper No. 2420.
Shonfeld, Andrew. 1965. *Modern Capitalism: The Changing Balance of Public and Private Power*. Oxford: Oxford University Press.
Silva, Patricio. 1991. Technocrats and Politics in Chile: From the Chicago Boys to the CIEPLAN Monks. *Journal of Latin American Studies* 23: 385–410.
Simmons, Beth, Frank Dobbin, and Geoffrey Garrett. Forthcoming. The International Diffusion of Liberalism. *International Organization*.
Stigler, George and Claire Friedland. 1975. The Citation Practices of Doctorates in Economics. *Journal of Political Economy* 83: 477–508.
Strang, David. 1991. Adding Social Structure to Diffusion Models. *Sociological Methods & Research* 19: 324–53.
Strang, David and Patricia M. Y. Chang. 1993. The International Labour Organisation and the Welfare State: Institutional Effects on National Welfare Spending, 1960–80. *International Organization* 47: 235–62.
Tangri, Roger. 1999. *The Politics of Patronage in Africa. Parastatals, Privatization, and Private Enterprise*. Oxford: James Currey (Kampala: Fountain).
Thatcher, Margaret. 1993. *The Downing Street Years*. London: HarperCollins.
Tuma, Nancy and Michael Hannan. 1984. *Social Dynamics: Models and Methods*. Orlando: Academic Press.
Valdes, Juan Gabriel. 1995. *Pinochet's Economists: The Chicago School in Chile*. Cambridge: Cambridge University Press.
van den Bulte, Christophe and Gary L. Lilien. 2001. Medical Innovation Revisited: Social Contagion versus Marketing Effort. *American Journal of Sociology* 106: 1409–35.
Vickers, J. and G. Yarrow. 1988. *Privatization: An Economic Analysis*. Cambridge, MA: MIT Press.
Vreeland, James Raymond. 2002. *The IMF and Economic Development*, New York: Cambridge University Press.
Wade, Jacoby. 2000. *Imitation and Politics: Redesigning Modern Germany*. Ithaca: Cornell University Press.
Williamson, John. 1990. What Washington Means by Policy Reform. In *Latin American Adjustment: How Much Has Happened?* edited by John Williamson, 5–20. Washington, DC: Institute for International Economics.
World Bank. 1995. *Bureaucrats in Business: The Economics and Politics of Government Ownership*. Washington, DC: International Bank for Reconstruction and Development.
World Bank. 2002. *World Development Indicators* (CD-ROM). Washington, DC: World Bank.
Yergin, Daniel and Joseph Stanislaw. 1998. *The Commanding Heights: The Battle Between Government and the Market Place that is Remaking the Modern World*. New York: Simon & Schuster.
Ziegler, Nick. 1997. *Governing Ideas*. Ithaca: Cornell University.

4 The international diffusion of public sector downsizing: network emulation and theory-driven learning*

Chang Kil Lee and David Strang

The twentieth century as a whole, and particularly the three decades after the Second World War, witnessed steady growth in government size and responsibility. States developed extensive social safety nets, actively managed aggregate demand, and regulated a widening swath of economic and social life. This trajectory of expansion was linked to powerful forces of economic development and demographic change, and anchored in a broad political consensus.[1]

The 1980s and 1990s saw a sea change in the rate of public sector growth. British Prime Minister Margaret Thatcher and US President Ronald Reagan led the way with privatization, outsourcing, and load shedding of public responsibilities. But the shift in direction was not limited to radicals on the right. Country reports to the Public Management Committee (PUMA) of the Organization for Economic Cooperation and Development (OECD) – itself an outspoken advocate of downsizing – point to widespread efforts to reduce the public sector. In 1995, for example, Denmark commercialized its railways and gave business autonomy to its postal service; Finland diminished the size of its Forestry Administration; France suppressed 7,400 public sector jobs; Greece froze new government appointments; Norway promoted competition between public agencies and private firms; Spain decentralized core

* An earlier version of this article was given at the International Diffusion of Political and Economic Liberalization Conference, Harvard University, October 2003. We thank Frank Dobbin, Geoffrey Garrett, and Beth A. Simmons for organizing the conference and this volume; Sarah Babb, Jeeyang Baum, Torben Iversen, Michael Mann, Steve Morgan, Fred Pampel, Deok-Seob Shim, conference participants, and *International Organization*'s editor and reviewers for their helpful comments; and Thomas Cusack for his generosity in sharing public employment data.

[1] See, for example, Wilensky 1975; Flora and Heidenheimer 1981; Pampel and Williamson 1988.

government functions; and Sweden reduced public sector employment by 62,000.[2]

During the same period, discourse on the appropriate size, role, and functioning of government underwent an even sharper transformation. On the left, O'Connor and Offe depicted state growth as driven by contradictory demands for accumulation and legitimation that were ultimately unsustainable.[3] But radical critiques were soon drowned out by conservative ones. Neoliberals advocated limiting government and importing market mechanisms into the public arena. Proponents of the "New Public Management" argued for lean public agencies that would be responsive to citizen customers. A consensus on shrinking government seemed to have replaced a consensus on growing it.

Figure 4.1 gives public sector employment as a percentage of the working-age population from 1965 to 1994 across OECD member states.[4] It shows that aggregate growth in government employment continued throughout the last third of the twentieth century. There is no general reversal in the size of the public sector, at least when we count heads. To the contrary: on average, government employment doubled during the last thirty years of the century, from about 6 percent of the working-age population in 1965 to about 12 percent thirty years later.[5]

But Figure 4.1 also shows the slackening pace of public sector growth. Annual increases of about 4.5 percent in the 1960s and 1970s were reduced to increases of a little more than 1 percent in the 1980s, and less than 1 percent in the 1990s. Growth steadily decelerates with no identifiable inflection point. In 1994, net change in the size of the public sector across OECD countries turned negative for the first time.

Considerable heterogeneity in national experiences underlies the aggregate trend. Great Britain's reduction of more than 30 percent of its public sector workforce was the most dramatic, while New Zealand and Sweden also conducted large-scale downsizing. By contrast, a number of governments increased sharply in size. The fastest growers were developing states

[2] OECD 1995. The Public Management Committee was renamed the Public Governance Committee in 2004.

[3] See O'Connor 1973; Offe 1984.

[4] Data collected by Thomas Cusack from OECD and other sources; see Cusack, Notermans, and Rein 1989. Analyses reported below employ a parallel data series covering the period 1980–1997. Figure 4.1 displays Cusack's data series to provide a sense of the broader trajectory.

[5] A similar pattern appears in the corporate world, where a reform movement centered around downsizing is even more palpable. Baumol, Blinder, and Wolff 2003 show that downsizing in major corporations is on average counterbalanced by upsizing, with many of the largest workforce reductions followed by subsequent growth.

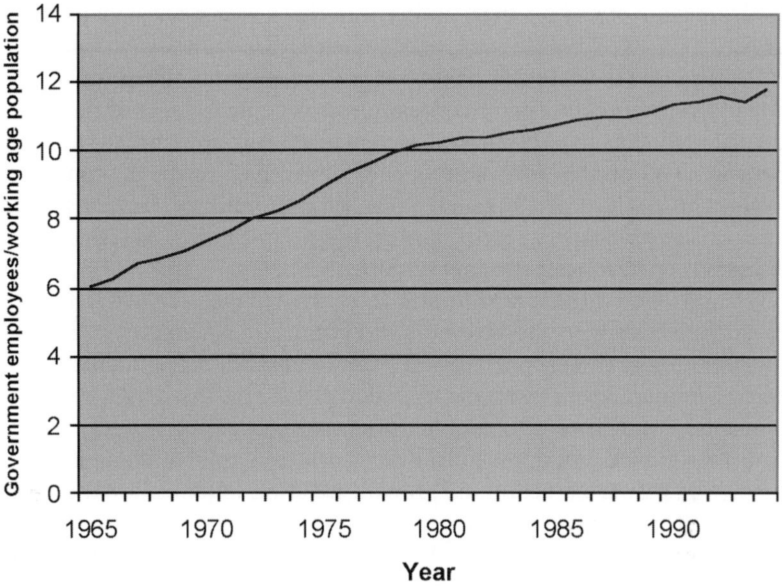

Figure 4.1 Public sector employment; OECD member nations, 1965–1994

with small public sectors in 1980; public employment per capita more than doubled in Greece, and rose some 75 percent in Portugal. But growth was not restricted to cases of late development; the relative size of government also expanded in countries such as Norway and Austria that possessed large public sectors at the beginning of the period.

We work with this heterogeneity to model change in the size of the public sector between 1980 and 1997 across twenty-six OECD countries.[6] The overall size of government is a composite outcome of administrative, economic, and political processes at many levels and is influenced by a welter of "named reforms" such as privatization, outsourcing, and private–public partnerships. But a net shrinking of the state was an explicit goal of many in the 1980s and 1990s, and an outcome that deserves attention. Government employment provides a

[6] Members of the OECD provide a good comparison set because they stand in structurally similar positions to public sector change, and because comparative data is widely available. We do not assume that government employment change outside the OECD mirrors that within the OECD, particularly given the different cast of international and domestic forces operating in poor and middle-income countries. We return in the discussion section to speculate on the forms that policy diffusion might take outside the OECD.

good omnibus measure that emphasizes the direct provision of public services.[7]

The analytic focus in this chapter is on international diffusion. We ask whether there is evidence of contagious change in the size of the public sector, such that expansion and retrenchment in government employment in one country affects others. We then investigate the pattern of linkages to better specify causal mechanisms. Internal factors such as fiscal crisis, economic growth, and ruling party politics are included in all models to develop a stronger empirical test.

We approach diffusion processes from the perspective of sociological institutionalism, with a focus on the way contagion is shaped by dominant understandings of appropriate and effective behavior.[8] This theoretical starting point leads us to attend to policy discourses that characterize the nature and functioning of public administration. In the period under study, neoliberal economic orthodoxy asserted that a bloated public sector was a drag on economic growth. Leading organizational theories contended that all enterprises, public and private, should become leaner and more decentralized. This chapter argues for and discovers a close connection between these discourses and the structure of international policy diffusion.

Diffusion research strategies and case study evidence

"Process tracing" and "pattern finding" strategies can be distinguished in the study of diffusion. Process tracing research follows the spread of a policy or practice from one location to another. This approach permits inspection of the role played by external models, and inquiry into why and how a concrete instance of learning or mimicry occurs. By contrast, pattern finding research tests *a priori* hypotheses about diffusion channels. Rather than demonstrate that actors in country A were aware of and influenced by country B, this strategy asks whether structures of

[7] Government expenditures also follow a trajectory of decelerating growth during the 1980s and 1990s and provide a second index of the size of the public sector. But expenditures are more heavily influenced by business cycle dynamics (such as automatic increases in unemployment insurance during economic slowdowns) than are measures of public sector employment. Reductions in public employment speak directly to discussions of the relative efficiency of the public and private sectors, and the overall advantages of lean organizations, which are central to the argument we advance here.

[8] Sociological institutionalism has mainly entered the study of international relations through the "world polity" perspective developed by Meyer and colleagues, which views the historical evolution of the state as informed by a cultural project of social rationalization and expansion of the rights and competence of the individual. See Thomas *et al.* 1987; Meyer *et al.* 1997.

covariance and temporal ordering are generally consistent with a theoretically specified model of influence.

This chapter works within the pattern finding approach. Before considering what patterns to test for, however, we note two cases of civil service reform that permit explicit process tracing. Both John Halligan's discussion of Australian policymaking and the Republic of Korea's benchmarking program provide insight into the rationales and organizational structures that support international diffusion.

Halligan argues that international policy networks provide channels for the spread of public management policies between the United States, the United Kingdom, and Australia.[9] These include bilateral relationships, such as regular meetings and exchange of personnel between Commonwealth countries, as well as broader intergovernmental fora such as the OECD and its Public Management Committee. Organizational linkages foster the transfer of knowledge about the programs of others and their rationales.

The policies traced by Halligan all involve "managerialist" efforts to reform public administration. Most relevant for present purposes are initiatives to improve government efficiency and eliminate waste. The approach devised in 1979 by Thatcher – ninety-day investigations aimed at time, money, and staff savings, conducted by an independent Efficiency Unit – was adopted virtually wholesale by Australia in 1986. Diffusion here is more than a correlation: "the methodology [of the scrutinies] follows the basic approach of the United Kingdom Efficiency Unit established by Sir Derek Raynor … The Unit acknowledges the assistance given by Sir Robin Ibbs, now head of the United Kingdom Unit."[10] The US Senior Executive Service, an effort to develop an elite corps of civil servants, was similarly mimicked by the state of Victoria, the federal government of Australia, and New Zealand.

A Korean effort to benchmark international "best practice" in public administration provides a second opportunity to trace policy diffusion. Between 1994 and 1997, the Republic of Korea's Task Force for Reengineering Governmental Functions collected information about policies in the United Kingdom, Canada, the United States, Australia, New Zealand, Japan, and Germany. The program advocated a variety of downsizing and restructuring initiatives that contributed to sweeping organizational change. Between 1998 and 2002, public sector

9 Halligan 1996.

10 Department of the Prime Minister and Cabinet, *Annual Report 1986–87* (Canberra: Australian Government Publishing Service), 35 (cited in Halligan 1996: 300).

employment in Korea was reduced by 20 percent and 209 projects of public entities were contracted out to the private sector.[11]

This benchmarking program sheds valuable light on the interpretive frames that surround public sector change. Korean policy analysts did not seek to determine the ideal size of government relative to population, nor did they study success stories involving public sector expansion. Instead, they began with downsizing as an objective. In fact, the task force investigated eight reform areas, the first of which was "reduction of government employees"![12]

This interpretive frame helped identify the countries and policies that benchmarkers focused on. The task force paid close attention to downsizing "pioneers" such as England and New Zealand. Within countries, benchmarkers focused on generalizable reform strategies that could be adapted to the Korean context:

> Korea should take lessons from ... the strong leadership for enforcing government reforms like that of Roger Douglas, New Zealand's Minister of Finance ... the argument for reducing the role of government through functional reengineering between public and private organizations as in Great Britain ... cutting back to basics as a criterion for the role of government as in the USA ... consensus process for reform as in Canada ... the simplification of administrative procedures in Germany.[13]

The status of downsizing as a desirable reform also shaped the inferences that benchmarkers drew from apparent success and failure. For example, the coincidence of government downsizing and economic growth in Canada was treated as a straightforward instance of cause and effect. New Zealand's experience of rapid downsizing followed by continuing economic difficulty, by contrast, prompted cautions about the complexity of causal inference in the macroeconomic sphere.[14] Given

[11] Republic of Korea, Ministry of Planning and Budget 2003:53, 122. Note that the above calculation excludes non-administrative personnel such as teachers, police officers, and security staff in the central and local governments. For discussions of Korean government reforms and the role of new public management principles, see Kim and Moon 2002; Ha 2004.

[12] Republic of Korea, Ministry of Government Administration 1997. The eight reform areas identified by the task force were "reduction of government employees," "restructuring government operations," "human resource management reforms," "budget and finance reforms," "performance management," "service quality and introduction of the market principle," "information technology in government," and "regulatory reform."

[13] Ibid. Translations from the Korean conducted by the first author.

[14] "It is not easy to observe the causal effects of downsizing or government reform in New Zealand. The central government has reduced employment over 60 percent, from 85,278 employees in 1985 to 32,639 employees in 1996. In 1993–94, the government finally attained budgetary surplus which seems the result of government reforms. New Zealand's economy worsened right after government reforms in 1988–89, however, and then switched direction towards growth since 1992. It is difficult to clarify the effect of government reforms on the economy." Ibid.

this interpretive frame, it is hardly surprising that Korea's task force advocated downsizing strategies in use elsewhere.

Policy diffusion, we should note, does not imply a world without agency. In both of the cases described above, key actors – most notably Australia's Prime Minister Bob Hawke and Korea's President Young-Sam Kim – allied themselves with foreign exemplars to achieve their policy goals.[15] International influences are integrally connected to national politics; they are particularly important, we think, in concretizing policy options and in strengthening the case for change.

These episodes provide insight into the way public policies spread internationally. Diffusion took somewhat different forms in the two cases: Australia explicitly borrowed a British organizational vehicle for promoting efficiency, while Korea drew on a wide range of national initiatives to support and reinforce a broad restructuring campaign. Substantively, however, the parallels are strong. In both cases, concrete policies "moved" because policymakers actively attended to and learned from their counterparts in other countries. Policy borrowing did not occur haphazardly, but was instead informed by a common interpretive frame that linked one country's experience to another's agenda. And of the many national policies that could have served as international exemplars, both Australia and Korea focused on reform initiatives aimed at downsizing.

While providing evidence that policy diffusion is a concrete reality and not merely an academic conceit, process tracing studies have important limitations. They tell us little about the underlying network structure of influence. For example, Australia might have attended to the UK because of its colonial heritage, close economic and political ties, economic competition, or a host of other linkages; we cannot discriminate between these alternatives by knowing more about the Raynor scrutinies. Nor does process tracing provide a measure of the relative scale of international versus domestic forces; mimicry might be an omnipresent but minor ingredient in organizational decision making. We thus consider how to represent diffusion processes in formal terms, and assess their significance in a quantitative analysis of government employment.

[15] In Korea, for example, President Young-Sam Kim was engaged in an effort to promote market reforms and counter bureaucrats who opposed his agenda; see Baum 2002. Moon and Ingraham 1998 develop a model of administrative reform in East Asia that incorporates both internal and external factors.

Diffusion mechanisms

Diffusion mechanisms are conceptualized here within the framework proposed in this volume by Simmons, Dobbin, and Garrett, focusing on the role of emulation, competition, and vicarious learning.[16] In addition to briefly noting the logic of each mechanism, we emphasize its structural implications for observable patterns of influence.

Emulation centrally involves the social construction of appropriate behavior, where actors model their behavior on the examples provided by others. One key set of connections are peer-based reference groups. Much sociological work shows that communication between peers leads them to "take the view of the other" and converge in their perceptions.[17] While these lines of argument originally developed to explain interpersonal interaction within communities (American farmers evaluating new varieties of seed corn, Andean villagers weighing the benefits of boiled water), they are also visible in Halligan's account of elite networks. The notion of peer-based emulation implies that countries will influence each other more when they are engaged in closer interaction, and when they share background characteristics such as a common language.

The sociological literature on innovation diffusion also points to asymmetric emulation of community leaders. Within the OECD, the United States stands out as the dominant political and economic power. Its potential influence can also be seen in Halligan's account of administrative initiatives. It is notable, for example, that Australian policymakers learned about and duplicated US President Jimmy Carter's Senior Service, rather than the other way around.[18]

A second mechanism is rivalry between competitors. This idea is elaborated by Burt, who points to the implicit mimicry that often arises among actors who can potentially replace or supplant each other.[19] In the

[16] This classification overlaps substantially with the others proposed in the diffusion literature. In sociology, the most influential classification scheme, from DiMaggio and Powell 1983, contrasts coercive, mimetic, and normative sources of isomorphism. Strang and Soule 1998 point to a variety of relational linkages (strong versus weak tie arguments, spatial proximity, and cultural proximity) as well as the role of agents of diffusion such as the media and professional communities.

[17] Rogers 1995.

[18] Asymmetric influence always raises the possibility of "coercive" rather than "emulative" diffusion, and some readers may interpret the empirical impact of the United States in this light. A review of OECD public sector reform does not suggest political pressures emanating from Washington (for a welcome change).

[19] Burt 1987.

international arena, competition for trade partners or foreign investment may promote policy diffusion as rivals adjust to each other's actions.

A third mechanism is vicarious learning. Policymakers may treat the behaviors of other countries as experiments whose outcomes provide useful information. If changes in the size of the public sector elsewhere are followed by economic benefits, for example, states may imitate the actions that appear to produce success. By the same logic, policies that are accompanied by undesirable outcomes should be avoided.

Simmons, Dobbin, and Garrett also elaborate a fourth mechanism, coercion, where policies are explicitly or implicitly imposed by powerful actors. This is likely to be a central mechanism in shaping the public sectors of middle- and low-income countries, particularly via loan conditionality and aid dependence. Within the OECD community studied in this chapter, however, coercion seems likely to play a limited role.

What diffuses?

While all policies have some probability of spreading, some are more contagious than others. What gives real force to observation of what others do, and leads one practice to spread rapidly while another does not? A purely relational analysis does not respond to this question: it helps us understand why Sweden would have a larger impact on Norway than on Portugal, but does not explain what kinds of practices are likely to flow from Stockholm to Oslo.

Work in organizational sociology argues that legitimate practices diffuse more readily than illegitimate ones. Prior adopters are likely to broadcast information about behaviors that are normatively approved, while illegitimate practices tend to be hidden. Potential adopters are also more likely to actively seek out information about legitimate practices, and to be swayed by relatively weak positive signals.

Davis and Greve's analysis of the diffusion of two corporate innovations designed to ward off hostile takeovers provides a case in point.[20] They find that the poison pill, which was legitimated as "shareholder defense," diffused rapidly through the weak ties of board interlocks. The golden parachute, which was viewed as a giveaway to incompetent executives, spread more slowly through the thicker medium of municipal business communities. Davis and Greve argue that the spread of an illegitimate practice requires greater social reinforcement than a legitimate practice does.

[20] Davis and Greve 1997.

Strang and Meyer develop a parallel argument about the cognitive supports of diffusion. They suggest that practices spread more rapidly and less relationally when they are theorized in terms of general models of behavior and cause–effect schemes.[21] By explaining how and why particular practices should work, theories promote the development of context-independent innovations that can and should be adopted everywhere. In American health policy, for example, economic analyses led to the invention of the "health maintenance organization" (HMO) as a vehicle for controlling runaway costs. (Because they combine the health insurance and delivery functions traditionally separated in American medicine, it was argued that self-interest would lead HMOs to proactively maintain health rather than profit from curing illness.) Efficiency analyses of incentives within self-regulating markets were so compelling that supportive legislation diffused across the American states faster than HMOs could be formed.[22]

In the 1980s and 1990s, discourse on the public sector legitimated and theorized downsizing. The neoliberal turn in public policy celebrated market mechanisms and challenged the efficacy of government action. For example, public choice theory delegitimated public servants as self-interested agents. The Chicago School argued that even natural monopolies were disciplined by the threat of competitive entry, providing a rationale for privatizing state enterprises and outsourcing government functions.[23]

Emerging theories of organization also supported downsizing. Public bureaucracies had been built around a Weberian ideal of a detailed division of labor, formally specified rules, and an ethos of professional service. The 1980s and 1990s saw a turn toward opposing ideals, first in the corporate sector, and then in public administration. Theorists spoke of "network organizations" and "virtual organizations," arguing for the advantages of flexibility and rapid response over standardization and reproducibility.[24] Osborne and Gaebler offered a best-selling roadmap for how public agencies could become entrepreneurial and customer focused.[25]

The dominance of these discourses is palpable in Korea's benchmarking of public sector downsizing as a reform (a term defined in the *Oxford English Dictionary* as "the amendment of some faulty state of things, esp.

[21] Strang and Meyer 1993. Theorization also implies that policy experts and professionals play a key role as "change agents," as we see in the Korean benchmarking program described above.

[22] See Brown 1983; Strang and Bradburn 2001. [23] Niskanen 1971.

[24] Piore and Sabel 1984. [25] Osborne and Gaebler 1993.

of a corrupt or oppressive political institution or practice"). Even where champions such as Korea's Young-Sam Kim were absent, policy debate in the 1980s and 1990s was framed in economistic and managerial terms. In describing Denmark's selective adoption of neoliberalism, for example, Kjaer and Pedersen note that "in order to be a participant in the structural policy debate, actors now had to legitimize themselves by reference to being familiar and comfortable, if not masterful, with particular and somewhat exclusive bodies of scientific knowledge."[26]

Given the asymmetry between prevailing interpretations of upsizing and downsizing, we argue that the latter should spread more contagiously. While in epidemiology the disease rather than the remedy is infectious, in public policy the reverse is true. Ideas about market efficiency and organizational empowerment indicated what sorts of policies should be attended to and learned from. Efforts to reduce staff, to decentralize government agencies and draw them into competition with the private sector, and to privatize became virtues to be emulated. By the same token, cases of public sector expansion became vices to be shunned.

Internal factors

While our main concern is to develop and test diffusion arguments, we briefly review major lines of argument about internal sources of public sector downsizing. Incorporation of these factors makes for a stronger test of a diffusion hypothesis and sharpens our ability to detect the role of international influences.

Fiscal stress is one important internal source of government downsizing. Budget deficits may pressure politicians to freeze or shrink state spending and government employment. Or politicians (such as Reagan in 1980, and US President George W. Bush twenty years later) who wish to cut public programs may foster deficits to provide political cover. Fiscal stress also helps explain why Sweden and other countries with large public sectors may move to decrease government employment.

A related argument points to the impact of poor economic performance. Governments presiding over slow growth rates and worsening balances of trade may downsize to improve economic competitiveness, while those doing well may maintain a pattern of economic expansion. This is especially true if the public sector is viewed, not as providing the infrastructure needed for economic growth, but as a luxury and drag on private enterprise.

[26] Kjaer and Petersen 2001:239.

Party politics and the strength of key interest groups provide a third internal source of government downsizing. Thatcher put privatization, deregulation, and managerialism on the map, and the affinity between small governments and the conservative agenda is clear. Rightist governments should be more likely to downsize than leftist governments. As defenders of employment protections and the welfare state, trade unions stand out as a likely source of organized opposition to downsizing, especially as public sector unions are the fastest growing segment of the union movement, and in some countries the only growing segment.

Beyond explicit economic and political differences, efforts to shrink the state can be identified with their cultural underpinnings. Castles speaks ironically of "the awfulness of the English" in describing shifts in public management from the 1960s to the 1980s.[27] Neoliberal and managerialist ideas are rooted in the background assumptions of Anglo-American political culture, and have been directly pursued not only in the United States and the UK but in Australia, New Zealand, and Canada.

Data and variables

Dependent variable

We study annual change in public sector employment from 1980 to 1997 among twenty-six OECD member countries: Austria, Australia, Belgium, Canada, Denmark, Finland, France, Germany, Greece, Iceland, Ireland, Italy, Japan, Korea, Luxembourg, Mexico, New Zealand, the Netherlands, Norway, Portugal, Spain, Sweden, Switzerland, Turkey, the United Kingdom, and the United States.

The dependent variable is the annual rate of change in government employment:

$$\Delta GE_{it} = \frac{GE_{it} - GE_{it-1}}{GE_{it-1}} \times 100. \quad (1)$$

The scope of public sector employment is "general government" as defined in the UN's Systems of National Accounts. This includes employees of federal, state, and local governments; it does not include military forces and employees of public enterprises. Data on government employment was taken from country reports to the International Monetary Fund (IMF). Data points not available from the IMF were drawn from Public Sector Pay and Employment data assembled by the OECD.

27 Castles 1989.

Diffusion effects Our general approach to estimating diffusion effects is to model outcomes in each country as a function of prior outcomes elsewhere. For example, change in government employment at *t* in the United Kingdom is related to prior changes in government employment in the United States, France, Sweden, and the twenty-two remaining OECD countries.

Hypotheses about the structure of diffusion are represented by weighting influence in an appropriate way. Consider a matrix $\mathbf{W}_{ij,t}$ that gives the influence of each country *j* on every country *i*. The aggregate diffusion effect on a focal country *i* is then a weighted sum of outcomes across countries *j*, $\sum_{j=1}^{J}(\mathbf{W}_{ij,t}\Delta GE_{j,t-1})$.

The simplest structure that diffusion might take is homogeneous mixing, which produces a pattern of GLOBAL DIFFUSION where all countries influence each other equally (here, $\mathbf{W}_{ij,t}$ equals 1 in all off-diagonal cells). While this is a possible empirical pattern, the results of homogeneous mixing are easily confused with those of external shocks and common environmental stimuli that show stability over time. We thus regard global diffusion as a baseline from which to investigate more structured patterns of influence.

To represent peer-based emulation, we employ economic exchange and spatial proximity as weights that index the degree to which two countries are likely to interact extensively, to be aware of each other's public policies, and to serve as prominent referents for each other. (Concrete exemplars of this sort of relationship include Norway and Sweden, Belgium and the Netherlands, and Belgium and France.) TRADE PARTNERSHIP is measured as the ratio of imports from the influencing country to all imports received by the influenced country (annual trade data is drawn from the IMF's Direction of Trade tables). Spatial proximity is indexed in two ways: COMMON BORDER, a binary variable that equals 1 if countries are geographically adjacent, and CAPITAL CITY PROXIMITY, an inverse function of great circle distance.[28]

To study "follow the leader" emulation, we examine the degree to which OECD countries are influenced by prior downsizing or upsizing in the United States. Rather than treat all countries as equally susceptible,

[28] An alternative way to measure peer-based emulation makes use of shared cultural characteristics like language, religion, and colonial heritage. This approach is difficult to implement in a study of OECD member states, due to much variation in national tongues and religions and a paucity of colonial ties. We opt for ease of comparability and operational transparency by focusing on trade and geographic proximity as two measures that are empirically associated with many forms of cultural similarity.

however, we weight the relationship by the strength of their economic links to the dominant world power. TRADE WITH USA equals the fraction of each country's imports and exports that come from and go to the United States.

To model mimicry between rivals, we develop a measure of competition that weights dyads by the extent to which they trade with the same countries. For example, Korea and Australia would score high on this measure if they both traded a great deal with the United States, Germany, and Japan, even if they did not trade much with each other. This sort of index is often used in sociological research as a measure of structural equivalence that captures competitively driven diffusion.[29] TRADE COMPETITION equals the normed correlation between the import and export shares of each pair of countries across all trade partners.

Finally, vicarious learning argues that countries respond not only to "who does what" but to "what happens when they do it." Learning is modeled by multiplying lagged employment change in each country by an economic outcome of interest, and cumulating this term across influencers. Since knowledge of and learning from external outcomes occurs over time, we work with three-year moving averages. The overall process is thus one of backward-looking adaptation, where positive coefficients indicate that countries move toward policies that were followed by success in the recent past.

Three economic outcomes serve as "evidentiary weights." LEARNING FROM ECONOMIC GROWTH weights lagged employment change by the rate of GDP growth. LEARNING FROM BUDGETARY HEALTH uses the state's budgetary position (for example, positive values give surpluses, negative values deficits). Finally, LEARNING FROM TRADE BALANCES uses the country's import–export differential as a third signal of strong economic performance.[30]

The above measures imply a symmetrical analysis of downsizing and upsizing. For example, the signal sent by an upsizing neighbor is assumed to have the same impact as the signal sent by a downsizing neighbor. Similarly, the effects of economic success after upsizing and after downsizing are assumed to have the same magnitude – only the direction differs.

To examine whether upsizing and downsizing are differentially contagious, we distinguish these cases. For network diffusion, we measure

[29] Burt 1987 motivates and illustrates this analytic strategy.

[30] Our goal here is not to identify an optimal learning strategy, but to construct indicators that reflect the sorts of information that decision makers are likely to treat as salient. Short-run trends are readily available and easily interpreted, while sophisticated data analysis plays a minor role in most policymaking. A fuller analysis might consider the particular salience of well-rehearsed success stories and paradigm-challenging anomalies; see Kuhn 1970; Hall 1993; Strang and Macy 2001.

linkages to upsizers and downsizers separately. For example, if four of the six OECD members with which France shares a common border decreased government employment in 1995 and two increased the size of their public sectors, aggregate employment change in the four is used to construct a score of proximity to downsizing, while change in the other two is summed to measure proximity to upsizing.

To study asymmetries in vicarious learning, we separate evidence that supports downsizing from evidence that supports upsizing. EVIDENCE FOR DOWNSIZING is restricted to those cases where either employment reductions are accompanied by strong performance (rapid economic growth, strong trade balances, or fiscal health) or where upsizing is accompanied by poor performance.[31] EVIDENCE FOR UPSIZING cumulates the converse cases, where either decreases in government employment are followed by poor outcomes or where employment increases are followed by good outcomes.

Internal factors Indicators of national economic performance include the rate of growth in gross domestic product (GDP), the trade balance (exports minus imports, standardized by total trade), and the unemployment rate. In addition, a measure of the state's fiscal position is calculated as the central government's balance of revenues and expenditures (surpluses have positive values, deficits negative values). All fiscal measures are taken annually from the International Finance Statistics of the International Monetary Fund.

Indicators of the size of the public sector include the ratio of government expenditure to GDP and the ratio of national population to government employment (an inverse measure), both drawn from IMF statistics.

An index of left party power codes the composition of governing parties on a 1 to 5 scale (1 = right party dominance, 5 = left party dominance).[32] Union density measures the fraction of the non-agricultural workforce that is unionized, taken from International Labor Organization (ILO) statistics.

We count the number of governmental reforms announced by each country each year, based on the OECD's *Issues and Developments in Public Management*. (Reform initiatives in recent years are also collected in the OECD website.) These initiatives include not only measures focused

[31] In any given year, strong (weak) performers are those whose economic growth is above (below) the mean for OECD member states for that year, or where the value of exports is greater (less) than imports, or where government revenues are greater (less) than expenditures.

[32] See Woldendorp, Keman, and Budge 1998 for construction of this index.

Table 4.1. *Descriptive statistics*

Variable	Mean	Standard deviation
ΔGE_{IT-1}	1.26	3.88
(log) GDP	5.32	1.54
GOVT EXPENDITURE/GDP	0.32	0.10
POPULATION/PUBLIC EMPLOYMENT	17.74	10.40
BUDGET DEFICIT	−0.11	0.11
UNEMPLOYMENT RATE	6.85	4.21
TRADE BALANCE	0.01	0.15
GDP GROWTH RATE	0.02	0.02
LEFT PARTY POWER	2.43	1.46
UNION DENSITY	42.23	21.22
PUBLIC SECTOR REFORM INITIATIVES	2.58	2.93
EC MEMBER	0.69	0.46
ENGLISH-SPEAKING	0.26	0.44
GLOBAL DIFFUSION	1.35	1.01
NETWORK DIFFUSION: TRADE WITH USA	1.88	4.67
NETWORK DIFFUSION: TRADE PARTNERSHIP	0.83	1.14
NETWORK DIFFUSION: COMMON BORDER	1.09	1.90
NETWORK DIFFUSION: CAPITAL CITY PROXIMITY	134.18	94.06
NETWORK DIFFUSION: TRADE COMPETITION	15.92	13.89
LEARNING FROM ECONOMIC GROWTH	0.04	0.04
EVIDENCE FOR DOWNSIZING	−0.44	0.26
EVIDENCE FOR UPSIZING	0.65	0.52
LEARNING FROM TRADE BALANCES	−0.04	0.19
EVIDENCE FOR DOWNSIZING	−0.92	0.28
EVIDENCE FOR UPSIZING	0.63	0.22
LEARNING FROM BUDGETARY HEALTH	−0.16	0.17
EVIDENCE FOR DOWNSIZING	−2.46	1.32
EVIDENCE FOR UPSIZING	2.05	0.59

on public sector employment but also initiatives involving deregulation, privatization, information technology, and human resources management.

Table 4.1 provides descriptive statistics for all variables.

Estimation

We estimate models of the form

$$\Delta GE_{it} = \beta_{1k} X_{it-1,k} + \beta_2 \Delta GE_{it-1} + \beta_3 \sum_{i=1}^{N} (W_{ijt} \Delta GE_{jt-1}) + \varepsilon_{it}. \quad (2)$$

Two main threats to inference arise. The first is spatial correlation, the statistical problem raised by diffusion. Most diffusion processes (including the majority postulated here) involve reciprocated interdependence, where case *i* affects case *j* and case *j* affects case *i*. Because each outcome enters as a regressor in the model for the other, a correlation is constructed between explanatory variables and the error term for each country. As is well known, the result is a form of simultaneity bias which generally leads regression coefficients to be overestimated and standard errors underestimated.

Our strategy is to avoid simultaneity bias by relating each country's current upsizing or downsizing to prior upsizing or downsizing in other countries. Case *i*'s outcome at $t-1$ thus affects *j* at *t*, while the outcome for *j* at $t-1$ affects *i* at *t*. By lagging diffusion influences, we sever the direct connection between regressors and model error. A lag structure also makes substantive sense given the outcome studied here: changes in the size of the public sector can only be accomplished over time and are constrained by the bureaucratic structure of the process.[33]

The second threat to inference is serial correlation, where unmodeled case-specific factors lead the error term to be correlated with the lagged dependent variable. This is the characteristic problem of time-series analysis, and the subject of a large econometric literature. The main statistical remedy is to employ instrumental variables constructed from prior lags of exogenous variables. We adopt this strategy, estimating models within a general method of moments (GMM) framework. GMM estimators have been shown to outperform standard two-stage least squares estimators and to be robust in the absence of knowledge of the structure of heteroskedasticity and serial correlation.[34] Analyses are performed with ETS/SAS.

Results

All tables present GMM regression analyses of change in government employment between 1980 and 1997. Table 4.2 includes only national characteristics, while subsequent analyses add diffusion influences. Because the former have stable effects across all models, we present them once and review them first.

[33] Lagged diffusion effects would not make sense where feedback occurs instantaneously or in shorter intervals than those separating panel observations. For example, financial markets react so quickly that interdependence in exchange rates would be appropriately treated as simultaneous.

[34] See Hansen 1982; Arellano and Bond 1991. Many familiar techniques, such as ordinary least squares (OLS), are methods of moments estimators and thus special cases of GMM. The attraction of GMM is that it identifies parameters based on multiple model assumptions to minimize asymptotic variance. See Greene 1993 for an overview.

Table 4.2. *GMM analysis of the annual rate of change in government employment: influence of national characteristics only, twenty-six OECD countries, 1980–1997*

B_0	2.41***
(log) GDP	−0.21***
BUDGET DEFICIT	−0.02
GOVT EXPENDITURE/GDP	−0.31***
POPULATION/PUBLIC EMPLOYMENT	−0.85
UNEMPLOYMENT RATE	0.04*
TRADE BALANCE	0.32
GDP GROWTH RATE	7.81
LEFT PARTY POWER	0.20***
UNION DENSITY	−0.06
PUBLIC REFORM INITIATIVES	−0.03
EC MEMBER	−0.47*
ENGLISH-SPEAKING	−1.14***
$\Delta\ GE_{it-1}$	0.29***
R^2	.38
N	441

***p < .01;
**p < .05;
*p < .10.

Most economic and political factors influence public sector employment in the anticipated direction. The most substantial relationships involve economic development (wealthier countries are more likely to reduce the size of their public sectors), government size (countries with larger governments tend to downsize more), and political leanings (leftist party rule promotes public sector growth, rightist rule leads toward contraction).

Table 4.2 also shows the proclivity for public sector downsizing among English-speaking countries, net of economic and political conditions. We interpret this effect as a product of the centrality of neoliberal and managerial visions in Great Britain, the United States, Canada, Australia, and New Zealand. One indicator of the strength of these affinities is the weak impact of party politics within the English-speaking members of the OECD. Conservatives led the movement toward reducing and restructuring government in three of the five countries, while Labor parties oversaw downsizing in Australia and New Zealand.

Members of the European Community (EC) also tend to decrease public employment more than other OECD states do. Supplementary analyses exploring differences by decade (not shown) indicate that this effect appears in the 1990s but not the 1980s. Downsizing within the Community may thus index the Maastricht Treaty's Article 104c(1) provision that member states "shall avoid excessive government deficits." Downsizing among members of the EC may also reflect responses to the more general problem of structural competitiveness in the context of European integration.

A non-effect of particular interest is the negative but statistically insignificant impact of reform initiatives. This result is compatible with the notion that formal public sector reforms (not unlike private sector ones) often lack real consequences. Some governments may have announced vigorous programs for change that accomplished little. We should not leap to the conclusion that reforms are necessarily mere show, however; many initiatives focused not on the size of the public sector but its functioning.

Table 4.3 reports models that include diffusion influences in addition to internal factors (we do not continue to report coefficients for the latter, which change little from those shown in Table 4.2). The strong positive effect of global diffusion indicates that change in government employment within the OECD as a whole is followed by movement in the same direction in each focal country. One interpretation is that all OECD members influence each other. But external shocks or broad environmental changes might lead countries to act in similar ways over time, producing a relationship that is hard to distinguish empirically from homogeneous mixing.

Socially structured patterns of influence can be interpreted more positively. Table 4.3 indicates that diffusion generally follows the lines of economic interaction and geographic proximity. Net of aggregate trends, the rate of change in government employment in a focal country during a given year was significantly influenced by prior employment change among trade partners. Similarly, spatial measures (common border and great circle distances between capitals) indicate that geographically proximate countries tend to move in the same direction.[35] Because trade and geographic proximity are reciprocated relationships, they imply not only that policies diffuse across borders but that influence boomerangs back to its source.

Table 4.3 also links public sector shifts in the United States to subsequent shifts in other OECD countries. US government employment grew slowly in the early 1980s, rapidly in the late 1980s, and moved toward

[35] Lee 2001 further examines the lag structure of diffusion influences, which are strongest in the immediately preceding year and fall off smoothly over a three-year period.

Table 4.3. *GMM analyses of the annual rate of change in government employment: diffusion effects for twenty-six OECD member states, 1980–1997*

GLOBAL DIFFUSION	$.29^{***}$	$.20^{**}$	.20	$.30^{**}$	.02	$.45^{**}$	$.31^{***}$	$.29^{**}$	$.29^{***}$
Network diffusion									
TRADE WITH USA		$.15^{***}$							
TRADE PARTNERSHIP			$.25^{**}$						
COMMON BORDER				$.09^{*}$					
CAPITAL CITY PROXIMITY					$.004^{*}$				
TRADE COMPETITION						.23			
Learning from									
ECONOMIC GROWTH							2.09		
TRADE BALANCES								−.13	
BUDGETARY HEALTH									−.30

Notes: All models control for national characteristics shown in Table 4.2. $N = 441$ country/years.
$^{***}p < .01$;
$^{**}p < .05$;
$^{*}p < .10$.

downsizing through the 1990s. Other countries tended to follow suit, with the greatest movement occurring in member nations whose economies were most closely linked to the United States. (Additional analyses found a similar but weaker effect of unweighted imitation of the United States.)

By contrast, there is little evidence that diffusion is structured by trade competition. While countries that trade extensively with each other tend to move in tandem, countries that trade with the same third parties (and so compete for markets) do not. This is striking, particularly because the two measures of trade patterns are positively correlated; countries that trade with each other also tend to possess similar global trade profiles.

We also find little support for a simple form of vicarious learning, where countries adopt whatever policies appear to work for others. There is much variation over the 1980–1997 period in the empirical relationship between public employment change and key macroeconomic outcomes like economic growth, trade balances, and fiscal health. In some years, downsizers grew faster than upsizers, while in others they grew more slowly. But these signals are not systematically related to subsequent shifts in the size of the public sector.

Table 4.4 examines asymmetries in the diffusion of public sector upsizing and downsizing. As described above, we do so by distinguishing the

Table 4.4. *GMM analyses of the annual rate of change in government employment, upsizing versus downsizing diffusion effects for twenty-six OECD member states, 1980–1997*

GLOBAL DIFFUSION	.19**	.14	.31***	.20	.28	.32***	.31***	.31***
Network diffusion								
TRADE WITH USA								
DOWNSIZING	.18***							
UPSIZING	.13***							
TRADE PARTNERSHIP								
DOWNSIZING		.003**						
UPSIZING		.001						
COMMON BORDER								
DOWNSIZING			.15*					
UPSIZING			−.10					
CAPITAL CITY PROXIMITY								
DOWNSIZING				.004				
UPSIZING				−.001				
TRADE COMPETITION								
DOWNSIZING					.034			
UPSIZING					.002			
Learning from								
ECONOMIC GROWTH								
EVIDENCE FOR DOWNSIZING						.65**		
EVIDENCE FOR UPSIZING						−.14		
TRADE BALANCES								
EVIDENCE FOR DOWNSIZING							.99**	
EVIDENCE FOR UPSIZING							−.47	
BUDGETARY HEALTH								
EVIDENCE FOR DOWNSIZING								.04
EVIDENCE FOR UPSIZING								−.04

Notes: All models control for national characteristics shown in Table 4.2. $N = 441$ country/years.

*** $p < .01$;

** $p < .05$;

* $p < .10$.

impact of proximate countries that downsize from those that upsize, and separating evidence that downsizing is economically beneficial from evidence that it is harmful. All models continue to control for the full set of national characteristics reported in Table 4.2.

Downsizing appears to be contagious, while upsizing does not. Reductions in government employment by a trade partner or neighbor lead to reductions in the size of the public sector. But increases in government employment by the same partners or neighbors have negligible effects. We also find larger effects of downsizing than upsizing when proximity is measured between capitals and as a function of trade competition, though none of these effects are statistically significant at conventional levels.

Even more striking asymmetries appear in vicarious learning. Table 4.4 indicates that countries act as though they are influenced by evidence that downsizing works: they are more likely to diminish public employment when recent downsizers experienced rapid growth and improving trade balances, and when recent upsizers faced slow growth and worsening trade.[36] But they appear unmoved by countervailing information. Neither strong economic performance by upsizers nor weak performance by downsizers leads to upsizing. Shifts in government budgets follow the same asymmetric pattern, though these coefficients are not statistically significant.

These asymmetries emerge even though the overall economic record of upsizers and downsizers was in fact roughly equivalent. The correlation between change in public employment and GDP growth is .04; for trade balance, it is −.16; and for budgetary surpluses, it is −.05. Downsizers thus experienced slightly slower rates of economic growth than upsizers, somewhat better trade balances, and slightly healthier fiscal positions.

Deductions from these negligible and statistically insignificant relationships, we think, say more about the interpreter than the evidence. For example, proponents of vigorous government action might conclude from the first correlation that an enlarged public sphere provides a social and material infrastructure that promotes economic success. Neoliberals could counter that states often shrink in response to sluggish growth, and that a negligible correlation should be interpreted as evidence that downsizing helped prevent a bad situation from getting worse.[37] Our interpretation of Table 4.4 is that neoliberals dominated the debate.

[36] All measures are constructed so a positive coefficient indicates movement in the direction of the signal. A positive impact of EVIDENCE FOR DOWNSIZING indicates a reduction in public employment (since the interaction of positive economic outcomes and employment decreases produce negative values, as do those of negative outcomes and employment increases). A positive effect of EVIDENCE FOR UPSIZING indicates a rise in public employment (since the two terms are either both positive or both negative).

[37] Similarly, in a discussion of the collapse of Southern Cone economies that had enacted liberalization experiments in the 1980s, Kahler 1990:45 notes that "evaluations have typically varied according to initial sympathies."

Table 4.5. *GMM analyses of the annual rate of change in government employment, various diffusion effects for twenty-six OECD member states, 1980–1997*

GLOBAL DIFFUSION	$.38^{***}$	$.22^{**}$	$.26^{**}$	$.25^{**}$	$.35^{***}$	$.21^{*}$
Network diffusion						
TRADE WITH USA						
UPSIZING AND DOWNSIZING	.03	.02				
TRADE PARTNERSHIP						
DOWNSIZING			$.004^{***}$	$.002^{*}$		
SHARED BORDER						
DOWNSIZING					.10	.10
Learning from						
ECONOMIC GROWTH						
EVIDENCE FOR DOWNSIZING	$.66^{*}$		.30		.56	
TRADE BALANCES						
EVIDENCE FOR DOWNSIZING		$.88^{**}$		.52		$.88^{**}$

Notes: All models control for national characteristics shown in Table 4.2. $N = 441$ country/years.
$^{***}p < .01$;
$^{**}p < .05$;
$^{*}p < .10$.

The one network relationship that generates mimicry in both directions is imitation of the world's dominant power. When the United States upsizes, countries that trade a great deal with her are more likely to upsize. When the United States downsizes, they are more likely to downsize. This suggests that a dominant actor's behavior may be self-legitimating in a way that those of neighbors or trading partners are not.

Table 4.5 combines the major diffusion mechanisms identified above: peer-based emulation of downsizers, evidence that downsizing works, and trade with the United States. We see strong effects of trade-based proximity to downsizers net of vicarious evidence that downsizing works, and strong effects of evidence for downsizing's economic benefits net of the influence of the US and of border adjacency. Border adjacency and trade with the US have weaker effects in these combined models, though all estimated effects are larger than their standard errors. On the whole, diffusion effects appear remarkably robust.

Discussion

Contemporary governments are immensely complex organizations. Net shifts toward their expansion or contraction are the result of multiple pressures and decisions made at different levels. Yet it is clear that the overall trajectory of these decisions shifted within OECD member states in the 1980s and 1990s, as a long process of public sector expansion slowed and in some countries, reversed direction.

Regression analyses indicate that change in the size of the public sector is linked not only to domestic economic and political conditions but also to international policy diffusion. Influence is particularly strong between neighbors and countries that trade extensively with each other, which is suggestive of an underlying process of emulation linked to information flow and cultural similarity. We see correspondingly little sign of competitively driven influence between trade rivals. An asymmetric pattern of contagion also emerges where the trading partners of the United States tend to follow its lead.

This chapter's key findings, however, concern not the network structure of international diffusion but the sorts of policies that flow. As Table 4.6 summarizes, downsizing appears to be contagious while upsizing does not. We find that proximity to downsizers promotes downsizing, but that proximity to upsizers does not promote upsizing. We also find that evidence of the economic benefits of downsizing stimulates more downsizing, while evidence of the economic benefits of upsizing has no observable impact. Only the influence of the United States suggests an interpretively unmediated diffusion pattern, though this effect is weak once we control for vicarious learning.

The differential contagiousness of upsizing and downsizing makes sense given their diametrically opposed statuses within policy discourse.

Table 4.6. *Empirical asymmetries in emulation and learning*

	Network emulation	Theory-driven learning
Downsizing		
Proximity to downsizing peers	Promotes downsizing	
Proximity to a downsizing US	Promotes downsizing	
Strong economic performance among downsizers		Promotes downsizing
Weak economic performance among downsizers		No impact
Upsizing		
Proximity to upsizing peers	No impact	
Proximity to an upsizing US	Promotes upsizing	
Strong economic performance among upsizers		No impact
Weak economic performance among upsizers		Promotes downsizing

The dominant neoliberalism of the 1980s and 1990s argued that the public sector was wasteful and inefficient, and that markets could replace planning in many more contexts than had previously been recognized. Students of organizations contended that smaller was better, and advocated administrative reforms that would foster an entrepreneurial ethos within public servants. Examples of downsizing were broadcast as success stories to be mimicked, while examples of public sector growth were treated as parochial.

A Korean official of considerable experience provided us with an inside view of the routine way that interpretive frames enter into policy discussions. This official noted that when speaking about his country's experience at international meetings such as OECD/PUMA, he sensed in himself "some kind of desire to exaggerate the contents and numbers of reforms." The same impulse to "overstate the examples or ideas of reforms in the member countries" resurfaced when he relayed OECD experiences to government leaders at home.

The pattern of differential contagiousness shown here speaks to core theoretical issues in the study of diffusion. It reinforces Davis and Greve's finding that socially legitimated innovations are highly contagious. And this chapter's results go beyond prior research by showing that vicarious learning is theory-driven. Empirical outcomes that confirm expectations reinforce behavior, while outcomes that contradict expectations are discounted. In short, when theories and evidence come into conflict, theories win.

While we are unaware of prior demonstrations of theory-driven learning in national policy, social psychologists have identified similar processes in individual inference. In one classic study, for example, Lord, Ross, and Lepper exposed subjects to different reports concerning the deterrent effects of capital punishment.[38] Subjects found research whose conclusions jibed with their original views to be more convincing than research that came to opposing conclusions, and were more influenced by the former than the latter. Indeed, when subjects were supplied not only with research results but also exposure to discussion of procedures and possible critiques, they interpreted both confirming and disconfirming evidence as strengthening their initial positions.

Theory-driven learning poses a challenge to naive models of rational choice. As Simmons, Dobbin, and Garrett point out, most discussions of vicarious learning assume that information is used to update beliefs and increase their accuracy. But if only evidence that confirms beliefs is

[38] Lord, Ross, and Lepper 1979. For a review of cognitive and inferential biases, see Gilovich 1993.

believed, learning is neither rational nor adaptive! And while a short-term lag in response to mixed signals might seem reasonable, our results over two decades suggests that theories have great staying power.

As a process of interest in its own right, theory-driven learning provides an opportunity to combine insights from different theoretical and disciplinary perspectives. Cognitive research on attention, pattern recognition, and inference seems fundamental. Work on communication and social influence can detail how individual biases are propagated and reinforced within different kinds of groups. And political and cultural analyses can probe why particular theories tend to be dominant.

In considering how to put the many pieces of the puzzle together, Thomas Kuhn's analysis of normal science and paradigm change provides a powerful set of insights.[39] As Hall argues in applying Kuhn's ideas to public policy, most choices are made within an officially maintained interpretive frame.[40] Experience gained from past policies and their outcomes routinely feeds back into everyday target setting, but seldom calls the framework into question. Paradigm shifts, on the other hand, require a special kind of evidence – the accumulation of anomalies that challenge the internal logic of the extant paradigm. They also require demographic change. As Kuhn points out, established models are not so much rejected as left unvoiced when their adherents fail to reproduce themselves.

Implications

Three empirical implications of the diffusion pattern identified here stand out. First, downsizing's contagiousness should produce greater reductions in government employment than would occur otherwise. Since downsizing elsewhere has a reinforcing effect while upsizing does not, downsizing pressures should expand over time. And because the benefits of downsizing are treated as consequential while parallel evidence for upsizing is ignored, the international community should increasingly shift toward downsizing.

Second, contagion generates a tendency toward homogeneity. If countries move in the direction of each other's actions, under most conditions (including the models estimated here) they will tend to converge. And if countries learn vicariously from the same lessons, they will move in relative lockstep.

Third, the interpretively mediated form of policy diffusion that appears to characterize administrative reform suggests growing convergence in

[39] Kuhn 1970. [40] Hall 1993.

the qualitative strategies used to achieve downsizing. We would anticipate, not a process of blind imitation, but a professionally driven dynamic where policy experts select and codify "best practice."[41] By contrast, modes of expanding the public sector are likely to be less standardized and more nation- and context-specific.

We should emphasize that contagion does not imply uniformity. Since the size of government is not driven solely by diffusion but is anchored in internal conditions as well, the contagiousness of downsizing will neither drive public employment to its natural limit nor lead to the elimination of national differences. And systems of interdependence can in fact generate heterogeneity rather than isomorphism, both cross-sectionally and over time, though to achieve this outcome we would need to complicate the feedback structure considered here.[42]

Comparisons and extensions

One of the attractive features of diffusion models is that they travel well. The spread of the same policy in different domains, or of different policies in the same domain, often reveals substantial regularities.[43] The contextual variations that diffusion analyses identify are often theoretically generalizable.

One natural comparison is between public and private sector downsizing. During the period studied here, many firms engaged in planned, radical workforce reductions (though a simple pattern of net employment decline is no more true for corporations than governments). For example, IBM downsized by about 36 percent, or 150,000 employees, between 1991 and 1994. Despite the fervor of its advocates, much research also shows that downsizing bears a heavy cost: it negatively affects the psychological health and motivation of survivors, disrupts intra-firm networks that get things done, and often diminishes organizational performance.[44]

[41] Movement in this direction can be seen in the work of Korea's task force, which criticized simplistic approaches to cutting government employment: "the downsizing programs of each country tend to be arbitrarily enforced without some scientific analysis of the process and decision in advance. Just setting a short-term or long-term ceiling for cutbacks, ignoring the costs of downsizing, or neglecting the downsizing process, is an easy option."

[42] See Haunschild and Miner 1997; Strang and Macy 2001; Strang and Kim 2005.

[43] Walker 1969 provides a classic analysis of regularities in policy diffusion across the American states; within the international arena, see Thomas *et al.* 1987 and other work by Meyer and colleagues on education, welfare, and human rights policy.

[44] See De Meuse and Vanderheiden 1994.

Studies of corporate downsizing suggest factors that parallel those documented here for the public sector.[45] Internal precipitants include weak corporate performance (mirroring negative effects of GDP growth), organizational size (mirroring measures of government size), and the philosophy of the CEO (mirroring measures of ruling party politics). These combine with palpable forms of mimicry. Decisions to eliminate personnel in some companies makes it easier for others to follow suit – and later, hard for others not to follow suit. As Budros details,

> when few downsizings had occurred in the early 1980s, these acts were regarded as "puzzling" (*Hartford Courant* August 6, 1983) and it took "guts" to commit them (*Business Week* August 4, 1983:43). In the mid 1980s, staff trims were "in fashion" and so CEOs were "far less reluctant" to do some trimming. Indeed, downsizers began to hear the words: "Everyone else is doing this; how come you aren't?"[46]

By the mid-1990s, observers noted that downsizing continued apace in organizations that showed a healthy profit.

As in the public sector, the corporate downsizing movement appeared within a supportive cultural context. Theories of organizational effectiveness extolled the virtues of lean organizations while an older line of analysis stressing the benefits of "organizational slack" was forgotten. Ideologies of employee self-reliance supplanted notions of organizational commitment.[47] Survivors of downsizing were described as empowered, and even those who lost their jobs were regarded as the ultimate beneficiaries of a necessarily harsh lesson.

Diffusion analysis also seems appropriate in public sector contexts beyond the one examined here. This chapter has studied downsizing among OECD members, the world's richest and most powerful states. We suspect that analysis of downsizing outside the OECD also involves a combination of internal and external influences, but that different mechanisms are involved.

In particular, the World Bank and the IMF are key advocates and enforcers of neoliberal arrangements in poorer and economically indebted countries. Conditionality agreements that restrict government debt have direct implications for public expenditure and government employment. The scope of these requirements grew over the 1980–1997 period studied here, with structural reforms related both to market institutions and to governance increasing in prominence. Since the most stringent conditions are generally applied to the poorest countries and those least able to obtain credit elsewhere, coercion seems likely

[45] Budros 1997. [46] Budros 1997:233. [47] McKinley, Mone, and Barker 1998.

to play as large a role outside the OECD as emulation does within the OECD.[48]

Finally, it would be useful to compare determinants of the size of the public sector in different historical periods. The 1950s and 1960s gave rise to a rich analysis of public sector growth as resulting from socioeconomic change, social democratic politics, and supportive political institutions. Is an integrated model of the two eras plausible, or do institutional expansion and retrenchment operate in fundamentally disparate ways? While some mechanisms surely differ,[49] others are presumably implicated in both growth and decline. Pursuing this chapter's analysis of theory-driven learning one step further, we can venture a hypothesis: during the era when "reform" referred to an expansion of the state's power and capacity, upsizing and not downsizing would have been contagious.

References

Arellano, Manuel and Stephen Bond. 1991. Some Tests of Specification for Panel Data: Monte Carlo Evidence and an Application to Employment Equations. *Review of Economic Studies* 58 (2):277–97.

Babb, Sarah and Ariel Buira. 2004. Mission Creep, Mission Push and Discretion in Sociological Perspective: The Case of IMF Conditionality. Paper presented at the XVIII G24 Technical Group Meeting, March, Geneva.

Baum, Jeeyang R. 2002. Presidents Have Problems Too: The Logic of Intra-Branch Delegation in New Democracies (Korea, Taiwan, China). Ph.D. dissertation, University of California, Los Angeles.

Baumol, William J., Alan S. Blinder, and Edward N. Wolff. 2003. *Downsizing in America: Reality, Causes, and Consequences*. New York: Russell Sage.

Brown, Lawrence D. 1983. *Politics and Health Care Organization*. Washington, DC: Brookings.

Budros, Art. 1997. The New Capitalism and Organizational Rationality: The Adoption of Downsizing Programs, 1979–1994. *Social Forces* 76 (1):229–50.

Burt, Ronald S. 1987. Social Contagion and Innovation: Cohesion versus Structural Equivalence. *American Journal of Sociology* 92 (6):1287–335.

Castles, Francis. 1989. Big Government in Weak States: The Paradox of State Size in the English-Speaking Nations of Advanced Capitalism. *Journal of Commonwealth and Comparative Politics* 27 (3):267–93.

Cusack, Thomas R., Ton Notermans, and Martin Rein. 1989. Political-Economic Aspects of Public Employment. *European Journal of Political Research* 17 (4):471–500.

48 See Mosley, Harrigan, and Toye 1991 on the bargaining game between the IMF and recipient countries. As the IMF's conditions for loans grew more stringent, wealthy countries that could receive financing elsewhere largely opted out. Babb and Buira 2004 provide a close analysis of shifts in IMF conditionality that we draw on here.

49 Pierson 1994.

Davis, Gerald F. and Henrich R. Greve. 1997. Corporate Elite Networks and Governance Changes in the 1980s. *American Journal of Sociology* 103 (1):1–37.

De Meuse, Kenneth P. and Paul A. Vanderheiden. 1994. Announced Layoffs: Their Effect on Corporate Financial Performance. *Human Resource Management* 33 (4):509–30.

DiMaggio, Paul J. and Walter W. Powell. 1983. The Iron Cage Revisited: Institutional Isomorphism and Collective Rationality in Organizational Fields. *American Sociological Review* 48 (2):147–60.

Flora, Peter, and Arnold J. Heidenheimer, eds. 1981. *The Development of Welfare States in Europe and America*. New Brunswick, NJ: Transaction.

Gilovich, Thomas. 1993. *How We Know What Isn't So: The Fallibility of Human Reason in Everyday Life*. New York: Free Press.

Greene, William H. 1993. *Econometric Analysis*. New York: Macmillan.

Ha, Yeon-Seob. 2004. Budgetary and Financial Management Reforms in Korea: Financial Crisis, New Public Management, and Fiscal Administration. *International Review of Administrative Sciences* 70 (3):511–25.

Hall, Peter A. 1993. Policy Paradigms, Social Learning, and the State: The Case of Economic Policymaking in Britain. *Comparative Politics* 25 (3):275–96.

Halligan, John. 1996. The Diffusion of Civil Service Reform. In *Civil Service Systems in Comparative Perspective*, edited by Hans A. G. M. Bekke, James L. Perry, and Theo A. J. Toonen, 288–317. Bloomington: Indiana University Press.

Hansen, Lars Peter. 1982. Large Sample Properties of Generalized Method of Moments Estimators. *Econometrica* 50 (4):1029–54.

Haunschild, Pamela R. and Anne S. Miner. 1997. Modes of Interorganizational Imitation: The Effects of Outcome Salience and Uncertainty. *Administrative Science Quarterly* 42 (3):472–500.

Kahler, Miles. 1990. Orthodoxy and Its Alternatives: Explaining Approaches to Stabilization and Adjustment. In *Economic Crisis and Policy Choice: The Politics of Adjustment in the Third World*, edited by Joan M. Nelson, 33–62. Princeton, NJ: Princeton University Press.

Kim, Pan Suk and M. Jae Moon. 2002. Current Public Sector Reform in Korea: New Public Management in Practice. *Journal of Comparative Asian Development* 1 (1):49–70.

Kjaer, Peter and Ove K. Pedersen. 2001. Translating Liberalization: Neoliberalism in the Danish Negotiated Economy. In *The Rise of Neoliberalism and Institutional Analysis*, edited by John L. Campbell and Ove K. Pedersen, 219–48. Princeton, NJ: Princeton University Press.

Kuhn, Thomas. 1970. *The Structure of Scientific Revolutions*. Chicago: University of Chicago Press.

Lee, Chang Kil. 2001. The Institutionalization of Growth and Decline in Government Employment: Economics, Politics, and Imitation. Ph.D. dissertation, Cornell University.

Lord, Charles G., Lee Ross, and Mark R. Lepper. 1979. Biased Assimilation and Attitude Polarization: The Effects of Prior Theories on Subsequently Considered Evidence. *Journal of Personality and Social Psychology* 37 (11):2098–109.

McKinley, William, Mark A. Mone, and Vincent L. Barker III. 1998. Some Ideological Foundations of Organizational Downsizing. *Journal of Management Inquiry* 7 (3):198–212.

Meyer, John W., John Boli, George M. Thomas, and Francisco O. Ramirez. 1997. World Society and the Nation-State. *American Journal of Sociology* 103 (1):144–81.

Moon, Myung-Jae and Patricia Ingraham. 1998. Shaping Administrative Reform and Governance: An Examination of the Political Nexus Triads in Three Asian Countries. *Governance* 11 (1):77–100.

Mosley, Paul, Jane Harrigan, and John Toye. 1991. *Aid and Power: The World Bank and Policy-based Lending*. London: Routledge.

Niskanen, William. 1971. *Bureaucracy and Representative Government*. Chicago: Aldine.

O'Connor, James. 1973. *The Fiscal Crisis of the State*. New York: St. Martin's Press.

Organization for Economic Cooperation and Development (OECD). 1995. *Governance in Transition: Public Management Reforms in OECD Countries*. Paris: OECD.

OECD/PUMA, *Issues and Developments in Public Management, 1993–1998*. Paris: OECD.

Offe, Claus. 1984. *Contradictions of the Welfare State*. Cambridge, MA: MIT Press.

Osborne, David and Ted Gaebler. 1993. *Reinventing Government: How the Entrepreneurial Spirit is Transforming the Public Sector*. New York: Plume.

Pampel, Fred C. and John B. Williamson. 1988. Welfare Spending in Advanced Industrial Democracies, 1950–1980. *American Journal of Sociology* 93 (6):1424–56.

Pierson, Paul 1994. *Dismantling the Welfare State?: Reagan, Thatcher, and the Politics of Retrenchment*. New York: Cambridge University Press.

Piore, Michael J. and Charles F. Sabel. 1984. *The Second Industrial Divide: Possibilities for Prosperity*. New York: Basic Books.

Republic of Korea. Ministry of Government Administration. 1997. *Sin Jungbu Hyuksinron ("New Government Reforms")*. Seoul: DonMyungSa.

Republic of Korea. Ministry of Planning and Budget. 2003. *How Korea Reformed the Public Sector*. Seoul: Ministry of Planning and Budget.

Rogers, Everett M. 1995. *Diffusion of Innovations*. 4th ed. New York: Free Press.

Strang, David and Ellen M. Bradburn. 2001. Theorizing Legitimacy or Legitimating Theory? Neoliberal Discourse and HMO Policy, 1970–89. In *The Rise of Neoliberalism and Institutional Analysis*, edited by John L. Campbell and Ove K. Pedersen, 129–58. Princeton, NJ: Princeton University Press.

Strang, David and Young-Mi Kim. 2005. The Diffusion and Domestication of Managerial Innovations: The Spread of Scientific Management, Quality Circles, and Total Quality Management Between the United States and Japan. In *The Oxford Handbook of Work and Organization*, edited by Stephen Ackroyd, Rosemary Batt, Paul Thompson, and Pamela S. Tolbert, 177–99. Oxford, England: Oxford University Press.

Strang, David and Michael W. Macy. 2001. In Search of Excellence: Fads, Success Stories, and Adaptive Emulation. *American Journal of Sociology* 107 (1):147–82.

Strang, David and John W. Meyer. 1993. Institutional Conditions for Diffusion. *Theory and Society* 22 (4):487–511.

Strang, David and Sarah A. Soule. 1998. Diffusion in Organizations and Social Movements: From Hybrid Corn to Poison Pills. *Annual Review of Sociology* 24:265–90.

Thomas, George M., John W. Meyer, Francisco O. Ramirez, and John Boli. 1987. *Institutional Structure: Constituting State, Society, and the Individual.* Newbury Park, CA: Sage.

Walker, Jack L. 1969. The Diffusion of Innovations Among the American States. *American Political Science Review* 63 (3):880–99.

Wilensky, Harold L. 1975. *The Welfare State and Equality: Structural and Ideological Roots of Public Expenditures*. Berkeley: University of California Press.

Woldendorp, Jaap, Hans Keman, and Ian Budge. 1998. Party Government in 20 Democracies: An Update (1990–1995). *European Journal of Political Research* 33 (1):125–64.

5 Global ideology and voter sentiment as determinants of international financial liberalization*

Dennis P. Quinn and A. Maria Toyoda

Introduction

Scholars have long argued that the spread of ideas and values matters for the adaptation and reform of government policies. (See, for example, the essays in Hall 1989.) In this chapter, we investigate whether and how either liberal or restrictive international financial policies on capital account regulation spread globally, both through the direct effects of changes in global ideology on government policy and indirectly, through policy diffusion between other states.

In the following sections we: (1) provide a detailed account of the mechanisms of diffusion, focusing on the theoretical basis for the global, grassroots spread of ideas that affect government policies; (2) identify valid indicators of ideological change that will aid in identifying the mechanisms through which it is diffused; (3) discuss our models and methods, focusing on how ideology is diffused indirectly and globally through influence on other governments' policies; and (4) report the results of our study, and offer concluding remarks.

* We are grateful for financial assistance provided by the National Science Foundation (SBR-9729766 and SBR-9810410), the McDonough School of Business, and the Graduate School of Arts and Sciences, Georgetown University. This project has evolved from several other projects, done in collaboration with Carla Inclán and John Woolley. We would especially like to thank the participants at the May 2002 conference on diffusion held at Yale University, organized by Geoff Garrett and Beth A. Simmons, participants at a panel at the August 2002 Annual Meeting of the American Political Science Association in Boston, as well as the UCLA and Harvard conferences in March and August 2003, respectively (organized by Garrett, Simmons, and Frank Dobbin). Beth A. Simmons, Geoff Garrett, and Frank Dobbin provided very detailed and helpful suggestions. Keith Ord deserves special thanks for assisting us with methods for the analysis of common variance. We also thank Barry Eichengreen, Lars Jonung, Jeff Macher, John Mayo, John Meyer, Pietra Rivoli, Ronald Rogowski, Andy Sobel, Tom Willett, and Bennet Zelner for their comments. Sarah Zhu provided able assistance with the data set. The authors are responsible for all errors. Part of this chapter previously appeared in Quinn and Toyoda, Ideology and Voter Preferences as Determinants of Financial Globalization in *American Journal of Political Science* 51, April 2007:344–63. Reprinted with permission from Blackwell Publishing.

How ideas spread

While global convergence toward political and economic liberalism might be a defining story of the last two decades of the twentieth century, we find scant evidence that convergence around a particular set of policies regarding capital account liberalization is consistent over time or space. During the entire twentieth century, many distinct waves of international financial openness and closure diffused worldwide.

Based upon the work of many scholars, we know many of the domestic and international political and economic forces that account for change in international financial openness.[1] While this rich literature explains many of the determinants of policy liberalization and closure, to our knowledge scholars have not undertaken an empirical study of the effects of the *global* spread of ideas as an influence on a government's policy choices.

We hypothesize that capital account regulation in a range of countries is directly, significantly, and systematically influenced by changes in global ideology and sentiment, a non-state-centered form of diffusion. That is, the regulation of international financial transactions is likely to be more (less) restrictive as anti-capitalist (pro-capitalist) sentiment is widespread. That sentiment is revealed in part through fair and open electoral competition, and we posit that voting outcomes over time provide a valid and reliable indicator of the depth of anti- and pro-capitalist sentiment. The effects of this sentiment should be distinguished from the effects of democracy, however, which we will also assess.

Simmons, Dobbin, and Garrett (this volume; hereafter, SDG) define international policy diffusion as one where states are influenced by the behavior of other states in the system.[2] We extend their analysis, and hypothesize that part of ideology's effects on a given nation are diffused through its influence on other governments' policies, which in turn influence the home country. We consider below several propositions for global policy diffusion.

Global influence

Two major sets of perspectives are revealed in this book, and both rest on the roles of dominant or elite actors. On the one hand, the realist perspective is primarily operationalized in terms of a rational, unitary state

[1] For general literature reviews on capital account liberalization, see Eichengreen 2001; IMF 2001. Examples of papers on the determinants of liberalization are Brune, Garrett, Guisinger, and Sorens 2001; Li and Smith 2002; Quinn and Inclán 1997; Rector and Kasner 2002; Simmons and Elkins 2004; Zhang 2002.

[2] That is, the choices governments make about policies are interdependent.

responding to external pressure. A less statist, but still "pressure-focused" view is that activism of domestic pressure groups is the impetus for policy changes by the state. The constructivist perspectives in this volume, on the other hand, identify cultural channels of diffusion. These analyses, however, also rely heavily on the existence of dominant or elite actors who are the propagators and the receptors of ideas. These elite identities are formed through what Lee and Strang, in this volume, refer to as "peer-based reference groups." An example of this is the activity of professional groups or associations, be they formal or informal. Epistemic communities, transnational networks of elites, or international organizations offer similar channels for policy diffusion by espousing certain orthodoxies or "schools of thought" that are largely interpreted in the same ways across societies.

Another possibility is offered by the world society approach in sociology, which offers insights into non-elite channels for diffusion. The state is conceived not as a bounded and unitary actor, but as an entity exogenously constructed by individuals and groups, both inside and outside the state, engaging in state and policy formation.[3] Meyer (2004) further conceptualizes the state as embedded in the "ether" of world society. The ether may emanate and diffuse at the grassroots level. Moreover, as Acharya (2004) and Risse, Ropp, and Sikkink (1999)[4] note, global beliefs are often transformed or reconstructed in the process of "localization" in order for them to achieve greater congruence at the national or local level.

The "world civic politics" perspective offers yet another non-elite channel for influencing policy through the activism of a global civil society.[5] World civic politics distinctly treats activist organizations as political actors who lobby not just the state, but also seek to influence non-state actors. Policy influences filter upwards through changes enacted in conditions and practices at the grassroots level rather than through direct appeal to the state. Wapner (1995), for example, suggests that sensibilities in favor of environmental conservation and recycling, or against the hunting of baby seals, become internationalized through the work of non-governmental organizations that seek to raise the level of public awareness. In some cases, the state is swayed by public opinion into adopting new policies. In other cases, no action is taken by the state, but market (societal) actors might change their behavior to fall in line with the new public sensibility.

These non-elite channels of diffusion suggest that states should not be conceived solely as "rational actors." Government officials rely on

[3] Meyer, Boli, Thomas, and Ramirez 1997. [4] Especially pp. 6–18.
[5] See e.g. Wapner 1995 and 1996, especially Chs. 1 and 6.

heuristic shortcuts (bounded rationality),[6] retrospective learning biased toward the most recent events, and "error-learning" (i.e. through adjustments based on perceived past mistakes).[7]

The state-centered, elite-centered, and society-centered channels of diffusion therefore recall the earliest studies of the diverse means through which ideas diffused.[8] The classical diffusion model, developed by Rogers in the early 1960s, defines diffusion as the spread of innovations (ideas, practices, objects) "through certain channels over time among the members of a social system."[9] In our study, states are one channel and members of one type of social system, among many channels and social systems through which policy ideas diffuse in the world social system.

We draw upon these perspectives to offer a possible mechanism for policy diffusion based on changes in sentiment among elites and citizens alike about international capitalism. Pro- and anti-capitalist theories and values wax and wane in their relative popularity over time. The ether of global sentiment about capitalism, we hypothesize, influences government officials to respond through policy changes. Their actions are motivated by more than simple economic or technocratic considerations. As alternatives to the global spread of ideas, our study also tests the effects of other mechanisms such as coercion, emulation, learning, and competition that may also influence government behavior.

To examine the direct effect of anti- and pro-capitalist sentiment as an important force shaping national response to the broad spread of global liberalism, we consider changes in electoral support for Communist parties (CPs) worldwide as indicative of changes in global ideology. CPs were ideologically consistent in their hostile stance toward international economic liberalism for a long period of time. Their electoral performance should tell us something about global and national sentiments regarding those policies in which the party maintains consistent views. We expect that their domestic support will matter in the choices made by a democratic government. Of equal interest here is whether change in their support worldwide will affect a particular government's regulatory policies.

Coercion

Coercion by influential actors is one commonly suggested mechanism for affecting government behavior. We study three plausible possibilities.

[6] Weyland 2005. [7] Jonung 2005. [8] See e.g. Ryan and Gross 1943.
[9] Rogers 1983:5.

The financial policies of leading economies The literature on economic globalization is peppered with assumptions, rooted in structural dependency theory, that Organization for Economic Cooperation and Development (OECD) countries have influenced or compelled developing countries to pursue liberal policies in trade and finance.[10] Even those who assert that states retain policy autonomy still assume that national policies must be adjusted in response to the fait accompli of liberalized capital.[11] The degree of international financial openness of the world's leading economies might therefore affect the international financial policies of other nations. But why and how it does is open to interpretation.

The mechanisms of influence include the demonstration effects of the results of their policies (learning or emulation); enhanced difficulties in trading with partners with a given financial payments regime (network externalities); development of profit opportunities for economic agents in arbitraging differences in regulatory systems (strategic competition); the threat or reality of capital flight (indirect coercion of market forces); and overt political pressure from the governments of the leading economies to permit their firms greater economic freedoms in the host country (direct coercion).

The options we listed present a problem of definition, of course. There is little to distinguish coercion from structural dependency arguments regarding the imposition of policy from those related to learning or emulation, or recognition of the ways mechanisms interact (Meseguer and Gilardi 2005). Some theorists may further claim that only learning and emulation constitute diffusion (see Stallings 1992) or that coercion is clearly not diffusion (Meseguer 2003). In this chapter, though, we follow the other contributors to this volume, and include coercion as a diffusion mechanism worth exploring.

One inference, therefore, is that once the leading economies deregulated more or less completely, other countries would come under increasing pressure to do the same. This logic underpins much of the literature on structural dependence, as well as the logic in the realist/dominant actors school of international relations theory.

Many emerging market countries, however, explicitly rejected the model of financial openness advocated by leading economies, at least in the 1960s through the 1980s. They did so partly in accordance with a

[10] See e.g. Evans 1997; Drezner 2001; Gwynne and Kay 1999; Fourcade-Gourinchas and Babb 2002. The starting point for claims of liberal convergence, as many of these authors note, is the collapse of national Keynesianism following the first oil shock in the early 1970s, notably in Britain, and its subsequent repudiation in France and Sweden in the 1980s, where it was supposedly even more deeply embedded.

[11] See e.g. Mosley 2003.

world systems or *dependencia* interpretation of modern capitalism. This view suggested that "peripheral" countries were better situated if they isolated themselves from "core" countries, whose exploitation of the periphery was central to core nation wealth but resulted in peripheral nation poverty. In this constructed understanding of development, closely associated with Raul Prebisch and Immanuel Wallerstein, peripheral nations should undertake import substitution industrialization to improve their terms of trade, which requires partial financial closure. Other theorists advocated nationalizing industries owned by core country residents or blocking "core" capital flows as a means of establishing economic independence. (See J. Quinn 2002 for a discussion of ideology and nationalization in Sub-Saharan Africa in the 1960s.)

Policy preferences of the International Monetary Fund It is widely argued that the International Monetary Fund (IMF) is able, through negotiated terms of conditionality[12] to impose its policy preferences.[13] Be that as it may in many policy areas, the Fund rarely to almost never imposed capital account liberalization on nations as part of conditionality.[14] Moreover, Abiad and Mody[15] show that various financial reforms in thirty-five countries from 1973 to 1996 (including capital account liberalizations) were uncorrelated with whether a country was in an IMF program.

In contrast, the Fund has long argued that governments, before liberalizing capital accounts, should have sound macroeconomic outcomes. Dreher[16] reports, for example, that reducing external debt appeared in 96 percent of conditionality agreements. Maintaining a positive balance of payments is generally a precondition for a government's capital account liberalization, and we use that indicator as a rough proxy for IMF policy preferences for whether a particular country should liberalize its capital accounts. Consistent with that view, Abiad and Mody (2005) found that balance of payments crises spurred a variety of financial reforms.

[12] See Conway 2004 for a discussion of the fundamental endogeneity of IMF conditionality programs.

[13] Henisz, Zelner, and Guillen 2004 find this to be increasingly the case over time as later beneficiaries of multilateral aid face greater pressures than earlier ones to conform to practices that are also more widespread over time.

[14] Dreher 2002:51, 62 shows that, from 1988 to 1992, capital account liberalization appeared in 18.75 percent of conditionality agreements, and between 1999 and 2001 in only slightly more than 3 percent of conditionality agreements. Beginning with Thailand (August 14, 1997), the IMF has made public the details of the Letters of Intent and the terms of conditionality. We undertook a content search of the hundreds of Letters of Intent from August 1997 to November 2004, and found only seven that mentioned capital account liberalization.

[15] 2005:73. [16] 2002:62.

European Union membership Members of the European Union commit to reducing internal barriers to movements of goods, people, and capital. Capital account liberalization should likely follow, once a nation joins the EU.

Emulation, learning, and competitive pressures

We should also consider that the source of pressure may not simply be coercion, but that learning by policymakers is somehow involved. Moreover, there are different types of learning to consider.

Emulation Nations are influenced by the experiences of neighbors,[17] and we expect capital account policies to follow this pattern. Governments that adopt policy through emulation are assumed to be taking informational shortcuts, without fully assessing the range of available policies and their expected outcomes, or are part of a network of countries where "acceptable policies" are regionally defined. Perhaps this could be characterized as weak learning. We therefore introduce a regional variable for capital account openness to test for emulation. We recognize that governments within regions also have reasons beyond emulation for adopting regionally common, coordinated economic policies.[18]

Learning Capital account liberalization produces complex results. Governments are likely to consider the experience of their near neighbors, and adopt successful, and avoid unsuccessful, policies. Learning, in contrast to emulation, involves progressive rethinking about policies, sometimes involving "natural experiments" (SDG). For learning to take place, there should be plausible reasons of comparability for why states draw on each other's experiences.[19] We explicitly test for informed learning (as opposed to heuristic or political "shortcuts") by interacting regional capital account regulation with regional economic growth, assuming that regional emulation processes can be distinguished from learning with the additional information about economic performance.

Competitive pressures Nations compete with each other for goods and resources. As SDG note, many of the studies of competitive

[17] Simmons 2000.
[18] See e.g. the discussions in Mansfield and Milner 1997 and Abiad and Mody 2005.
[19] SDG; Meseguer 2003.

dynamics have not specified clearly a competition hypothesis where policy changes in one country are linked to those in competitor countries (one exception being Simmons and Elkins 2004). Capital account liberalization offers a reasonably clean test of the competitive linkage hypothesis among countries with structural similarities.[20] We test this by including a variable that measures capital account liberalization for potential export competitors. The measure is analogous to a "potential competitor" indicator, and allows for dynamism in economic relations.

Measuring anti- and pro-capitalist global sentiment

Measuring anti-capitalist sentiment

Anti-capitalist sentiment[21] was widespread in the interwar and immediate postwar periods. Parties committed to anti-capitalist agendas fared well in electoral competition. Moreover, many respected economists doubted the long-term viability of capitalism, particularly internationalized capitalism, as an economic system.[22] Another cycle of anti-capitalist sentiment spread post-Second World War as colonies received independence.

But how do we measure worldwide anti-capitalist sentiment? The difficulty of measuring the force of ideas is legendary. Two problems are particularly salient. First, how do we know which ideas and values are held by whom, when, and where? Second, how forceful are the ideas?

A standard solution to the first problem has been to rely on polling data. This is inadequate for current purposes. Respondents frequently have an incentive to deceive about beliefs, especially beliefs regarded by elites as dangerous.[23] Polling data, moreover, give us few insights about

[20] It might be the case, as Meyer 2004 points out, that "[t]he idea that interaction might diffuse differentiated or oppositional roles, is not considered, though it can certainly happen in the world." Fortunately, for our study, capital account liberalization and its alternatives (relative degrees of closure) are not complementary states that might induce one set of countries to adopt policies opposite to those of possible competitors. We can imagine several possibilities, such as differences in industrial policy, which could give rise to conscious differentiation.

[21] We make a distinction between our conceptualization of anti-capitalist sentiment and other associated sentiments such as anti-globalization, anti-Americanism (Stiglitz 2002), or anti-protectionism (see Rodrik 1995, 1997; Scheve and Slaughter 2001). Anti-capitalist sentiment, for our purposes, is not as all-encompassing an idea as anti-globalization, as chauvinistic as anti-Americanism, or an idea that primarily targets trade. The principal reaction of anti-capitalist sentiment is that of opposition to the free flows of international capital.

[22] Keynes 1933 and Schumpeter 1942 were prominent examples.

[23] See Bonardi and Keim 2002.

the influence of reported beliefs on government policies. More to the point, we have been unable to find relevant polls on sentiments about capitalism, with consistent questionnaires, offering sufficient cross-sectional and temporal data points to allow an econometric study.

One solution to both problems has been to observe behavior in political and economic markets in settings where actors have choices and privacy is protected. Simply put, voting results give us some insight into the political beliefs of individuals. Because political markets are contested in democracies, we can expect widely held beliefs to influence public policy.[24]

Many political parties have, at varying times and places, adopted anti-capitalism as part of their electoral platform. One political party stands out, however, as having had a consistent line through time and space, particularly about international capital movements. As shown below, one of the world's leading agents of globalization, the Communist Party of the Soviet Union, and Soviet-line Communist parties had consistent ideas and values regarding international capitalism.[25]

Other political parties have shown less consistency. While many social democratic parties rhetorically opposed international capitalism, socialist and labor parties tended to liberalize international finance when their countries had abundant highly skilled labor.[26] Right-wing parties often restricted international finance when their domestic capitalists were at an international disadvantage. Indeed, no common pro-free market political party has taken root in multiple countries! Hence, it is harder to answer the related question – how widespread was the global *support* of internationalized capitalism?[27] (We propose a validation test for our measures below that draws on some measures of the spread of free market ideas.)

The ideological consistency of Soviet-line CPs

Anti-international capitalism, rooted in Leninist ideology, was a common doctrine for CPs following the Soviet line, at least through the

[24] For discussions, see Page and Shapiro 1992; Stimson, Mackuen, and Erikson 1995; Wittman 1995.

[25] This was the case, at least, until the 25th International Communist Party Congress in 1989. Italy's CP, however, began its break with the hard-line Soviet position earlier than most other CPs in reaction to the Soviet invasion of Czechoslovakia in 1968.

[26] Quinn and Inclán 1997; Li and Smith 2002.

[27] Not that we, and others, didn't try. We began to collect data on worldwide subscriptions to leading economics journals, and admission to leading economics Ph.D. programs by country of origin. Apart from collection problems, these efforts stumbled against the valid objection that the content of economics as a discipline is itself affected by the global spread of anti-capitalist and pro-capitalist ideas. Please see Chwieroth 2002 for another valiant attempt.

1980s.[28] Lenin, following Hilferding's analysis,[29] understood the export of capital by Western firms to be the key mechanism of First World imperialism. If a nation were to accept the export of Western capital, it sets itself up for, at best, economic colonialism. Leninist theory, hence, proscribes international capital mobility, a motif echoed later by Prebisch and Wallerstein.

More practical than Leninist ideology for solidifying the anti-international capital ideology of the Soviet CP and its follower parties was the autarkic economic system established through Soviet central planning. While scholars have debated about whether the Soviet system required trade autarky,[30] almost everyone agrees that currency inconvertibility and prohibitions on private capital transactions were central to the system. Indeed, the two Soviet bloc members who were also members of the IMF, Poland and Czechoslovakia, either withdrew or were expelled (respectively) over non-compliance with IMF rules mandating the easing of international financial restrictions. Within the Soviet bloc, most retained full capital account restrictions until the 1980s. The Soviet government forbade inward foreign direct investment until January 1987.[31] Not surprisingly, foreign direct investments in the former Soviet bloc nations were zero to negligible.[32]

The former Soviet-bloc nations liberalized international finance in the 1990s. Russia began liberalization in 1990, and had, by 1994, substantially liberalized.[33] None of these developments reflected an ideological change of heart by the Russian CP, however.[34] Many Western European CPs edged away from the Soviet line, with major breaks occurring from the late 1980s into the 1990s. Even so, as of 1993, all CPs continued to rank on the extreme to far left of the Huber and Inglehart (1995) party space location continuum.[35]

Therefore, to measure global anti-capitalist sentiment, we use the percentage of the votes across countries garnered by CPs (hereafter "CP votes"). We include data only from countries where all parties, including the CP (or a renamed subsidiary) have been free to compete

[28] See especially Ch. V, "Export of Capital," in Lenin 1916. [29] 1910.

[30] See LaVigne 1991. [31] See Hart and Dean 1994.

[32] *East European Business Law* 1991.

[33] European Bank for Reconstruction and Development 1994.

[34] In the 1996 election campaign, *The Economist* (June 15, 1996) said of its leader, Gennady Zyuganov, that "Mr Zyuganov thinks Russia must resist being drawn into a world economic system that may leave it dependent on hostile outside forces. The enemy here is the West's 'trading and financial cosmopolitan oligarchy.'"

[35] Their left to right scale ranged from 1 (extreme left) to 10 (extreme right). The sixteen CPs on the 1993 list had a mean ideological spatial position of 2.19. The Ukrainian CP, in power at the time, was the most "rightward" CP, at 3.67, and the CP of France was at the mean. The CP of Brazil was the most left-leaning at 1.33.

in secret balloting from 1949–1952 through 1999.[36] There are twenty-three such countries in the data set.[37]

For the twenty-three countries with home CPs, we expect that their governments will be responsive to changes in home CP vote shares. For those countries, we seek to identify separately the influences of change in global sentiment and change in domestic support for anti-capitalist policies.

Measuring pro-capitalist sentiment

As noted above, it is harder to compile valid measures of pro-capitalist sentiment. Using available data on party manifestos, however, we validate our results regarding our central measure of anti-capitalism. The authors of the Comparative Manifesto Project (CMP) provide content analyses of the party election platforms of more than 150 parties in 20 countries for 56 wide-ranging policy issues.[38] The data from the project begin in a few cases in the 1920s and end as late as 1988. A relatively complete set of data is available from 1945 to the early 1980s.

The CMP authors did not code party platforms on the issue of capital account liberalization. They did, however, include a related survey category on economic affairs, which is "Item 401." Item 401 assesses a party's statement of support for economic liberty, free enterprise, and free trade.[39] (Item 401 is worded "Favorable mentions of

[36] The data are provided in an appendix available from the authors. Let us note some data problems: (1) The German CP was banned for ten years in the late 1950s and early 1960s. Germany's data are excluded, therefore. (2) CPs frequently joined in alliance with other parties. Where, as in the case of Finland in 1991 and 1995, the CP is the dominant partner (of the Left-Wing Alliance), the Left-Wing Alliance's total votes are entered as CP votes. Italy in 1948 and Denmark (Unity List) are treated that way. In other cases, such as Sri Lanka where the CP is a junior partner in the People's Alliance, the CP vote total is entered as zero. The CP of Netherlands (Green Left) is treated this way. (3) CPs frequently fissure. Where the resulting parties describe themselves as loyal to Marxist–Leninist theory, the vote totals are summed. This is the case for India, where the CP of India (pro-Soviet) and the CP-Marxist (pro-Chinese) split in 1964. In Israel, Maki and Rakah are summed. Hadash is treated as the successor party. (4) A few CPs, notably the Vansterpartiet in Sweden and Italy's CP, which was the largest and most successful one in Western Europe, have gradually broken with Leninism. (See their history at www.vansterpartiet.se/ and www.fact-index.com/i/it/italian_communist_party.html.) For the purposes of this paper, they are treated as being a CP.

[37] These are Austria, Belgium, Denmark, Finland, France, Iceland, Ireland, Italy, Luxembourg, Malta, Netherlands, Norway, Sweden, Switzerland, United Kingdom, Australia, New Zealand, Canada, the United States, Israel, India, Japan, and Sri Lanka.

[38] See Budge 1992; Kim and Fording 2003; Volkens 1995.

[39] The project coders count favorable mentions (called "quasi-sentences") of free trade in party manifestos and other sources. These scores are standardized by dividing by the length of the document. Zero represents no positive mention of economic liberty and free enterprise.

free enterprise capitalism, superiority of individual enterprise over state and control systems, favorable mentions of private property rights, personal enterprise and initiative, need for unhampered individual enterprises.")

We use the CMP Item 401 data to construct a "pro-capitalism" indicator. If a party manifesto contains a standardized score of at least "1" in the favorable mention of economic liberty and free markets, we sum its vote share with those of other parties with favorable mentions of economic liberty. Joining vote share data to the CMP data allows us to develop a global measure of the support of pro-capitalist parties. The data for eighteen countries from 1945 to 1980 are available.[40]

Models and methods

Investigative strategy Our general empirical strategy was originally outlined in Dobbin, Garrett, and Simmons.[41] They proposed:

$$LIB_{it} = \beta_1 \sum X_{it-1} + \beta_2 \sum X_{it-1} + \beta_3 \sum LIB_{jt-1} + \mu \qquad (1)$$

where the three determinants of country *i*'s policy choice of capital account liberalization are domestic conditions β_1 at t–1; external shocks β_2 t–1, and the liberalization of policies of j other countries β_3 (trade liberalization, democratization, tax restructuring, etc.) at t–1.

We adapt their model by distinguishing between domestic economic and domestic political conditions (β_1 (economic) at s–1 + β_2 (political, electoral, and previous levels of policy) at s–1) in a five year average panel(s). We explicitly model changes in global sentiment (β_4 at s–1). We also hypothesize that either liberal or illiberal policies can diffuse: change in policy is the dependent variable, and we allow for either liberalization or closure policies by other countries (β_3 at s–1). See Equation 2:

$$\begin{aligned} \Delta Policy_{i,s} = &\beta_1 \sum Economic_{i,s-1} + \beta_2 \sum Political_{i,s-1} \\ &+ \beta_3 \sum Policy_{j,s-1} + \beta_4 \sum WorldViews_{j,s-1} + \mu \end{aligned} \qquad (2)$$

We also allow for the effects of global change in sentiment ($\beta_4 \sum WorldViews_{j,s-1}$) to be diffused through the $\beta_3 \sum Policy_{j,s-1}$ term

[40] The countries for which data are available include Austria, Australia, Belgium, Canada, Denmark, France, Germany, Ireland, Israel, Italy, Japan, Luxembourg, New Zealand, the Netherlands, Norway, Sweden, the United Kingdom, and the United States.

[41] 2003:14.

(as well as others), by assessing the relative contribution of the variables to the common pool of variance among them and the dependent variable, and by using exogeneity tests.

The prospect that international finance might be liberalized could induce economic and political actors to alter their current behavior. Hence, we also estimate a simultaneous model, Equation 3:

$$\begin{aligned}\Delta Policy_{i,s} &= \beta_1 \sum Economic_{i,s} + \beta_2 \sum Political_{i,s} \\ &+ \beta_3 \sum Policy_{j,s} + \beta_4 \sum WorldViews_{j,s} + \mu\end{aligned} \tag{3}$$

Models The base model seeks to explain change in a government's capital account policies from one time period to another. The model incorporates domestic and international political economic variables and ideology measures. We develop a second model that introduces other diffusion mechanism variables. We continue with robustness checks to account for the collapse of the Soviet bloc (by omitting data from the 1990s) and the effects of other conditions (such as unionization rates for non-agricultural workers, factor advantage, and oil shocks).

We use five-year non-overlapping panel data starting at 1955–1959 and continuing to 1995–1999. We employ the notation, $i = 1, 2, \ldots, 82$, and the index s, representing five-year intervals. This means, for example, that $\Delta CAPITAL_{i,s}$ for the $s = 1985$–1989 period is examined using data from the s–$1 = 1980$–1984. Five-year panels are employed both for econometric reasons (discussed below), and in recognition of the uncertainty of the timing of the effects of economic and political variables on a government's regulatory decisions. (For comparison purposes, we also report the results of OLS (ordinary least-squares) models estimated using annual data.)

Our dependent variable is $\Delta CAPITAL$. The key independent variables are the indicators of global sentiment and policy diffusion: changes in global CP vote totals, changes in national CP vote totals, the degree of financial openness of the world's leading economies, a country's balance of payments position, changes in policy within a region, EU accession, the capital account policies of a nation's competitors, and a measure of the economic results of prior liberalization experiences. (See Appendix 5.1.)

Changes in global sentiment are theoretically more relevant in this investigation than levels since we hypothesize that government officials are influenced by changes in global beliefs. Moreover, because variables measured in levels are frequently collinear with other political economy processes, change indicators have more desirable estimation properties.[42]

Other independent variables in the investigation include levels and changes in a country's domestic political economic variables,[43] as well as country fixed effects.[44] The subscript *s* denotes a five-year time period such that, for example, dependent variable data for the 1995–1999 period are examined using independent variables measured in 1990–1994 in an error correction-style model. The base model (Equation 4) is as follows:

$$
\begin{aligned}
\Delta \mathrm{CAP}_{\mathrm{i,S}} = \; & \\
& \beta_0 + \beta_1(\mathit{Capital}_{\mathrm{i,S}-1}) + \beta_2(\mathrm{Growth}_{i,S-1}) + \beta_3(\mathit{Income}_{i,S-1}) \\
& + \beta_4(\Delta \mathit{Investment}_{i,S-1}) + \beta_5(\mathit{Investment}_{i,S-1}) \\
& + \beta_6(\mathit{Population\ Growth}_{i,S-1}) \\
& + \beta_7(\Delta \mathit{Trade\ Openness}_{i,S-1}) + \beta_8(\mathit{Trade\ Openness}_{i,S-1}) \\
& + \beta_9(\mathit{RevolutionsCoups}_{i,S-1}) + \beta_{10}(\Delta \mathit{Democracy}_{i,S-1}) \\
& + \beta_{11}(\mathit{Democracy}_{i,S-1}) \\
& + \beta_{12}(\Delta \mathrm{WorldCPVote5}_{\Sigma j,S-1}) + \beta_{13}(\Delta \mathrm{HomeCPVote5}_{i,S-1}) \\
& + \beta_{14}(\mathrm{Time\ Trend}) \\
& + \beta_{15,\,16\ldots}(\mathrm{Country\ Dummy\ Variables}) + \varepsilon_{\mathrm{i,S}} \\
& i = 1, 2, \ldots, 82;\ s = 1955-1959, .., 1995-1999. \qquad (4)
\end{aligned}
$$

We also estimate models where the party manifesto free enterprise measures[45] – ß12(WorldFreeEcon$5_{\sum j,s-1}$) + β_{13}(HomeFreeEcon$5_{i,s-1}$) –

[42] One way of measuring the collinearity among variables is to examine a variable's Variance Inflation Factor (VIF) in a multivariate regression. The VIF for CP vote totals in levels on other variables in the models reported below is 47.2, whereas the VIF for CP vote in changes is 3.09.

[43] We use an error correction representation for the economic variables to allow for short-term vs. longer term economic effects: a wealthy nation, for example, might have a long-run tendency toward financial openness, but a short-term growth shock might have an independent, contrary effect in the same country. Trade and investment are treated similarly with levels and changes. Unit roots tests (Augmented Dickey-Fuller and Phillips-Perron, available from the authors) reject the null hypotheses of a unit root in these (logged) economic data.

[44] The Hausman test for the appropriateness of fixed vs. random effects strongly rejected the random effects models. The sample analyzed is, in any event, the full sample of all the data that are available.

[45] This variable is not expressed in changes because its construction contains information about the changing platform content of parties. The variable also contains little information overlap with other independent variables.

replace the CP Vote measures.[46] To the base model, we add measures of variables meant to capture diffusion processes described in DGS (2003):

$$\beta_{15}\,(\text{FiveCap5}_{S-1}) + \beta_{16}(\text{EU Membership}_{i,S-1}) + \beta_{17}\,(\text{Regional Capital Policies}_{j,S-1}) + \beta_{18}\,(\text{Competitor Capital Policies}_{j,S-1}) + \beta_{19}\,(\text{Balance of Payments}_{i,S-1}) + \beta_{20}\,(\text{Capital Account Liberalization}* \text{Economic Growth for Regional Neighbors}_{j,S-1}) \qquad (5)$$

Regression methods Most models are fixed effects models estimated with OLS. We report panel-corrected standard errors. None of the independent variables in Equation 4 are contemporaneous with the dependent variable.

The OLS estimations are potentially plagued by several methodological problems, including multicollinearity (discussed below), serial correlation,[47] and possible endogeneity in the relationships between capital account liberalization and several independent variables. Five-year lags in independent variables attenuate the possible endogeneity bias.

To further address endogeneity concerns, we also use the Generalized Method of Moments system estimator (GMM-SYS) proposed in Arellano and Bover (1995) and Blundell and Bond (1998).[48] GMM-SYS models use internal instruments to account for endogenous relationships, and also employ information from the fixed effects.[49]

The base GMM-SYS model (Equation 6) is:

[46] The panel correlation between ΔCPVote$5_{\sum}$ and FreeEcon$5_{\sum}$ is $-.66$.

[47] We assess serial correlation in the OLS models by computing the residuals of a model, and running a model with the lagged residuals on the residuals.

[48] All dynamic panel modeling is done using *PCGive 10* with GMM models with levels and differences.

[49] For a discussion and application of GMM-SYS models, see Eichengreen and Leblang 2003. The GMM-SYS estimation combines transformed and level equations. The model explicitly treats all the independent variables as endogenous, and uses internal instruments and fixed effects to account for these endogenous relationships. The instruments for the transformed equation are lags 2 through 5 of the right-hand-side variables. The instruments for the levels equations are lag one of the right-hand-side variables and the country fixed effects. Lags of *CAPITAL* are explicitly modeled, and for this variable, the GMM levels lags are set to two, and the GMM lags are 3 . . . 5. Fixed effects are entered as GMM level instruments. The diffusion variables are treated as being endogenous.

$$\Delta \mathrm{CAP}_{\mathrm{i,S}} = \beta_0 + \beta_1 \Delta \mathit{Capital}_{\mathrm{i,S}-1}[\beta_1 \Delta \mathit{Capital}_{\mathrm{i,S}-2}] + \beta_2(\Delta \mathrm{Growth}_{i,S}) + \beta_3 \Delta(\mathit{Income}_{i,S}) + \beta_4(\Delta \mathit{Investment}_{i,s}) + \beta_6(\Delta \mathit{Population\ Growth}_{i,s}) + \beta_7(\Delta \mathit{Trade\ Openness}_{i,s}) + \beta_9(\Delta \mathit{RevolutionCoups}_{i,s}) + \beta_{10}(\Delta \mathit{Democracy}_{i,s}) + \beta_{12}(\Delta \mathrm{Global\ CPVote}_{\Sigma j,s}) + \beta_{12}(\Delta \mathrm{Home\ Country\ CPVote}_{i,s}) + \beta_{13}(\mathrm{Time\ Trend}) + \varepsilon_{\mathrm{i,S}}\ i = 1, 2 \ldots, 82;\ s = 1955\text{–}1959, .., 1995\text{–}1999. \quad (6)$$

In the GMM-SYS models, we use either one- or two-period lagged changes, or Δ*Capital(s–1, s–2)* in the GMM system estimation. The need to achieve uncorrelated residuals drives the lag choices.[50]

As with the OLS models, we also estimate GMM-SYS models with the free enterprise manifesto party measures – $\beta_{12}(\Delta \mathrm{FreeEcon}5_{\sum j,s-1}) + \beta_{13}(\Delta \mathrm{FreeEcon}5_{i,s-1})$, as well as models with various diffusion variables entered: β_{14} (ΔFiveCap5_s) + β_{15} (ΔEU Membership $_{i,s}$) + β_{16} (ΔRegional Capital Policies $_{j,s}$) + β_{17} (ΔCompetitor Capital Policies $_{j,s}$) + β_{18} (ΔBalance of Payments $_{i,s}$) + β_{19} (ΔCapital Account Liberalization*Economic Growth for Regional Neighbors $_{j,s}$). These are treated as endogenous to the system, which allows for some of the cross-national correlations to be accounted for in the analysis.

Each methodological approach has strengths and weaknesses.[51] Because of the potential weaknesses of each approach offset each other, we have greatest confidence in results found in both OLS and GMM-SYS models.

Detecting diffusion processes through an analysis of common pool variance As noted above, multicollinearity is a standard problem of multivariate analysis, which occurs when two independent variables

[50] No serial correlation is indicated in GMM-SYS models when the Arellano-Bond test for second-order serial correlation is not significant, and the AR1 test shows evidence of significant negative serial correlation in the differenced residuals. For a discussion, see Doornik and Hendry 2001:69.

[51] In the presence of various forms of endogeneity, OLS coefficient estimates are potentially biased, as Franzese and Hays 2004 point out. However, the validity of IV procedures, including GMM procedures, depends on the investigator finding good instruments for the endogenous explanatory variables. Bound, Jaeger, and Baker 1995 show that in the presence of weak correlation between an instrument and explanatory variables, OLS outperforms IV (e.g. 3SLS) estimations. It is not evident what valid instrument we might use for changes in global public opinion.

are highly correlated. As is well known, the parameters of each variable are calculated based upon the unique variance of each independent variable, X, with the dependent variable, Y, and variation common to X_1 and X_2 and with Y (known as the common pool variance or common variance) is excluded from the estimation of parameters and standard errors. The common pool of variance of X_1 and X_2 with Y is, however, used to calculate the R-square of the regression, useful information that we exploit below.

In most panel time-series investigations, a large common pool of variance (or multicollinearity) is regarded as a moderate to severe nuisance as it impedes the assessment of the hypothesized empirical relationships. Indeed, the generalized methods of moments procedures used here, like all instrumental variable regressions, orthogonalizes the data – or, removes common pool variation.

In this analysis of diffusion, however, the common pool variance of X_1 and X_2 with the dependent variable, instead of being a nuisance, offers an unusual window into assessing possible mechanisms of diffusion. The variation common to two independent variables and Y might be a diffusion mechanism – variable X_1 could covary with variable X_2 because of the influence of X_2 on X_1, either contemporaneously or with some lags. Hence, part of X_1's effects on Y could be due to X_2's effect on X_1.

Putting this in terms of our investigation, we assess whether the effects of change in global sentiment on a nation's capital account policies are diffused through changes in other governments' policies: (1) those of regional partners, (2) competitors, and (3) leading economies. That is, if a home country's policies are influenced by changes in the global climate of opinion, so too should be the policies of other regional governments, which in turn influences home country policies.

To investigate the diffusion of global sentiment through the influence of other countries' policies, we: (1) establish whether there is common variance between X_1 and X_2; (2) test whether, over time, one of the independent variables is exogenous to the other; and (3) most importantly, assess what proportion of the independent effects plus the common pool variance with Y is attributable to X_1 vs. X_2. Regarding the first point, we run an OLS regression of the values of X_1 on X_2 used in the analysis to estimate common variance of X_1 with X_2. We assess exogeneity[52] between X_1 and X_2 by estimating the effects of lagged X_1 on contemporaneous X_2, and vice versa.

[52] Kennedy 1998:92 describes this as a test of "strong exogeneity."

Regarding (3): because an equation's R-square is not affected by multicollinearity among variables,[53] we use an analysis of variance of R-squares of different equations to examine common pool of variance of X_1 and X_2 with Y, and to assess the proportion of adjusted R^2 attributable to which element of a pair of variables.[54] We undertake an analysis of variance by examining Equation 7:

$$\left(R^2_{(\text{model 1})} - R^2_{(\text{model 3})}\right) / \left(R^2_{(\text{model 2})} - R^2_{(\text{model 3})}\right) \tag{7}$$

compared to Equation 8:

$$\left(R^2_{(\text{model 4})} - R^2_{(\text{model 3})}\right) / \left(R^2_{(\text{model 2})} - R^2_{(\text{model 3})}\right) \tag{8}$$

where model 3 omits both X_1 and X_2 variables but includes all others, model 2 includes both X_1 and X_2 variables and all others, model 1 omits only X_2 (e.g. Δ *World CP Vote Share*), and model 4 omits only X_1 (e.g. *Regional Average of Capital Account Openness*). The closer the value of an equation approaches to 1, the *lesser* the contribution of the *omitted* variable to both the explanatory power of the overall model and the variance in the dependent variable due to the common pool variance of the two independent variables. In contrast, the closer the value of an equation approaches zero, the *greater* the contribution of the *omitted* variable to both the explanatory power of the overall equation and the variance in the dependent variable due to the common variance of the two indepedent variables. (We give a numerical example below.)

Results

Are CPs ideologically homogenous on international economic liberalization?

We first assess a starting assumption of our project, which is that CPs were ideologically homogenous regarding economic liberty and international economic affairs among themselves, but different when compared with other types of parties. On Item 401, party manifesto codings are available for eight CPs.[55] In order to assess the degree of ideological

[53] The R-square is generally computed as the explained variation of the dependent variable from all of the independent variables together (accounting for both unique and common variation of variables) to the total variation.

[54] We thank Keith Ord for discussions about strategies for handling common pool variance, and for suggesting the analysis of variance approach. Any errors are the responsibility of Dennis Quinn, not his.

[55] Denmark, France, Israel, Italy, Japan, Luxembourg, Norway, and Sweden.

homogeneity on international economic issues, we match the manifesto data for these eight CPs to those for left, right, and center parties in the same countries over the same periods of time.[56] We ask whether the average number of favorable mentions of economic liberty differs by type of party or by country or both.

Table 5.1a assigns parties into Communist, left, right, and center groupings.[57] Seven countries have left, right, center, and CPs with data for Item 401. (Luxembourg had no "right" party, and is not included in the first part of the analysis.) The analysis of variance rejects cross-national variation as a source of variability in the data. In contrast, type of party is highly statistically significant, which implies that the main differences within the party manifesto data on Item 401 are partisan and ideological, not national.

In Table 5.1b, we undertake pairwise analyses of variance to assess whether CPs in eight countries differ in terms of support of Item 401 from left, right, and center parties. The analysis strongly supports the claim that the CPs show great ideological homogeneity in opposition to economic liberty, free enterprise, and free trade during the period of data availability, and that they systematically differed from other types of parties, including other left-wing parties.[58]

We next assess a second key assumption, which is that CP vote totals are useful in revealing shifts in public opinion preferences either for or against economic liberalism. We examine the contemporaneous within-country correlation of votes for CPs compared to votes for parties supporting Item 401 within those countries where both sets of data are available.[59] If we observe a negative, statistically significant correlation between CP votes and votes for liberalizing parties, we propose that CP voting reflects changes in policy preferences for the political spectrum. If, in contrast, we observe a positive, statistically significant correlation,

[56] We used Huber and Inglehart 1995 ideological spectrum rankings to group parties into left, right, and center groupings, and supplemented their analysis with data from Swank's party grouping data set, described below.

[57] The assignment of ideological grouping is primarily taken from Swank's "Codebook for 21-Nation Pooled Time-Series Data Set" accessed at www.marquette.edu/polisci/Swank.htm, which is based on Castles and Mair 1984. Israel's parties are assigned according to data found in Krayem (n.d.), and www.country-data.com/cgi-bin/query/r-6788.html, in Appendix B.

[58] Left and center parties differed from each other at a statistically significant level, with center parties showing greater support for free enterprise. Center and right of center parties, however, did not differ at statistically significant levels.

[59] These countries are Australia, Austria, Belgium, Canada, Denmark, France, Ireland, Israel, Italy, Japan, the Netherlands, New Zealand, Norway, Sweden, the United Kingdom, and the United States. The panels are the five-year averages used in this investigation, the correlations are for within country, the series are from 1945 (or earliest available) to 1979, and $n = 108$.

Table 5.1a. *National differences or ideological differences in free trade positions?*

SUMMARY	Types of parties	Sum of mentions	Average mentions	Variance
Denmark	4	8.770277	2.192569	6.154963
France	4	5.424834	1.356209	2.427759
Israel	4	2.141722	0.53543	0.269268
Italy	4	5.525975	1.381494	1.641198
Japan	4	0.313043	0.078261	0.024499
Norway	4	15.35487	3.838718	41.65522
Sweden	4	18.28731	4.571828	39.98022
CPItem401	7	0.425424	0.060775	0.017612
LeftItem401	7	1.649063	0.23558	0.026661
CenterItem401	7	16.40776	2.343966	2.83335
RightItem401	7	37.33578	5.333684	33.18738

ANOVA

Source of variation	SS	df	MS	F	*p*-value
Countries	66.66812	6	11.11135	1.335839	0.292361
Types of parties	126.7375	3	42.24584	5.078917	0.0101
Error	149.7219	18	8.317883		
Total	343.1275	27			

Table 5.1b. *F-test of the hypothesis that means from two or more samples are equal (mean positive mentions of free trade in party manifestos; CPs compared to other national parties by ideology type)*

	F	*p*-value
Communist parties vs. left parties	6.841	0.02**
Communist parties vs. center parties	16.174	0.001***
Communist parties vs. right parties	6.755	0.02**
Left parties vs. center parties	13.479	0.003***
Center parties vs. right parties	2.068	0.174
Right parties vs. left parties	6.275	0.026**

* *p*-value <.10
** *p*-value <.05
*** *p*-value <.01.

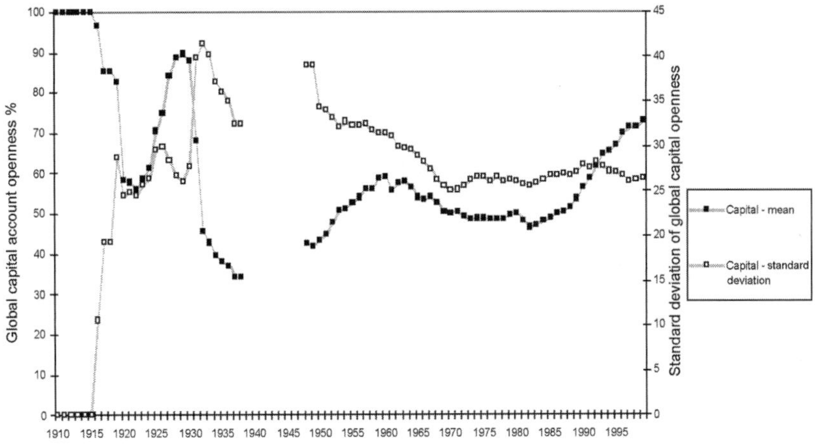

Figure 5.1 The global level of capital account openness, mean and standard deviation, 1910–1999

increases in both CP voting and voting for parties supporting international economic liberalization might instead reflect a political polarization. The Pearson's *r* between the two series is − .21, which is statistically beyond the .05 level using a two-tailed test. These results, combined with the above result on CP ideological homogeneity versus other parties, suggest that changes in CP voting provide information about changing voter preferences regarding international capitalism.

Means and standard deviations of CAPITAL

Figure 5.1 shows worldwide means and standard deviations by year from 1910 to 1999 for levels of capital account openness as measured by *CAPITAL*. Seven distinct periods are evident, four of which are beyond the scope of this chapter: universal openness to 1914, partial closure during wartime and reconstruction (1915 to 1922), liberalization and a return to the gold standard (1923 to 1929), and deepening closure during the depression (1930 to 1937).[60]

The late 1940s through 1960 was a period of liberalization, with some of the largest postwar increases in the annual global mean occurring in the early to mid-1950s. The 1960s through the early 1980s, in contrast, were characterized by a retreat from international financial openness, as

[60] See Quinn 2003 for a discussion of the 1890 to 1937 period.

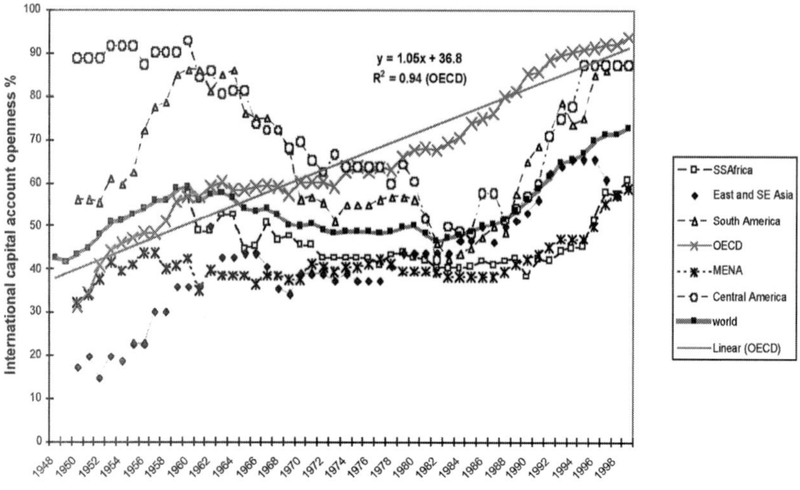

Figure 5.2 Mean levels of capital account openness by region, 1948–1999

were – more sharply – the 1930s. Unlike the 1930s, however, but like the 1950s, the closure from 1961 to the early 1980s was accompanied by decreases in the annual standard deviation of *CAPITAL*. The smallest post-Second World War values of the standard deviation are for 1969 to 1972, and the three next low values are found in 1981, 1982, and 1983. The early 1980s are associated with the lowest global mean values of *CAPITAL* since 1951. In the 1960s through the early 1980s, it was financial *closure* that diffused worldwide.

The mid-1980s through the 1990s are widely described as a period of liberalization, and accurately so. Not since 1929 and 1930 had the world been so open to international capital transactions as it was in the late 1990s. The global standard deviation, while not as low as that for the early 1970s and 1980s, also decreased.

Figure 5.2 overlays the global means in *CAPITAL* with regional trend lines, and these regional trends show very different patterns of liberalization and closure over time. Only among OECD member nations is there anything like a steady linear trend toward liberalization in international financial openness.[61]

[61] A simple linear trend line with a coefficient of 1.05 explains 94 percent of the variance in the mean among OECD member nations.

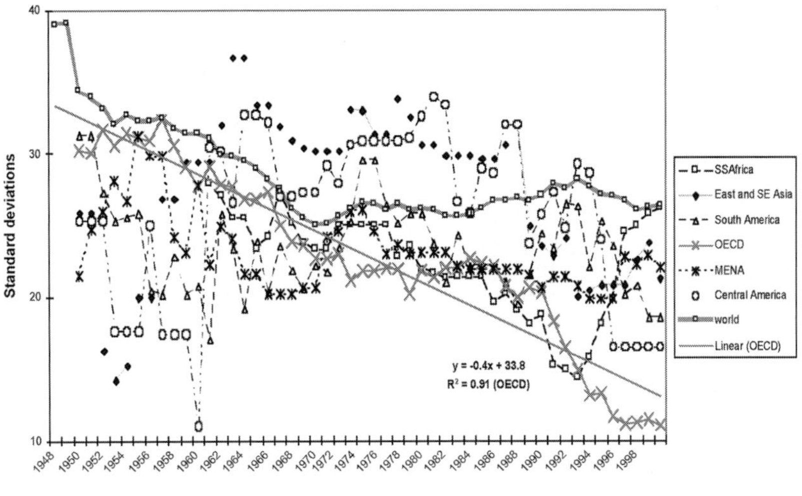

Figure 5.3 Standard deviations of capital account openness by region, 1948–1999

Figure 5.3 overlays the global annual standard deviation in *CAPITAL* with similar annual regional standard deviations. Again, the OECD experience is unique in that the within region standard deviation has steadily and incrementally fallen over time.[62] The divergence in the behavior of the standard deviation data is not just across space but also time. The Appendix Figure 5.4 divides the post-Second World War annual standard deviations for *CAPITAL* into two periods, 1948 to 1970, and 1971 to 1999. The first several decades showed marked decreases in annual standard deviations. But, with the collapse of the Bretton Woods regime, the post-1970 trend has generally been flat or slightly increasing, suggesting a continuing diversity in international financial regulatory policies during this era of liberalization.

Regression results

Our main interest is estimating the effects of diffusion and global ideology variables on capital account liberalization. In Table 5.2, we present three fixed-effects models: one for the full sample of 82 nations (2.1), another

[62] A linear trend with a coefficient of – .4 explains 91 percent of the variance in annual standard deviations over time.

Table 5.2. *Base models. Dependent variable = change in capital account regulation (ΔCAP). Unbalanced panel estimated using OLS with panel correct standard errors*

Variable	A. Communist Party votes, 1955–1999			B. Party manifesto (PM) support of free enterprise, 1955–1984		
	Model 2.1	Model 2.2	Model 2.3	Model 2.4	Model 2.5	Model 2.6
	Full sample 82 nations	61 nations with no CP	21 nations with a CP	Full sample	Countries with no PM data	Countries with PM data
Capital (S–1)	– 0.439***	– 0.502***	– 0.325***	– 0.586***	– 0.603***	– 0.526***
	(0.044)	(0.053)	(0.059)	(0.056)	(0.063)	(0.097)
Growth (S–1)	– 0.077	– 0.107	0.399	– 0.741***	– 0.838***	0.534
	(0.241)	(0.261)	(0.560)	(0.290)	(0.299)	(0.781)
Income (S–1)	– 1.30	– 0.402	4.763	17.533***	21.594***	7.303
(Per capita, PPP-adjusted)	(3.149)	(3.414)	(6.050)	(4.519)	(4.649)	(11.630)
Change in investment (S–1)	0.973*	1.381**	– 0.759	1.406**	1.681**	– 0.122
	(0.541)	(0.621)	(1.018)	(0.626)	(0.729)	(1.367)
Level of investment (s–1) (share of GDP)	– 0.602	0.017	– 4.153	6.065**	8.957***	– 5.169
	(1.981)	(2.160)	(4.992)	(2.853)	(2.991)	(13.000)
Population growth (s–1)	– 2.553***	– 2.915**	0.618	– 6.000***	– 7.820***	0.770
	(1.039)	(1.226)	(1.572)	(1.550)	(1.913)	(3.353)
Change in openness (s– 1)	– 0.067	– 0.091	0.143	– 0.500*	– 0.589**	2.307
	(0.169)	(0.176)	(0.723)	(0.269)	(0.287)	(1.652)
Level of trade openness (s– 1)	5.002**	5.086**	– 10.205**	4.262	– 0.989	– 10.691**
	(2.001)	(2.248)	(4.849)	(3.187)	(3.387)	(5.215)
Revolutions and coups (s– 1)	0.671	0.676	0.615	– 0.178	– 0.071	
	(0.533)	(0.601)	(0.792)	(0.588)	(0.611)	
ΔDemocracy (s– 1)	0.271	0.371**	2.451*	0.259	0.319	
	(0.187)	(0.192)	(1.498)	(0.233)	(0.235)	
Level of democracy (s– 1)	0.458***	0.566***	0.222	0.081	0.033	
	(0.176)	(0.182)	(1.307)	(0.272)	(0.268)	

Change in vote share of home Communist Party, s–1	**– 0.976***** **(0.320)**		**– 1.263***** **(0.319)**			
Change in vote share of Communist parties, s–1 (**ΔCPVote5$_s$**)	**– 9.410***** **(1.421)**	**– 10.108***** **(1.460)**	**– 3.385**** **(1.520)**			
Home CP countries*change in vote share of Communist parties, s-1 **(HomeCP*ΔCPVote5$_s$)**	**4.787**** **(1.987)**					
Free enterprise support worldwide, s-1				**0.286*** **(0.167)**	0.232 (0.169)	**0.604*** **(0.321)**
Domestic free enterprise support, s-1				**0.176*** **(0.099)**		**0.181**** **(0.082)**
Interaction term (free enterprise support worldwide*dummy/ countries with manifesto data)				– 0.188 (0.327)		
Time trend	0.135 (0.086)	0.030 (0.098)	0.435*** (0.152)	– 0.969*** (0.157)	– 1.227 (0.168)	0.324 s(0.416)
Adj. R^2	40.82%	46.83	37.44%	53.82%	55.11%	54.42%
Number of countries	82	61	21	78	63	15
Number of observations	621	437	184	382	295	87

* *p*-value <.10
** *p*-value <.05
*** *p*-value <.01.

for the 61 nations without CPs that have competed continuously in elections ("no home CPs," 2.2), and a third for 21 nations with continuous home CPs ("home CPs," 2.3). Models 2.1 and 2.2 show broadly consistent signs and levels of statistical significance for the coefficients, but Model 2.3, which looks only at the home CP sample, shows some differences in parameter estimates. Our key variable, the coefficients for change in the vote share of CPs worldwide, is negatively and statistically significantly associated with capital account liberalization in all three models. The coefficients for change in home country CP are also negative and statistically significant in the two relevant models. The interaction term for the effects of world CP votes in countries with a home CP has a positive and statistically significant term, which indicates that the slope estimates differ. The world CP vote share has a negative and statistically significant effect in countries with a home CP, but the estimated coefficient is a third to half the size of the coefficients in the other model. The democracy variables, consistent with previous findings, are positive and statistically significant. (We treat the other domestic economic and political variables as control variables and limit our discussion of these variables.)

For comparison purposes, we re-estimate Models 2.1, 2.2, and 2.3 with annual data where the independent variables are lagged one year. (Please see Appendix Table 5.7). The coefficient estimates for global CP vote remain negative and statistically significant at the .1 level or beyond in all three models with annual data. The home CP vote share variables remain negative and statistically significant at beyond the .01 level. The level of a nation's democracy score remains a positive and highly statistically significant influence on its subsequent capital account liberalization.[63]

Table 5.2 Models 2.4 through 2.6, re-estimate Models 2.1, 2.2, and 2.3, substituting the "pro-capitalist" global and domestic opinion indicators for the anti-capitalist indicators. The "pro-capitalist" indicators are positive and statistically significant at the .1 level in the overall model combining types of countries (Model 2.4). In the model including countries without party manifesto data (Model 2.5), the pro-capitalist indicator is not statistically significant, but is correctly signed and larger than its standard error. In the models using data for countries with party

[63] We also estimate a model where the dependent variable is annual change in the global mean of *CAPITAL*, and the regressors are the global values of most of the variables used in Appendix Table 5.7. Despite few degrees of freedom, the adjusted R-square of the regression is 36.7 percent, and change in world CP vote has a statistically significant t-stat of – 1.756. Results available on request.

manifesto data, the pro-capitalist sentiment indicators are both positive and statistically significant. These results suggest that the results of the analysis are not driven by choice of ideology measure.

In Table 5.3, we re-examine the six models from Table 5.2 using system GMM estimation methods. We report one-step GMM-system with robust standard errors and fixed effects. The diagnostic statistics are good. The disturbances show no sign of serial correlation, and the Sargan test fails to reject the null hypothesis of the validity of the instruments. The joint Wald-test and adj. R^2 indicate that the model explains much of the variance in growth.

The results once again show that world CP vote has a negative and significant coefficient in all three models. The coefficient estimates are substantially smaller and the standard errors are somewhat larger compared to the OLS estimates (as expected for GMM-system estimations). The estimated effects of home country CP vote share continues to be negative and statistically significant. This confirms again that governments in democratic societies respond directly to voter sentiment as measured by home CP.

The GMM-SYS pro-capitalist indicators show a very similar substantive result to the companion OLS indicators. As the global support for parties favoring "free enterprise" increases, governments appear to have increasingly liberalized their capital accounts in all three models (3.4, 3.5, and 3.6). The coefficient estimate for the variable indicating increasing domestic support for free enterprise is not statistically significant in the overall model (Model 3.4), but is positive and highly statistically significant in the more relevant model (3.6), which restricts the analysis to the countries with domestic parties where Item 401 is present in party manifesto data.

In Table 5.4, we used OLS-PCSE methods, and entered the diffusion variables to the base models in Table 5.2. Global CP vote share and home CP vote share continue to have negative and highly statistically significant coefficient estimates. The indicator of the capital account policies of the leading economies has a negative and highly statistically significant coefficient in all three models – a result utterly at odds with the coercion hypothesis, but fully consistent with a constructivist understanding. Regional capital account openness has a positive and statistically significant coefficient in two models, and is near statistical significance in the third, lending support for the regional emulation hypothesis. The interaction term between capital account openness and economic growth in neighboring countries is positive and statistically significant, suggesting that nations adapted their policies in light of the successes and failures of neighboring countries.

Table 5.3. *GMM-system estimator, dependent variable = ΔCAPITAL models with CP vote and free enterprise variables*

	A. Communist Party votes, 1955–1999			B. Party manifesto support of free enterprise, 1955–1979		
	Model 3.1	Model 3.2	Model 3.3	Model 3.4	Model 3.5	Model 3.6[1]
Variable	All countries	Countries without home CPs	Countries with home CPs	All countries	Countries without manifesto data	Countries with manifesto data
ΔCAPITALt− 1	-0.277^{***} (0.075)	-0.333^{***} (0.087)	*Variable omitted because of correlated residuals*	*Variable omitted because of correlated residuals*	*Variable omitted because of correlated residuals*	0.067 (0.105)
ΔCAPITALt−2	-0.246^{***} (0.059)	-0.220^{***} (0.062)	-0.469^{***} (0.060)	-0.4661^{***} (0.054)	-0.449^{***} (0.074)	-0.356^{***} (0.102)
ΔGROWTH	0.637^{**} (0.252)	0.797 (0.241)	−0.244 (0.434)	0.144 (0.453)	0.0492 (0.463)	3.064^{**} (1.233)
ΔINCOME (PER CAPITA, PPP-ADJUSTED)	3.897 (3.577)	1.835 (3.415)	14.406^{*} (8.465)	18.052^{***} (6.472)	17.701^{***} (6.460)	11.919^{*} (6.145)
ΔINVESTMENT	−0.840 (2.768)	1.516 (2.902)	-10.451^{**} (4.585)	−1.910 (4.834)	3.719 (4.880)	-13.538^{***} (3.579)
ΔPOPULATION GROWTH	−0.575 (0.937)	−0.913 (1.059)	2.349 (2.278)	0.785 (2.057)	0.533 (2.482)	−0.256 (1.231)
ΔTRADE OPENNESS (IMPORTS + EXPORTS)/ GDP	7.504^{***} (1.995)	6.312^{***} (2.224)	−3.493 (4.079)	6.559^{*} (3.828)	3.285 (3.801)	2.612 (2.417)
ΔREVOLUTIONS and COUPS	0.037 (0.684)	−0.151 (0.734)	1.174 (0.971)	−0.048 (0.790)	0.239 (0.890)	1.507 (1.043)
ΔDemocracy	−0.231 (0.317)	0.112 (0.260)	1.093 (1.592)	−0.687 (0.435)	−0.528 (0.404)	2.271 (3.067)
Δ EU membership			7.758^{**} (3.667)			

Δ*Communist Party vote share worldwide*	**−6.500***** **(1.410)**	**−7.920***** **1.757**	**−2.029**** **(1.017)**			
Δ *Domestic Communist Party vote share*	**−1.252**** **(0.622)**		**−0.768**** **(0.358)**			
Free enterprise support worldwide				**0.416***** **(0.161)**	**0.357*** **(0.188)**	**1.120***** **(0.290)**
Domestic free enterprise support				**−0.010** **(0.084)**		**0.109*** **(0.052)**
Time trend	−0.297**	−0.451***	−0.038	−0.667***	−0.805***	0.186
	(0.139)	(0.171)	(0.268)	(0.228)	(0.236)	(0.243)
Adj. R^2	54.46%	51.50%	54.71%	52.36%	55.86%	42.56%
Wald (joint)	244.3**	240.5***	182. 8**	214.3**	55.47**	2064.0**
AR1	−3.371**	−2.522*	−3.623**	−3.640**	−3.380**	2.499*
AR2	−0.686	−0.215	1.008	−1.457	−1.522	0.7454
Sargan	93.29	46.05	7.766	358.9	52.23	3.571
	[1.000]	[1.000]	[1.000]	[0.691]	[1.000]	[1.000]
Number of countries	80	59	21	80	64	16

Note: All models, except where noted, are fixed effects models. The results are from the 1-step estimations except the Sargan test and AR1/AR2 tests, which are taken from the 2-step estimations. The R-square is defined as 1–rss/tss. Estimates in Tables 5.3 and 5.5 are based on Blundell and Bond, 1998. A negative and statistically significant AR1 term plus a statistically insignificant AR2 term indicates NO serial correlation.

[1]Model 3.6 is a random effects model. There are too few degrees of freedom for fixed effects.

* p-value <.10

** p-value <.05

*** p-value <.01.

Table 5.4. *Models with diffusion variables, dependent variable = change in capital account regulation (ΔCAP)*

	A. Communist Party votes, 1955–1999			B. Party manifesto support of free enterprise, 1955–1984		
	Model 4.1	Model 4.2	Model 4.3	Model 4.1b	Model 4.2b	Model 4.3b
Variable	Full model with full sample	Full model no CP countries	Full model for HomeCP countries	Full sample	Countries with no PM data	Countries with data
Capital (s −1)	$-.499^{***}$	-0.534^{***}	-0.376^{***}	-0.660^{***}	-0.692^{***}	-0.399^{***}
	(0.048)	(0.059)	(0.057)	(0.061)	(0.068)	(0.099)
Growth (s −1)	−0.124	−0.170	0.074	-0.739^{***}	-0.733^{**}	0.154
	(0.237)	(0.261)	(0.581)	(0.296)	(0.309)	(0.823)
Income (s −1)	−3.264	−2.787	6.509	14.324^{***}	18.702^{***}	-34.955^{*}
(Per capita, PPP-adjusted)	(3.008)	(3.440)	(5.867)	(4.552)	(4.979)	(18.06)
Change in investment (s −1)	1.256^{**}	1.300^{**}	0.340	1.838^{***}	1.847^{***}	1.227
	(0.534)	(0.627)	(0.977)	(0.633)	(0.725)	(1.136)
Level of investment (s −1) (share of	1.423	1.394	0.154	6.903^{**}	8.983^{***}	−7.522
GDP)	(1.929)	(2.102)	(5.065)	(2.921)	(3.036)	(10.09)
Population growth (s −1)	-3.412^{***}	-2.900^{*}	−1.948	-6.233^{***}	-6.236^{***}	−2.6557
	(1.169)	(1.619)	(1.760)	(1.473)	(1.824)	3.341
Change in openness (s −1)	−0.272	−0.269	0.124	-0.849^{***}	-0.790^{***}	0.206
	(0.170)	(0.177)	(0.709)	(0.272)	(0.283)	(1.822)
Level of trade openness (s −1)	2.961	4.144^{*}	−4.549	2.315	−0.058	22.789^{**}
	(2.087)	(2.271)	(5.057)	(3.357)	(3.458)	(12.10)
Revolutions and coups (s−1)	0.613	0.683	0.469	−0.118	−0.004	
	(0.510)	(0.588)	(0.761)	(0.586)	(0.630)	
ΔVote share of Home CP, s −1	$\mathbf{-0.951}^{***}$		$\mathbf{-1.160}^{***}$			
	(0.323)		**(0.331)**			
ΔVote share of global Communist parties, $_{s-1}$ **(ΔCPVote5$_s$)**	$\mathbf{-11.019}^{***}$	$\mathbf{-11.469}^{***}$	$\mathbf{-4.964}^{***}$			
	(1.475)	**(1.637)**	**(1.538)**			

Countries with Home CPs*Δ**CPVote5$_s$**	4.686**					
	(1.858)					
ΔLevel of **DEMOCRACY(ΔDem5$_{s-1}$)**	0.261	0.303	−0.403	0.141	0.1593	
	(0.183)	(0.194)	(1.688)	(0.235)	(0.238)	
Level of *DEMOCRACYs−1*	0.375**	0.417**	−1.838	0.003	−0.062	
	(0.177)	(0.206)	(1.488)	(0.281)	(0.280)	
Free enterprise support worldwide				**0.273***	0.241	**0.246**
				(0.166)	(0.170)	**(0.291)**
Domestic free enterprise support				**0.125***		**0.117****
				(0.077)		**(0.059)**
Interaction term (free enterprise support worldwide*dummy/ countries with manifesto data)				−0.104		
				(0.282)		
CA openness 5 leading economies	−0.667***	−0.747***	−0.396***	−0.246**	−0.129	−0.519**
	(0.112)	(0.164)	(0.145)	(0.122)	(0.147)	(0.213)
European Union	2.392	5.020	−1.991	9.563***	2.003	−0.605
	(2.565)	(5.159)	(3.236)	(3.697)	(6.757)	(4.135)
Regional CA openness	0.244***	0.135	0.256***	0.309***	0.224**	0.367**
	(0.062)	(0.092)	(0.093)	(0.088)	(0.103)	(0.164)
CA openness of competitors	−0.050	0.108	−0.290***	−0.011	0.070	−0.312*
	(0.068)	(0.108)	(0.098)	(0.088)	(0.110)	(0.161)
Balance of payments	7.400	2.954	21.054	20.332	28.259	−7.744
	(10.93)	(12.980)	(21.07)	(16.11)	(21.84)	(27.59)
ΔCA openness*growth	0.0273**	0.027*	0.040**	0.047***	0.047***	0.088**
	(0.0125)	(0.015)	(0.018)	(0.014)	(0.016)	(0.026)
Time trend	0.748***	0.733***	0.483***	−0.644***	−0.947***	1.014***
	(0.125)	(0.179)	(0.182)	(0.204)	(0.240)	(0.473)
Adj. R2	45.90%	47.09%	47.85%	57.11%	57.54%	65.83%
Number of countries/obs	81/612	60/428	21/184	77/374	63/293	14/81

*p-value <.10
**p-value <.05
***p-value <.01.

We re-estimate Models 4.1, 4.2, and 4.3, ending the analysis in 1989 and omitting the two former Soviet bloc countries in the data set. The R-square for all three equations increases markedly (to 53.2–56.2 percent), and the coefficient estimates for the CP vote share variables remain stable, negative, and two and a half to nearly six times their standard errors. The other coefficient estimates are similar, except for the democracy indicators, which are no longer statistically significant, and the balance of payments indicator, which is now positive and statistically significant in two models. We re-ran Models 4.1, 4.2, and 4.3 adding oil prices variables, and the results reported here do not change. (Full results are available upon request.)

The OLS models using "free enterprise" global ideology measures, used in Models 4.4, 4.5, and 4.6, show a similar pattern to that found in 4.1, 4.2, and 4.3. Global and domestic support for free enterprise is positively associated with subsequent liberalization. The capital account indicators of the leading economies (negative) and regional neighbors (positive) are associated with subsequent liberalization. The interaction term between *CAPITAL* and economic growth in neighboring countries continues to be positive and statistically significant.

In Table 5.5, we re-examine the models from Table 5.4 using system-GMM estimation. Once again, the world CP vote share has negative and statistically significant coefficients. The indicator for home CP had a negative and statistically significant coefficient in the model restricted to the countries with a home CP, but not in the overall model. The regional emulation indicator had positive and statistically significant coefficients in the overall model and in the no home CP sub-sample. The other state-centered diffusion coefficient estimates are not statistically significant or show no consistent pattern.

The GMM estimations using the free enterprise party manifesto vote total data (Models 5.4, 5.5, and 5.6) indicate that global changes in the support for pro-free trade parties is associated with capital account liberalization. The domestic ideology indicators have positive coefficients, but are not statistically significant. The EU membership coefficients and, in two cases, the regional capital account variables, have positive and statistically significant coefficients.

Common pool variance and diffusion

The results reported above, whether by OLS or by GMM-SYS, report the effects of independent variables that are due only to their unique variation with the dependent variable. We turn now to assessing the common pool

Table 5.5. *GMM-system estimator, dependent variable = ΔCAPITAL full models*

Variable	A. Communist Party votes			B. Party manifesto support of free enterprise		
	Model 5.1	Model 5.2	Model 5.3	Model 5.4	Model 5.5	Model 5.6
	All countries	Countries without Home CPs	Countries with Home CPs	All countries	Countries without manifesto data	Countries with manifesto data
ΔCAPITALt-1	−0.352***	−0.154*				
	(0.082)	(0.079)				
ΔCAPITALt-2	−0.230***	−0.121*	−0.449***	−0.473***	−0.404***	−0.497***
	(0.063)	(0.071)	(0.070)	(0.054)	(0.069)	(0.055)
Δ GROWTH	0.467**	0.404*	−0.409	0.261	0.138	1.973***
	(0.233)	(0.228)	(0.338)	(0.354)	(0.404)	(0.703)
ΔINCOME (PER CAPITA, PPP-ADJUSTED)	4.503	1.205	9.687	7.054	9.543*	10.054**
	(4.003)	(1.449)	(7.735)	(5.485)	(5.667)	(4.982)
ΔINVESTMENT	0.015	0.879	−4.814	2.450	7.503**	−11.058***
	(2.737)	(1.591)	(5.876)	(4.029)	(3.736)	(4.100)
ΔPOPULATION GROWTH	−0.152	−.199	1.688	0.513	0.093	−1.552
	(1.223)	(0.930)	(2.162)	(1.894)	(1.871)	(1.158)
ΔTRADE OPENNESS	4.771**	2.061*	−0.388	4.522	2.365	−2.559*
(IMPORTS + EXPORTS)/GDP	(2.023)	(1.227)	(4.469)	(3.385)	(3.189)	(1.323)
ΔREVOLUTIONS and COUPS	−0.374	−0.312	1.719**	0.271		0.147
	(0.610)	(0.529)	(0.802)	(0.741)		(0.606)
ΔDemocracy	−0.187	0.171*	−0.796	−0.677**		−4.917
	(0.256)	(0.099)	(0.936)	(0.290)		(5.832)
ΔEU membership	7.809	2.179	2.650	12.966**	13.141	7.820***
	(5.188)	(5.049)	(3.831)	(6.220)	(14.440)	(1.875)
ΔOpenness five leading economies	−0.108	0.046	0.029	−0.090	−0.136	0.009
	(0.222)	(0.325)	(0.247)	(0.259)	(0.334)	(0.103)
ΔRegional CA openness	0.239***	0.233***	−0.009	0.242***	0.129	0.226***
	(0.085)	(0.076)	(0.106)	(0.083)	(0.098)	0.060)
ΔCA openness in competitors	0.042	0.032	−0.200	0.155	0.239*	−0.190**
	(0.112)	(0.114)	(0.126)	(0.119)	(0.137)	(0.075)

Table 5.5. (*cont.*)

Variable	A. Communist Party votes			B. Party manifesto support of free enterprise		
	Model 5.1	Model 5.2	Model 5.3	Model 5.4	Model 5.5	Model 5.6
	All countries	Countries without Home CPs	Countries with Home CPs	All countries	Countries without manifesto data	Countries with manifesto data
ΔCA openness*growth	0.017	0.030	−0.059	0.007	0.042	−0.102**
	(0.020)	(0.022)	(0.043)	(0.044)	(0.060)	(0.046)
ΔBalance of payments	−16.018	−13.626*	16.929	32.901	30.453	−4.845
	(11.41)	(7.660)	(15.980)	(20.710)	(18.580)	(25.770)
$\Delta Year_{t-1}$	−0.150	−0.168	−0.104	−0.213	−0.348	−0.172
	(0.174)	(0.242)	(0.308)	(0.274)	(0.320)	(0.188)
ΔCommunist Party vote share world	**−4.289***	**−3.643**	**−3.986**			
	(1.652)	**(1.734)**	**(1.692)**			
Δ Domestic CP vote share	−0.484		**−0.871***			
	(0.616)		**(0.308)**			
Free enterprise support world				**0.402**	**0.295***	**0.696***
				(0.165)	**(0.180)**	**(0.153)**
Domestic free enterprise support				0.072		0.018
				(0.104)		(0.050)
Adj. R^2	51.88%	69.63%	52.09%	50.91%	54.73%	34.55%
Wald (joint)	296.4 **	144.0**	2357.0**	212.0**	130.8**	1057**
AR1	−2.829**	−2.041*	−2.369*	−3.729**	−3.668**	−1.975*
AR2	−1.055	−1.603	−1.383	−1.387	−1.522	0.950
Sargan	60.64	43.03	0.000	401.1	32.95	0.000
Number of obs./parameters	631/97	444/18	187/37	392/94	315/78	82/18

Note: Please see Table 5.3 notes. Model 5.3 has very few degrees of freedom.
* *p*-value <.10
** *p*-value <.05
*** *p*-value <.01.

variation between key independent variables as a means of identifying diffusion processes.

We focus on the pairwise common variation between world CP vote share and other possible diffusion independent variables. In general, world CP vote share is negatively and highly statistically significantly correlated with most of the diffusion variables. Only balance of payments and home CP vote shares fail to show a statistically significant relationship with world CP vote shares across the samples. (Please see Appendix Table 5.8.)

Table 5.6 reports the evidence on attributing common pool variance between pairs of variables. We provide here a numerical example of our procedure using 6.2. (1) World CP vote share and regional average of capital account openness co-vary at a statistically significant level (see Appendix Table 5.8 2b). (2) CP vote share is strongly exogenous to regional capital openness (Table 5.6 2). (3) Omitting world CP vote share gives Equation 7 (above) a value of 0.099 (or (0.4062–0.3991)/(0.4709–0.3991)), and omitting regional average of capital account openness gives Equation 8 (above) a value of 0.96 (or (0.4677–0.3991)/(0.4709–0.3991)). The increase in adj. R^2 from including both variables over excluding both is 7.2 percent (or (0.4709–0.3991)). The ratio of .099 to .96 gives the proportion of the increase in adj. R^2 from including both attributable to regional capital account openness and world CP vote share respectively: 8% (.099/(.099 + .96)) and 92% (.96/(.099 + .96)). That is, the unique contribution of world CP vote share, *plus* the share of the common pool variation attributable to it, is an increase in overall adj. R^2 of 6.6% (.92*7.2), and the unique contribution of regional average of capital account openness, *plus* the share of the common pool variation attributable to it, is an increase in overall adj. R^2 of 0.6% (.08*7.2). Considering the analysis of common pool variance and the exogeneity tests, we can conclude that part of the effect of change in global anti-capitalist sentiment is *diffused through* its effects on regional capital account openness, which then influences a country's capital account liberalization.

The relationship between world CP vote shares and the capital account policies of regional neighbors is characterized by substantial negative common variance and by the exogeneity of CP vote shares (6.1 and 6.3, in addition to 6.2 discussed above). When both variables are in the model, the adjusted R-square of the overall equations increases by between 4.4% and 8.2%. Using the analysis of variance described above, we see that world CP vote shares account for two-thirds to 92% of the increase in R-square from including both variables in the model. Put simply, part of the effects of regional capital account openness on a country's liberalization decisions derive from how regional neighbors have themselves reacted to

Table 5.6. *Assessing indirect effects through common pool variation and exogeneity tests*

Pair of variables with common pool variation	Sample	Exogeneity test (exogenous relationship, if any, in bold)	Adj. R^2 of exogeneity tests	Increase in adj. R^2 when both variables in model over omission of both	Proportion of overall adj. R^2 increase attributable to which variable (dominant element, if any, in bold)?
1. ΔCPVoteShare & Regional Capital Openness	**81**	**ΔCPVoteShare(s– 1) → -RegionalCap** RegionalCap(s– 1) ΔCPVoteShare	**2.8%** 0%	8.2%	**ΔCPVoteShare(s – 1) = 79%** RegionalCap(s– 1)= 21%
2. ΔCPVoteShare & Regional Capital Openness	**60**	**ΔCPVoteShare(s – 1) → -RegionalCap** RegionalCap(s– 1) ΔCPVoteShare	**9.5%** 0%	7.2%	**ΔCPVoteShare(s– 1)= 92%** RegionalCap(s – 1)= 8%
3. ΔCPVoteShare & Regional Capital Openness	**21**	**ΔCPVoteShare(s – 1) → -RegionalCap** RegionalCap(s– 1) ΔCPVoteShare	**14.7%** 0.8%	4.4%	**ΔCPVoteShare(s– 1)= 67%** RegionalCap(s– 1)= 33%
4. ΔCPVoteShare & 5 Country Capital Openness	**81**	ΔCPVoteShare(s– 1)→ -5Capital 5Capital(s– 1) → -ΔCPVoteShare	10.2% 2.0%	7.7%	**ΔCPVoteShare(s– 1)= 77%** 5Capital(s– 1)= 23%
5. ΔCPVoteShare & 5 Country Capital Openness	**60**	ΔCPVoteShare(s – 1)→ -5Capital 5Capital(s – 1) → -ΔCPVoteShare	15.1% 4.8%	7.4%	**ΔCPVoteShare(s– 1)= 82%** 5Capital(s– 1) = 18%
6. ΔCPVoteShare & 5 Country Capital Openness	**21**	**ΔCPVoteShare(s – 1) → -5Capital** 5Capital(s – 1) ΔCPVoteShare	**2.8%** 0.2%	3.9%	**ΔCPVoteShare(s – 1)= 67%** 5Capital(s – 1) = 33%
7. ΔCPVoteShare & Competitor Cap Openness	**81**	**ΔCPVoteShare(s – 1)→ -Competitor Cap**	**24.8%** 0.7%	6.0%	**ΔCPVoteShare(s – 1) = 107%** Competitor Cap(s – 1) =– 7%

		Competitor Cap(s – 1) ΔCPVoteShare			
8. ΔCPVoteShare & Competitor Cap Openness	**60**	**ΔCPVoteShare(s – 1)→ -Competitor Cap** Competitor Cap(s– 1) ΔCPVoteShare	**30.1%** 0.6%	7.2%	**ΔCPVoteShare(s – 1)= 82%** Competitor Cap(s– 1)= 18%
9. ΔCPVoteShare & Competitor Cap Openness	**21**	**ΔCPVoteShare(s – 1) Competitor Cap** **Competitor Cap(s – 1) ΔCPVoteShare**	0.3% 0.8%	5.9%	ΔCPVoteShare(s – 1)= **53%** Competitor Cap(s– 1)= 47%
10. ΔCPVoteShare & Regional Cap*Regional Growth	**81**	ΔCPVoteShare(s – 1)→ -RegCapRegGr RegCapRegGr(s– 1) → -ΔCPVoteShare	2.0% 1.0%	7.8%	**ΔCPVoteShare(s– 1)= 84%** RegCapRegGr(s– 1)= 16%
11. ΔCPVoteShare & Regional Cap*Regional Growth	**60**	ΔCPVoteShare(s– 1)→ -RegCapRegGr RegCapRegGr(s– 1) → -ΔCPVoteShare	1.7% 1.8%	8.5%	**ΔCPVoteShare(s– 1)= 85%** RegCapRegGr(s– 1)= 15%
12. ΔCPVoteShare & Regional Cap*Regional Growth	**21**	**ΔCPVoteShare(s– 1)→ -RegCapRegGr** RegCapRegGr(s– 1) ΔCPVoteShare	**2.0%** 0%	5.1%	**ΔCPVoteShare(s – 1)= 65%** RegCapRegGr(s – 1)= 35%

Note: Because an equation's R^2 is not affected by multicollinearity among variables, it is possible to assess the contribution of two independent, but collinear, variables (i.e. with common pool variation). The proportion of R^2 attributable to which element of a pair of variables is assessed through an analysis of variance of the contribution to the R^2 of four equations, one of which omits both variables, one of which includes both, and the other two dropping one or the other. The precise tests are described in the text. Thanks to Keith Ord for suggesting this approach.
Exogeneity is assessed by estimating the effects of lagged X_1 on X_2., and vice versa.

changes in global sentiment. Regional capital account openness is a diffusion mechanism for changes in global sentiment.

The relationship between world CP vote shares and the capital account policies of the five leading economies (6.4, 6.5, and 6.6) is also characterized by substantial common negative variance. When both variables are in the model, the adjusted R-square of the overall equations increases by between 3.9% and 7.7%. Only in the sample with home CPs, however, do we see evidence of exogeneity: CP vote shares are exogenous to the liberalization policies of the leading economies. Two-thirds to 82% of the increase in adjusted R-square from including both variables is due to CP voting. It is unclear, based on this evidence, to what extent changes in global sentiments are diffused through the policies of the leading economies.

The relationship between world CP vote shares and competitor capital account policies (6.7, 6.8, and 6.9) is once again characterized by substantial common negative variance. When both variables are in the model, the adjusted R-square of the overall equations increases by between 5.9% and 7.2%. CP vote shares are exogenous to competitor capital account policies in two models (overall sample and the no home CP sample). In the same two models, 82% to all of the increase in adjusted R-square from including both variables is due to CP voting. Competitor capital account openness is, based on this evidence, a strong diffusion mechanism for changes in global sentiment in a large part of the sample.

The relationship between world CP vote shares and the interaction of capital account policies of regional neighbors with regional growth is, yet again, characterized by substantial negative common variance (6.10, 6.11, and 6.12) and by the exogeneity of CP vote shares in the home CP countries (6.12). When both variables are in the model, the adjusted R-square of the overall equations increases by between 5.1% and 8.5%. Using the analysis of variance described above, we see that world CP votes shares account for two-thirds to 85% of the increase in R-square from including both variables in the model. On this evidence, we are unclear whether diffusion characterizes the relationship.

Conclusion

The aim in this chapter was to develop measures of worldwide anti-capitalist and pro-capitalist sentiment, and to establish whether, where, and by how much that sentiment influenced international financial liberalization. We proposed that CP votes in free elections provide an exogenous measure of global anti-capitalist sentiment, allowing us to study its direct effects, as well as to study some mechanisms of diffusion of capital account openness and closure. We also employed an indicator of domestic opposition to financial globalization in using home country CP vote share. We also developed a pro-capitalist indicator, though the resulting data are far thinner. We used two methods, OLS in a pooled, cross-section, time-series framework, and system-GMM estimators. We developed an approach for analyzing the common pool of variance between independent variables to assess diffusion influences.

The results offer strong support for the proposition that global anti-capitalist and pro-capitalist sentiment directly affected the capital account policies of many countries. In addition, domestic anti-capitalist sentiment robustly influenced capital account liberalization. We find evidence for regional diffusion processes, along the lines developed in SDG and evident in Simmons (2000). We see some evidence for the learning and emulation diffusion hypotheses, at least as measured by regional growth*regional liberalization and regional capital account openness, whose coefficients were positive and frequently statistically significant. Everett Rogers' original conception of diffusion as the spread of ideas through multiple levels of social systems via numerous channels remains relevant to understanding international finance policymaking.[64]

We found no evidence of "competitive" effects, unlike some chapters in this volume. Our period of study, and hence our indicator of a country's "competitors," necessarily differed from that used by some other chapters in this volume, however.

We show further that the spread of anti-capitalist ideas also has indirect effects through their influences on state-centered diffusion variables. Indeed, the coefficient estimates of the financial policies of the leading economies were usually negatively signed and statistically significant. At a time when leading economies were liberalizing, many emerging market economies were closing. In light of this result, we note that policy innovations need not originate and spread uni-directionally from the core to periphery or from experts to non-experts, as is seemingly implied by the prevailing accounts in the world polity approach. A form of anti-capitalism appears to have emerged at the periphery and diffused in reaction to international financial liberalization in core countries.

It might appear, on a preliminary reading, that these results regarding the absence of "coercive" effects of the leading economies are at variance with the results reported in Swank's chapter in this volume and Elkins, Guzman, and Simmons (2004; EGS). But, this would be a misreading.

[64] Rogers 1983.

Swank examines tax policies in OECD nations 1981–1998, and finds that changes in the US statutory tax rate influenced the statutory tax rates of other advanced industrial countries. Considering Figures 5.2 and 5.3 we also find that OECD nations moved together toward liberalization. It is between emerging market countries and OECD nations that we find policy divergence occurring, a possibility not examined in the Swank chapter. EGS provide an interesting counterpoint to our findings about policies in leading economies. They correctly note that emerging market nations, at least prior to the 1990s, resisted both unilateral national capital liberalizations and a new international agreement on capital movements. At the same time, trade liberalization enhanced the value of certain types of manufacturing foreign direct investments. Bilateral investment treaties (BITs), EGS show, allow some emerging market countries to gain export manufacturing advantage over competitors by attracting certain types of foreign direct investment, but without throwing open their borders. The *selective* liberalization associated with the BIT occurs, in part, because of the absence of the more *general* forms of liberalization represented by *CAPITAL*.

The regression results are based on an analysis of each variable's unique variation with the dependent variable. When we analyze further the common variance among variables, and consider exogeneity tests as well, we find that the capital account policies of regional neighbors and competitor nations are diffusion mechanisms for global sentiments. In all cases, world CP votes account for the majority or, in some cases, the vast majority, of a pair of variables' contribution to the explanatory power of the models.

Our main conclusion is that the force of ideas, while difficult to measure, is powerful both directly and, through diffusion processes, indirectly.

Appendix 5.1 Data and data sources

We operationalize international financial regulation through two indicators of change in international financial openness or closure, which are described in Quinn 1997 and 2003. *Capital* and *Current* are the main components of *Openness* created from the text of an annual volume published by the International Monetary Fund (IMF), *Exchange Arrangements and Exchange Restrictions*. The measure is available from 1950 to 1997 for 58 countries, and for a shorter period for 33. *Capital* is scored 0–4, in half-integer units, with 4 representing an economy fully open to inward and outward capital flows. We transformed the measures into a 0 to 100 scale taking 100*(*Capital*/4). The data on CP vote totals are taken from these sources: Mackie and Rose 1991, 1997; www.electionworld.org; *Keesings' Contemporary Archive*, various issues; and

Table 5.7. *Base models. Dependent variable = change in capital account regulation (ΔCAP). Unbalanced panel estimated using OLS with panel correct standard errors*

	A. Communist Party votes, 1955–1999		
	Model A1.1	Model A1.2	Model A1.3
Variable	Full sample 82 nations	61 nations with no CP	21 nations with a CP
ΔCAP(t − 1)	0.000	0.005	− 0.004
	(0.023)	(0.027)	(0.033)
Capital (t− 1)	− 0.065***	− 0.077***	− 0.053***
	(0.008)	(0.009)	(0.013)
Growth (t− 1)	0.035	0.049	− 0.077
	(0.033)	(0.037)	(0.056)
Income (t − 1)	0.057	0.053	1.16***
(Per capita, PPP-adjusted)	(0.285)	(0.323)	(0.437)
Change in investment (t− 1)	− 0.004	0.013	0.024
	(0.065)	(0.078)	(0.116)
Level of investment(t− 1)	− 0.329	− 0.341	− 0.384
(share of GDP)	(0.309)	(0.363)	(0.541)
Population growth (t− 1)	− 0.067	− 0.117	− 0.146
	(0.146)	(0.129)	(0.242)
Change in openness (t− 1)	0.001	0.003	0.092
	(0.285)	(0.023)	(0.06)
Level of trade openness	0.27	0.573**	− 0.337
(t− 1)	(0.232)	(0.285)	(0.254)
Revolutions and coups	− 0.073	− 0.109	0.18***
(t− 1)	(0.077)	(0.083)	(0.07)
ΔDemocracy (t− 1)	0.002	− 0.005	0.997**
	(0.056)	(0.056)	(0.409)
Level of democracy (t − 1)	0.076***	0.082***	0.228***
	(0.025)	(0.03)	(0.119)
Change in vote share of home Communist Party, t − 1	**− 0.164***** **(0.0622)**		**0.211***** **(0.075)**
Change in vote share of Communist parties, t − 1 (**ΔCPVote5$_s$**)	**− 0.907**** **(0.38)**	**− 0.731*** **(0.433)**	**− 1.205*** **(0.736)**
Time trend	0.052***	0.048***	− 0.211***
	(0.012)	(0.015)	(0.075)
Adj. R^2	4.8%	5.2%	4.9%
Number of countries	82	61	21
Number of observations	3408	2422	986

Note: All models include a lagged endogenous variable, which precludes the use of fixed effects, but which achieved serially uncorrelated residuals in all cases. We enter regional dummy variables, whose coefficient estimates are not reported to save space, but are available from the authors. The interaction term between a dummy variable for the presence of a home country CP and the world CP vote share in model A1.1 was far from statistical significance (t-stat of − 0.636), and was therefore excluded from the final model.

* *p*-value <.10

** *p*-value <.05

*** *p*-value <.01.

Table 5.8. *Estimating pairwise common variance of ΔCP vote share worldwide with other key variables*

Variable	Sample	t-statistic	R-square
1. ΔVote share of Home CP	1.a 81	1.578	0.4%
	1.b 21	1.51	1.1%
2. Capital account openness of the world's five leading economies	**2.a 81**	**− 7.182**	**7.7%**
	2.b 60	**− 7.546**	**11.7%**
	2.c 21	**− 2.548**	**3.2%**
3. Regional average of capital account openness	**3.a 81**	**− 3.241**	**1.7%**
	3.b 60	**− 3.183**	**2.3%**
	3.c 21	**− 2.934**	**4.5%**
4. Competitor capital account openness	**4.a 81**	**− 6.095**	**5.7%**
	4.b 60	**− 6.14**	**8.0%**
	4.c 21	**− 1.969**	**2.1%**
5. Balance of payments	5.a 81	− 1.260	0.3%
	5.b 60	.557	0.1%
	5.c 21	**− 1.96**	**2.1%**
6. Δ Regional capital account openness *Regional growth	**6.a 81**	**− 4.104**	**2.6%**
	6.b 60	**− 3.581**	**2.8%**
	6.c 21	**− 1.961**	**2.0%**

Note: Estimated relationships are OLS. Statistically significant relationships (at $p < .1$) denoted with **BOLD** formatting.

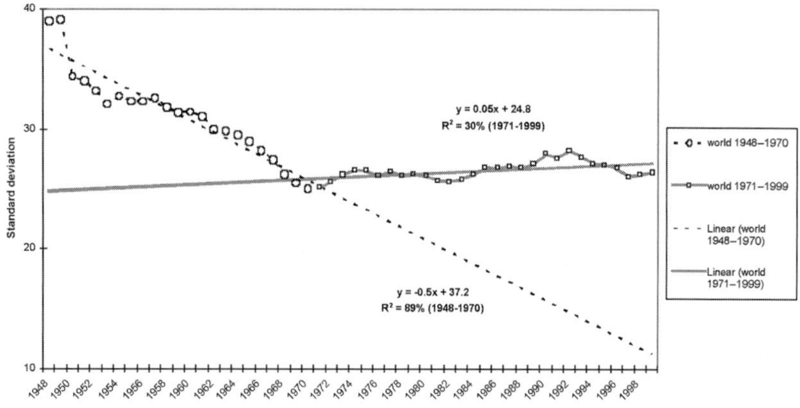

Figure 5.4 Standard deviations of world capital account openness, 1948–1970 vs. 1971–1999

www.polisci.com/almanac/nations/nation/FI.htm. The economic data are from Penn World Tables Mark 6.1, by Heston, Summers, and Aten (2001). The data on revolutions, coups, etc. are updated Cross-National Times Series data from Arthur S. Banks (2001). The democracy indicators are from Polity II. We use the World Bank's regional codes in creating regional dummy variables. Competitor capital policies are nations identified by the World Bank as offering similar export products to a home country's, and are meant to capture competitive dynamics.[65]

References

Abiad, Abdul and Ashoka Mody. 2005. Financial Reform: What Shakes It? What Shapes It? *American Economic Review* 95 (1):66–88.

Acharya, Amitav. 2004. How Ideas Spread: Whose Norms Matter? Norm Localization and Institutional Change in Asian Regionalism. *International Organization* 58 (2):239–75.

Arellano, Manuel and Olympia Bover. 1995. Another Look at the Instrumental Variables Estimation of Error-Components. *Review of Economic Studies* 68 (1):277–97.

Banks, Arthur S. 2001. Cross-National Time-Series Data Archive. Available through www.databanks.sitehosting.net/.

Blundell, Richard W. and Stephen R. Bond. 1998. Initial Conditions and Moment Restrictions in Dynamic Panel Data Models. *Journal of Econometrics* 87 (1):115–43.

Bonardi, Jean-Philippe and Gerald Keim. 2002. Nonmarket Strategies in Election Issues: A Theoretical Framework Based on Information and Reputation Cascades. Paper presented at Strategy and the Business Environment Conference, Graduate School of Business, Stanford University, Stanford, California.

Bound, John, David A. Jaeger, and Regina M. Baker. 1995. Problems with Instrumental Variables Estimations when the Correlation Between the Instruments and the Endogenous Explanatory Variable is Weak. *Journal of the American Statistical Association* 90: 443–50.

Brune, Nancy, Geoff Garrett, Alexandra Guisinger, and Jason Sorens. 2001. The Political Economy of Capital Account Liberalization. Paper presented at the 97th Annual Meeting of the American Political Science Association, San Francisco, California.

Budge, Ian. 1992. *ECPR Party Manifestos Project* [computer file]. 3rd ed. Colchester: ESRC Data Archive.

[65] The World Bank Development Report (in the "yellow sheets fixed factors") classifies nations in terms of their competitive position. It lists nations as exporters of manufactures, exporters of non-fuel primary products, exporters of fuels (mainly oil), exporters of services, diversified exporters, not classified by export category. While this indicator of a nation's competitor is less precise than the measures used in Simmons and Elkins 2004, the categorization is consistent with the theoretical categories in Dunning 1988.

Castles, Francis G. and Peter Mair. 1984. Left-right Political Scales: Some Expert Judgments. *European Journal of Political Research* 12: 73–88.

Chwieroth, Jeffrey M. 2002. Neoliberalism's Role in Capital Account Liberalization in Emerging Markets. Paper presented at the Annual Meeting of the American Political Science Association, Boston, MA.

Conway, Patrick. 2004. Endogenous IMF Conditionality: Theoretical and Empirical Implications. Paper presented at the Annual Meeting of the American Economic Association, San Diego, California.

Dobbin, Frank, Geoffrey Garrett, and Beth A. Simmons. 2003. Introduction: The International Diffusion of Democracy and Markets. Paper presented at the Weatherhead Center for International Affairs Conference on International Diffusion of Political and Economic Liberalism, Harvard University, Cambridge, MA.

Doornik, Jurgen and David F. Hendry. 2001. *Econometric Modeling Using PCGive 10: Volume III.* London: Timberlake Consultants.

Dreher, Axel. 2002. The Development and Implementation of IMF and World Bank Conditionality. Hamburg Institute of International Economics Discussion Paper # 165.

Drezner, Daniel. 2001. Globalization and Policy Convergence *International Studies Review* 3: 53–78.

Dunning, John H. 1988. The Eclectic Paradigm of International Production: A Restatement and Some Possible Extensions. *Journal of International Business Studies* 19: 1–31.

East European Business Law. 1991. The Evolution of Business Law in the USSR. March 1.

Eichengreen, Barry. 2001. Capital Account Liberalization: What Do the Cross-Country Studies Tell Us? *World Bank Economic Review* 15 (3):341–65.

Eichengreen, Barry J. and David Leblang. 2003. Capital Account Liberalization and Growth: Was Mr. Mahathir Right? *International Journal of Finance and Economics* 8 (3):205–24.

Electionworld.org. n.d. Available from http://www.electionworld.org [accessed February 2003].

Elkins, Zachary, Andrew Guzman, and Beth A. Simmons. 2004. The Diffusion of Bilateral Investment Treaties. Paper presented at a conference on International Diffusion of Political and Economic Liberalization, Weatherhead Center for International Affairs, Harvard University, Cambridge, MA.

European Bank for Reconstruction and Development. 1994. Transition Report: Foreign Direct Investment. October.

Evans, Peter. 1997. The Eclipse of the State? Reflections on Stateness in an Era of Globalization. *World Politics* 50: 62–87.

Fourcade-Gourinchas, Marion and Sarah Babb. 2002. The Rebirth of the Liberal Creed: Paths to Neoliberalism in Four Countries. *American Journal of Sociology* 107(9): 533–79.

Franzese, Jr., Robert J. and Jude C. Hays. 2004. Modeling International Diffusion: Inferential and Methodological Challenges (with an Application to International Tax Competition). University of Michigan manuscript.

Gwynne, Robert N. and Cristobal Kay, eds. 1999. *Latin America Transformed: Globalization and Modernity*. Cambridge: Cambridge University Press.

Hall, Peter A., ed. 1989. *The Political Power of Economic Ideas: Keynesianism Across Nations*. Princeton: Princeton University Press.

Hart, Gary and Richard N. Dean. 1994. Doing Business in Russia: Risk and Reward. *Legal Times*, September 5.

Henisz, Witold, Bennet Zelner, and Mauro F. Guillen. 2004. International Coercion, Emulation and Policy Diffusion: Market-Oriented Infrastructure Reforms, 1977–1999. Unpublished manuscript, Georgetown University, Washington, DC and Wharton School of Business, University of Pennsylvania, Philadelphia, PA.

Heston, Alan, Robert Summers, and Bettina Aten. 2001. The Penn World Table, Version 6.0. Center for International Comparisons at the University of Pennsylvania (CICUP).

Hilferding, Rudolf. 1910[1981]. *Finance Capital: A Study of the Latest Phase of Capitalist Development*. Edited by Tom Bottomore; translated by Morris Watnick and Sam Gordon. Boston: Routledge, Kegan, Paul.

Huber, John and Ronald Inglehart. 1995. Expert Interpretations of Party Space and Party Locations in 42 Societies. *Party Politics* 1 (1):71–111.

International Monetary Fund. *Annual Report on Exchange Restrictions*. Washington: IMF. Various years, 1950 on. Continued by *Annual Report on Exchange Arrangements and Exchange Restrictions* after 1979 and *Exchange Arrangements and Exchange Restrictions* after 1989.

International Monetary Fund. 2001. International Financial Integration and Developing Countries. *World Economic Outlook* October: 145–73.

Jonung, Lars. 2005. How Do Policy-makers Learn? The Case of Swedish Stabilisation Policy, 1970–2000. Paper presented at Midwest Political Science Association's 63rd Annual National Conference, Chicago, IL.

Keesings' Contemporary Archive. Harlow: Longman, various years.

Kennedy, Peter. 1998. *A Guide to Econometrics*. 4th ed. Cambridge, MA: MIT Press.

Keynes, John Maynard. 1933. National Self-Sufficiency. *The Yale Review* 22: 755–69.

Kim, Heemin and Richard C. Fording. 2003. Voter Ideology in Western Democracies: An Update. *European Journal of Political Research* 42 (1): 95–105.

Krayem, Hassan. n.d. Political Parties and Electoral Systems in Lebanon and Israel: Interactive Reinforcement. Available at http://ddc.aub.edu.lb/projects/pspa/krayem/krayem.html [accessed August 2003].

LaVigne, Marie. 1991. *International Political Economy and Socialism*. Trans. David Lambert. New York: Cambridge University Press.

Lenin, V. I. 1916[1971]. *Imperialism, the Highest Stage of Capitalism*. In *Selected Works: One Volume Edition*. New York: International Publishers.

Li, Quan and Dale Smith. 2002. The Dilemma of Financial Liberalization: State Autonomy and Societal Demands. *Journal of Politics* 64 (3):764–90.

Mackie, Thomas T. and Richard Rose. 1991. *The International Almanac of Electoral History*. Washington, DC: Congressional Quarterly Inc.

Mackie, Thomas T. and Richard Rose. 1997. *A Decade of Election Results: Updating the International Almanac*. Glasgow: Center for the Study of Public Policy, University of Strathclyde.

Mansfield, Edward D. and Helen Milner. 1997. The Political Economy of Regionalism: An Overview. In *The Political Economy of Regionalism*, edited by Edward D. Mansfield and Helen Milner, 1–19. New York: Columbia University Press.

Meseguer, Covandonga Y. 2003. Rational and Bounded Learning in the Diffusion of Policy Innovations. Paper presented at the 99th Annual Meeting of the American Political Science Association, Philadelphia, PA.

Meseguer, Covandonga Y. and Fabrizio Gilardi. 2005. What is New in the Study of Policy Diffusion: A Critical Review. Paper presented at the 2005 ISA Meetings, Hawaii.

Meyer, John W. 2004. Sociological Perspectives on Diffusion. Unpublished manuscript, Stanford University, Stanford, CA.

Meyer, John W., John Boli, George M. Thomas, and Francisco O. Ramirez. 1997. World Society and the Nation-State. *American Journal of Sociology* 103: 144–81.

Mosley, Layna. 2003. *Global Capital and National Governments*. Cambridge: Cambridge University Press.

Page, Benjamin I. and Robert Y. Shapiro. 1992. *The Rational Public*. Chicago: University of Chicago Press.

Polisci.com. n.d. Available at www.polisci.com/almanac/nations/nation/FI.htm [accessed December 2002].

Prebisch, Raul. 1950. *The Economic Development of Latin American and its Principal Problems*. New York: United Nations.

Quinn, Dennis. 1997. The Correlates of Change in International Financial Regulation. *American Political Science Review* 91 (3):531–51.

Quinn, Dennis P. 2003. Capital Account Liberalization and Financial Globalization, 1890–1999: A Synoptic View. *International Journal of Finance and Economics* 8: 189–204.

Quinn, Dennis P. and Carla Inclán. 1997. The Origins of Financial Openness: A Study of Current and Capital Account Liberalization. *American Journal of Political Science* 41 (3):771–813.

Quinn, John James. 2002. *The Road Oft Traveled: Development Policies and Majority State Ownership of Industry in Africa*. Westport, CT: Praeger.

Rector, Chad and Scott Kasner. 2002. Partisan Cycles and the Timing of Capital Controls Regulatory Changes. Unpublished manuscript, University of California, San Diego.

Risse, Thomas, Stephen C. Ropp, and Kathryn Sikkink. 1999. *The Power of Human Rights*. Cambridge: Cambridge University Press.

Rodrik, Dani. 1995. The Political Economy of Trade Policy. In *Handbook of International Economics*. Volume 3, edited by G. Grossman and K. Rogoff, 1457–94. Amsterdam: North-Holland.

Rodrik, Dani. 1997. *Has Globalization Gone Too Far*? Washington, DC: Institute for International Economics.

Rogers, Everett M. 1983. *Diffusion of Innovations*. 3rd ed. New York: The Free Press.

Ryan, Bryce and Neal C. Gross. 1943. The Diffusion of Hybrid Seed Corn in Two Iowa Communities. *Rural Sociology* 8: 15–24.

Scheve, Kenneth and Matthew J. Slaughter. 2001. What Determines Individual Trade-Policy Preferences? *Journal of International Economics* 54: 267–92.

Schumpeter, Joseph A. 1942. *Capitalism, Socialism, and Democracy*. New York: Harper.

Simmons, Beth A. 2000. International Law and State Behavior: Commitment and Compliance in International Monetary Affairs. *American Political Science Review* 94: 543–65.

Simmons, Beth A., Frank Dobbin, and Geoffrey Garrett. 2005. Introduction: The International Diffusion of Liberalism. *International Organization* 60: 781–810.

Simmons, Beth A. and Zachary Elkins. 2004. The Globalization of Liberalization: Policy Diffusion in the International Political Economy. *American Political Science Review* 98 (1):171–89.

Stallings, Barbara K. 1992. International Influence on Economic Policy: Debt, Stabilization, and Structural Reform. In *The Politics of Economic Adjustment: International Constraints, Distributive Politics, and the State*, edited by Stephan Haggard and Robert Kaufman, 41–88. Princeton: Princeton University Press.

Stimson, James A., Michael B. Mackuen, and Robert S. Erikson. 1995. Dynamic Representation. *American Political Science Review* 89: 819–35.

Volkens, Andrea. 1995. *Comparative Manifestos Project. Dataset CMPr3. Programmatic Profiles of Political Parties in 20 Countries, 1945–1988* (ESRC Data Archive study number F139–94). Science Center Berlin, Research Unit Institutions and Social Change (Director Hans-Dieter Klingemann) in cooperation with the Manifesto Research Group (Chairman Ian Budge).

Wallerstein, Immanuel. 1976. *The Modern World-System: Capitalist Agriculture and the Origins of the European World-Economy in the Sixteenth Century*. New York: Academic Press.

Wapner, Paul. 1995. Politics Beyond the State: Environmental Activism and World Civic Politics. *World Politics* 47 (3):311–40.

Wapner, Paul. 1996. *Environmental Activism and World Civic Politics*. Albany, NY: SUNY Press.

Weyland, Kurt. 2005. Theories of Policy Diffusion: Lessons from Latin American Pension Reform. *World Politics* 57 (2):262–95.

Wittman, Donald. 1995. *The Myth of Democratic Failure: Why Political Institutions are Efficient*. Chicago: University of Chicago Press.

World Bank. Various years. *World Development Report*. Washington, DC: World Bank.

Zhang, Hui. 2002. The Causes and Impacts of International Financial Liberalization. Unpublished manuscript, Claremont Graduate School, Claremont, CA.

6 Competing for capital: the diffusion of bilateral investment treaties, 1960–2000*

Zachary Elkins, Andrew T. Guzman, and Beth A. Simmons

The global market for productive capital is more integrated than ever before. The growth of foreign direct investment (FDI) is a clear example. According to World Bank data, gross FDI as a percentage of total world production increased seven-fold from 1.2 percent to 8.9 percent between 1970 and 2000. Though such investments tend to be highly skewed across jurisdictions – developed countries account for more than 93 percent of outflows and 68 percent of inflows[1] – foreign capital has come to play a much more visible role in many more countries worldwide.

It is widely recognized that economic globalization requires market-supporting institutions to flourish. But unlike trade and monetary relations, virtually no multilateral rules for FDI exist.[2] Direct investments in developing countries are overwhelmingly governed by bilateral investment treaties (BITs). BITs are agreements establishing the terms and conditions for private investment by nationals and companies of one country in the jurisdiction of another. Virtually all BITs cover four substantive areas: FDI admission, treatment, expropriation, and the settlement of disputes. These bilateral arrangements have proliferated over the past forty-five years, and especially in the past two decades, even as political controversies have plagued efforts to establish a multilateral regime for FDI.

Why the profusion of bilateral agreements? The popularity of BITs contrasts sharply with the collective resistance developing countries have shown toward pro-investment principles under customary international law and the failure of the international community to make progress on a

* For useful comments on earlier drafts of this chapter, we thank Bill Bernhard, Bear Braumoeller, Frank Dobbin, Robert Franzese, Jeffry Frieden, Geoffrey Garrett, Tom Ginsburg, Jude Hays, Lisa Martin, Bob Pahre, Mark Ramsayer, Steven Ratner, Susan Rose-Ackerman, and John Sides. For research assistance, we thank Elizabeth Burden, Raechel Groom, and Alexander Noonan.

1 UNCTAD. FDI/TNC Database. Available at www.unctad.org.

2 For a review of the relevant legal literature, see Dolzer 1981; Minor 1994; Sornarajah 1994; Vagts 1987.

multilateral investment agreement.[3] On its face, this seems to suggest that BITs do not simply reflect the ready acceptance of dominant international property rights norms. Our theory and findings support the competitive economic explanations described in the introduction to this volume:[4] the proliferation of BITs – and the liberal property rights regime they embody – are propelled in good part by the competition among potential host countries for credible property rights protections that direct investors require.

This chapter is organized as follows. The first section describes the spread of BITs in some detail. The second section presents a model of competition for investment that could lead to diffusion among competitors. The third section discusses the methods we use to test our propositions (and a range of alternatives), and the fourth section discusses our findings. Our data are consistent with competitive pressures for BIT proliferation: governments are influenced by competitors' policies and by the mobility of FDI in manufactures, which tends to intensify competition among hosts. We interpret our findings as evidence of pressure for certain governments to adopt capital-friendly policies in highly competitive global capital markets.

Securing investors' legal rights

From customary law to bilateral investment treaties

FDI has always been subject to contractual and political hazards that raise the expected costs of investing.[5] Before the use of BITs, few mechanisms existed to make state promises about the treatment of foreign investment credible.[6] Customary international law, expressed succinctly in the "Hull Rule," held that "no government is entitled to expropriate private property, for whatever purpose, without provision for prompt, adequate, and effective payment therefore."[7] Apart from the obvious problem of enforcement, this approach did not allow potential hosts voluntarily to signal their intent to contract in good faith.

[3] Guzman 1998. [4] Simmons, Dobbin, and Garrett 2006. [5] Henisz 2000.

[6] For a discussion of the historical protection of foreign investment, see Lipson 1985.

[7] See Cordell Hull's note to the Mexican Minister of Foreign Affairs during the 1938 dispute over land expropriations, reprinted in Green H. Hackworth, *Digest of International Law* v. 3, § 228 (1942). The Rule itself predates Cordell Hull's statement, and various statements of it can be found in decisions from the early part of the twentieth century. See Concerning the Factory at Chorzow (Ger. v. Pol.), 1926–29 P.C.I.L. (ser. A), Nos. 7, 9, 17, 19; Norwegian Shipowners Claims Arbitration (U.S. v. Nor.) 1 Rep. Int'l Arb. Awards 307 (1922).

Both customary international law and its practice were under attack by developing country hosts by the 1950s. The nationalization of British oil assets by Iran in 1951, the expropriation of Liamco's concessions in Libya in 1955, and the nationalization of the Suez Canal by Egypt a year later served notice of a new militancy on the part of investment hosts. The nationalization of sugar interests by Cuba in the 1960s further undercut assumptions about the security of international investments.[8] Meanwhile, collective resistance to the Hull Rule in the United Nations was on the rise. In 1962 the UN General Assembly adopted the "Resolution on Permanent Sovereignty over Natural Resources" that provided for merely "appropriate" compensation in the event of expropriation. Several more United Nations resolutions followed in the 1970s,[9] along with a string of under-compensated expropriations around the world.[10]

Bilateral treaties made their debut in the late 1950s, just as consensus on customary rules began to erode. BITs were innovative in a number of respects.[11] They require an explicit commitment on the part of the potential host government and involve direct negotiations with the government of potential investors. In this way, BITs up the political ante for the host government and raise expectations of performance. The typical BIT offers a wider array of substantive protections than did the customary rule. For example, BITs typically require national treatment and

[8] Guzman 1998.

[9] These are discussed in Lipson 1985. In 1966 the General Assembly reaffirmed states' rights to nationalize resources without reference to international legal principles. In 1972 the UN General Assembly passed Resolution 3041 (XXVII), which contained an endorsement of the Trade and Development Board's Resolution 88 (XII) of October 19, 1972, regarding permanent sovereignty over natural resources, and claimed that compensation for natural resource nationalization cases was to be fixed by the nationalizing state with jurisdiction for such cases falling within the sole jurisdiction of the nationalizing country's courts. The 1973 Resolution on Permanent Sovereignty over Natural Resources (Resolution 3171) stated that in the event of nationalization "each State is entitled to determine the amount of possible compensation and the mode of payment." The Charter of Economic Rights and Duties of States (GA Res. 3281(xxix), UN GAOR, 29th Sess., Supp. No. 31 (1974: 50)), which specified the right of each state "To nationalize, expropriate or transfer ownership of foreign property, in which case appropriate compensation should be paid by the State adopting such measures, taking into account its relevant laws and regulations and all circumstances that the State considers pertinent" with national courts taking jurisdiction in case of disputes (Art. 2(c)).

[10] See Kobrin 1980.

[11] Other mechanisms have been used to try to protect foreign investment, of course. One possibility since 1988 is to apply for insurance through the World Bank's Multilateral Insurance Guarantee Agency (MIGA). MIGA covers risks associated with transfer restriction, expropriation, breach of contract, and risks relating to war and civil disturbances. See www.miga.org/. [Accessed June 20, 2006.] US businesses can also insure against risks associated with currency inconvertibility, expropriation, and political violence by applying for investment insurance from the Overseas Private Investment Corporation (OPIC), a US government agency. See www.opic.gov/Insurance/. [Accessed June 20, 2006.]

most-favored-nation treatment of foreign investments in the host country,[12] protect contractual rights,[13] guaranty the right to transfer profits in hard currency to the home country, and prohibit or restrict the use of performance requirements.[14] Finally, and perhaps most importantly, BITs provide for international arbitration of disputes between the investor and the host country,[15] typically through the International Center for Settlement of Investment Disputes (ICSID) or the United Nations Commission on International Trade Law (UNCITRAL).

The spread of BITs

Despite the aggressive campaign waged by some developing countries against the relevant customary international law, BITs were embraced by many potential host governments.[16] Figure 6.1 documents the geometric growth of both investment treaties and mean inflows of FDI as a percentage of gross domestic product (GDP) from 1959 to 1999. Early BITs typically involved a midsized European power and one of the least developed countries, often in Africa (see Table 6.1). The negotiation of BITs proceeded at a moderate pace until the mid-1980s, rarely exceeding twenty new treaties per year. Late in the decade, however, the rate of signings accelerated dramatically, with an average of more than one hundred new treaties a year throughout the 1990s.

The United States embraced BITs later than did its West European counterparts. Between 1962 and 1972, during which time West Germany entered into forty-six BITs and Switzerland entered into twenty-seven, the United States eschewed such treaties and signed only two Friendship Commerce and Navigation Treaties – with Togo and Thailand.[17] One

12 For example, the 1994 US Prototype Bilateral Investment Treaty, Office of the Chief Counsel for International Commerce, US Department of Commerce, Article 2(1), 2(2)(a). For convenience, throughout this chapter we label the more developed partner in a BIT the "home" country (meaning the home of investors) and the less developed partner the "host." The treaty obligations bind both parties, but in the vast majority of treaties there is a developed country that will be the source of most FDI and a developing country that will be the recipient.

13 For example, 1994 US Prototype BIT, Article I(d)(ii).

14 For example, 1994 US Prototype BIT, Article V(1–2).

15 For example, 1994 US Prototype BIT, Article IX.

16 It is interesting to note, however, that some of the most vociferous opponents of the Hull Rule were in fact latecomers to the BITs movement. As of the late 1990s, Mexico for example had signed only two BITs, with Spain and Switzerland. Brazil did not sign a BIT until 1994, and as of the late 1990s none of its ten bilateral agreements had entered into force. India's pattern is similar to that of Brazil. See www.worldbank.org/icsid/treaties/treaties.htm. [Accessed December 10, 2003.]

17 Vandevelde 1988.

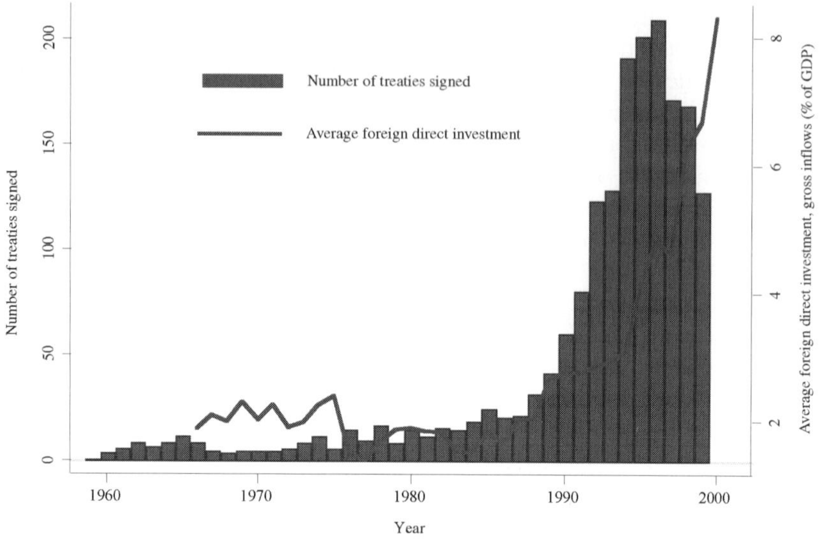

Figure 6.1 Number of bilateral investment treaties signed and mean global foreign direct investment as a proportion of GDP, by year, 1959–1999

reason for the delayed US participation in bilateral arrangements may have been the hope of retaining a multilateral approach. The United States was one of the most aggressive proponents of the Hull Rule and may have feared that BITs represented a threat to its claim that investment was already protected under customary international law. Moreover, potential hosts may have had incentives to resist the relatively onerous provisions the US government typically tried to secure. One of the prime differences between the terms typically offered by the Europeans and the United States at this time was the former's emphasis on investment protection and the latter's additional insistence on liberalization.[18]

It was not until 1981 that the United States changed its view on BITs. There is evidence that some officials in the administration of US President Ronald Reagan viewed BITs as an alternative way to protect the principles contained in the embattled Hull Rule. Secretary of State

[18] "Multilateral or Bilateral Investment Negotiations: Where Can Developing Countries Make Themselves Heard?" Briefing Paper No. 9. Available at http://cuts-international.org/9-2002.pdf. [Accessed July 12, 2006.] Some observers note that the insistence on liberalization explains the inability of the United States to secure agreements with East and Southeast Asian countries until quite recent years; see Reading 1992.

Table 6.1. *The first forty bilateral investment treaties signed*

Investing country	Host country	Year BIT signed
Germany	Dominican Republic	1959
Germany	Pakistan	1959
Germany	Malaysia	1960
Germany	Greece	1961
Switzerland	Tunisia	1961
Germany	Togo	1961
Germany	Thailand	1961
Germany	Liberia	1961
Germany	Morocco	1961
Switzerland	Niger	1962
Switzerland	Côte d'Ivoire	1962
Switzerland	Guinea	1962
Germany	Cameroon	1962
Switzerland	Congo	1962
Switzerland	Senegal	1962
Germany	Guinea	1962
Germany	Turkey	1962
Germany	Madagascar	1962
Switzerland	Rwanda	1963
Netherlands	Tunisia	1963
Switzerland	Liberia	1963
Switzerland	Cameroon	1963
Germany	Sri Lanka	1963
Germany	Tunisia	1963
Germany	Sudan	1963
Italy	Guinea	1964
Switzerland	Togo	1964
Germany	Senegal	1964
Germany	Niger	1964
Switzerland	Madagascar	1964
Belgium-Luxembourg	Tunisia	1964
Germany	South Korea	1964
Switzerland	Tanzania	1965
Switzerland	Malta	1965
Germany	Sierra Leone	1965
Switzerland	Costa Rica	1965
Germany	Ecuador	1965
Netherlands	Cameroon	1965
Netherlands	Côte d'Ivoire	1965
Sweden	Côte d'Ivoire	1965

George Schultz argued that BITs were designed "to protect investment not only by treaty but also by *reinforcing traditional international legal principles* and practice regarding foreign direct private investment."[19] By the mid-1980s, the United States pursued investor protection in the same fashion as did the Europeans. Schultz noted in his communication with the president after completion of six BITs in 1986[20] that, "[o]ur approach followed similar programs that had been undertaken with considerable success by a number of European countries, including the Federal Republic of Germany and the United Kingdom since the early 1960s."[21] By the late 1980s, most analysts would agree that governments in countries home to large multinational corporations (MNCs) had nearly converged on a single treaty model. Developing countries could, increasingly, opt to take it or to leave it. As Figure 6.1 attests, many did the former.

Early on, BITs were primarily agreements between countries of starkly varying developmental levels and political traditions. Figure 6.2, which plots the mean difference in GDP per capita between BIT partners as well as that between states in all other dyads "at risk" of signing in a given year, demonstrates that the economic differences within these dyads have declined fairly substantially over time, even while the wealth disparities between non-BIT dyads have increased. As is the case with wealth, the "political gap" between new BIT signers has also diminished significantly over the past thirty years. Figure 6.3 plots the mean difference in the level of democracy (as measured by Polity scores) of BIT partners in the year of their signing against that of all other dyads at risk of signing. Over time new BIT partners have become more similar, evidence that the institution is spreading to a population of dyads of similar political and economic structure and, presumably, with less reason to sign such agreements.

By the late 1990s, there emerged a few twists to the basic theme of wealthy countries picking off potentially lucrative but risky venues one at a time. From about 1999, developing countries began a rather more proactive effort to create bilateral investment treaties among themselves. These activities have been coordinated through the United Nations Conference on Trade and Development (UNCTAD), and sometimes with the assistance of a major capital-exporting country, such as Germany

[19] Emphasis added. George P. Schultz, transmission letter to the president recommending transmission of the US–Turkey Bilateral Investment Treaty, 1985. Available at www.state.gov/documents/organization/43615.pdf. [Accessed July 12, 2006.]

[20] Turkey, Morocco, Haiti, Panama, Senegal, and Zaire.

[21] George P. Schultz, transmission letter to the president recommending transmission of the US–Turkey Bilateral Investment Treaty, 1985. Available at www.state.gov/documents/organization/43615.pdf. [Accessed July 12, 2006.]

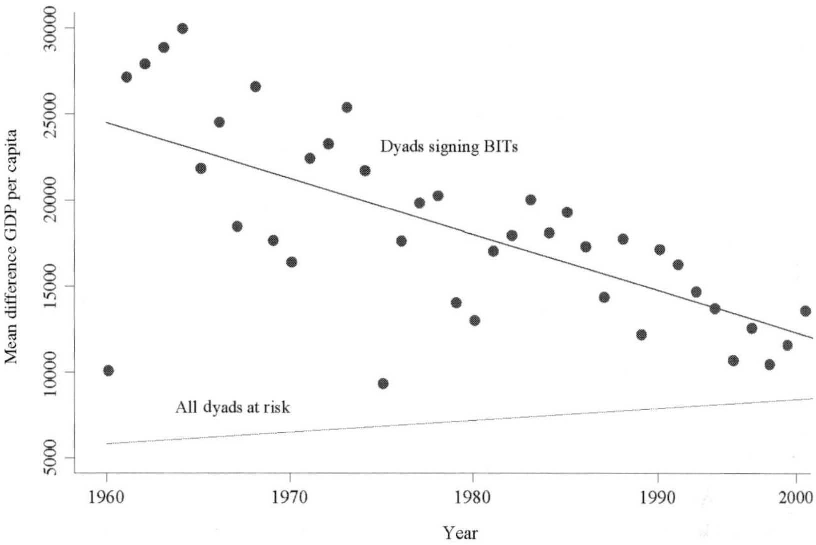

Figure 6.2 Mean difference in GDP per capita between dyad members
Notes: Data points shown are for dyads signing BITs.

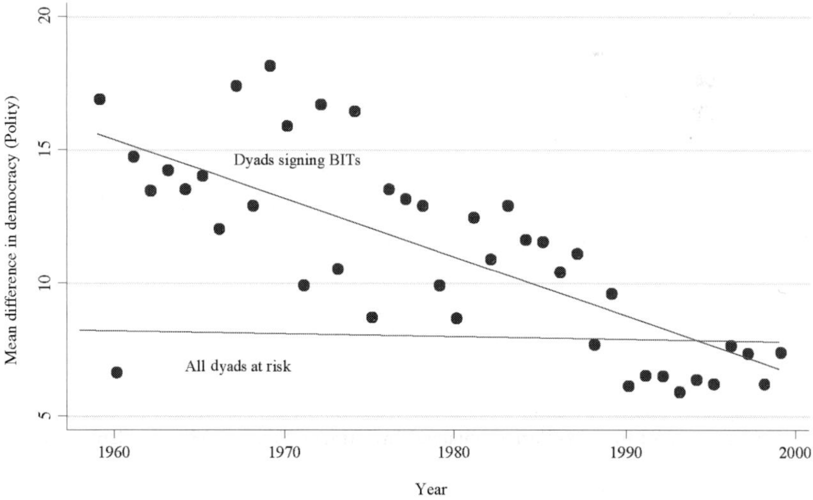

Figure 6.3 Mean difference in democracy between dyad members
Notes: Data points shown are for dyads signing BITs.

or France. During a meeting jointly sponsored by UNCTAD, the Swiss government, and a group of fifteen developing countries (G-15), seven developing countries signed eight bilateral treaties among themselves.[22] Individual developing countries soon began to seize the initiative. At the request of Thailand, a minilateral conference yielded nine more developing country BITs,[23] and furthered discussions on several more. Bolivia (2000), India (2001), and Croatia (2001) initiated minilateral discussions on a similar model. France financed a round of discussions primarily among the francophone countries in 2001 that attracted twenty participants and yielded forty-two BITs, many of which involved non-contiguous, poor, highly indebted African countries for which it is difficult to imagine much benefit. (What are the chances that capital from Burkina Faso would flow to Chad, or investors from Benin would soon demand entrée to Mali?) More understandable, from an economic point of view, was the German-funded and -supported meeting in October 2001 that drew together seven capital-poor countries (five of which were officially "highly indebted poor countries") and four wealthy European countries,[24] yielding both understandable (Belgium–Cambodia) and bizarre (Sudan–Zambia) bilateral treaty combinations.[25] This recent turn toward BITs between developing states is more difficult for our theory to explain. It does seem to suggest that more political or sociological explanations may be increasingly relevant quite recently in some regions. However, these cases are still relatively few and of such recent vintage that they do not affect the broader relationships we report below.

Leaders and followers in BIT agreements

BITs present potential benefits for both capital-exporting and capital-importing countries. But which group of countries initiates and drives the signing of such agreements? Our theory, to anticipate the following section, assumes that potential host countries have an important

[22] Egypt, India, Indonesia, Jamaica, Malaysia, Sri Lanka, and Zimbabwe.

[23] Thailand–Zimbabwe, Thailand–Croatia, Thailand–Iran, Zimbabwe–Croatia, Zimbabwe–Sri Lanka, Croatia–Iran, Thailand–Kazakhstan, Zimbabwe–Kazakhstan, and Croatia–Kazakhstan. Sweden also participated and concluded a BIT with Thailand.

[24] Participants included Cambodia, Eritrea, Malawi, Mozambique, Sudan, Uganda, and Zambia. Upon the request of these countries, Belgium, France, the Netherlands, and Sweden were invited to participate and responded affirmatively.

[25] Notice that even multilateral meetings of this sort have not yielded multilateral treaties on investment. The states involved have always chosen instead to sign a series of BITs. The question of why multilateral approaches are not adopted is interesting, but we leave it for another day.

(although not exclusive) role in initiating or nurturing BIT negotiations. Is this a plausible assumption? After all, power-based theories – or "coercive" theories in the language of Simmons, Dobbin, and Garrett[26] – suggest that dominant capital-exporting countries such as Germany or the United States control the agenda and begin BIT negotiations according to their schedule and needs. Indeed, the chronology described above suggests that some home countries establish BIT "programs" and sign agreements with a slate of developing countries in concentrated periods of time.

If the dominant powers determine the BIT schedule, then we should see evidence of home country "programs" when we look at BITs, by country, across time. Programs would look like clusters, or peaks, of activity in certain eras in a home country's history. By the same logic, if host countries take a lead role in producing BITs, their histories would also show some evidence of concerted, programmatic activity. Figures 6.4 and 6.5 chart the number of BITs signed since 1959 for the twelve most active BIT signatories from both home (Figure 6.4) and host (Figure 6.5) countries. It appears that most home countries have BIT activity that lasts at least twenty years; most of these countries, in fact, sign BITs throughout the forty-year period. Spain is an exception, with a short spate of BITs in the 1990s only. Potential hosts, however, demonstrate a different pattern: their BIT signings spike up in a more clustered pattern, one indicative of programmatic activity (Figure 6.5).[27]

Evidence of programmatic activity can be established statistically as well. Comparing the average kurtosis[28] for the historical distribution of BITs among both home and host countries, it is clear that the distribution of BITs over the past forty years is significantly more peaked (less uniform) for the host than it is for home countries (9.11 and 4.48, respectively). The standard deviation of their distributions over time is also lower for host countries than it is for home (7.08 versus 9.39, respectively), suggesting a more clustered pattern of activity for the host. If BITs are driven by home country programs, it is not especially apparent in the data. Rather, it appears that potential hosts are more likely to sign in clusters – suggesting that while the major capital exporters stand ready with model treaties in hand, the decision whether and when to sign is left to a large extent to the host.

[26] Simmons, Dobbin, and Garrett 2006.

[27] Appendices 1 and 2, available online [https://netfiles.uiuc.edu/zelkins/www], also organized by capital-exporting and importing countries, summarize the BIT history for all 178 countries that have ever signed a BIT.

[28] Kurtosis is the degree to which a distribution is peaked, or clustered, with high kurtosis indicating clustered data, and low kurtosis indicating a more uniform distribution.

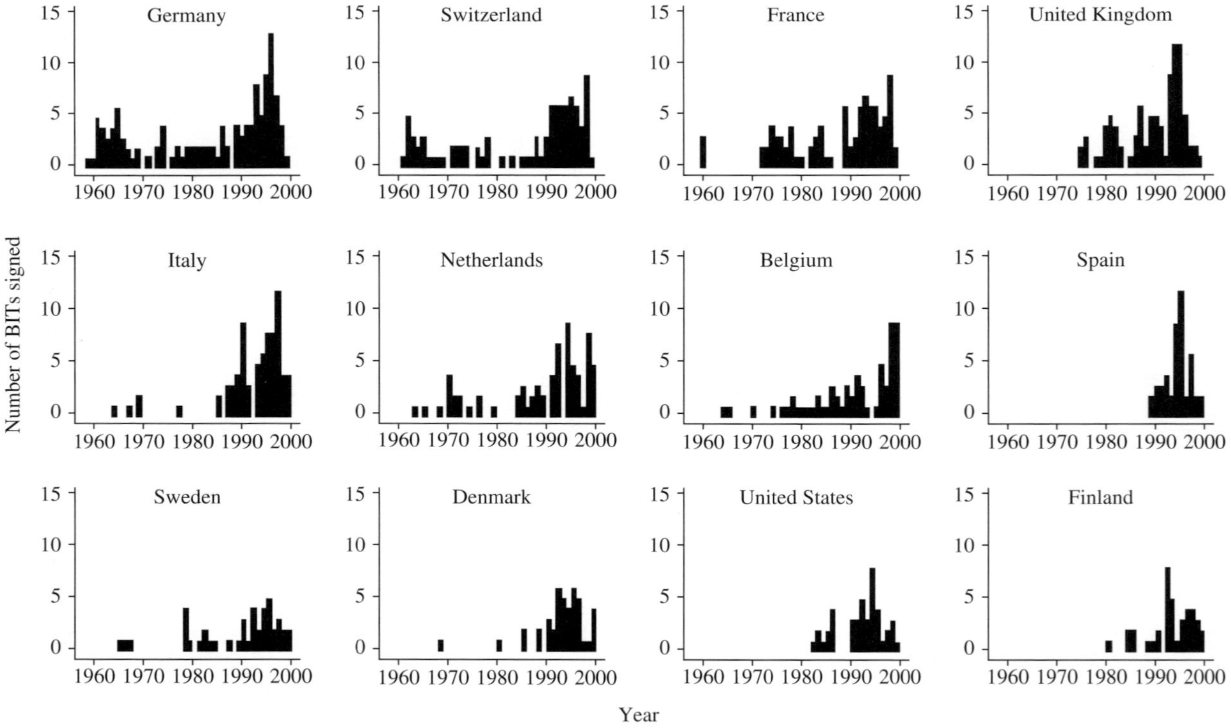

Figure 6.4 Number of BITs signed, by country, 1959–1999
Notes: Figure includes the twelve most active BIT signers of capital-exporting countries.

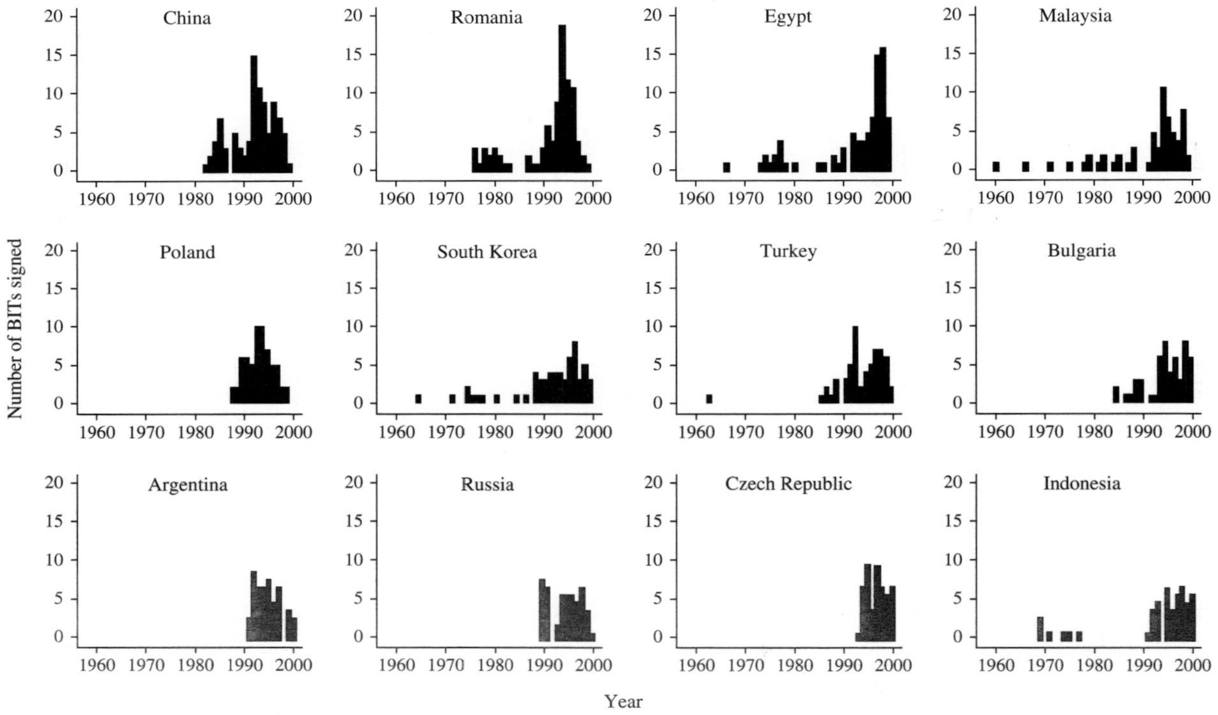

Figure 6.5 Number of BITs signed, by country, 1959–1999
Notes: Figure includes the twelve most active BIT signers among capital-importing countries.

The notion that home countries make take-it-or-leave-it offers to potential hosts and that hosts eventually decide to sign BITs is also consistent with the observed content of BITs. These treaties tend to provide consistent terms, even across different home countries. In particular, the core terms of the treaties are almost always present: mandatory dispute resolution before an international arbitration body, a private right of action for investors, monetary compensation in the event of a violation, national treatment, and most-favored-nation treatment. This uniformity suggests that host countries are "price-takers" with respect to the terms of these treaties, consistent with our assumptions. In essence, each home country has market power over the terms that will govern investment by its locals. Host countries, on the other hand, realize that they must compete with other potential hosts, and therefore cannot demand changes to the core provisions of the treaties.

A competitive theory of BIT diffusion

Our theory of BIT diffusion[29] has a simple structure. BITs are viewed by host governments and by investors as devices that raise the expected return on investments. The treaties do this by assisting governments in making credible commitments to treat foreign investors "fairly" – as described in the previous section. BITs give host governments a competitive edge in attracting capital[30] if there are otherwise doubts about their willingness to enforce contracts fairly. Accordingly, governments with little inherent credibility are more likely to sign BITs than are governments known for their fair treatment of foreign capital. The result is a competitive dynamic among potential hosts to reduce the risks and enhance the profitability of investing.

BITS as a credible commitment

Governments may have many motives to sign a BIT, but the most significant is to make a credible commitment to treat foreign investors fairly. BITs allow governments to make credible commitments because they raise the *ex post* costs of non-compliance above those that might be

[29] See Elkins and Simmons 2005 for a further elaboration of the concept of "diffusion."

[30] There is debate in the literature about the impact of BITs on investment flows. The small number of papers on the subject have generated inconsistent results. The most recent and sophisticated study of which we are aware, however, concludes that BITs do indeed increase FDI and serve as a substitute for good domestic institutional quality; Neumayer and Spess 2005. Other relevant studies include Hallward-Driemeier 2003; Tobin and Rose-Ackerman 2003; UNCTAD 1998.

incurred in the absence of the treaty. They do this by: (1) clarifying the commitment; (2) explicitly involving the home country's government; and (3) enhancing enforcement.[31]

BITs raise *ex post* costs of reneging on contracts by reducing the ambiguity of the host government's obligations. BITs are much more precise than customary international law in this area. They also provide a broader legal framework in which to interpret specific contractual obligations. Precision removes potential avenues of plausible deniability, making it clearer to a broader range of audiences (domestic audiences, other foreign investors, other governments), that an obligation has been disregarded. Clear violations imply a much greater reputational cost than do actions not clearly barred by law.[32]

The second way BITs raise *ex post* costs of reneging is by involving the investor's government as a treaty party. BITs are negotiated between sovereign states. State-to-state legal arrangements implicate the interests of the home government more directly than do simple investment contracts between private parties and host governments. The home government has an interest in broader principles of good-faith treaty observance. Treatment that violates a BIT qualifies as a breach of the fundamental principle of international law: *pacta sunt servanda* (treaties are to be observed). Reneging on a contract governed by a treaty arrangement can damage important foreign policy interests.

Finally, BITs raise *ex post* costs by significantly enhancing contract enforcement. These agreements contain mandatory dispute settlement provisions that investors are entitled to use when they feel the host state has violated the relevant BIT. Significantly, investors can begin arbitration proceedings without the approval or support of their home government. Moreover, the host can neither prevent the legal proceeding from going forward, nor control the final decision of the international arbitration tribunal. The international tribunal can require a host found to be in violation of its obligations to pay monetary damages. The sovereign host state could, of course, refuse to pay, but that decision could have even more profound reputational consequences: when a government spurns

31 We cast our argument in the credible commitments framework, but our competition argument may be compatible with signaling theories as well. Some of the empirical implications would be different than those we describe here, however. If a BIT is a signaling device, we would expect more reliable rather than less reliable property rights protectors to sign them. We might also expect less reliable governments to sign one, rather than multiple treaties, since one should suffice to send the signal. Empirically, we tend to observe multiple signings per host, which leads us to frame the issue as one of credible commitments rather than costly signals that reveal type. Both frameworks could, however, explain a competitive dynamic to sign BITs.

32 See Abbott *et al.* 2000; Lipson 1991; Guzman 2002.

the decision of a neutral authoritative third party with which it has voluntarily precommitted to comply, a range of important actors – public and private – are likely to infer that that government is an unreliable economic partner. By giving private parties a right to pursue and receive a legal remedy, BITs boost the credibility of the host government's commitment. As a result, we would expect some violations to be deterred by a BITs commitment and expected returns to investments to increase accordingly.

Do these formal dispute settlement mechanisms actually come into play in the way we have described? Theoretically, we should expect such arbitrations to be rare, because fully informed parties should be able to settle "out of court" and avoid litigation costs. When we do observe arbitration, it would be more likely to indicate information asymmetries than the seriousness of the case.[33] Nonetheless, a significant number of cases have in fact gone to arbitration. A recent conservative estimate puts the number at least 160 cases.[34] Due largely to controversial measures taken by its government in early 2002, Argentina alone has recently been a party to some thirty BIT arbitrations, most of them under ICSID and the rest under UNCITRAL rules.[35] BIT arbitrations have given rise to a number of significant awards, including recent decisions against the governments of the Czech Republic ($350 million), Lebanon ($266 million), and Ecuador ($70 million).[36]

In short, BITs represent a credible commitment because of the range of *ex post* costs – diplomatic costs, sovereignty costs, arbitration costs, and reputational costs – involved in both their observance and their violation. We argue below that some governments have incentives to increase these costs in order to attract FDI.

Competitive BIT signings: logic and implications

In the previous section we argued that BITs allow governments credibly to commit themselves to protect investors' property rights. The ability to do so lowers risks and increases expected returns to investment. If this is the

[33] This point has long been recognized in the law and economics literature, see Bebchuk 1984.

[34] UNCTAD 2004. This number omits, of course, disputes that were resolved prior to the arbitration stage.

[35] See www.bomchilgroup.org/argmar04.html#16. [Accessed June 20, 2006.]

[36] For examples of awards, see reports of the International Institute for Sustainable Development, available at www.iisd.org/investment. [Accessed June 20, 2006.] See also *The National Law Journal*, Arbitration Survey, "Global Litigation," September 15, 2003. See also http://blog.lewrockwell.com/lewrw/archives/Friedman-BITs-9-15-03.pdf. [Accessed June 20, 2006.]

case, BITs can be a mechanism – such as favorable tax treatment, lower wages, and efficient infrastructure – for making a jurisdiction a more attractive place in which to invest. As with these other mechanisms, committing to a BIT involves costs for the host government. We characterize these as "sovereignty costs." They are the costs any government pays when it negotiates, ratifies, and complies with an investment treaty. We would include here the political costs of assembling a coalition in support of foreign investors' rights, as well as the costs associated with giving up a broad range of policy instruments relevant to domestic social or developmental purposes (taxation, regulation, performance requirements, property seizure, and currency and capital restrictions). Most striking are the sovereignty costs associated with the delegation of adjudicative authority: virtually any legal change or rule that affects foreign investors is potentially subject to review by a foreign tribunal. The decision to sign a BIT always involves an assessment by the host of whether the expected benefit of attracting an additional increment of foreign capital outweighs these costs. In many cases, the answer is no. In this section, we discuss the conditions under which the expected benefits for a particular government might outweigh these sovereignty costs.

BITs can attract capital from two broad resource pools. First, they can shift resources from consumption or domestic investment, effectively stimulating new international capital investments that would not have been made absent the treaty. Secondly, and more importantly for our theory, BITs can redirect international capital flows from one venue to another. A BIT gives the host signatory a "reputational advantage" over otherwise comparable rivals in the competition for (re)distribution of an existing investment pool.[37] The possibility of investment diversion means that governments may have competitive reasons to implement BITs. It is the ability of a BIT – or at a minimum, its perceived ability – to give one country an advantage over other similarly situated countries in the competition for capital that we hypothesize provokes many BIT signings.[38]

The strategic structure we are describing creates serious collective action problems among potential host countries. Collectively, they might be better off resisting the demands of investors (avoiding the sovereignty costs described above), but individually it is rational to sign in hopes of stimulating capital inflows. In recognition of this dynamic,

[37] This redistributive effect contrasts with customary international law, under which all potential hosts have the same obligations and enjoy the same benefits.

[38] Guzman 1998 provides a more complete discussion of the potential impact of competition on BITs.

one finds cases of regional attempts to coordinate host resistance. In the Caribbean, for example, collective efforts have been made to reduce BIT concessions,[39] though predictably the "cartel" has been difficult to maintain.[40] The breakdown of such efforts is consistent with the competitive context we believe accounts for the proliferation of BITs over the past several years.

A competitive theory of BITs has at least four observable implications. First, BITs should diffuse among host country competitors – countries that, from an investor's point of view, are closely substitutable venues for investment. It is precisely these countries that should display the clearest evidence of interdependent decision making. This is a unique prediction of competitive theory. No other diffusion mechanism – whether hegemonic, cognitive, or ideational – makes this specific prediction.

Second, BITs should spread most readily to countries where the competition for capital is the most intense. Competition intensifies where the number of plausible hosts for a particular investment project is greatest. For this reason, host competition for investment in extractive goods is far less intense than in light manufactures: while the number of countries in which bauxite mining is profitable is quite limited, almost any jurisdiction can host a Nike plant. If our competition hypothesis is correct, these treaties should be more prevalent where host competition is most fierce: in light manufactures rather than in primary production or extractive industries. This prediction is the exact opposite of what one might expect were BITs propelled in a "hegemonic" fashion, by the home country. From a home government's point of view, theories of obsolescing bargaining should predict the need for enforceable investment protections precisely in those industries that involve large upfront difficult-to-relocate investments. Obsolescing bargaining[41] suggests investors are more likely

[39] CARICOM (Caribbean Community) countries, for example, produced a document entitled "Guidelines for Use in the Negotiation of Bilateral Treaties" that states, among other things, that CARICOM countries should not accept any restriction on the use of performance obligations and that they should retain the right to nationalize and to "determine at the time of nationalization the quantum of compensation and the terms of payment." Source: Caribbean Community Secretariat, reproduced in "UNCTAD, International Investment Instruments: A Compendium," vol. III.

[40] Jamaica, a member of CARICOM when the guidelines were adopted, signed a string of BITs with important partners in the late 1980s and early 1990s, including the United Kingdom (1987); Switzerland (1990); the Netherlands (1991); Germany (1992); France (1993); Italy (1993); the United States (1994); Argentina (1994); and China (1994). These BITs include performance requirements and compensation provisions that are inconsistent with the CARICOM guidelines.

[41] See Vernon 1971, 1977.

to demand treaties to protect their extractive and primary production investments, at least relative to easier-to-relocate light manufactures.[42]

Third, BITs should spread as the pool of available capital grows. As the pool of global capital grows, any competitive advantage (such as that conferred by a BIT) should yield a larger marginal increase in FDI inflows. Thus, the expected return per BIT should increase with the size of the investment pool, which encourages hosts to scramble to improve access to a share of the bigger "pie." While other researchers have suggested that BITs may contribute to a growth in FDI,[43] our theory suggests a possible feedback loop: the expectation of greater payoffs may stimulate more treaties. This relationship is not predicted by more sociological explanations, which might expect BITs to proliferate as a function of the density of BITs themselves, rather than the growing volume of investment. Nor is it predicted by learning theories, which would presumably require a demonstration that BITs actually "work" in attracting capital.

Finally, while all countries should be subject to some degree to the competitive pressures we have theorized above, BITs should diffuse somewhat more readily among host governments that lack credibility. For these countries, a BIT can be expected to make a real difference to investors, other factors held constant. In countries that already have institutions and practices that are favorable to investors, transparent, and predictable, a costly BIT adds relatively little value. These states may be able to compete for capital on the basis of their "inherent" credibility. This relationship is in principle consistent with power-based explanations (powerful home governments may be more likely to demand BITs from unreliable hosts than inherently reliable ones), but it is much less consistent with more sociological accounts discussed in Simmons, Dobbin, and Garrett in this volume. If governments have been "socialized" to accept the dominant paradigm for investor protection, there would be no reason for the more credible host governments to largely exempt themselves.

A competitive theory of BITs predicts that the host countries most likely to sign treaties will be those whose competitors have signed, those who depend on manufacturing over extractive production, and those with a credibility gap. More generally, a competitive theory predicts increased treaties as the pool of available capital grows. In the following section, we develop an empirical strategy for testing these hypotheses against alternative explanations.

42 Kobrin 1987 finds that manufacturing is not characterized by the inherent, structurally based and secular obsolescence that is found in the natural resource-based industries.

43 Neumayer and Spess 2005.

Empirical methods and data

Analytical design

We use an event history framework to estimate the duration of time before two countries sign a BIT. Our analysis begins in 1958, the year before the first BIT, and includes those BITs concluded up to January 1, 2000, the last year for which we have accurate data. Since the focus of the analysis is a bilateral agreement between governments in a given year, the appropriate unit of analysis is the country dyad-year. In each dyad, we identify the potential "home" and the potential "host" country based on their relative level of development, as measured by GDP per capita. Of course, such designations become less meaningful the closer the members of the dyad are in their level of development. But treaties among countries of a similar level of development – especially at the higher end – are considerably less likely. In the reported analyses we exclude "developed dyads" from the sample in order to minimize the bias from estimates derived from "irrelevant dyads."[44] Otherwise, our sample includes all independent states, as identified by Gleditsch and Ward.[45]

Event history methods offer a convenient way to incorporate time dependence in models of policy or innovation adoption. Our formulation is slightly more complicated than most since the unit of analysis is the country dyad and the model includes variables measured for one or the other member of the dyad as well as for the dyad itself. We estimate the following equation:

$$y_{ij,t} = \alpha X_{i,t} + \beta Z_{j,t} + \delta V_{ij,t} + \rho W y^{*}_{t-1} + \varepsilon_{ij} \qquad (1)$$

where y_{ij} is the number of years without a BIT between countries i (host) and j (home), X is a vector of conditions that affect country i's calculations, Z is a vector of conditions that affect country j's calculations, V is a

[44] We exclude dyads in which both members are classified as "high income countries" by the World Bank (that is, dyads in which both members have a GDP per capita of over $6,000 (in 1987 US$) in a given year), thus excluding 125 BITs in the analysis.

[45] Gleditsch and Ward 1999. Restricting our sample to those states (and their dates of existence) identified by Gleditsch and Ward means that we exclude eighteen BITs listed in the UNCTAD data such as the fourteen to which Hong Kong was party as well as those involving states such as the United Arab Emirates and Slovenia, which occur several years prior to the dates that Gleditsch and Ward list the states as independent. The relatively inclusive sample ensures that we will encounter missing data, particularly for smaller countries. We experiment with several methods of managing missing data, none of which alter the substantive findings. For the results below, we have estimated missing values of time-varying covariates with decade means where possible and appropriate. Such extrapolations buy a more inclusive sample at the expense of potentially underestimated standard errors; see King *et al.* 2001.

vector of characteristics of the relationship between countries *i* and *j*, and $Wy^\star$ is a vector of spatial lag terms in which a count of BITs among other host countries in the previous year ($y^\star$) is weighted by various measures of their distance (W) to country *i* (see our discussion of spatial lags below). We estimate this equation with a Cox proportional hazard model, a useful estimator when one does not have strong assumptions about the effect of time on the baseline hazard.

Data and measures

Our dependent variable is the number of years a dyad goes without a treaty, marked by the year of a treaty's signing, rather than the year in which it enters into force.[46] We reason that the signing not only approximates the moment during which a government deliberates over the treaty, but is also the more important event for purposes of sending a pro-investment signal to international markets.[47] Both UNCTAD and the World Bank's ICSID track the date and signatories of BITs. While the two sources basically agree, UNCTAD's list is more recent and more comprehensive.[48] As the equation above indicates, our independent variables take on one of four analytic forms: (1) independent factors associated with the "home" country; (2) independent factors associated with the "host" country; (3) factors associated with the relationship between host and home countries; and (4) spatial lags of the dependent variable.

Spatial lags of the dependent variable: competition and cultural emulation To assess the source and strength of the various influences of policy diffusion, we construct a series of spatial lags, modeled largely after those in Simmons and Elkins.[49] Spatial lag models treat spatial dependence in the same way time-series models treat serial correlation.[50] Instead of (or, in our case, in addition to) lagging the value of the dependent variable one unit in time, one "lags" it one (or more) unit in space to capture the behavior of neighbors. Thus, the general formulation of the spatial lag above, $Wy^\star$, in which W is an N by N by T spatial weights

[46] While approximately forty dyads have entered into second and, in one case, third treaties, we predict the duration until the first treaty.

[47] "As the great majority of BITs are ratified, it is reasonable to assume that, in the perception of investors, signing a BIT is the crucial action: Once a BIT is signed, or expected to be signed, the market has absorbed it or begins to absorb it" (UNCTAD 1998:106).

[48] Our comparison of the two data sets found that, for the years they overlapped (1959–1997), UNCTAD included over two hundred treaties not included in the ICSID database.

[49] Simmons and Elkins 2004. [50] Anselin 1988.

matrix that maps the distances between units for each year and y⋆ is an N by T matrix of values that represent some function of the dependent variable for all countries other than i. In our case, y⋆ represents the sum total of BITs in force for each host country in a given year.[51] We then compute the weighted average of y⋆ by dividing the sum of its product with W, by a row sum of W. Thus, the spatial lag for country i using the weight w is as follows:

$$= \frac{w_{ij}y_j^* + w_{ik}y_k^* + \ldots + w_{in}y_n^*}{w_{ij} + w_{ik} + \ldots + w_{in}} \quad (2)$$

This computation of Wy⋆ allows an intuitive interpretation of the spatial lag: it is the average number of BITs in force among other host countries, weighted by some distance to country *i*. Since the spatial lag is endogenous, we lag it one year to capture the behavior of other host countries in the previous year, a chronology that makes more sense for the causal logic of diffusion as well.[52] Note that the W matrix can represent not only geographic distances, but also economic, cultural, or political distances among countries.[53]

Our theory predicts interdependent decision making among host countries that compete for the same sources of global capital. Thus, we need to determine the "competitive distance" between hosts. We create spatial weights that capture this distance in three ways. The first measures the degree to which host governments compete in the same foreign markets; that is, whether they have the same export trade relationships.[54] (All data

[51] This formulation assumes that it is the accumulation of treaties among peers, not the "event" of their recent signing, that provokes a response. We also experimented with an event trigger by calculating the number of BITs signed by others in the previous year. In fact, the results were largely comparable.

[52] While spatial lags are common solutions to estimating the relational effects that we hypothesize, they do introduce a potential degree of endogeneity. Unless non-diffusion predictors are included in the model, spatial lags can absorb these effects when the domestic variables are correlated within the network. For this reason, some scholars have moved toward simultaneous equation modeling, in order to model the endogeneity. Recent monte-carlo evidence reported in Franzese and Hays (2004) suggests that the costs associated with such models may outweigh their benefits in large samples. Our solution is to specify the non-diffusion components as completely as possible and to lag the spatial lag one year. Nonetheless, we recognize that effects from spatial lags may be slightly inflated.

[53] Elkins and Simmons 2004; Beck, Gleditsch, and Beardsley 2006.

[54] We use the IMF Direction of Trade data to produce an N by N by T matrix of correlations (between countries) across the countries' proportion of exports to each of the 182 partner countries. Two countries that export goods in the same proportions to 182 countries will have a score of 1; while those with entirely opposite relationships will have a score of –1. For a similar approach, see Finger and Kreinin 1979. Network analysts often use this sort of measure to identify competitors; see Wasserman and Faust 1994.

sources and descriptive statistics are provided in Appendix 6.1.) This is a useful indicator because trade competitors are also likely to be competitors for FDI and empirical studies show that the two are strongly correlated. We reason that countries that compete for export markets are structurally positioned to compete for the same sources of FDI as well. The second measure records the degree to which nations export the same basket of goods.[55] This measure captures the idea that investors choose between alternative locations for direct investment that they consider close substitutes with respect to the countries' traditional export products. For example, an automobile manufacturer might consider investing in countries that produce steel but will be unlikely to consider those whose leading export is cocoa. Our third measure captures the degree to which countries have similar educational and infrastructure resources. Assuming that potential foreign direct investors are concerned with a country's human assets as well as its technological and communications infrastructure, we reason that countries with similar educational and infrastructural profiles will compete for the same pool of capital.[56] For all three competition measures, we compute a spatial lag by anchoring the distances (measured as correlations) at zero by adding 1 to each score and then using these distances to calculate a weighted sum of BITs in force in all other host countries in the previous year.

The competition distances themselves appear to have a fair degree of validity. For example, Figure 6.6 plots the values for the "distance" in export products between Brazil and select countries across time. If these values are to be believed, Brazil's products correlated quite highly with those of most Latin American countries in the 1960s and 1970s. This correlation decreased in the 1990s, at which time Brazil's export profile began to resemble that of the United States and Canada more than that of its Latin American neighbors. This finding is consistent with the common interpretation of the increasingly diversified Brazilian economy, whose exports in everything from technology to agriculture now compete

[55] We calculate the distance between countries according to their export products, using information from the World Bank's *World Development Indicators* (WDI) CD-ROM that describes a country's export mix. These indicators tap the value of exports (in 1995 US$) in sectors such as food, fuel, agricultural raw materials, ores and metals, and arms. We calculate the correlation between countries for each year across thirteen such indicators. The result is a measure, ranging from −1 to 1, of the similarity between countries according to the products they export.

[56] We compare such investment profiles by calculating correlations, by year, between countries across roughly fifteen educational and infrastructural variables selected from the WDI. These distances range from −1 to 1.

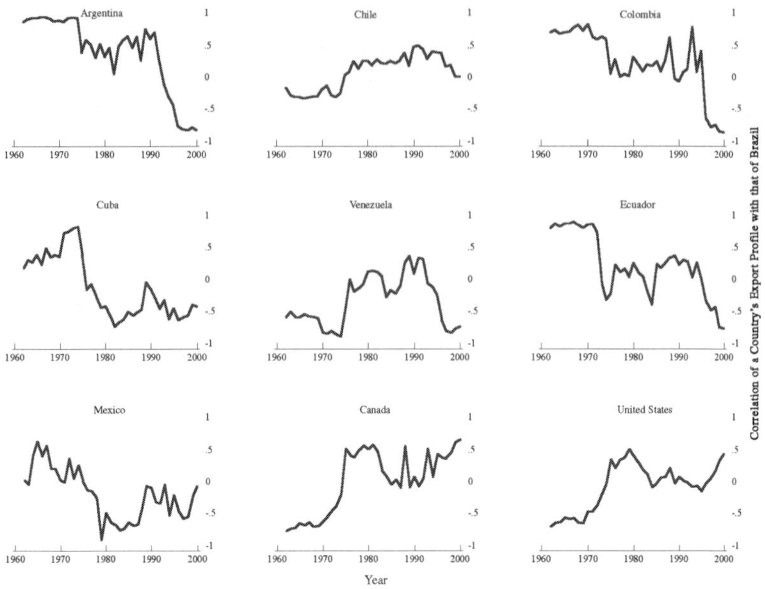

Figure 6.6 A measure of export market similarity; the Brazilian case

directly with the United States and less directly with smaller Latin American states.[57]

We also use spatial lags in a similar way to measure the influence of an important alternative explanation suggested in Simmons, Dobbin, and Garrett,[58] that of cultural peers. We use three measures of "cultural distance": predominant religion, colonial heritage, and predominant language. The spatial lag for these "distances" is calculated in the same weighted-average manner as for the competitive distances. Unlike the competition measures, the cultural distances are binary; a country either shares a common language with another, or it does not. The cultural spatial lags, therefore, are equivalent to the mean number of BITs in force among those host countries with the same cultural identity (religion, language, or colonial heritage). These measures capture an important possibility: that BITs result more from socially constructed emulation of policies of important reference groups than from hard-nosed economic competition. Note that this measure does not capture whether BITs are more likely between cultural peers, an effect we test with the cultural distance variables themselves (see below).

[57] Baer 2001. [58] Simmons, Dobbin, and Garrett 2006.

Alternative diffusion mechanisms: learning and coercion Finally, we seek to capture the effects of policy learning and coercion. Our notion of learning, consistent with that articulated in Simmons, Dobbin, and Garrett,[59] implies that policymakers from host countries are motivated to sign BITs based on the treaties' demonstrated benefits (specifically, increased FDI). Our model does not assume policymakers have Herculean powers of observation or analysis; nor does it treat them as remedial statisticians. We assume simply that policymakers assess the success of countries in attracting investment over recent years given the countries' level of development and their number of treaties in force during this time. We replicate this cognitive process by regressing, each year, the average FDI inflows as a percentage of GDP for the previous five years on the average number of treaties in force for that country during that period as well as its average GDP per capita. The standardized regression coefficient for the BITs variable in each of these yearly equations is our indicator of a policymaker's estimate of the payoff of these treaties in terms of increased investment.[60] Thus, we assume that each year decision makers observe and draw conclusions about the effects of BITs on investment, controlling for a country's level of development, and that all actors observe the same signal.

Because FDI data is sparse in the 1960s, the effect of the treaties is incalculable with any degree of certainty, both for us and for policymakers at the time. Throughout the 1970s and most of the 1980s, the apparent effect of BITs is effectively zero or even negative. However, by the early 1990s – the period in which more than half of existing BITs were signed – BITs appear to have obvious payoffs. Those countries with BITs in force in those years are clearly also the recipients of investment.[61] The coefficient in 1990, for example, suggests that each BIT in force is associated with an extra .05 percent of GDP in investment. Thus, BITs in a country with fifty such agreements (for example, Chile) would account for added investment roughly equivalent to 2.5 percent of the country's GDP (that is, for Chile, more than a $1 billion). This is the difference between having no foreign direct investment and having the worldwide average for a low- or middle-income country, for which gross FDI averages

59 Ibid.

60 In order to compute these results, we use only those data that are immediately available to us (and, more to the point, to policymakers). We reason that our informational constraints should match those of policymakers. As such, we use data reported in the World Bank's WDI and do not make efforts to impute or otherwise fill in missing data in these equations.

61 Such mixed results do not seem surprising given the discrepant findings of scholars on this question (see note 30).

around 2.3 percent of GDP. To an observant host country in 1990, BITs would certainly appear to have some demonstrable benefits.

We consider one final interdependent mechanism, coercion. It may be that potential hosts are coerced or at least strongly encouraged to enter into BITs. If so, a likely juncture for the application of such pressure is at the time a country seeks International Monetary Fund (IMF) credits. We incorporate a dichotomous measure of whether or not a country has drawn on IMF resources in a given year. Though we do not believe the pursuit of or entry into BITs is explicitly stipulated in formal loan conditions, there may be more subtle pressures on a state in balance of payments difficulties to use these treaties to attract foreign capital.

Home country considerations The proliferation of BITs could be explained by two home country considerations: the desire to protect existing overseas capital, and the desire for additional investments. These considerations could significantly influence the pool of BITs that is potentially available, independently of any competitive dynamic among potential hosts. In the analysis that follows we control for the total FDI "exposure" of the home country; that is, the degree to which a country's capital is actually invested abroad. For this we use a measure of net FDI outflows as a proportion of GDP (scored positively when outflows outweigh inflows and negatively when inflows outweigh outflows). On average, we expect high outflows to produce a greater willingness to supply BITs on the part of investors' governments.

In models not reported here, we also include country dummies for the identity of home governments with the most active BIT programs (Germany, Switzerland, France, the United Kingdom, Italy, and the United States) in order to absorb any idiosyncratic tendencies to pursue BITs and to capture the effect of large BIT programs.

Host country considerations Our competitive story of the proliferation of BITs suggests that competitive reputation building, through BITs, can set off a sequence of treaty signings among countries that compete with one another. Although all countries may be subject to such competitive pressures to some degree, we expect governments with greater indigenous credibility to be less willing to pay the sovereignty and other political costs associated with concluding BITs. We capture this idea by using an indicator of investors' perceptions of corruption in the host country. The more corrupt a state is perceived to be, the more necessary it becomes to lure investors with an explicit promise to delegate adjudication to an authoritative third party. We complement this measure with one of the nature of the legal system itself. Some research suggests common law systems tend to provide better property rights protections;[62] civil law systems are more likely, these scholars argue, to implement regulatory solutions to perceived social conflict[63] – arguably, the kind of approach likely to make external capital flinch. If civil law systems are less oriented toward credible rules of capital protection, governments in those systems should more frequently reach for an external commitment mechanism, such as a BIT.[64] Finally, we would like to use a measure of the extent to which the host's legal system is perceived by foreign investors as strong and impartial. Unfortunately, the measure that appears to be most appropriate for tapping legal strength and impartiality ("law and order") is confounded by the inclusion of investors' assessment of popular observance of the law, which likely has little to do with the judiciary's attitude toward foreign investors. Nonetheless, our argument implies that a reputation for "law and order" should reduce a host's need to sign a BIT.

Another important factor, and one with implications for our competition story, has to do with a country's exposure to competition. If BITs are driven by competition for capital, they should be most prevalent where that competition is most fierce. We have argued that competition for capital is most cutthroat in manufacturing; by comparison, there are limited sites worldwide that produce copper or other extractive commodities. The fewer the alternative investment sites, the more protected the host from international competition, and the less likely a host is to sign a BIT. To capture this idea, we construct a measure of extractive industry dependence by summing the share of each country's exports of both fuel and "ores and metals," as recorded in the World Bank's *World Development Indicators* (WDI) CD-ROM. Approaches emphasizing the coercive role of dominant powers would anticipate a positive coefficient for extractive industries, since these are most subject to obsolescing bargaining and hence intensified political risks. Our expectation, however, is that this effect will be swamped by competition among hosts for manufacturing FDI, and we anticipate a negative effect. The outcome on the extractive industry variable thus provides a fairly crisp test of the importance of competition among hosts in explaining the proliferation of BITs.

62 La Porta *et al.* 1997, 1998. 63 Botero *et al.* 2002.

64 We use an indicator of a English common law tradition generated by the World Bank and used by La Porta *et al.* 1997, 1998; see Easterly and Sewadeh 2001. We have some misgivings about using this measure to capture reputation for property rights protections, especially since Simmons (forthcoming) has shown that common law countries are much less likely to sign human rights treaties, which points to a more general orientation toward international treaties of all kinds.

Quite aside from indicators of the need for a credible commitment discussed above, a number of economic conditions make particular hosts especially attractive BIT partners. We control for the economic desirability of the investment site by controlling for market size of the host country (log of the host's GDP),[65] the host's level of development (GDP per capita),[66] the quality of the host's workforce (rate of illiteracy), and the host's growth (GDP growth rate).[67] We also include a rather direct measure of the host's attractiveness for capital, FDI net inflows in the previous year, as a percentage of GDP.[68]

Finally, we control for other political and policy conditions in the host country. Since investors may see democracies as less capricious, we control for the host's level of democracy. It is possible that the pattern of BITs is driven by a few countries' aggressive privatization programs, and so we control for the value of privatized assets in a given year. Finally, we recognize that to sign BITs requires a certain degree of diplomatic capacity. We account for the diplomatic and legal capacity to enter into BITs by controlling for the total number of embassies a country hosts and has established in foreign countries.[69] A host with extensive diplomatic representation is more likely to have the international political and legal capacity to conclude a larger volume of treaties.

Characteristics of country pairs In this analytic category we identify the relational variables that might be associated with the likelihood of an agreement between the two nations. We focus on three kinds of relationships: business, security, and cultural relationships. Since firms are likely to want to invest in or near their export markets and to otherwise take advantage of vertical downstream linkages,[70] we control for the intensity of business transactions, proxied by the extent of trade

65 Kobrin 1976; Wheeler and Mody 1992. 66 Henisz 2000.

67 See Kobrin 1976; Wheeler and Mody 1992.

68 The literature on agglomeration economies, stressing the increasing benefits of colocation by economic units, provides a justification for including prior FDI inflows; see Wheeler and Mody 1992. As current and future FDI is likely affected by the very agreements we predict in this model, we lag the measure one year.

69 See Guzman and Simmons 2005.

70 The literature that has focused on firm and industry level explanations for the location of FDI emphasizes that firms that depend on foreign sales are more likely to invest overseas. For example, some research suggests that a firm's decision to deepen its presence in a particular country is influenced by the extent of its prior experience in that jurisdiction; see Ball and Tschoegl 1982. Others have found that firms are more likely to invest where they have strategic advantages, and these are plausibly connected with vertical downstream linkages; see Kimura 1989. The measure proposed here assumes these effects may show up in the aggregate trade relationships at the national level.

between the two countries. Investment agreements may also have a foreign policy[71] or even a security rationale as well. To address this possibility, we include a measure of the intensity of the alliance relationship for each pair. We also consider the possibility that BITs reflect cultural relationships, although this variable could have opposing effects. On the one hand, it may be easier for states with cultural similarities to negotiate successfully. On the other hand, if cultural similarities also reduce the perceived risks of investment, a common culture might operate in the opposite direction, reducing the need for a BIT. We test the relationship between cultural characteristics and BIT signing by coding country pairs with shared language and colonial traditions. Note that these variables should not be confused with the cultural spatial lags, which are measures of a host's peers' treaty activity.

Findings

We present estimates (as hazard ratios) from three specifications of our model (Table 6.2). A hazard ratio of more than 1 represents a positive effect on the odds of a BIT; less than 1, a negative effect. The first regression includes the export partner lag together with the full set of covariates described above. The last two regressions include one of the remaining two competitive spatial lags (export product similarity and infrastructure/workforce similarity) in a reduced form of the model. Several clear empirical patterns begin to emerge. There is fairly consistent and convincing evidence of the importance of competition for capital among developing countries in explaining the proliferation of BITs over the past four decades. In all cases, higher rates of BIT signing among competitors (however measured) appear to have increased the rate at which a given country itself enters into a BIT at statistically significant levels. One can appreciate the size of these effects in Figure 6.7a, which plots the survival curve for two different values of the spatial lag calculated from the "export product similarity" measure, the competition variable with the largest impact. In this illustration, a country whose competitors average fifteen agreements has a markedly increased risk of signing an agreement compared with a country whose competitors have refrained from signing. In the late 1990s (forty years after the inception of BITs), the difference between such countries in their probability of signing is almost 0.20. The results of these three competition variables alone

[71] See Gowa 1994; Pollins 1989.

Table 6.2. *A model of BIT signings: Cox proportional hazard model*

Explanatory variables	Model 1	Model 2	Model 3
Competitive theory			
BITS AMONG EXPORT MARKET COMPETITORS	1.05***		
	(0.01)		
BITS AMONG EXPORT PRODUCT COMPETITORS		1.11***	
		(0.04)	
BITS AMONG INFRASTRUCTURE COMPETITORS			1.04**
			(0.02)
AVERAGE ANNUAL GLOBAL FDI FLOWS	1.32***	1.53***	1.46***
	(0.12)	(0.14)	(0.13)
HOST EXTRACTIVE INDUSTRIES/EXPORTS	0.73**	0.73**	0.72***
	(0.09)	(0.09)	(0.09)
PERCEPTIONS OF HOST CORRUPTION	1.03	1.01	1.01
	(0.04)	(0.04)	(0.04)
HOST LEGAL TRADITION (COMMON LAW)	0.66***	0.65***	0.66***
	(0.05)	(0.05)	(0.05)
Alternative diffusion explanations			
BITS AMONG THOSE WITH SAME RELIGION	0.99	0.98	0.99
	(0.01)	(0.01)	(0.01)
BITS AMONG THOSE WITH SAME LANGUAGE	1.01		
	(0.06)		
BITS AMONG THOSE WITH SAME COLONIZER	0.99		
	(0.04)		
LEARNING FROM SUCCESS	1.85**	1.83*	2.13*
	(0.42)	(0.61)	(0.94)
COERCION: HOST USE OF IMF CREDITS	1.44***	1.39***	1.43***
	(0.12)	(0.11)	(0.12)
Host control variables			
HOST GDP (LN)	1.07**	1.03	1.04
	(0.04)	(0.04)	(0.04)
HOST GDP/CAPITA	1.00	1.00	0.99
	(0.03)	(0.03)	(0.03)
HOST GDP GROWTH	0.97***	0.97***	0.97***
	(0.01)	(0.01)	(0.01)
HOST NET FDI INFLOWS (% OF GDP), T−1	1.01	1.01	1.01
	(0.01)	(0.01)	(0.01)
HOST ILLITERACY RATE	0.34***	0.30***	0.30***
	(0.06)	(0.05)	(0.06)
HOST CAPITAL ACCOUNT/GDP	1.01	1.01**	1.01**
	(0.01)	(0.01)	(0.01)
HOST LAW AND ORDER	1.34***	1.39***	1.38***
	(0.05)	(0.05)	(0.05)
HOST DEMOCRACY	0.99	0.99	0.99
	(0.01)	(0.01)	(0.01)

Table 6.2. (*cont.*)

Explanatory variables	Model 1	Model 2	Model 3
HOST DIPLOMATIC REPRESENTATION	1.01***	1.01***	1.01***
	(0.00)	(0.00)	(0.00)
HOST PRIVATIZATION RECORD	1.05***	1.06***	1.06***
	(0.02)	(0.02)	(0.02)
Home control variables			
HOME NET FDI OUTFLOWS (% OF GDP)	1.13***	1.14***	1.14***
	(0.02)	(0.02)	(0.02)
Dyadic control variables			
DYADIC TRADE (% OF HOST'S GDP)	1.59*	1.61	1.64
	(0.35)	(0.56)	(0.57)
COMMON COLONIAL HERITAGE	0.41***	0.40***	0.41***
	(0.09)	(0.09)	(0.09)
COMMON LANGUAGE	1.57***	1.55***	1.54***
	(0.19)	(0.19)	(0.19)
ALLIANCE	1.18*	1.20*	1.18
	(0.10)	(0.11)	(0.14)
Common "shocks"			
COLD WAR	0.37***	0.31***	0.32***
	(0.08)	(0.06)	(0.06)
NUMBER OF BITS GLOBALLY, BY YEAR	1.03	1.00	1.01
	(0.03)	(0.03)	(0.03)
Observations	206766	208610	201073
Number of country pairs analyzed	6781	6831	6828
Number of BITs	1125	1140	1137
Log likelihood	−8723.114	−8858.474	−8823.590

Note:
Standard errors in parentheses.
*significant at 10%;
**significant at 5%;
***significant at 1%.

provide preliminary evidence that competition is central to the spread of BITs.

The evidence also suggests that as global FDI has increased, potential hosts have been more willing to sign BITs. One interpretation of this finding is that as the pool of FDI has increased, the competitive stakes for a share have grown. The pattern with respect to countries with predominantly extractive industries also provides corroboratory evidence for the competition theory. The results show that higher extractive production by the potential host reduces the propensity to negotiate a BIT (contrary

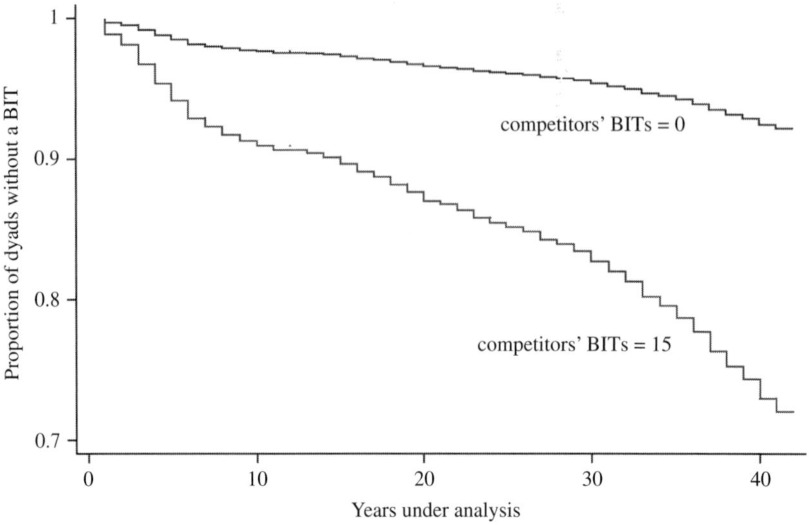

Figure 6.7a Survival estimates according to the average number of BITs of host's competitors (measured by export product similarity)
Notes: Estimates derived from Model 2 in Table 6.2.

to expectations based on investors' demands to address obsolescing bargains endemic to primary and extractive production). Figure 6.7b, which compares the signing rates for a government with a largely extractive-based economy versus one with an exclusively manufacturing-based economy, suggests that – ceteris paribus – signing rates can differ by as much as ten percentage points depending on a state's level of extractive material exports. Both the magnitude and stability of this effect across models suggests that it is a fairly robust finding.

We found inconsistent evidence, however, to support our expectation that host countries with a credibility gap are most likely to sign a BIT. Contrary to expectation, BITs were more likely to be signed by countries with better reputations for "law and order." We have already noted that this indicator only partially reflects our argument, as it conflates perceptions of the strength of the court system with perceptions of popular willingness to obey the law. Even so, the strong positive result is surprising. One possibility is that this measure is picking up the relatively favorable orientation of some countries toward legal solutions to conflicts generally. As we expected, perceptions of corruption were in the correct direction, although the hazard ratio is not statistically significant in any

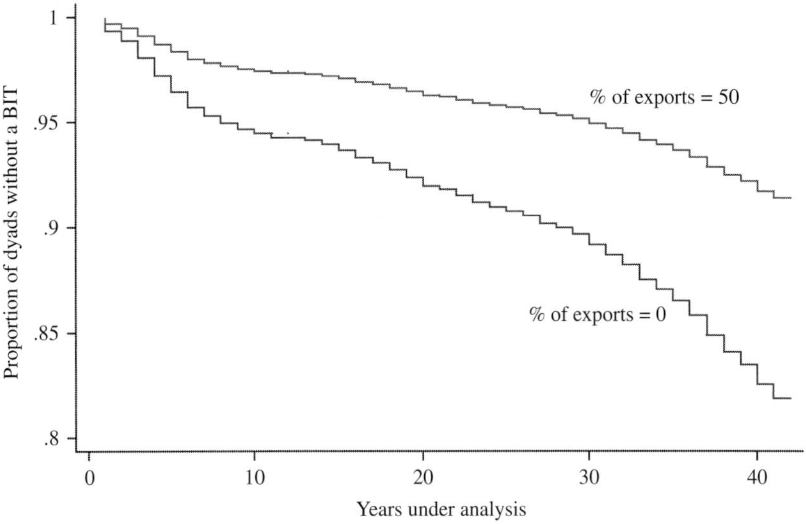

Figure 6.7b Survival estimates according to host's percent of exports in extractive industries
Notes: Estimates derived from Model 2 in Table 6.2.

specification that also contains "law and order." We should note that corruption is a significant determinant of signing a BIT whenever the law and order variable is not included. The common law variable did work as anticipated, but in light of the above findings, we think the prudent conclusion is that common law countries also refrain from entering into these agreements for reasons other than the reputational concerns developed here.[72]

In addition to the competition variables, our coercion variable (use of IMF credits) is significant in each of the models. This may mean that states seeking assistance from the IMF are encouraged to enter into BITs. Alternatively, it may be that the conditionality of IMF loans overlaps with the obligations of the BIT, reducing the costs of the latter. Interestingly, there is some evidence of learning from BIT outcomes. BITs are significantly more likely to be signed during years in which signatory states appear to be benefiting (in terms of FDI) from the treaties than when they are not. Such a pattern, of course, is consistent with our general theory of

[72] Simmons forthcoming.

competition over shares of FDI. We found no evidence, however, that countries sign agreements in response to signings in their cultural networks. None of the spatial lags along religion, language, or colonial heritage had consequential effects.

Many of the variables that would predict home country interest in offering a BIT to a developing country had somewhat unpredictable, and muted, effects. The size of the host economy and previous FDI inflows (as a percentage of host GDP) showed effects in the predicted direction, although rarely statistically significant across the models we tested. Meanwhile GDP per capita and economic growth had, if anything, the opposite effects of what we would expect, although only the economic growth coefficients were significant. On the other hand, we did find evidence that countries with a high quality workforce, as measured by literacy rates, and with an export orientation (current accounts tending toward surplus), were more likely to sign BITs (illiteracy is associated with a reduced likelihood of a BIT). Our prediction that privatization programs in a host country would coincide with BIT agreements was borne out as well. Similarly, host countries with a larger diplomatic presence were also more likely to enter into BITs. Finally, host's degree of democracy had practically no effect.

Certain control variables describing the relationships between home and host countries were important predictors of BITs. While the direction of dyadic trade is as hypothesized, the effect is statistically insignificant in two of three models. Political and cultural relationships seem to be more important. In accordance with expectations, BITs are more likely among allies, which could suggest a somewhat coercive element to their conclusion. A common language within the dyad makes it much more likely a pair of countries will negotiate a BIT, but a colonial link reduces by about two-thirds the likelihood that a country pair will do so. Perhaps investors in home countries perceive the risk in their colonial "families" to be lower than in other states. After all, colonies' legal institutions are likely to be similar to, if not partially overlap with, legal institutions in the mother country and fellow former colonies. This fits with our conception of BITs as being created to establish a credible legal framework for investment that is otherwise lacking.

In models not reported here, we attempted also to control for the BIT "programs" of particularly active countries by including country dummy variables for the five most active hosts and the five most active home countries. All were highly significant, with the partial exceptions of Germany and the United States. Their inclusion reduced substantially the effect of two variables, the volume of bilateral trade between country pairs and the home country net foreign direct investment. The robustness of the other results to the country dummies, however, reassures us that our results are not driven by idiosyncratic policies in a few of the most active countries.

Finally, we consider the potential impact of commonly experienced "shocks" on the propensity to sign BITs. All countries could have been affected by the Cold War, and our results indicate a significantly lower propensity to sign BITs during that era. Our more general measure of BIT period effects (the number of BITs signed in a given year), however, is insignificant in the company of our fairly comprehensive model. Whatever temporal clusters were evident in Figure 6.1 are accounted for by predictors in our model.

Conclusion

The use of bilateral investment treaties has grown significantly since the early 1960s. Their growth is especially remarkable given the outright rebellion many hosts have staged against customary law understandings and multilateral codifications of investors' rights that are quite similar to those contained in these proliferating bilateral accords. Why the disjuncture? How can we understand the spread of these pro-market agreements across time and space?

The diffusion mechanisms spelled out by Simmons, Dobbin, and Garrett in the introduction to this volume suggest a broad range of empirically verifiable hypotheses about movement toward BITs. Both theoretically and empirically, the competition model seems most apt in this case. These treaties are meant to improve conditions under which global capital relocates, prospers, and repatriates. They are also meant to raise the reputational stakes for governments of capital-poor economies by committing them to respect property and contractual rights of foreign investors and to agree to arbitration – effectively clipping their sovereignty – in the event of any disagreement over subsequent investment contracts. There are clearly possibilities here for mutual gain for hosts and investors, though we are agnostic about the global welfare effects of these treaties, given their potential redistributive consequences. We admit that some of the more recent treaties between very poor countries do not square with our straightforward competitive model; nonetheless, the strongest case can be made for a competitive diffusion dynamic in this case.

Let us begin with the project's null hypothesis: that country characteristics or commonly experienced shocks explain the pattern of BIT signings. There was plenty of support in the data for traditional economic explanations. Some of the most important drivers of the spread of BITs are likely factors that drive investment decisions more generally. The pattern of BITs shows that home governments want to secure investments in developing markets that are large, somewhat open, with high-quality labor. On the other hand, BITs are most valuable where political risk is endemic. China, which has concluded a large number of BITs with both rich and poor partners, would be the quintessential BIT partner, according to our model.

We also found strong evidence that dyadic characteristics explain BITs. BITs are much more likely to be negotiated among country pairs of the same culture (at least as measured by shared language) and among country pairs with strong security commitments. But if cultural linkages explain home–host pairs, cultural emulation is much less in evidence among potential hosts. Not one indicator of cultural emulation among hosts had any purchase at all on the adoption of BITs. These cultural arguments may in the end be a more satisfying account available for the growing category of "strange BITs" between highly indebted, capital poor, non-contiguous country pairs. We know anecdotally that third parties (France, UNCTAD) facilitated many of these agreements, indicating that in many cases external political or cultural forces may be crucial. The strong positive effect of IMF borrowing and alliance relationships on the propensity to sign a BIT also reminds us that a certain degree of coercion may be at play in some cases.

We do not doubt that multiple motives exist for the spread of this form of protection for foreign investors. But the competitive explanation has strong theoretical foundations and is the most consistently supported by the data. First, it was well supported by three different measures of "competitive space": by export market, export product, and workforce/infrastructural quality. When more of a host's closest competitors have signed BITs, that country is much more likely do so itself. The remarkable consistency across these three highly nuanced measures of competitive space provide strong initial evidence of a tendency to match the policy choices of competitors.

Second, the size and character of markets for foreign direct investment have fed the competitive atmosphere in predictable ways. The sheer size of the available pool of investment has greatly raised countries' stakes in securing a share. More BITs are signed when the global capital pool increases. This finding is of course consistent with home countries' concern to protect their investors as well as hosts' desire to increase their access. But a second finding much more clearly indicates that the impetus for signing is host-country driven. Our theory of competition among hosts predicts more BITs where the market for FDI is most competitive – the manufacturing sector. We found, in contrast to what theories of obsolescing bargaining would predict, that dependence on extractive industries reduced the probability that a host would make such a commitment.

Finally, a theory of host-driven competition was supported by some of our findings about the qualities associated with those hosts most likely to sign. We expected BITs to be pursued most assiduously by host governments whose domestic institutions render them least able to make credible commitments to protect property rights. When we excluded the possibly confounded "law and order" variable from our analysis, hosts were much more likely to sign if their regime was perceived as corrupt by foreign investors. They were also more likely to sign depending on the nature of their legal institutions. Common law countries – legal systems that some well-documented empirical work has shown to be associated with better legal protection for property rights – are much less likely to sign than are civil law countries. We recognize there are other reasons for common law countries to be reluctant to enter into international treaty obligations generally, but it remains possible that the differential ability of various legal traditions indigenously to protect property rights is at work as well. In this context, our finding on "law and order" is somewhat puzzling. But we are far less convinced that this indicator captures the domestic institutional guarantees of protection and fairness that foreign direct investors seek.

The diffusion of norms that protect investment has been further advanced by host governments' desire to attract a share of the global capital pool. We have doubts that this phenomenon can be explained by the appeal of liberal ideas alone, for we have witnessed the proliferation of BITs just as multilateral and customary law approaches have foundered. Most governments would prefer to avoid the explicit commitments contained in these treaties; there continue to be few concluded between the wealthiest countries of the world. In some regions, developing countries have tried to coordinate their responses to BITs in hopes of gaining more favorable terms, with notably limited success. In short, we base our conclusions on the importance of competition for capital not just on statistical relationships that show up in the quantitative analysis, but also on the broader context in which our analysis is nested.

BITs are part of a larger process of globalization that has been furthered by the dynamics of competition. This competition is driven by the desire of developing countries to participate in the global capitalist system. But has this uncoordinated strategy of signing away the sovereign right to regulate a growing segment of national economic activity yielded the results developing countries have hoped for? The evidence whether BITs actually succeed in attracting capital is unclear on this point. Our

Appendix 6.1. *Summary statistics and sources for variables included in the analysis*

	Variables	Mean	Standard deviation	Minimum	Maximum	Data sources
Dependent variable	BILATERAL INVESTMENT TREATY (SURVIVAL RATE)*	0.97	0.17	0	1	(1)
Explanatory variables						
Competition	BITS AMONG EXPORT MARKET COMPETITORS	2.79	3.72	0.00	36.57	(1), (2)
	BITS AMONG EXPORT PRODUCT COMPETITORS	3.70	4.12	0.00	19.20	(1), (3)
	BITS AMONG INFRASTRUCTURE COMPETITORS	3.41	3.84	0.03	18.21	(1), (3)
	AVERAGE ANNUAL NET FDI INFLOWS (% OF GDP)	1.26	1.28	− 1.17	3.90	(3)
	HOST EXTRACTIVE INDUSTRIES/EXPORTS	0.23	0.28	0.00	1.00	(3)
	PERCEPTIONS OF HOST CORRUPTION	3.27	1.23	0.00	6.00	(4)
	HOST LEGAL TRADITION (COMMON LAW)	0.32	0.47	0.00	1.00	(5)
Other diffusion mechanisms	BITS AMONG THOSE WITH SAME RELIGION	2.82	3.50	0.00	32.00	(1), (7), (8), (9)
	BITS AMONG THOSE WITH SAME LANGUAGE	3.12	3.54	0.00	43.25	(1), (7), (8), (9)
	BITS AMONG THOSE WITH SAME COLONIZER	2.59	3.59	0.00	56.39	(1), (7), (8), (9)
	LEARNING FROM SUCCESS	−0.15	0.22	−0.59	0.17	(1), (3)
	COERCION: HOST USE OF IMF CREDITS	0.74	0.41	0.00	1.00	(3)
Host country controls	HOST GDP (LN)	22.25	2.08	17.24	29.79	(3)
	HOST GDP/CAPITA	2.21	4.70	0.00	52.71	(3)
	HOST GDP GROWTH	3.89	5.54	−61.59	85.90	(3)
	HOST NET FDI INFLOWS (% OF GDP), T−1	1.32	3.95	0.00	145.13	(3)
	HOST ILLITERACY RATE	0.40	0.28	0.00	1.00	(3)
	HOST CAPITAL ACCOUNT/GDP	−4.74	8.54	−120.60	65.30	(3)
	HOST LAW AND ORDER	2.24	1.41	0.00	6.00	(4)
	HOST DEMOCRACY	−1.71	6.85	−10.00	10.00	(10)
	HOST DIPLOMATIC REPRESENTATION	38.08	32.25	0.00	158.00	(11)
	HOST PRIVATIZATION RECORD	0.18	0.80	0.00	14.80	(12)

Home country controls	HOME NET FDI OUTFLOWS (% OF GDP)	0.31	1.60	−26.06	14.65	(3)
Dyadic controls	DYADIC TRADE (% OF HOST'S GDP)	0.01	0.07	0.00	6.68	(2), (3)
	COMMON COLONIAL HERITAGE	0.05	0.21	0.00	1.00	(7), (8), (9)
	COMMON LANGUAGE	0.07	0.25	0.00	1.00	(7), (8), (9)
	ALLIANCE	0.05	0.22	0.00	1.00	(13)
Common "shocks"	COLD WAR	0.72	0.45	0.00	1.00	—
	NUMBER OF BITS GLOBALLY, BY YEAR	4.47	5.14	0.00	17.72	(1)

Notes:
*Summary statistics for the dependent variable expressed as average survival rates (rate of not signing a BIT).
Data sources: (1) UNCTAD, available at www.unctad.org/en/docs/poiteiiad2.en.pdf; (2) International Monetary Fund, Direction of Trade Statistics; (3) World Bank, *World Development Indicators* CD-ROM; (4) The PRS Group, available at www.prsgroup.com/; (5) La Porta, Lopez-De-Silanes, Shleifer, and Vishny 1997; La Porta, Lopez-de-Silanes, Shleifer, and Vishny 1998; (6) Alvarez, Cheibub, Limongi, and Przeworski 1996; Political and Economic Database Codebook, available at www.ssc.upenn.edu/~cheibub/data/ACLP_Codebook.PDF; various country websites; (7) Countries of the World and Their Leaders Yearbook 2000; (8) The Europa World Year Book 1999; (9) Central Intelligence Agency, CIA World Factbook. available at https://www.cia.gov/library/publications/the-world-factbook/index.html; (10) Polity IV, available at www.cidcm.umd.edu/polity/; (11) Tagish Diplomatic Directory, available at www2.tagish.co.uk/Links/embassy1b.nsf/; (12) Brune, Garrett, and Kogut 2004; (13) Correlates of War Project, available at http://cow2.la.psu.edu/; Gibler and Sarkees 2004.

research suggests why this may be the case. Competition for capital has important redistributive consequences. The result of the BIT competition may be only minimally improved access to capital at a high cost to national sovereignty.

References

Abbott, Kenneth, Robert O. Keohane, Andrew Moravcsik, Anne-Marie Slaughter, and Duncan Snidal. 2000. The Concept of Legalization. *International Organization* 54 (3):401–19.

Alvarez, Michael, José Antonio Cheibub, Fernando Limongi, and Adam Przeworski. 1996. Classifying Political Regimes for the ACLP Data Set. *Studies in International Comparative Development* 31: 3–36.

Anselin, Luc. 1988. *Spatial Econometrics: Methods and Models.* Dordrecht, Netherlands: Kluwer Academic.

Baer, Werner. 2001. *The Brazilian Economy: Growth and Development.* Westport, CT: Praeger.

Ball, Clifford A. and Adrian E. Tschoegl. 1982. The Decision to Establish a Foreign Bank Branch or Subsidiary: An Application of Binary Classification Procedures. *Journal of Financial and Quantitative Analysis* 17 (3):411–24.

Bebchuk, Lucian A. 1984. Litigation and Settlement Under Imperfect Information. *Rand Journal of Economics* 15 (3):404–15.

Beck, Nathaniel, Kristian Skrede Gleditsch, and Kyle Beardsley. 2006. Space is More than Geography: Using Spatial Econometrics in the Study of Political Economy. *International Studies Quarterly* 50 (1): 27–44.

Botero, Juan, Simeon Djankov, Rafael La Porta, Florencio Lopez-de-Silanes, and Andrei Schleifer. 2002. The Regulation of Labor. Available at www.econ.ucla.edu/workshops/papers/History/flopslabor.3.pdf [accessed July 9, 2006].

Brune, Nancy, Geoffrey Garrett, and Bruce Kogut. 2004. The International Monetary Fund and the Global Spread of Privatization. *IMF Staff Papers* 51 (2):195–219.

Dolzer, Rudolph. 1981. New Foundations of the Law of Expropriation of Alien Property. *American Journal of International Law* 75 (3):553–89.

Easterly, William and Mirvat Sewadeh. 2001. *Global Development Network Growth Database.* Washington, DC: World Bank. Available at http://econ.worldbank.org/WBSITE/EXTERNAL/EXTDEC/EXTRESEARCH/0contentMDK:20701055~pagePK:64214825~piPK:64214943~theSitePK:469382,00.html [accessed June 20, 2006].

Elkins, Zachary and Beth A. Simmons. 2005. On Waves, Clusters, and Diffusion: A Conceptual Framework. *Annals of the American Academy of Political and Social Science* 598: 33–51.

Finger, Joseph M. and M. E. Kreinin. 1979. Measure of Export Similarity and Its Possible Uses. *Economic Journal* 89 (356):905–12.

Franzese, Robert J. and Jude C. Hays. 2004. Modeling International Diffusion: Inferential Benefits and Methodological Challenges, with an Application to

International Tax Competition. WZB Markets and Political Economy Working Paper No. SP II 2004–12. Available at http://ssrn.com/abstract=560581 [accessed June 20, 2006].

Gibler, Douglas M. and Meredith Reid Sarkees. 2004. Measuring Alliances: The Correlates of War Formal Interstate Alliance Dataset, 1816–2000. *Journal of Peace Research* 41 (2):211–22.

Gleditsch, Kristian S. and Michael D. Ward. 1999. Interstate System Membership: A Revised List of the Independent States since 1816. *International Interactions* 25 (4):393–413.

Gowa, Joanne S. 1994. *Allies, Adversaries, and International Trade*. Princeton, NJ: Princeton University Press.

Guzman, Andrew. 1998. Explaining the Popularity of Bilateral Investment Treaties: Why LDCs Sign Treaties That Hurt Them. *Virginia Journal of International Law* 38: 639–89.

Guzman, Andrew. 2002. International Law: A Compliance Based Theory. *California Law Review* 90 (6):1823–88.

Guzman, Andrew and Beth A. Simmons. 2005. Power Plays and Capacity Constraints: The Selection of Defendants in WTO Disputes. *Journal of Legal Studies* 34 (2):557–98.

Hallward-Driemeier, Mary. 2003. Do Bilateral Treaties Attract FDI? Only a Bit ... And They Could Bite. Unpublished manuscript, World Bank, Washington, DC.

Henisz, Witold J. 2000. The Institutional Environment for Multinational Investment. *Journal of Law, Economics, and Organization* 16 (2):334–64.

Kimura, Yui. 1989. Firm-Specific Strategic Advantages and Foreign Direct Investment Behavior of Firms: The Case of Japanese Semiconductor Firms. *Journal of International Business Studies* 20 (2):296–314.

King, Gary, James Honaker, Anne Joseph, and Kenneth Scheve. 2001. Analyzing Incomplete Political Science Data: An Alternative Algorithm for Multiple Imputation. *American Political Science Review* 95 (1):49–69.

Kobrin, Stephen J. 1976. The Environmental Determinants of Foreign Manufacturing Investment: An Ex Post Empirical Analysis. *Journal of International Business Studies* 7 (2):29–42.

Kobrin, Stephen J. 1980. Foreign Enterprise and Forced Divestment in the LDCs. *International Organization* 34 (1):65–88.

Kobrin, Stephen J. 1987. Testing the Bargaining Hypothesis in the Manufacturing Sector in Developing Countries. *International Organization* 41 (4):609–38.

La Porta, Rafael, Florencio Lopez-De-Silanes, Andrei Shleifer, and Robert W. Vishny. 1997. Legal Determinants of External Finance. *Journal of Finance* 52 (3):1131–50.

La Porta, Rafael, Florencio Lopez-De-Silanes, Andrei Shleifer, and Robert W. Vishny. 1998. Law and Finance. *Journal of Political Economy* 106 (6):1113–55.

Lipson, Charles. 1985. *Standing Guard: Protecting Foreign Capital in the Nineteenth and Twentieth Centuries*. Berkeley: University of California Press.

Lipson, Charles. 1991. Why Are Some International Agreements Informal? *International Organization* 45 (4):495–538.

Minor, Michael S. 1994. The Demise of Expropriation as an Instrument of LDC Policy. *Journal of International Business Studies* 25 (1):177–88.

Neumayer, Eric and Laura Spess. 2005. Do Bilateral Investment Treaties Increase Foreign Direct Investment to Developing Countries? *World Development* 33 (10):1567–85.

Pollins, Brian M. 1989. Conflict, Cooperation, and Commerce: The Effect of International Political Interactions on Bilateral Trade Flows. *American Journal of Political Science* 33 (3):737–61.

Reading, Michael R. 1992. The Bilateral Investment Treaty in ASEAN: A Comparative Analysis. *Duke Law Journal* 42 (3):679–705.

Simmons, Beth A. Forthcoming. *International Human Rights: Law, Politics and Accountability*. Cambridge: Cambridge University Press.

Simmons, Beth A., Frank Dobbin, and Geoffrey Garrett. 2006. Introduction: The International Diffusion of Liberalism. *International Organization* 60 (4):781–810.

Simmons, Beth A. and Zachary Elkins. 2004. The Globalization of Liberalization: Policy Diffusion in the International Political Economy. *American Political Science Review* 98 (1):171–89.

Sornarajah, M. 1994. *The International Law of Foreign Investment.* New York: Cambridge University Press.

Tobin, Jennifer and Susan Rose-Ackerman. 2003. Foreign Direct Investment and the Business Environment in Developing Countries: The Impact of Bilateral Investment Treaties. Unpublished manuscript, New Haven, Yale University.

United Nations Conference on Trade and Development (UNCTAD). 1998. *Bilateral Investment Treaties in the Mid-1990s.* New York: United Nations.

United Nations Conference on Trade and Development (UNCTAD). 2004. *Occasional Note: International Investment Disputes on the Rise.* Geneva: UNCTAD.

Vagts, Detlev F. 1987. Foreign Investment Risk Reconsidered: The View from the 1980s. *ICSID Review – Foreign Investment Law Journal* 2 (1):1–18.

Vandevelde, Kenneth J. 1988. The Bilateral Investment Treaty Program of the United States. *Cornell International Law Journal* 21 (2):201–76.

Vernon, Raymond. 1971. *Sovereignty at Bay; the Multinational Spread of U.S. Enterprises*. New York: Basic Books.

Vernon, Raymond. 1977. *Storm over the Multinationals: The Real Issues.* Cambridge, MA: Harvard University Press.

Wasserman, Stanley and Katherine Faust. 1994. *Social Network Analysis: Methods and Applications*. Cambridge: Cambridge University Press.

Wheeler, David and Ashoka Mody. 1992. International Investment Location Decisions. *Journal of International Economics* 33 (1):57–76.

World Bank. 2002. *World Development Indicators* (CD-ROM). Washington, DC: World Bank.

7 Diffusion and the spread of democratic institutions*

Kristian Skrede Gleditsch and Michael D. Ward

Democracy and democratization in time and space

In 1989, a series of popular protests in the German Democratic Republic (GDR) forced the resignation of Erich Honecker and the fall of the wall separating the East German capital from West Berlin. The speed of the organization of the opposition and the fall of the regime surprised many Western observers.[1] Although dissatisfaction with economic and political conditions was assumed to be widespread in the GDR, the repressive character of the state made opposition very costly. Yet, it grew. The dramatic increase in the open opposition to the regime stemmed in part from changes in external conditions, as liberalization in other Eastern European states facilitated organizing protest in the GDR. The Soviet leader Mikhail Gorbachev had begun to let the countries in the Soviet bloc deal more independently with their own internal and foreign politics. The declining Soviet commitment to the Honecker regime lowered the perceived costs of protest, as a military response and invasion became less likely. Neighboring countries such as Hungary had initiated moves toward open, competitive elections. Since Hungary was a popular travel destination for East Germans, the opportunities for emigration to the German Federal Republic through neighboring states presented a huge problem to the regime in East Berlin. By the middle of 1989, many East Germans were heading to Hungary on "vacation" with all their worldly

* We are grateful for comments from Brian A'Hearn, Kyle Beardsley, Nathaniel Beck, Scott Gates, Håvard Hegre, David Lektzian, Jon Pevehouse, Dan Reiter, Kenneth Schultz, Heather Smith, Håvard Strand, and Kaare Strøm, as well as the editors of this volume and the participants at the Conferences on the International Diffusion of Democracy and Markets, University of California, Los Angeles, March 7–8, 2003, and the International Diffusion of Political and Economic Liberalization at the Weatherhead Center for International Affairs, Harvard University, Cambridge, MA, October 3–4, 2003. Beth A. Simmons, Lisa Martin, and anonymous reviewers have sought to focus our attention on making our theoretical and empirical arguments more compelling, and we thank them for their efforts.

[1] See Kuran 1991; Lohmann 1994.

possessions, having locked one last time their East German apartments. Lohmann argues that the extent of the emigration through neighboring countries also helped signal the extent of popular dissatisfaction with the regime, thereby altering people's expectations that others would participate in protests.[2] During the celebrations of the fortieth anniversary of the GDR there were massive demonstrations throughout the country. Although Honecker himself is reported to have been willing to use massive military force to defeat the protests – and indeed offered public praise for the Chinese solution in Tiananmen Square – others in the Politburo eventually intervened and ousted him from power. Even fundamentalist members of the Supreme Soviet viewed this tremendous change in Germany as both a harbinger and a result of massive structural change in international and regional politics.

In retrospect, it is easy to look back on the momentous change in the GDR as being ineluctable. Indeed, one prominent scholar has remarked that "it would appear that popular attitudes in East Germany were so powerfully influenced by messages transmitted neutrally from the West that democratization became unavoidable."[3] However, the collapse of the GDR was neither ineluctable nor completely explained by forces at work within the Democratic Republic, or for that matter the two "Germanies" alone. Few would dispute the influence of popular dissatisfaction in promoting the protest movement in the GDR. However, even fewer would ignore the importance of Gorbachev's renunciation of the Brezhnev doctrine and his commitment to eschew military interventions in support of failing regimes in the Soviet bloc. The former neighborhood bully changed the course of democracy in the former members of the Soviet bloc by scrambling the balance of forces between the socialist rulers and the ruled in cities such as Dresden, Leipzig, and Berlin.

Although any particular transition to democracy is always big news and on some level a unique event with its particular characteristics, both scholars and policymakers alike have sought to see beyond the idiosyncrasies of individual events and come up with generalizations on the conditions facilitating democratic rule and the circumstances under which transitions to democracy are more likely. So far, however, an understanding of the causes for the emergence of democratic political institutions has remained elusive. Is democracy "caused" by economic or social factors, political culture, or do transitions come about by just plain luck? Can democracy be promoted by other states directly? The best-known theory to explain the origins and genesis of democracies is Lipset's

[2] Lohmann 1994. [3] Whitehead 1996:6.

"social requisites" hypothesis, which holds a high level of development to be a key precondition for democratic rule.[4] Other perspectives give prominence to cultural aspects, norms, or values held to favor the development and durability of democratic rule.[5] Still others emphasize distributional aspects such as material inequality or the relative strength of groups or classes.[6] Another class of transition theories stresses political factors such as the timing of national development, negotiated pacts between elites, or forms of path dependence or "critical junctures" in a country's political development.[7] More recently, Przeworski and Limongi and Przeworski *et al.* have argued that any relationship between social and economic factors and democratic institutions stem simply from democracy being more likely to survive under certain conditions, and that transitions to democracy are random events.[8]

These explanations differ considerably from one another and entail quite different predictions about where certain political institutions should be more or less common.[9] At the same time, these explanations are in another sense all "similar" in that they relate a country's prospects for democratization or sustaining democracy to various *domestic* factors, internal to the democratizing society itself. Focusing exclusively on processes within states, these theories either explicitly or implicitly assume that external events and processes in other countries do not affect the political institutions of a country or the likelihood of transitions.[10]

In this chapter, we argue that international factors and processes taking place between countries influence the prospects for democracy and the likelihood of transitions. We demonstrate that the global distribution of democracy as well as transitions to democracy cluster in time and space. This strongly suggests that diffusion mechanisms exert important influences on domestic political institutions and transition processes.

4 Lipset 1960.
5 See, e.g., Almond and Verba 1963; Muller and Seligson 1994; Putnam 1993.
6 See, e.g., Muller 1988, 1995; Rueschemeyer, Stephens, and Stephens 1992; Vanhanen 1990.
7 See, e.g., Bollen 1979; Casper and Taylor 1996; Moore 1973; O'Donnell, Schmitter, and Whitehead 1986; Przeworski 1991; Rueschemeyer *et al.* 1992.
8 Przeworski and Limongi 1997; Przeworski *et al.* 2000.
9 See, e.g., Vanhanen 1990 for a comprehensive review.
10 Some may argue that studies of how position in the so-called "World-System" influences prospects for democracy provide a possible exception; see, e.g., Bollen 1983; Wallerstein 1979. However, leaving other doubts about the usefulness of these theories aside – see, e.g., Weede 1996 for a critique – this tradition usually holds that external dependence primarily influences national economies and prospects for democracy only indirectly through its impact on the domestic conditions seen as relevant for democracy. Somewhat ironically, the domestic processes held to hinder or help democratization are usually similar to those highlighted by the social requisites school.

Diffusion is an encompassing term that in its general form simply indicates that there are enduring, cross-boundary dependencies in the evolution of policies and institutions. We consider the role of diffusion in light of current theories of democratization, emphasizing how external factors can change the relative balance of power between regimes and opposition forces as well as the preferences and relative evaluations that different groups hold over particular forms of governance. In line with the theme of this volume,[11] we examine how democratic rule and transitions may diffuse as a result of diffusion mechanisms such as coercion, competition, learning, and/or social emulation in light of the general theory. Our results suggest that although democratization could come about in multiple different ways and involve a wide range of potentially important actors in any one particular instance, external factors are generally better indicators of the prospects for transition than domestic country attributes. Even if no single factor or mechanism may characterize all transitions, however, efforts to account retrospectively for why the relative power and balance of competing forces at the domestic level changes in transition countries almost invariably point to changes and shocks in the external environment that states face. The evidence we present indicating that transitions cluster spatially and that diffusion processes appear to play a prominent role in transitions to democracy undermines Przeworski and Limongi's claim that transitions to democracy are random events.[12]

Democratization: international contexts and stylized facts

We start by reviewing some empirical facts about the distribution of democracy to establish the plausibility of diffusion relative to other theories of democratization where international factors are presumed not to be important. Although democracy has been defined in many ways, emphasizing somewhat different criteria, we see democracy as a form of governance where the power of executives is limited by other institutions and where governments are selected either directly or indirectly through competitive elections, with open or unrestricted entry for candidates.[13]

[11] See Simmons, Dobbin, and Garrett Introduction, this volume.
[12] Przeworski and Limongi 1997.
[13] Alternative definitions of democracy may emphasize other features such as protection of political rights or the inclusiveness of participation. For overviews, see, e.g., Beetham 1994; Doorenspleet 2001; Vanhanen 1990. Some definitions of "substantive" democracy also include outcomes that procedural democracy is assumed to lead to; see Shapiro 2003.

There are many efforts to measure democracy empirically. The Polity data, based on Gurr and Gurr, Jaggers, and Moore,[14] provide an additive scale of a state's degree of democracy, ranging from a minimum of −10, for the most autocratic forms of governance, to a maximum of 10 for polities where government selection is based on open competitive elections and executives are constrained by independent legislatures.[15] Figure 7.1 shows the distribution of democracy for independent states in the world over the last two centuries in terms of the global average of the Polity scale and the proportion of countries that are considered democratic by common criteria.[16] Whereas only about 5 percent of the states in the world could be considered democracies in 1816, countries with democratic institutions outnumbered states with autocratic institutions at the end of the 1990s. The share of democracies in the system has not expanded in a gradual fashion, but expanded and contracted over time in what Huntington has called three "waves of democracy."[17]

A comparison of democracy in the world based on all states in the system, as the measures displayed in Figure 7.1, however, reflects not only changes within existing states, but also changes stemming from new states entering the system. Accordingly, it has been argued that what

[14] Gurr 1974; Gurr, Jaggers, and Moore 1990.

[15] We use a modified and expanded version of the Polity IV data, available from http://privatewww.essex.ac.uk/~ksg/polity.html. Some other empirical measures of democracy include Alvarez *et al.* 1996; Bollen 1990; the Freedom House index (e.g. Gastil 1985); Vanhanen 2000. Many alternative measures, however, are only available for a smaller set of countries and a shorter time interval than the Polity data (1816–2002). Although definitions that emphasize other criteria such as broad participation can lead to somewhat different classifications of democracies in the late nineteenth and early twentieth centuries when women and many groups were denied voting rights – see Paxton 2000 – alternative criteria for democracy such as participation and protection of human rights tend to go together with competitive elections in the contemporary era.

[16] The threshold for "democracy" is here set to a score of seven or above, which corresponds to Jaggers and Gurr's suggested threshold for "coherent democracies," characterized by competitive executive recruitment, competitive political participation, and constraints on the chief executive; see Jaggers and Gurr 1995:479. The Polity project codes many countries as having institutions that are in transition or interrupted, and these states have not been accorded regular values on the 21-point scale. For the global means, we treat these countries as non-democracies and assign a numerical value of −10.

[17] Huntington 1991 dates the start of the third wave to the emergence of democracy in Southern Europe and the reestablishment of democracy in many Latin American countries. Whereas some consider subsequent democratization in Eastern Europe and the developing world an extension of the third wave, others such as Doorenspleet 2001 refers to the period since 1990 as a "fourth wave."

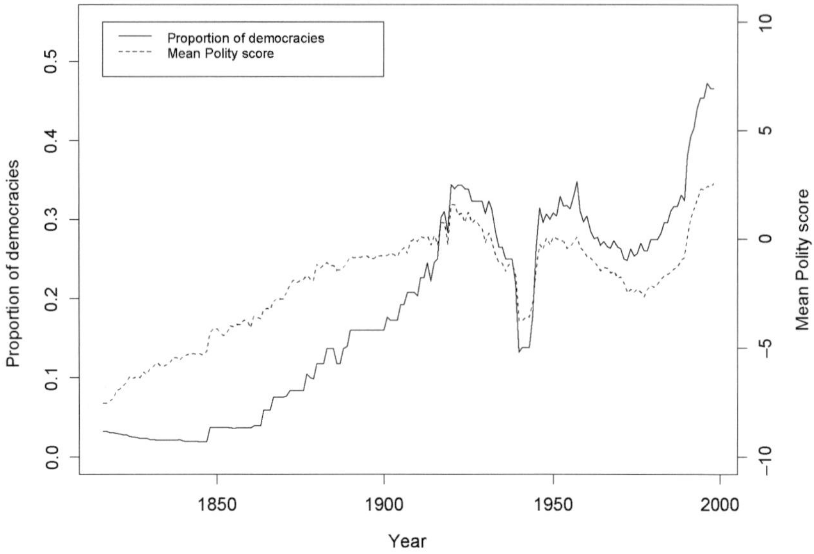

Figure 7.1 The global distribution of democracy, 1816–1998

Huntington and others infer to be "waves" of democracy are merely artifacts following changes in the population of states over time rather than reflecting changes in prevailing types of governance.[18] Figure 7.2 displays alternative measures of the distribution of democracy for a sample of only nineteen states that have been in continuous existence from 1816, based on the list of independent states in Gleditsch and Ward.[19] As can be seen, Figure 7.2 indicates similar trends in democracy over time as Figure 7.1. Whereas only Switzerland and the United States were democratic in 1816, sixteen of the nineteen states were democratic in 1998. There have been periods with large increases in the share of countries that are democratic as well as periods where many states have become less democratic, notably during the two World Wars and the period of decolonialization.

[18] See Doorenspleet 2000. Similarly, Alesina, Spolaore, and Wacizarg 2000 argue that a measure of globalization based on trade over gross domestic product (GDP) for the entire world understates the expansion of trade in the global economy, as it ignores the changing population of states and the fact that many former colonies tend to have less trade integration.

[19] Gleditsch and Ward 1999. The sample of independent states in continuous existence since 1816 includes Argentina, China, Denmark, France, Iran, Japan, Nepal, the Netherlands, Oman, Paraguay, Portugal, Russia/Soviet Union, Spain, Sweden, Switzerland, Thailand, Turkey, the United Kingdom, and the United States.

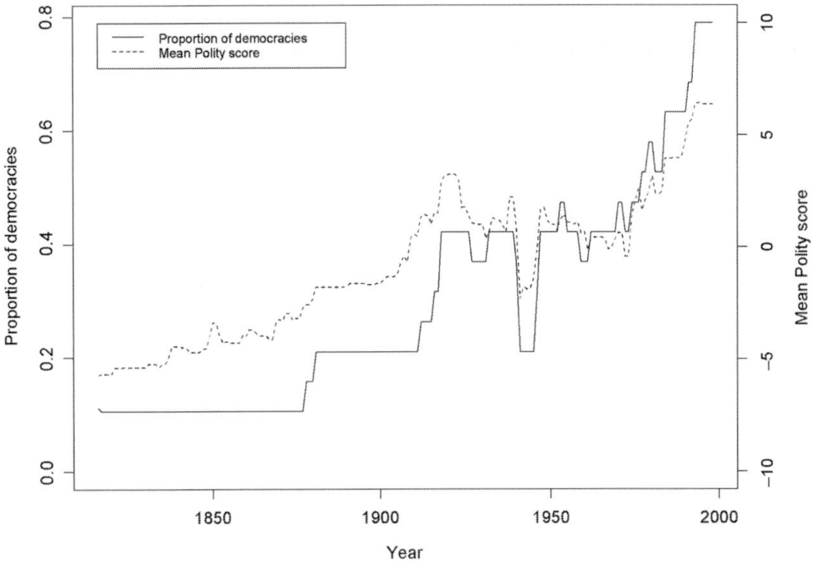

Figure 7.2 Measures of democracy for sample of nineteen continuously independent states, 1816–1998

Assessing the extent of democracy and changes over time based on independent states alone also understates how much of the world's population prior to growth of authoritarian states in the wake of decolonialization lived in colonized territories not under democratic rule. Figure 7.3 displays diffusion-based cartograms of the distribution of democracy, in which the shading indicates the value on the Polity score and the relative size of a country or an area is scaled according to population. Populations in non-sovereign (and non-democratic) entities are displayed as a residual block for each geographical region.[20] Comparing the maps for 1945 to 2002 suggests that democracy has become considerably more widespread in the world, both in industrialized and developing societies. Whereas most of Europe and the Western Hemisphere is currently governed by democratic regimes, many states in Europe and Latin America had autocratic regimes in 1945. The growth of the share of the world's population living in societies with higher levels of democracy

[20] These cartograms are based on a "density equalizing" approach developed by Gastner and Neuman 2004 and historical population estimates compiled by Gleditsch 2004. Global population in 1945 was only about 2.5 billion compared to the approximately 6 billion in 2002.

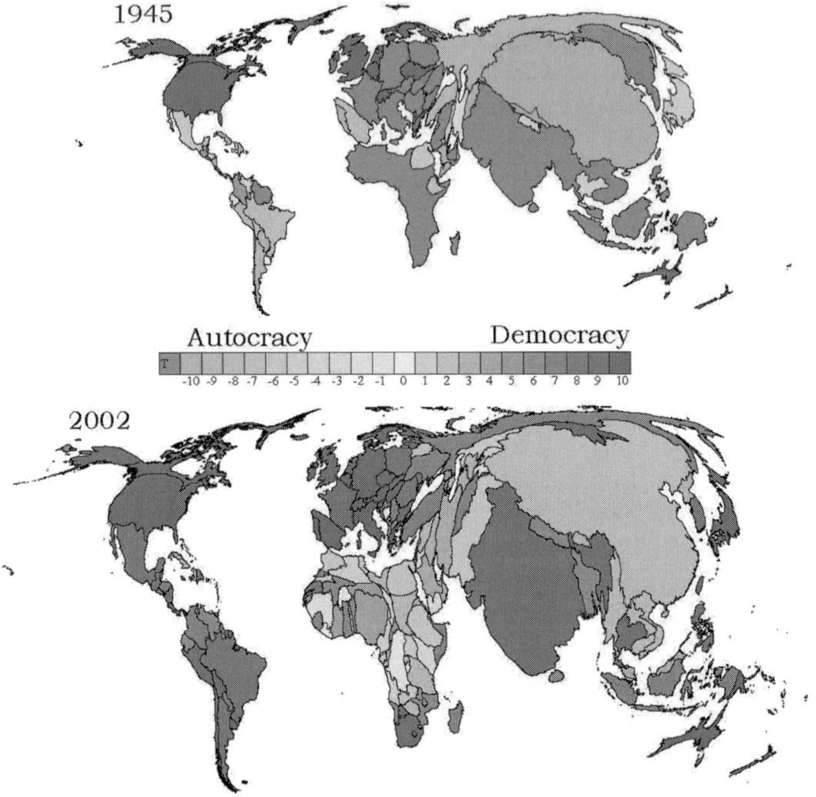

Figure 7.3 Cartogram of democracies and autocracies, proportional to population

is all the more remarkable, as population growth from 1945 to 2002 has been much higher in the low-income countries assumed to be less receptive to democratic forms of governance. However, even though the share of population living under democratic rule remains lower by comparison in Africa and Asia, nearly all geographic regions of the world have shown remarkable progress in democratization since 1945. The lone exception is the Middle East, which continues to be ruled almost exclusively by autocratic governments. Merely a cursory examination of the geographic distribution of democracy suggests that there are clear regional patterns and geographic clustering in both 1945 and 2002.

Whether genuine or artifacts, the notion of "waves" of democracy and autocracy has alerted researchers to the possibility that such global trends in democratization may reflect international influences.[21] For example, many point to how the second and third wave of democratization seemed to coincide with two major watersheds in world history, namely the end of the Second World War and the end of the Cold War. Similarly, the first wave of authoritarianism unfolded in the interwar period and the era of the global depression, and a second wave of autocracy emerged in the aftermath of decolonialization.[22] Others attribute the main changes to shifts in the relative status of political ideologies,[23] or the role of hegemony and the main global powers.[24]

Merely attributing democratization or autocratization to some "international context," however, explains little without clarifying the relevant international context and how this influences prospects for democracy. It is difficult to see any clear relationship between trends in democratization and most of the other global trends that researchers have alluded to. Greater participation in war, for example, seems to have preceded both democratization and autocratization, and there is no obvious relationship between the share of states at war and the share of democracies in the international system.[25] Attributing variation in the global distribution of democracy to exogenous shifts in political ideology or the changing position of the United States on democracy[26] in turn begs the question of why ideologies or foreign policy doctrines change in ways that sometimes favor democracy and sometimes favor autocracy.

In our view, international processes that influence democratization are not particularly likely to be found at a global level. Looking for a *Zeitgeist* or universal global influences that affect all countries alike is probably as ill-conceived as assuming identical and independent processes within each country. The global level is also an aggregate that masks large regional differences and variation within the international system. Whereas democracies dominate in some regions of the world at the present, political institutions that can be characterized as democratic remain scarce in other areas. Further, transitions to democracy have clearly been more frequent in certain areas at different periods of time.

We believe that taking a local or regional perspective can provide more insight into how external factors influence democratization and transition processes than an exclusive focus on global level influences. Figure 7.3

[21] Huntington 1991; Ray 1995. [22] See, e.g., Huntington 1991; O'Loughlin *et al.* 1998.
[23] See, e.g., Fukuyama 1992. [24] See, e.g., Modelski and Perry 1992; Robinson 1996.
[25] See Gleditsch 2002a; Mitchell, Gates, and Hegre 1999. [26] See Robinson 1996.

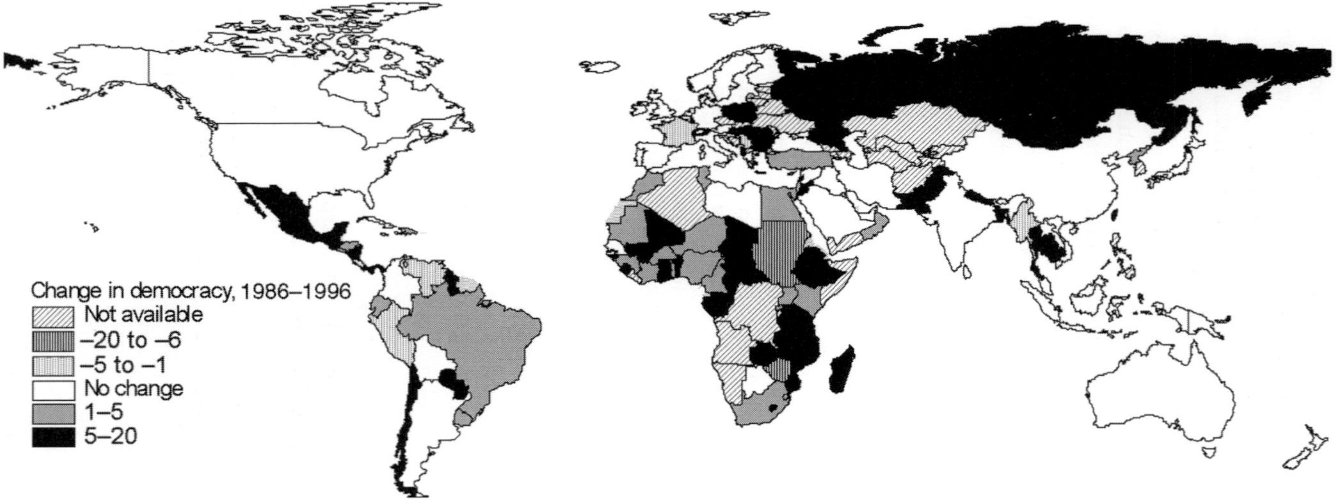

Figure 7.4 Changes on the Polity scale from 1986 to 1996

demonstrates clear regional patterns and geographic clustering in the geographic distribution of democracy in both 1945 and 2002, and similar patterns of clustering hold for other time periods as well. Over the range of all years in the Polity data we find that the probability that a randomly chosen country will be a democracy is about 0.75 if the majority of its neighbors are democracies, but only 0.14 if the majority of its neighbors are non-democracies. The clustering in democracy is not just a static pattern, but countries that are geographically proximate are also more likely to undergo transition and regime changes following transitions in neighboring states. Figure 7.4 displays countries' changes on the 21-point Polity scale over the decade from 1986 to 1996. This clearly illustrates the clustering of transitions to democracy in Eastern Europe, as well as the many changes toward less autocratic forms of governance, if not necessarily full-fledged democracy, in many African countries. Maps of earlier time periods would similarly suggest a diffusion of autocracy, as when many Latin America states experienced transitions to military rule in the 1960s.

It is possible to show more generally that the observed rates of transitions to democracy differ sharply depending on the makeup of other states in a country's spatial context. Figure 7.5 displays non-parametric local regression estimates of the probability of a transition from one regime type to another in a given year, given the proportion of other states that are democracies within a 500 km radius of a country.[27] The unconditional likelihood that an autocracy will be replaced by a democratic regime in any one year is very small, less than 0.015. However, as can be seen from Figure 7.5, the estimated probability that an autocracy will become a democracy, given by the solid line, increases sharply as an S-curve with higher proportions of democratic neighbors. More precisely, the estimated probability of transitions to democracy in a one-year period for a country in a relatively democratic region toward the right of the horizontal axis exceeds 0.1. Likewise, the risk that a democracy will break down and be replaced with an autocracy, indicated by the dashed line in Figure 7.5, also displays an S-shaped relationship with the regional context. As would be expected from the secular trend toward a higher proportion of democracies, the maximum probability that an autocracy will become a democracy reaches roughly twice the level of the likelihood of democracies going authoritarian.

[27] The geographic information is taken from the Gleditsch and Ward 2001 minimum distance data.

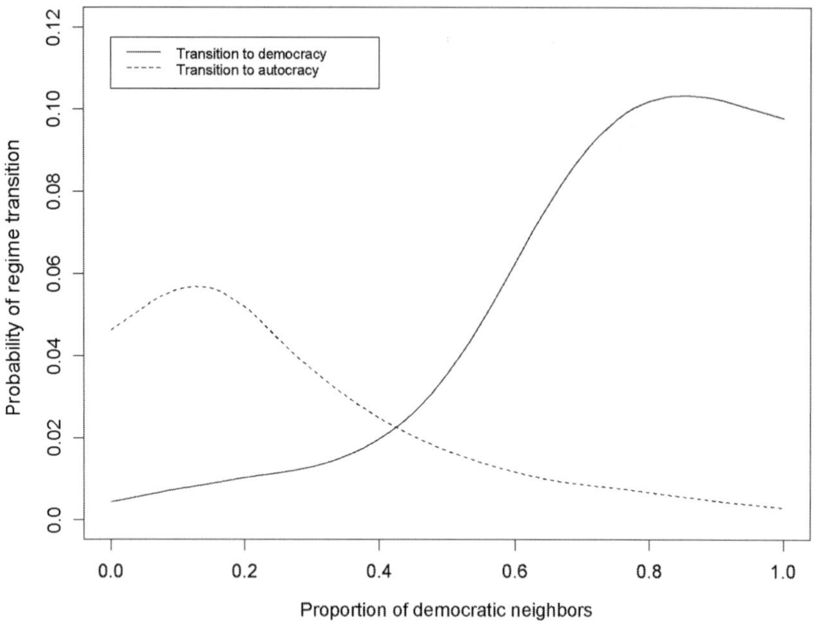

Figure 7.5 Transition probabilities by proportion of neighbors that are democratic

The diffusion of democracy

Our brief overview clearly indicates substantial changes in the distribution of democracy in the world over the last two centuries. Some of these changes may be attributed to increases in economic wealth and other social requisites held to be conducive to democracy. However, since the domestic and economic conditions that typically are assigned importance in theories of democratization tend to change slowly over time, it is difficult to see how stable relationships between social requisites and democracy alone could produce such seeming waves in the share of countries with democratic institutions. The observed geographic patterns in the distribution of democracy suggest that the likelihood of a transition in one country also depends on the international context and events in other states. Although numerous other studies have shown similar empirical evidence of "diffusion" in the sense of spatial and temporal clustering in the distribution of democracy and transitions,[28] it is less clear what this stems from, and what it is about

[28] See, e.g., O'Loughlin *et al.* 1998; Starr 1991.

democracy in one state that influences the prospects for democracy in another. In this section, we discuss possible mechanisms that may underlie the clustering in the distribution of democracy and what role external factors might play in the democratization processes.

We find it helpful to think of diffusion in the context of existing theories of democratization. The study of democratization is complicated by the many possible ways in which one regime may disappear and be replaced by another. Neither is it clear who should be regarded as the main agents. In some cases, the most interesting feature in explaining institutions is to account for how a new regime or political coalition seizes power and replaces existing institutions. The Soviet Union, for example, came into effect following a coup in which the Bolsheviks defeated the previous leadership of Russia and set up new institutions. At the same time, we also need to accommodate the fact that in other cases, different factors can influence the eventual collapse of an old regime and the kinds of institutions that eventually emerge after its downfall. For example, the military junta in Argentina essentially withdrew under widespread dissatisfaction with poor economic performance and the military's disastrous performance in the Falklands/Malvinas war. Yet, the dissatisfaction that led to the fall of the junta does not explain why a democratic regime emerged in the aftermath of the fall of the regime, as military juntas most frequently are followed by other military regimes. Some transitions involve popular uprising or mobilization, while other transitions are initiated by rulers themselves or carried out by actors closely associated with the previous leadership. In Paraguay, a military government made the initial steps toward democracy with little popular pressure; in Uruguay, a return to open elections in 1985 was negotiated at a meeting between representatives of the armed forces and politicians at the Naval Club. In other cases, such as the Philippines, democracy emerged as a result of popular contestation.

Although it perhaps is a stretch to talk about a canonical theory of democratization, the wide range of possibilities in which regime transitions can occur may be subsumed under a framework focusing on power, mobilization, and the preferences of important actors. Much of the literature on democratization argues that democracy emerges as an outcome of social conflict when no single actor or group possesses sufficient resources to impose its rule upon others.[29] Bueno de Mesquita *et al.* suggest that political coalitions survive in proportion to the ratio of the size of the winning coalition to the size of the group of individuals who

[29] See, e.g., Olson 1993; Przeworski 1988; Vanhanen 1990.

have a role in determining that winning coalition, the so-called selectorate.[30] Institutionalizing methods for sharing power and establishing political and civil rights become rational options when the selectorate expands so that actors are unable to fully dominate or control political power by repressive means or distributing private groups alone. Existing structural theories of democracy can from this perspective be seen as pointing to factors that influence the distribution of power and resources between groups, as well as preferences or support for democracy. Power tends to be generally more dispersed among different actors and groups in economically developed states with a more advanced division of labor than in agricultural societies where land is the primary source of wealth.[31] Similarly, values favoring democratic rule are more likely to be widespread when no group can achieve its unrestricted preferences and when democratic political systems are seen as well functioning relative to autocratic alternatives and less of a threat to powerful interests.[32] There is, however, no inherent reason why struggles over influence and the relevant resources should "stop at water's edge," or be confined within the boundaries of individual states. Accordingly, we can think of diffusion in terms of how linkages to external actors and events influence: (1) the relative power; and (2) the preferences of relevant groups in struggles over political institutions and outcomes.

In their introduction, Simmons *et al.*[33] propose a typology of four plausible mechanisms for the diffusion of liberal and neo-liberal institutions and policies: (1) *Coercion as diffusion* suggests that dominant actors impose institutions in a variety of ways, some subtle – others less so. In this way, a powerful state can impose conditions that effectively require adoption of a certain institutional framework. (2) *Competition as diffusion* posits that liberal institutions will be more effective, bringing greater benefits along with them. As a result, such institutions will be adopted widely and spread when national leaders seek the best paths to maintain or increase their competitiveness in the international system. (3) *Learning as diffusion* highlights changing beliefs about the world, such as the learning of decision makers that globalization now affects their local considerations in new and profound ways. (4) *Constructivist emulation as diffusion* presents the idea that the way in which policies are voluntarily instantiated will result in diffusion. This can occur via various mechanisms such as follow the leader and divining contingent policies for specific locales.

[30] Bueno de Mesquita *et al.* 2003. [31] See, e.g., Boix 2003; Vanhanen 1990.
[32] See, e.g., Almond and Verba 1963; Putnam 1993. [33] Introduction, this volume.

We will relate these mechanisms to our arguments about factors changing the relative power of groups as well as preferences and the evaluations of democracies relative to other forms of governance in the discussion below. Although we find their terms useful heuristics for thinking about diffusion and the interaction of domestic and transnational politics, it is clear at the outset that these four diverse ideas about how diffusion might work are neither mutually exclusive nor exhaustive. Just as we cannot single out certain types of actors as universally important in transition processes, no single international agent can be generally responsible for all these diffusion mechanisms. Applied to the case of East Germany, none of the mechanisms alone can account for the transition to democracy. The GDR fell as much because of the declining power and eventual collapse of the Soviet Union – not widely viewed as a democratic agent in the 1970s – as it did as a result of the power of the USA and Reagan's speech demanding the destruction of the Berlin Wall, or the acculturation and socialization of East Germans watching television broadcasts from the Federal Republic. Emulation at the government level does not seem to fully explain even this case either, since leaders could have emulated other potential models than political opening. Although poor by comparison to Western European economies, the GDR was the richest Soviet bloc country and the most competitive COMECON (Council for Mutual Economic Assistance) economy in global terms. The GDR was an important trading nation, and since the 1960s the regime had pursued a strategy of economic modernization and increased trade with the West. Other socialist states such as China "learned" in dramatically different ways, opening up to economic liberalization and openness without any willingness to permit political reforms. To anticipate our conclusion, none of these diffusion mechanisms appear to completely capture how democratic institutions and practices spread over time and space.

Diffusion and the distribution of power

Both domestic and external events and process can shift the distribution of power, thereby undermining existing regimes or assisting certain groups in determining the nature of subsequent regimes. The idea of foreign-imposed regime change represents an extreme case of what Simmons *et al.* call diffusion through coercion.[34] Despite the recent calls for regime change in rogue states, there are few clear cases where democracy has emerged as a result of foreign intervention. The Polity

[34] See Simmons, Dobbin, and Garrett's Introduction to this volume.

project identifies thirty-two cases where new polities where "imposed or prescribed by external agents" between 1816 and 1994.[35] Of the eleven cases where these polities were democratic, however, all but Austria, Japan, and Germany are former British dependencies where institutions were put in place immediately prior to independence.[36] Most imposed regimes are autocratic. The Soviet Union and its Warsaw Pact allies, for example, intervened in Hungary in 1956 and Czechoslovakia in 1968 partly out of fear that local reforms could lead to democracy and the abandonment of socialism. Accordingly, imposition through intervention does not seem an important source of democratization.

However, coercion may also take more subtle forms than direct intervention. The fear of Soviet intervention by itself generally sufficed to deter governments in Eastern Europe from initiating political reforms during the Cold War era, until the adoption of the so-called Sinatra doctrine, where countries could "do it their way," under Gorbachev.[37] Many other external shocks can also alter the domestic distribution of power. Notably, outside actors can promote democratization by providing assistance to domestic actors seeking democratic reform. States and transnational actors can promote democratization in other countries by providing assistance that weakens the power of the regime or strengthens groups favoring democratization.[38] We hypothesize that states will tend to support opposition movements and government reforms that would bring about more similar regimes. Likewise, we believe that opposition groups in autocracies that are connected to or interact with open, democratic societies are more likely to receive support from transnational actors.

External support may have a particularly dramatic impact on struggles for political power when there are shifts in the coalitions that hold power in neighboring entities. Schelling's "tipping model" suggests that merely small changes in external context may suffice to yield cascades that can generate a critical mass in political contestation.[39] Such processes are often held to have played out in the fall of socialism in Eastern Europe, where the initial political changes in Poland and Hungary spurred subsequent changes in Czechoslovakia and East Germany. Tipping effects

35 Gurr *et al.* 1989:22.

36 More specifically, these are Botswana, Cyprus, Ireland, Jamaica, Lesotho, Mauritius, Nigeria, and Uganda.

37 See Ash 1999.

38 See, e.g., Deutsch 1954; Keck and Sikkink 1999; Randle 1991; Smith, Pagnucco, and Lopez 1998; Solingen 1998.

39 Schelling 1971; Kuran 1989, 1991; Lohmann 1994.

should lead to a clustering of transitions, with one transition increasing the likelihood of subsequent transitions in connected states.

The military component of interstate coercion can also have implications for the prospects for democracy. Many researchers argue that regional conflict and insecurity severely constrains prospects for democratic rule. Critics have surmised that the democratic peace may be an artifact of democratic rule breaking down under the threat of conflict.[40] Thompson argues that initial political institutions were shaped by rulers' need to obtain resources and mobilize militarily.[41] Sustained rivalry and threats fostered authoritarianism as power became more centralized. By contrast, relative peace facilitated political pluralism, as internal political processes could unfold with more insulation from external threats. Barzel and Kiser argue that external threats hindered the development of voting institutions as insecure rulers were not in a position to make credible commitments and unable to make contracts with the ruled.[42] Mansfield and Snyder hold that leaders in transitional regimes with fragile institutions are likely to rely on nationalism and diversionary conflict to remain in power, thereby increasing the risk of democratic reversals.[43] The relative geographic isolation and protection from external threat may in part explain why early steps toward democracy were more durable in England than in France. Similarly, the initial "zones of peace" first emerged when powerful states were forced to abandon ambitions of regional hegemony and domination.[44] Accordingly, we should expect democracies to be more likely to emerge and thrive in regions with stable peace.

Diffusion and preferences

Theories of democratization can also be cast in terms of people's preferences for particular institutional arrangements. Even in situations where no single group can monopolize political power, power sharing need not lead to democratic institutions as powerful actors often fear the consequences of unmitigated popular rule and resist democracy. Many nineteenth-century theorists, such as Mill or Marx, expected that the expansion of suffrage to the labor class inevitably would lead to massive redistribution of private property and income.[45] Until the advent of the third wave, many elites in Southern Europe and Latin America similarly tended to be skeptical of the ability of democratic institutions to maintain

[40] See, e.g., Gates, Knutsen, and Moses 1996; Layne 1994. [41] Thompson 1996.
[42] Barzel and Kiser 1997. [43] Mansfield and Snyder 2002. [44] See Thompson 1996.
[45] See Mueller 1999.

order and property rights.[46] The war in Bosnia was in part driven by a perhaps exaggerated view of the effectiveness of democracy, as many ethnic Serbs clearly believed that they would be a perpetually repressed minority under majority rule.[47] Most predictions about radical changes following the introduction of majority rule, however, have failed to materialize in countries that have undergone transitions to democracy. Simmons *et al.*[48] point to how leaders tend to be reluctant to change, but may be more willing to initiate difficult reforms if the experiences of other states suggest that the costs and consequences of reforms may not be as bad as they had feared. In the case of democratization, the experiences of other states can convince leaders that democracy may not be the unwieldy monster often suggested, and that numerous former autocratic rulers have been able to hold on to power or retain influence under democratic rule. Accordingly, fears of democracy are likely to weaken, and support for democracy should increase as more reference countries become democratic. A related diffusion mechanism is what Simmons *et al.*[49] characterize as emulation of successful nations. In many circles, democracy and good governance have increasingly been seen as a prerequisite for economic growth and development. Although empirical research does not unambiguously support a relationship between democracy and economic performance,[50] as Mueller points out,[51] democracy might be facilitated if people believe that such a relationship exists and thereby remain supportive of democracy.

Finally, the likelihood of experiments with democracy depends not only on the perceived benefits from democracy, but also the expected costs of not being a democracy relative to other nations. As suggested by the idea of network externalities, there are strong reasons to suspect that the costs to leaders of not being a democracy have changed considerably over time. During the Cold War, ruling a country in an authoritarian fashion did not necessarily impose particular problems for a leader or a country's standing, as most countries were not democracies, especially in the developing world. Despite some token rhetorical phrases about the free world, democracy was clearly not a requirement in the selection of allies and aid recipients of the main democratic states.[52] After the Cold War, when the strategic importance of allies in the developing world has declined, however, many long-standing autocratic rulers who had enjoyed international support found themselves increasingly isolated.

[46] See Alexander 2002 on Spain; Pevehouse 2002a, 2002b on Latin America.
[47] See Mueller 2000.
[48] See Simmons, Dobbin, and Garrett's Introduction to this volume.
[49] See Simmons, Dobbin, and Garrett's Introduction to this volume.
[50] See, e.g., Inkeles 1991; Przeworski and Limongi 1993. [51] Mueller 1999.
[52] See, e.g., Meernik, Krueger, and Poe 1998; Reiter 2001/2002.

Hence, many leaders may seek to initiate democratic reforms in efforts keep on good terms with the rest of the world or not to look bad relative to other comparable states.

Relationship to alternative perspectives on democratization

Before turning to how external factors can influence diffusion mechanisms, we need to take seriously what alternative theories of democratization *without* diffusion would suggest about the role of international factors and their role in transitions. The general null hypothesis in this volume, as well as this particular chapter, is that policymaking and outcomes are determined based on domestic characteristics and processes, and are independent of international events and the outcomes in other states. Once the relevant domestic factors are taken into account, any residual variation should be randomly distributed across space and over time. In the case of democracy, the obvious alternative hypothesis would be varieties of theories in the modernization or social requisites approach, which hold that societies must develop a certain level of income or political values before transitions to democracy are likely or feasible to hold. Such theories would suggest that international factors such as foreign aid and trade could promote economic change and/or changes in values. Still, as in any form of social change, such processes would presumably be slow and require a long time to take hold. Greif and Laitin suggest that if institutions are understood as self-enforcing equilibria, under gradual social change, institutional reinforcement mechanisms can change the parameters that govern institutions, leading to institutions that adapt and persist and possible endogenous institutional change.[53] This is consistent with the revised version of modernization theory outlined by Przeworski *et al.*,[54] which emphasizes that better economic performance and higher income may stabilize autocracies, making them less susceptible to change.

By contrast, our perspective highlights how external factors are generally more likely to alter an equilibrium institution at the domestic level or a particular set of relations between the winning coalition and the selectorate than internal forces. In this sense, what is sometimes seen as random shocks from an external environment will tend to become key influences on domestic political contention. When Gorbachev indicated that the authorities in the GDR could not rely on Soviet intervention, and the regime had to take into account and deal with the challenges of a

[53] Greif and Laitin 2004. [54] Przeworski *et al.* 2000.

growing outflow of its citizens through Hungary, as well as the growing strength of the protests organized by the Lutheran Church, the country saw an expansion of the selectorate along with a plausible destruction of the winning coalition. Such changes in the balance between rulers and the ruled and the relative attractiveness of particular forms of governance are more likely to be affected from outside the domestic political system than within, as the logic of political survival ossifies the balance internally, even if it can change through small modifications as suggested by Greif and Laitin.[55]

Regional and international contexts of democratic diffusion

We have argued that the prospects for democracy should increase when connected states are democratic or experience transitions, but so far we have not discussed how to identify connected states. States may in principle be connected to all the other states in the international system, but there are strong reasons to suspect that some states will be more important than others. Assuming global or system-wide influences provides no explanation of why some states experience transitions in response to international factors while others remain irresponsive. We posit that geographically proximate states are likely to be particularly important influences on a country. Empirical studies show a strong link between geographic distance and interaction.[56] Whereas political events in Bulgaria are unlikely to exert much impact on Paraguay, events in Argentina and Brazil are highly relevant. Some factors in diffusion processes have a direct geographic component. With restrictions on air travel, migration out of the GDR would have to occur over land borders, and liberalization in Hungary and Poland, where their citizens could travel without restrictions, is hence more relevant than democratization in the Philippines. Likewise, Paraguay has greater opportunities for trade with its neighboring countries Argentina and Brazil than Malaysia. Not only do states interact more with geographically proximate states, but neighbors are likely to display similar features such as language, and may serve as role models that states can compare themselves against or emulate.[57] Assuming that states are connected to geographically close states has proved very useful for formal and empirical models of interdependence and interaction in social systems.[58]

[55] Greif and Laitin 2004. [56] See Olsson 1964. [57] See Axelrod 1984:158.
[58] See, for example, Cederman 1997; Cornes and Sandler 1996; Gleditsch and Ward 2000; Watts 1999.

In the case of linkages from conflict and security, the relevant factor that may impede democratization is the extent of threats to a country's vital security rather than conflict participation. The geographic locus of conflict involvement determines to what extent conflicts pose threats to a state's vital security. For example, we should not expect decisions to participate in United Nations peacekeeping forces or colonial wars far removed from a state's core territory to be related to the prospects for democracy, while territorial conflicts with neighboring states may be highly relevant.[59] We believe that many studies fail to find empirical evidence for hypothesized linkages between conflict involvement and democracy in part due to not identifying the locus of conflict.[60]

In this chapter, we consider global and regional contexts of diffusion as defined by geographic distance, although we note that clusters of connected states could be defined by non-geographic criteria such as similar language or ethnic composition. Many measures of "relevance" based on observed interactions, however, turn out to be less suitable measures for accounting for differences between states, since they tend to connect most countries to the same states. Trade-based networks, for example, tend to link all countries to the same large Organization for Economic Cooperation and Development economies. Stated differently, since most states tend to have large democracies such as the USA and the UK as their main trading partners, there is relatively little variance in the level of democracy among trading partners for different countries in the world. See Beck, Gleditsch, and Beardsley for an empirical analysis of alternative specifications of connectedness.[61]

Empirical analysis

In this section, we reexamine how international and regional factors influence the likelihood that a country will be democratic. Empirically, we can only observe the regimes that prevail in a country in a given year, and the specific mechanisms that lead to changes are of course not directly observable. However, we can observe whether transitions are more or less common following factors that reflect the causal mechanisms discussed in the previous section. We will test these propositions in an analysis of two-way transitions between democracy and autocracy. Gleditsch and Ward suggested that changes in political authority structures could be analyzed as a Markov chain process of transition between

[59] See Gibler and Wolford 2003; Gleditsch 2002a.
[60] See, e.g., Mousseau and Shi 1999; see Gleditsch 2002a for a more extended discussion.
[61] Beck, Gleditsch, and Beardsley 2006.

different states over time.[62] For simplicity, we here limit ourselves to two possible states, democracy and autocracy, which we define operationally by whether an observation has a value of seven or above on the institutionalized democracy scale.[63] In a transition model, the probability distribution of a variable $y_{i,t}$ for observation i at time t is modeled as a function of i's prior history or state at previous time periods *t–1*, *t–2*, . . . , *t–T*. If the observations are conditional only on the previous observations, we have a *first-order Markov chain*.[64] The transition matrix for a first-order Markov chain with a binary outcome can be written as

$$\begin{pmatrix} p_{00} & p_{01} \\ p_{10} & p_{11} \end{pmatrix} \tag{1}$$

where p_{01} indicates the probability of change from 0 to 1 (i.e. $y_{i,t} = 1$, $y_{it-1} = 0$), and p_{11} indicates the probability of remaining at 1 from *t–1* to *t* (i.e. $y_{it} = 1, y_{i,t-1} = 1$).

Our interest here lies in the conditional probability distribution given a set of covariates. Two-way transitions for repeatable events or spells of binary outcomes can be modeled by limited dependent variable models.[65] A matrix of conditional transition probabilities given some set of covariates of interest $\mathbf{x}_{it}$ can be derived by estimating

$$\Pr\left(y_{i,t} = 1 \middle| y_{i,t-1}, \mathbf{x}_{i,t}\right) = F\left[\mathbf{x}'_{i,t}\beta + y_{i,t-1}\mathbf{x}'_{i,t}\alpha\right] \tag{2}$$

where F is either a logit or a probit link. In this model, the vector β indicates the effects of the covariates in $\mathbf{X}$ on the probability of a 1 at time t given a 0 at time t–1, i.e. $\Pr(y_{i,t} = 1 | y_{i,t-1} = 0)$. The effects on the probability of a 1 at time t given a 1 at time t–1, $\Pr(y_{it} = 1 | y_{it-1} = 1)$, are given by the vector of parameters $\gamma = \alpha + \beta$. Such a model has been applied to democracy by Przeworski and Limongi and Gleditsch, and by Beck *et al.* to transitions between conflict and peace.[66] To facilitate

[62] Gleditsch and Ward 1997.

[63] As we have seen, transitions can come about in many possible ways. Hence, it could be argued that studies should try to distinguish between different types of transitions and disaggregate the actors in democratization processes. What drives a specific transition, however, is ultimately not observable, and although a typology of transitions could be constructed, different researchers may disagree on how individual cases should be classified. Moreover, since many actors potentially can exert power, it is difficult to identify *in advance* what actors should be considered relevant, even if a certain actor can be singled out as important *after* transitions. Many case studies of observed transitions thus sample relevant government–opposition dyads based on outcomes on the dependent variable.

[64] See, e.g., Harary, Norman, and Cartright 1965:371–7.

[65] See Beck *et al.* 2001; Yamaguchi 1991: Ch. 3.

[66] See Przeworski and Limongi 1997; Gleditsch 2002a; Beck *et al.* 2001.

comparison with Przeworski and Limongi's transition model, we let $y_{it} = 1$ if a state i is an autocracy at time t and $y_{i,t} = 0$ if it is a democracy. In this case, the estimated $\hat{\beta}$ coefficients can be interpreted as indicating the effects of a covariate on the likelihood that a democracy will become an autocracy, whereas the $\hat{\gamma}$ estimates indicate the effect of the covariate on the likelihood that autocracies will remain autocracies from one time period to another. Since the set of possible outcomes at time t given $y_{i,t-1} = 1$ must sum to unity, the likelihood that an autocracy at time t–1 will become a democracy at time t is given by $1 - \hat{p}_{11}$, or 1 minus the probability that an autocracy will endure.

We examine diffusion, or the influence of international factors, through four covariates. The first three pertain to local and global diffusion of regime types. If local diffusion processes operate, we should expect autocracies to be more likely to experience transitions to democracy the greater the proportion of democratic neighboring countries (i.e. $\gamma < 0$). We identify the local context by the proportion of neighboring states within a 500 km radius that are democracies, based on the minimum distance data.[67] Similarly, if global diffusion drives transitions to democracy, we should expect to find that autocracies become less likely to remain autocracies as the global proportion of democracies increases. We assume that transitions may be contagious, and increase the likelihood of transitions in other connected states. We further assume that democratic transitions in other states do not influence the likelihood that democratic states will become autocracies, but may influence the likelihood that autocracies become democracies. In light of this, we constrain the parameter β for this variable to be 0 and let $\gamma = \alpha$. We use a binary indicator of whether a transition to democracy takes place in a neighboring state within a 500 km radius.

Our final covariate reflecting diffusion pertains to the role of conflict. We have argued that conflict with other states may decrease the prospects for democracy. We have also emphasized how not all incidents of "war participation" and "peace" are qualitatively equivalent, and that threats to a state's territory must be distinguished from general conflict participation, which may reflect decisions to intervene in conflicts elsewhere in the international system. Moreover, it is a perception of insecurity rather than individual outbreaks of conflict that may influence the prospects for democracy. This means that we should not look for effects on regime type

[67] Gleditsch and Ward 2001. The 500 km threshold is somewhat arbitrary. However, the results do not look dramatically different for other distance thresholds, provided not overly restrictive cutoff points are used. See Gleditsch 2002a:94–5 for a discussion of sensitivity to varying thresholds.

at the time of conflict involvement only, but consider the more enduring forms of threats that do not necessarily break into open war at any given time. We use a simple count of the number of years that a country has remained at peace on its territory as a proxy for the stability of peace. Our conflict data is based on the Correlates of War data, with some modifications and updates.[68] We also consider an alternate measure, based on whether a country is part of an enduring interstate rivalry as identified by Diehl and Goertz.[69]

Whereas most previous studies that have examined diffusion or the role of international factors for transitions to democracy have disregarded the potential impact of domestic attributes and processes,[70] in this chapter we will consider both international and domestic factors. An aggregate relationship between a country's institutions and the countries in its regional context alone does not provide convincing evidence of diffusion processes. First, the principal social and economic conditions hypothesized to influence democracy such as differences in GDP per capita can also be shown to cluster geographically.[71] Second, individual countries may be responding to common trends rather than display interdependent transitions. As such, we face an inverse form of Galton's famous problem of distinguishing between independent functional relationships and interdependent diffusion processes: what existing studies that do not consider domestic characteristics attribute to diffusion may stem from geographic clustering in domestic attributes that influence prospects for democracy.[72] Accordingly, we need to demonstrate that the observed effects of regional context and diffusion do not merely stem from plausible omitted domestic factors.

The primary measure of "social requisites" is a country's GDP per capita, which we measure as the natural log of the lagged level of real GDP per capita, taken from the expanded trade and GDP data.[73] Many researchers have argued that negative economic performance or crises can affect the prospects for democracy. Countries that experience economic decline are more likely to experience regime transitions, and economic decline is often held to have undermined democracies in the wake of decolonialization and promoted transitions from autocracy to

[68] See Gleditsch 2004. [69] See Diehl and Goertz 2000.

[70] See O'Loughlin *et al.* 1998; Starr 1991; Starr and Lindborg 2003.

[71] See Gleditsch 2002a. [72] Galton 1889.

[73] Gleditsch 2002b. Przeworski and Limongi 1997 use a specification with GDP per capita and its square. We prefer the simpler natural log specification as there is no clear theoretical reason why GDP per capita should have a non-monotonic effect, and why democracy should become less likely beyond some level of income.

democracy in the third wave.[74] We consider the effect of growth in real GDP per capita as a measure of economic performance and crises, in the case of negative growth. Negative performance may also stem from a country's exposure to exogenous economic shocks such as changes in commodity prices, which in turn may induce social conflict that can undermine regime stability.[75] Based on Rodrik's suggested indicator of external exposure or sensitivity, we measure economic shocks by the volatility of a country's terms of trade over a five-year period, multiplied by a country's total trade as a proportion of its GDP.[76] Finally, democracy may also be related to domestic conflict and strife. Many civil wars revolve around control over the government. Other forms of violent conflict such as secessionist movements should also be expected to undermine existing regimes. The implications of civil war for democracy are ambiguous, however, since civil wars can topple autocracies, but also undermine democratic institutions and lead to the emergence of new autocratic regimes. We consider whether a state was involved in a civil war, based on the Correlates of War data, with some modifications and updates.[77]

Although the geographic and political data are available from 1875 to the present, the availability of data on lagged GDP per capita and economic growth constrains our sample to the years 1951 to 1998. Economic data are often missing for developing countries, socialist economies, and states involved in conflict in the standard data sources that have been used in most existing work.[78] Here, we use more comprehensive, expanded GDP data to prevent sample selection biases due to non-random missing data.[79]

Results

The results of our baseline model are shown as Model 1 in Table 7.1. Each row listing a covariate name displays the estimated $\hat{\beta}$ coefficient and the implied $\hat{\gamma} = \hat{\alpha} + \hat{\beta}$ coefficient for that covariate in the subsequent column fields. The standard errors for the coefficients are shown in

[74] See Gasiorowski 1995; Remmer 1991. [75] See, e.g., Rodrik 1999.

[76] We are grateful to Håvard Hegre for providing us with the data on terms of trade. These data are unfortunately available only after 1965.

[77] These are described in Gleditsch 2004.

[78] The analysis in Przeworski *et al.* 2000, for example, only includes countries that appear in the Penn World Data, leaving out many socialist and developing states. Although we can replicate the key points in our analysis in terms of sign and significance of estimating coefficients using the Alvarez *et al.* 1996 democracy measure, this source dramatically reduces sample size and possibly introduces problems of non-random sample attrition.

[79] See Gleditsch 2002b.

Table 7.1. *Results for estimation of transition model*

Covariates	Model 1 (1951–98)		Model 2 (1951–98)		Model 3 (1875–1998)	
	β	γ	β	γ	β	γ
Constant	2.276 (0.802)	3.675 (0.552)	1.863 (0.868)	3.682 (0.551)	−1.297 (0.234)	2.871 (0.196)
Logged GDP per capita	−0.501 (0.088)	−0.064 (0.062)	−0.401 (0.099)	−0.067 (0.062)		
Logged energy consumption per capita					−0.526 (0.126)	−0.073 (0.079)
Proportion of neighboring democracies	−0.525 (0.258)	−0.717 (0.21)	−0.483 (0.268)	−0.712 (0.209)	−0.591 (0.197)	−1.04 (0.179)
Civil war	0.379 (0.225)	−0.013 (0.157)	0.423 (0.233)	−0.016 (0.157)	0.381 (0.192)	0.07 (0.153)
Years of peace at territory	0.002 (0.002)	−0.004 (0.002)	0.003 (0.002)	−0.005 (0.002)	0.001 (0.002)	−0.002 (0.002)
Economic growth	−0.025 (0.013)	0.003 (0.008)	−0.021 (0.012)	0.003 (0.008)		
Global proportion of democracies	−0.512 (1.047)	−2.592 (0.672)	−1.025 (1.091)	−2.590 (0.672)	−0.575 (0.723)	−1.856 (0.559)
Neighboring transition to democracy		−0.172 (0.066)		−0.176 (0.066)		−0.251 (0.055)
Time as democracy			−0.023 (0.008)		−0.008 (0.004)	
Time as autocracy				0.001 (0.002)		0.002 (0.002)
N	6159		6159		8788	
Model LR-χ^2	6909.6 (df= 15)		6920.8 (df= 17)		9835.1 (df= 15)	
Test of H0: Constant slopes χ^2	4412.87 (df= 5)		2417.2 (df= 8)		3293.1 (df= 7)	

Notes: **β**: Effects on likelihood that a democracy at $t-1$ will be an autocracy, **γ**: Effects on likelihood that an autocracy at $t-1$ will remain an autocracy.

parentheses in the row below.[80] As can be seen at the bottom of Table 7.1, the likelihood ratio test of the null hypothesis of equal slopes

[80] We do not report the estimated $\hat{\alpha}$ coefficients, as these do not have a natural interpretation and are not independently informative. The variance for $\hat{\gamma}$ is given by $Var(\hat{\alpha}) + Var\left(\hat{\beta}\right) + 2Cov\left(\hat{\alpha}, \hat{\beta}\right)$.

across previous regime states (i.e. that $\beta = \gamma$ or that the parameters α are jointly insignificant) is clearly rejected. Hence, the covariates appear to have different effects on the likelihood that democracies will become autocracies and the likelihood that autocracies will remain autocracies.

Most of our hypotheses on diffusion and democratization are strongly supported by the results for Model 1 in Table 7.1. As can be seen from the negative estimates for $\hat{\gamma}$ and $\hat{\beta}$ in the fourth row of the main body of the table, a higher proportion of democratic neighbors significantly decreases the likelihood that autocracies will endure (i.e. $\hat{\gamma} = -0.717$) and increases the likelihood that democracies will break down (i.e. $\hat{\beta} = -0.525$). Moreover, a transition in a neighboring country significantly decreases the likelihood that an autocracy will endure. A more peaceful regional environment decreases the likelihood that an autocracy will endure, but does not have a statistically significant impact on the likelihood that democracies will break down.[81] Finally, we find evidence that transitions to democracy are more likely the higher the global proportion of democracies; however, the global proportion of democracies does not exert a significant effect on the survival rates of democracies.[82] Controlling for country-specific attributes and global characteristics does not remove the effects of the regional proportion of democracies and neighboring transitions. In contrast to Przeworski and Limongi's conclusion that transitions emerge exogenously as a "*deus ex machina*" out of the whims of history,[83] the results for Model 1 in Table 7.1 show that autocracies are significantly less likely to endure in a region with more democratic states, when a neighboring state experiences a transition to democracy, and when the international environment is relatively peaceful.

Other international factors than the processes that we have highlighted may influence the prospects for democracy. Pevehouse has stressed the role of international organizations dominated by democracies.[84] He argues that leaders in transition countries and new democracies rely on international organizations to "lock-in" policies and assuage elites who fear that democratic institutions will unleash unmitigated populism and

[81] Replacing the years at peace variable with Diehl and Goertz' measure of enduring rivals (not shown) likewise suggests that an enduring rivalry makes autocracies more likely to endure, but has no consistent effect on the survival of democracy.

[82] This contrasts somewhat with previous research, as Reiter 2001 and Pevehouse 2002a find that the regional proportion of democracies does not influence the duration of democracy while Kadera *et al.* 2003 find that a higher proportion of democracies increases the survival rates of democracies. The two first studies, however, use proportions within world regions as defined by the Correlates of War (COW) project rather than country-specific reference groups defined by a distance span. None of these studies consider both global and regional influences.

[83] Przeworski and Limongi 1997. [84] Pevehouse 2002a, 2002b.

instability. However, adding Pevehouse's IOScore measure of the democratic density of international organizations[85] to Model 1 (not reported) yields somewhat inconsistent results that do not confirm with Pevehouse's expectations. Although the $\hat{\gamma}$ coefficient for IOScore is negative, suggesting that autocracies connected to highly democratic international organizations are more likely to become democratic, the $\hat{\beta}$ coefficient is significantly positive and with a similar marginal effect, indicating that international organizations do not help to consolidate democracy.

Others have highlighted the role of non-governmental global actors, in particular, the Catholic Church. Although the Vatican in the nineteenth century denounced democracy and historically has played an important role in sustaining autocratic rule in Catholic societies, following changes in its official doctrine under the Second Vatican Council (1962–1965), the Catholic Church has become an active promoter of democracy with an extensive global network.[86] To consider the possible role of the Catholic Church, we re-estimated Model 1 including a measure of the Catholic percentage of the population from the CIA World Factbook, a dummy variable for the post-1965 period, and an interaction between the two terms.[87] Although our results (not shown) lend some support to the notion that democracy is more likely to endure in Catholic societies after the Second Vatican Council, the three terms are not jointly significant. Moreover, the net marginal effect on the transition probabilities of a greater share of Catholic population after the Second Vatican Council was positive, so there is no evidence that the shift in the Church's doctrine had a strong direct impact promoting transitions.

The effects of the domestic covariates are largely consistent with expectations and previous research. The results for Model 1 in Table 7.1 can be read as supporting Przeworski and Limongi's conclusion that although a higher GDP per capita does decrease the risk that democracies will break down, it does not significantly increase the likelihood that an autocracy will terminate (i.e. the estimated $\hat{\gamma}$ is relatively small and not significantly different from 0).[88] Likewise, economic growth strengthens the survival of democracies, but does not promote transitions in autocracies. Indeed, the estimated $\hat{\gamma}$ coefficient is positive, albeit not statistically significant. Civil wars significantly increase the

[85] Pevehouse measures the democratic density of international organizations by the average democracy score of the members of a state's most democratic international organization.
[86] See Huntington 1991.
[87] We thank Jorge Domínguez for suggesting this specification to us.
[88] Przeworski and Limongi 1997.

likelihood that democracies will break down in a one-tailed test, but this covariate has no statistically significant effect on the likelihood that autocracies will endure. Additional regressions (not shown) indicated that our measure of exogenous economic shocks was not significantly related to regime type or transitions after 1965; however, this may be due to the limited data available.

It may be questioned whether our data actually follow a first-order Markov process or all the information about transition and survival probabilities can be summarized by the previous states of regimes plus the covariates. We were unable to reject the null hypothesis that a second-order Markov specification did not fit the data significantly better than the first-order Markov process for Model 1. This is not particularly surprising as models for higher-order Markov processes invariably involve a very high number of parameters.[89] As a simpler alternative model of time dependence, we introduced two covariates counting the time that countries have remained democracies and autocracies respectively to the first-order Markov model. The results of this estimation are shown as Model 2 in Table 7.1. As can be seen, consistent with theories of democratic consolidation,[90] the estimates in the row for *Time as democracy* suggest that transitions to autocracy become increasingly less likely the longer countries have remained democratic. However, the survival rates of non-democracies do not appear to depend on time, as the coefficient for *Time as autocracy* is not significantly different from 0. This is perhaps not surprising, as the non-democracy categories lump together quite different regimes that share little in common beyond not being democracies and may display a great deal of instability. Using irregular transfers of power to identify regime changes within autocracies, Gleditsch and Choung find evidence that particular autocratic regimes become more likely to survive the longer they have held power.[91] The effects of the other covariates, however, do not qualitatively change when controlling for time dependence, and the impact of regional and international factors still appear to have important effects on transitions to democracy.[92]

Boix and Stokes have recently argued that Przeworski and Limongi's dismissal of modernization theory, or that development increases the prospects that autocracies will become democratic, is based not so

[89] See Berchtold and Raftery 2002. [90] See Gasiorowski and Power 1997.
[91] Gleditsch and Choung 2004.
[92] We also tried a non-parametric model specification, allowing for non-linear effects of time; see Beck, Katz, and Tucker 1998. However, our results suggested that this did not notably improve on the linear time dependence specification.

much on empirical evidence, but rather is an artifact of limiting their data to a post-1951 sample.[93] Since many countries that developed prior to the Second World War had already turned democratic before 1951, a sample based on this period may understate the role of development in the evolution of democracy in the first wave. Accordingly, one might ask whether the results shown here reflect a short time period. The Correlates of War project's estimates of energy consumption can serve as a proxy for economic wealth prior to 1945.[94] Model 3 in Table 7.1 displays the results for our model when estimated for the full time period 1875 to 1998, using logged energy consumption per capita rather than GDP per capita. As can be seen, the $\hat{\gamma}$ estimate for the log of energy consumption per capita is negative, but still not statistically significant.[95] More importantly, the coefficient estimates for the other covariates remain consistent, and our conclusions regarding the importance of the regional and international context do not change when we look at the extended time period.

Finally, to ensure that the Eastern European countries alone do not drive our results, we re-estimated our Model 3 excluding all the Eastern European states under Soviet influence after 1945. This yields a larger and significant negative coefficient estimate for the log of energy consumption per capita, but does not change our results with respect to the impact of international factors.[96]

93 Boix and Stokes 2003.

94 Energy consumption estimates are available in the COW National Military Capabilities data; Singer 1987. The current version (2.1) includes data only up to 1992. We extend the energy data to 1998 with estimates predicted from a linear regression of country's logged GDP per capita and a time trend.

95 Replacing energy consumption with the Maddison 1991 historical GDP per capita data used by Boix and Stokes (which are available only for a select number of countries) does not yield a significant impact of the log of GDP per capita on transition probabilities. Different model specification can change the statistical significance of an individual coefficient. Boix and Stokes include a number of dummy variables, such as oil-producing countries and Soviet zone of influence. Nonetheless, the implied marginal effect of GDP per capita from Boix and Stokes results is still very limited. Note that their reported Figure 5, which suggests large increases in transition probabilities by differences in GDP per capita, appears to have been generated setting the values of religious fractionalization and rate of leader turnover to the 99th percentile. Using less extreme scenarios such as mean or median values suggests a trivial impact on transition probabilities. We are grateful to Giacomo Chiozza for alerting us to this.

96 Readers may wonder whether our conclusion follows from the specification of the model and how the Markov transition model relates to other models used in empirical work on democratization, such as linear regression with a continuous dependent variable and event history analysis. The advantage of the transition model lies in allowing to test if covariates exert different effects on regime survival, i.e. $\Pr(y_{i,t} = 1 | y_{i,t-1} = 1)$, and transition probabilities, i.e. $\Pr(y_{i,t} = 1 | y_{i,t-1} = 0)$. Since predictions are dependent on state in the previous time period and the variance of logit/probit is scaled to 1 for identification, the estimates of the transition model will be identical to estimating separate models for

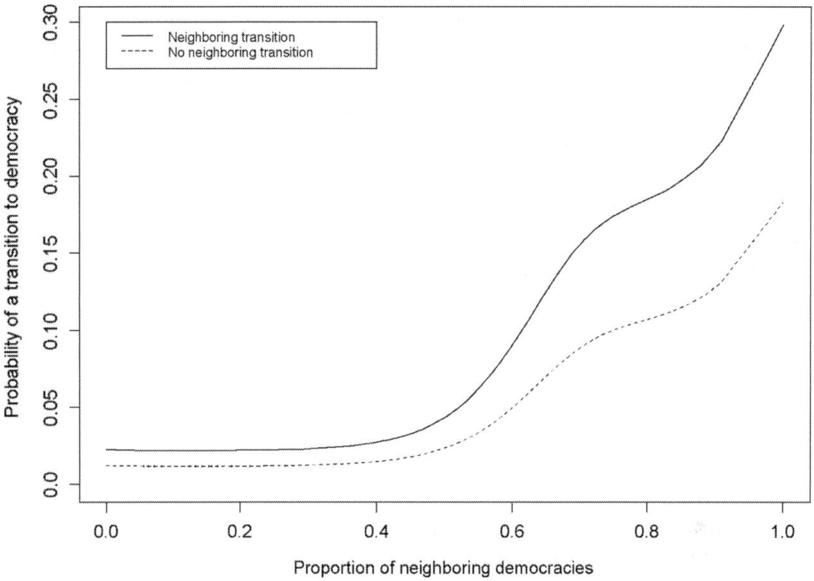

Figure 7.6 Transition probabilities by regional context, holding other covariates at their median

We have shown that the effect of differences in the regional context on transition probabilities, shown in Figure 7.3, still hold when we control for country-specific covariates and common trends, and that the probability that an autocracy will become a democracy increases markedly as more of its neighboring states are democracies or experience transitions to democracy. Figure 7.6 displays a non-parametric estimate of the marginal effects over differences in the proportion of neighboring democracies, based on Model 3 in Table 7.1, keeping the value of other variables at their medians. Substantively, this translates to a middle-income country that does not experience a civil war and has been an autocracy without experiencing conflict for over three decades. The solid line indicates the

observations that were autocracies and democracies in the previous time period; see Beck *et al.* 2001. There is little reason to expect that event history analysis will differ from a transition model, given the underlying similarity of event history analysis to logit/probit with time dependence; see Alt, King, and Signorino 2001; Beck *et al.* 1998. It is also possible to use some measure of degrees of democracy as a continuous variable, and linear regressions with the 21-point Polity score as the dependent variable for our data similarly suggest that the international and regional context increases the expected level of democracy. However, the possibility that covariates have a different effect on the likelihood of a qualitative outcome, depending on the previous state, as suggested by the transition model, is difficult to reconcile with a model of a continuous propensity for democracy. We are grateful to Nathaniel Beck for clarifying this point.

predicted probabilities of a transition to a democracy when there is a transition in a neighboring country. The dashed line indicates the transition probabilities for a case without a neighboring transition. As can be seen, the transition probabilities for a typical autocracy in a given year remain low, well below 0.015, when a small proportion of neighboring states are democracies – toward the left side of the horizontal axis – and there are no transitions in neighboring states. When the proportion of neighboring states exceeds one half, however, the transition probabilities increase quite dramatically. The likelihood of a transition to democracy exceeds 0.10 when more than 75% of the neighboring states are democracies, and is even higher when other countries in the region experience transitions to democracy.

How do the results from our transition model apply to the case of East Germany that we have previously discussed? Our model reflects how democracy became increasingly likely in East Germany as more of its neighboring countries became democratic. Indeed, in 1989 the majority of neighboring countries were either democratic or undergoing transitions. The predicted transition probabilities for the GDR from Model 1 in Table 7.1 is 0.25. Hence, the prospects for survival of the socialist regime were substantially changed from its seemingly stable outlook in the early 1980s. Recall that the predicted probabilities from the model refer to the likelihood of transitions in a given year, and that the likelihood of a transition occurring over a longer time period will be higher. For an autocracy that has a moderately high predicted likelihood of a transition to democracy in any one given year given its domestic and regional attributes (say 0.1), the implied likelihood that it will remain an autocracy for five years is $(1 - 0.1)^5$, which is less than 0.6.

Table 7.2 compares the observed regimes to the predictions of the model. As can be seen, the overall predictions of the models are generally good. The percentage of observations classified correctly by the models ranges from 98.1% to 98.2%. The share of democracies in the sample

Table 7.2. *Predicted versus observed regime status*

	Predicted regime					
	Model 1		Model 2		Model 3	
Observed regime	Autocracy	Democracy	Autocracy	Democracy	Autocracy	Democracy
Autocracy	2016	72	2016	72	2865	96
Democracy	41	4029	41	4029	64	5762

correctly classified varies from 96.55% to 96.75%. More importantly, the predicted transition probabilities are much higher for the cases where we observe transitions than the sets of autocracies and democracies in general.

Overall, these results provide clear support for our claims that the regional context of political institutions and structures exert strong effects on regime changes. Knowing a country's location and the characteristics of surrounding entities yields considerable predictive power. There is a marked tendency for cases to change in ways similar to their regional context over time, and transitions in one country often spill over to other connected states. Given such evidence of dependence and diffusion between countries, the claim that regime change is entirely random should not be accepted. Although transitions to democracy are relatively rare, they are clearly more common under some conditions than others. Like Monet's water lilies that look like random dots up close and only acquire shape with a change of perspective, the randomness of democratization may lie in the eye of the beholder.

Conclusion

We started our discussion by the example of East Germany, and how external forces conspired with domestic process to unseat a socialist regime that possessed both repressive means and relatively high degrees of many of the social and economic indicators believed to be associated with regime stability. We have argued that certain external and domestic conditions can make transitions more likely, even if the specific manner in which a transition occurs out of the range of possibilities cannot be determined in advance. We now turn to another case where a transition to democracy came about through entirely different dynamics than in the GDR, yet where the eventual outcome similarly was strongly influenced by changes in the regional environment. In Paraguay, a 1989 coup by young officers led by General Andrés Rodríguez deposed General Adolfo Stroessner, who had ruled the country since 1954. The coup was primarily motivated by the perceived poor treatment of the military, with low salaries and few opportunities for promotion. Given its military basis, one would expect such a coup to lead to a new military dictatorship. However, Rodríguez initiated surprising reforms, and announced that open parliamentary elections would be held within three months. Although the opposition was poorly organized and inexperienced following thirty-five years of authoritarian rule, the elections were deemed to be free by outside observers. The Colorado Party associated with both Stroessner and Rodríguez obtained about 75 percent of the votes, and has retained power in all subsequent elections, most recently in 2003.

Unlike the case of the German Democratic Republic, the transition to democracy in Paraguay cannot be attributed to an increase in the relative strength of the virtually non-existent opposition. Rather, we must consider how external changes influence actors' evaluations of the relative benefits associated with different forms of governance. Rodríguez could easily have chosen to set up an autocratic regime and enforced this without significant challenges, but changes in the position of Paraguay with its neighboring countries can help account for why he chose democratic reform. As a landlocked country, Paraguay is critically reliant on its neighbors Argentina and Brazil for economic exchange and communications. Whereas none of the neighbors of Paraguay were democracies as late as in 1981, following transitions in Argentina (1983), Brazil (1985), and Uruguay (1985), however, all of its neighbors had established democratic institutions, and the Stroessner dictatorship was increasingly becoming an anomaly. The new leaders in both Argentina and Brazil were advocating democracy as a prerequisite for membership in the efforts to expand their existing bilateral integration program (Programa de Integración y Cooperación Argentino–Brasileño, PICAB) to a multilateral common market, later realized as MERCOSUR. In this setting, enacting democratic reforms becomes a sensible measure for a leader who seeks greater integration with the outside world. Once again the regional and international context affected strongly the balance of power such that democratic change became possible. Based on the changes in external context, our model suggests that the end of the Stroessner regime was likely to be followed by steps toward democracy, and Paraguay has a predicted transition probability of 0.19 for 1989 based on Model 1 in Table 7.1.

Our results show that the prospects for democracy are not exclusively related to domestic attributes, but also appear to be affected by external conditions and events. Our most important finding is that democratization cannot be seen exclusively as a result of functionally similar processes unfolding independently within each country. We have argued that international events and processes can make democratization more likely by changing the relative power of actors and groups, and the preferences or relative payoffs for particular institutional arrangements. Domestic political processes are deeply affected by what goes on in neighboring societies, even if the specific ways in which external events influence transitions may vary from context to context. Our results indicate that diffusion processes among states at the regional level influence the distribution of democracy in the international system. There is a strong association between a country's institutions and the extent of democracy in the surrounding regional context. Not only do regimes tend to be similar within regions, but there is also a strong tendency for transitions to regimes more similar to the regional context. A history of prior regional conflict decreases the likelihood that a country will be democratic.

The US military attack on Iraq in 2003 and subsequent occupation has in part been defended as an effort to foster "regime change" and democracy in Iraq. In a speech at the National Endowment for Democracy after the fall of Saddam Hussein, for example, President Bush invoked the concept of democratic diffusion,[97] and argued that the establishment of a democratic regime in Iraq could help spread democracy to other countries in the greater Middle East region. Leaving aside all normative questions of whether military ventures to impose democracy are justifiable means or a worthy goal, the empirical results of our research on the international dimension of democracy in our view lend little support for the feasibility of this articulated vision of democratic diffusion.[98] In the first place, as noted by Bueno de Mesquita and Downs,[99] the goal of ensuring compliant policies in targets of intervention may be difficult to reconcile with democratic institutions where the local population actually can choose their preferred leaders and policies. Iraq clearly is not a democracy at the time of writing. Although a new government has been appointed based on competitive elections, the Iraqi government is essentially sovereign in name only, given its strong dependence on US military support and the rather strong oversight of the occupying authorities on selection of the country's leaders. However, even though Iraq conceivably could acquire democratic institutions by evolution or imposition at some point in the future, the international dimensions and mechanisms outlined here suggest that the prospects for sustaining democracy in Iraq at the present seem relatively unfavorable. Few other countries in the region have regimes that could be characterized as democracies or seem to be moving toward democratic reform. Moreover, few of Iraq's autocratic neighboring regimes have much interest in promoting democracy in Iraq, as democratization in Iraq could lead to increased demands for political freedom and undermine political stability on their home turf. Iraq has a

[97] Bush 2003.

[98] Peceny 1999:564 argues that imposed "conversions" to democracy are relatively common, and lists the Philippines, Germany, Japan, El Salvador, Cambodia, Grenada, Italy, Austria, Nicaragua, Honduras, Sudan, and Panama as countries that have become democracies after US intervention. However, the fact that the Philippines are listed three times in this grouping (1898–1936, 1985–1988, and 1949–1952) suggests that many such transformations may not be irreversible or particularly durable.

[99] Bueno de Mesquita and Downs 2004.

history of conflict, and is by some measures already at a state of civil war, which may be exacerbated by transnational linkages. All of these factors conspire to diffuse autocracy and make sustaining democracy generally more difficult.

Many transitions involve some element of surprise and their timing may not be fully predictable. Our ability to predict other changes in external context such as conflict and peace is also limited at best, and it may be difficult to accurately forecast how regions are likely to evolve over the near future. However, it is easier to predict an increase in the likelihood of transitions, conditional on transitions in other states and international events that influence the features shaping the prospects for democratization. Although it is difficult to fully specify the full range of possible microlevel processes of democratization and show how international factors influence these in a model at the aggregate level, it seems theoretically inappropriate to treat the domestic arena as isolated from or independent of the international context. Since the regional context is more permeable to changes in the short term than socio-economic factors, international influences on democracy are likely to be as important as the domestic "social requisites." We do not think that it will be feasible to sort through the multiple paths though transitions may come about and select one avenue as more likely than others in advance. However, we believe that our results allow us to firmly reject the idea that institutional change is driven entirely by domestic processes and unaffected by regional and international events. Likewise, it makes little sense to exclude the regional context and assume that transitions to democracy are random and exogenously determined when the regional context provided appears to play a dynamic influence in transition processes.

References

Alesina, Alberto, Enrico Spolaore, and Romain Wacizarg. 2000. Economic Integration and Political Disintegration. *American Economic Review* 90 (5):1276–96.

Alexander, Gerard. 2002. *The Sources of Democratic Consolidation*. Ithaca, NY: Cornell University Press.

Almond, Gabriel A. and Sidney Verba. 1963. *The Civic Culture: Political Attitudes and Democracy in Five Nations*. Boston, MA: Little, Brown.

Alt, James E., Gary King, and Curtis Signorino. 2001. Aggregation Among Binary, Count, and Duration Models: Estimating the Same Quantities from Different Levels of Data. *Political Analysis* 9 (1):21–44.

Alvarez, Michael R., Adam Przeworski, José Cheibub, and Fernando Limongi. 1996. Classifying Political Regimes. *Studies in Comparative International Development* 31: 3–36.

Ash, Timothy Garton. 1999. Ten Years After. *New York Review of Books* 46: 16–19.

Axelrod, Robert. 1984. *The Evolution of Cooperation*. New York: Basic Books.

Barzel, Yoram and Edgar Kiser. 1997. The Development and Decline of Medieval Voting Institutions: A Comparison of England and France. *Economic Inquiry* 35 (2):244–60.

Beck, Nathaniel, David Epstein, Simon Jackman, and Sharyn O'Halloran. 2001. Alternative Models of Dynamics in Binary Time-Series Cross-Section Models: The Example of State Failure. Paper presented to the Annual Meeting of the Society for Political Methodology, Emory University, July.

Beck, Nathaniel L., Kristian Skrede Gleditsch, and Kyle C. Beardsley. 2006. Space is more than Geography: Using Spatial Econometrics in the Study of Political Economy. *International Studies Quarterly* 50 (1):27–44.

Beck, Nathaniel, Jonathan N. Katz, and Richard M. Tucker. 1998. Taking Time Seriously: Time-Series Cross-Section Analysis with a Binary Dependent Variable. *American Journal of Political Science* 42 (4):1260–88.

Beetham, David, ed. 1994. *Defining and Measuring Democracy*. London: Sage.

Berchtold, André, and Adrian Raftery. 2002. The Mixture Transition Distribution Model for High-Order Markov Chains and Non-Gaussian Time Series. *Statistical Science* 17 (3):328–56.

Boix, Carles. 2003. *Democracy and Redistribution*. Cambridge: Cambridge University Press.

Boix, Carles and Susan C. Stokes. 2003. Endogenous Democratization. *World Politics* 55 (4):517–49.

Bollen, Kenneth A. 1979. Political Democracy and the Timing of Development. *American Sociological Review* 44 (4):572–87.

Bollen, Kenneth A. 1983. World System Position, Dependency, and Democracy: The Cross-National Evidence. *American Sociological Review* 48 (4):468–79.

Bollen, Kenneth A. 1990. Political Democracy: Conceptual and Measurement Traps. *Comparative Studies in International Development* 25 (1):7–24.

Bueno de Mesquita, Bruce and George Downs. 2004. Why Gun-Barrel Democracy Doesn't Work. *Los Angeles Times*, February 4 p. B13.

Bueno de Mesquita, Bruce, Alastair Smith, Randolph M. Siverson, and James D. Morrow. 2003. *The Logic of Political Survival*. Cambridge, MA: MIT Press.

Bush, George W. 2003. Remarks at the 20th Anniversary of the National Endowment for Democracy, 7 November, transcript available at www.whitehouse.gov/news/releases/2003/11/20031106-2.html.

Casper, Gretchen and Michelle M. Taylor. 1996. *Negotiating Democracy: Transitions from Authoritarian Rule*. Pittsburgh, PA: University of Pittsburgh Press.

Cederman, Lars-Erik. 1997. *Emergent Actors in World Politics: How States and Nations Develop and Dissolve*. Princeton, NJ: Princeton University Press.

Cornes, Richard and Todd Sandler. 1996. *The Theory of Externalities, Public Goods, and Club Goods*. Cambridge: Cambridge University Press.

Deutsch, Karl W. 1954. *Political Community at the International Level: Problems of Definition and Measurement*. Garden City, NY: Doubleday.

Diehl, Paul F. and Gary Goertz. 2000. *War and Peace in International Rivalry*. Ann Arbor, MI: University of Michigan Press.
Doorenspleet, Renske. 2000. Reassessing the Three Waves of Democratization. *World Politics* 52 (3):384–406.
Doorenspleet, Renske. 2001. *The Fourth Wave of Democratization: Identification and Explanation*. Den Haag: Institute of Social Studies.
Fukuyama, Francis. 1992. *The End of History and the Last Man*. New York: Free Press.
Galton, Francis. 1889. Comment on E. B. Tylor "On a Method of Investigating the Development of Institutions: Applied to Laws of Marriage and Descent." *Journal of the Royal Anthropological Institute* 18: 268–9.
Gasiorowski, Mark J. 1995. Economic Crisis and Political Regime Change: An Event History Analysis. *American Political Science Review* 89 (4):882–97.
Gasiorowski, Mark and Timothy Power. 1997. Institutional Design and Democratic Consolidation in the Third World. *Comparative Political Studies* 30 (1):123–55.
Gastil, Raymond D. 1985. *Freedom in the World: Political Rights and Civil Liberties, 1984–1985*. Westport, CT: Greenwood.
Gastner, Michael T. and Mark E. J. Newman. 2004. Diffusion-based Method for Producing Density-equalizing Maps. *Proceedings of the National Academy of Sciences* 101: 7499–504.
Gates, Scott, Torbjørn L. Knutsen, and Jonathon W. Moses. 1996. Democracy and Peace: A More Skeptical View. *Journal of Peace Research* 33 (1):1–10.
Gibler, Douglas M. and Scott Wolford. 2003. Like a Good Neighbor: Arms Races and Regime Diffusion Through International Borders. Typescript, Department of Political Science, University of Kentucky.
Gleditsch, Kristian Skrede. 2002a. *All International Politics is Local: The Diffusion of Conflict, Integration, and Democratization*. Ann Arbor, MI: University of Michigan Press.
Gleditsch, Kristian Skrede. 2002b. Expanded Dyadic Trade and GDP Data, 1946–92. *Journal of Conflict Resolution* 46 (4):712–24.
Gleditsch, Kristian Skrede. 2004. A Revised List of Wars Between and Within Independent States, 1816–2001. *International Interactions* 30 (4):231–62.
Gleditsch, Kristian Skrede and Jinhee L. Choung. 2004. Autocratic Transitions and Democratization. Paper presented at the 45th Annual Meeting of the International Studies Association, Montreal, Quebec, March 17–20.
Gleditsch, Kristian S. and Michael D. Ward. 1997. Double Take: Reexamining Democracy and Autocracy in Modern Polities. *Journal of Conflict Resolution* 41 (2):361–83.
Gleditsch, Kristian S. and Michael D. Ward. 1999. A Revised List of Independent States Since 1816. *International Interactions* 25 (4):393–413.
Gleditsch, Kristian S. and Michael D. Ward. 2000. War and Peace in Time and Space: The Role of Democratization. *International Studies Quarterly* 44 (1):1–29.
Gleditsch, Kristian Skrede and Michael D. Ward. 2001. Measuring Space: A Minimum Distance Database. *Journal of Peace Research* 38 (6):749–68.

Greif, Avner and David D. Laitin. 2004. A Theory of Endogenous Institutional Change. *American Political Science Review* 98 (4):633–52.

Gurr, Ted R. 1974. Persistence and Change in Political Systems, 1800–1971. *American Political Science Review* 68 (4):1482–1504.

Gurr, Ted R., Keith Jaggers, and Will H. Moore. 1989. Polity II Codebook. Center for Comparative Politics, Department of Political Science, University of Colorado. Modified online version available at http://privatewww.-essex.ac.uk/~ksg/polity.html.

Gurr, Ted R., Keith Jaggers, and Will H. Moore. 1990. The Transformation of the Western State: The Growth of Democracy, Autocracy and State Power. *Comparative Studies in International Development* 25(1): 73–108.

Harary, Frank, Robert Z. Norman, and Dorwin Cartright. 1965. *Structural Models: An Introduction to the Theory of Directed Graphs*. New York: Wiley.

Huntington, Samuel P. 1991. *The Third Wave: Democratization in the Late Twentieth Century*. Norman, OK: Oklahoma University Press.

Inkeles, Alex. 1991. *On Measuring Democracy: Its Consequences and Concomitants*. New Brunswick, NJ: Transaction.

Jaggers, Keith and Ted R. Gurr. 1995. Tracking Democracy's Third Wave with the Polity III Data. *Journal of Peace Research* 32 (4):469–82.

Kadera, Kelly M., Mark J. C. Crescenzi, and Megan L. Shannon. 2003. Democratic Survival, Peace, and War in the International System. *American Journal of Political Science* 47 (2):234–47.

Keck, Margaret E. and Kathryn Sikkink. 1999. Transnational Advocacy Networks in International and Regional Politics. *International Social Science Journal* 51 (1):89–101.

Kuran, Timur. 1989. Sparks and Prairie Fires: A Theory of Unanticipated Revolution. *Public Choice* 61 (1):41–74.

Kuran, Timur. 1991. The East European Revolution of 1989: Is It Surprising That We Were Surprised? *American Economic Review* 81 (1):121–5.

Layne, Christopher. 1994. Kant or Cant: The Myth of the Democratic Peace. *International Security* 19 (1):5–49.

Lipset, Seymour M. 1960. *Political Man: The Social Bases of Politics*. Garden City, NY: Anchor.

Lohmann, Susanne. 1994. The Dynamics of Informational Cascades: The Monday Demonstrations in Leipzig, East Germany, 1989–91. *World Politics* 47 (1):42–101.

Maddison, Angus. 1991. *Dynamic Forces in Capitalist Development: A Long-run Comparative View*. Oxford: Oxford University Press.

Mansfield, Edward and Jack Snyder. 2002. Democratic Transitions, Institutional Capacity, and the Onset of War. *International Organization* 56 (2):297–337.

Meernik, James, Eric L. Krueger, and Steven C. Poe. 1998. Testing Models of U.S. Foreign Policy: Foreign Aid During and After the Cold War. *Journal of Politics* 60 (1):63–85.

Mitchell, Sara McLaughlin, Scott Gates, and Håvard Hegre. 1999. Evolution in Democracy-War Dynamics. *Journal of Conflict Resolution* 42 (2):231–42.

Modelski, George and Gardner Perry. 1992. Democratization in Long Perspective. *Technological Forecasting and Social Change* 39 (1):23–34.

Moore, Barrington. 1973. *Social Origins of Dictatorship and Democracy: Lord and Peasant in the Making of the Modern World*. Boston, MA: Beacon Press.

Mousseau, Michael and Yuhang Shi. 1999. A Test for Reverse Causality in the Democratic Peace Relationship. *Journal of Peace Research* 36 (4):639–63.

Mueller, John E. 1999. *Capitalism, Democracy, and Ralph's Pretty Good Grocery*. Princeton, NJ: Princeton University Press.

Mueller, John. 2000. The Banality of 'Ethnic War'. *International Security* 25 (1):42–70.

Muller, Edward N. 1988. Democracy, Economic Development, and Income Inequality. *American Sociological Review* 50 (1):47–61.

Muller, Edward N. 1995. Economic Determinants of Democracy. *American Sociological Review* 60 (4):966–82.

Muller, Edward N. and Mitchell A. Seligson. 1994. Civic Culture and Democracy: The Question of a Causal Relationship. *American Political Science Review* 88 (3):635–52.

O'Donnell, Guillermo, Philippe C. Schmitter, and L. Whitehead. 1986. *Transitions from Authoritarian Rule*. Baltimore, MD: Johns Hopkins University Press.

O'Loughlin, John, Michael D. Ward, Corey L. Lofdahl, Jordin S. Cohen, David S. Brown, David Reilly, Kristian S. Gleditsch, and Michael Shin. 1998. The Diffusion of Democracy, 1946–1994. *Annals of the Association of American Geographers* 88 (4):545–74.

Olson, Mancur. 1993. Democracy, Dictatorship, and Development. *American Political Science Review* 87 (3):567–76.

Olsson, Gunnar. 1964. *Distance and Human Interaction: A Review and Bibliography*. Philadelphia, PA: Regional Science Research Institute.

Paxton, Pamela. 2000. Women's Suffrage in the Measurement of Democracy. *Studies in Comparative International Development* 35 (1):92–111.

Peceny, Mark. 1999. Forcing Them to Be Free. *Political Research Quarterly* 52 (3):546–82.

Pevehouse, Jon C. 2002a. Democracy from the Outside-in? International Organizations and Democratization. *International Organization* 56 (3):515–49.

Pevehouse, Jon C. 2002b. With a Little Help from My Friends? Regional Organizations and the Consolidation of Democracy. *American Journal of Political Science* 46 (3):611–26.

Przeworski, Adam. 1988. Democracy as a Contingent Outcome of Conflict. In *Constitutionalism and Democracy*, edited by Jon Elster and Rune Slagstad, 59–80. New York: Cambridge University Press.

Przeworski, Adam. 1991. *Democracy and the Market: Political and Economic Reforms in Eastern Europe and Latin America*. New York: Cambridge University Press.

Przeworski, Adam, Michael E. Alvarez, José Antonio Cheibub, and Fernando Limongi. 2000. *Democracy and Development: Political Institutions and Well-Being in the World, 1950–1990*. Cambridge: Cambridge University Press.

Przeworski, Adam and Fernando Limongi. 1993. Political Regimes and Economic Growth. *Journal of Economic Perspectives* 7 (1):51–69.

Przeworski, Adam and Fernando Limongi. 1997. Modernization: Theories and Facts. *World Politics* 49 (2):155–83.

Putnam, Robert D. 1993. *Making Democracy Work: Civic Traditions in Modern Italy*. Princeton, NJ: Princeton University Press.

Randle, Michael. 1991. *People Power: The Building of a New European Home*. Stroud: Hawthorn.

Ray, James L. 1995. Global Trends, State-Specific Factors and Regime Transitions, 1825–1993. *Journal of Peace Research* 32 (1):49–63.

Reiter, Dan. 2001. Does Peace Nurture Democracy? *Journal of Politics* 63 (3):935–48.

Reiter, Dan. 2001/2002. Why NATO Enlargement Does Not Spread Democracy. *International Security* 26 (4):230–5.

Remmer, Karen L. 1991. The Political Impact of Economic Crisis in Latin America in the 1980s. *American Political Science Review* 85 (3):777–800.

Robinson, William I. 1996. *Promoting Polyarchy: Globalization, US Intervention, and Hegemony*. Cambridge, New York: Cambridge University Press.

Rodrik, Dani. 1999. Where Did All the Growth Go? External Shocks, Social Conflict, and Growth Collapses. *Journal of Economic Growth* 4 (4):385–412.

Rueschemeyer, Dietrich, Evelyne Huber Stephens, and John D. Stephens. 1992. *Capitalist Development and Democracy*. Chicago, IL: University of Chicago Press.

Schelling, Thomas C. 1971. Dynamic Models of Segregation. *Journal of Mathematical Sociology* 1 (1):143–86.

Shapiro, Ian. 2003. *The State of Democratic Theory*. Princeton, NJ: Princeton University Press.

Singer, J. David. 1987. Reconstructing the Correlates of War Dataset on Material Capabilities of States, 1816–1985. *International Interactions* 14 (1):115–32.

Smith, Jackie, Ron Pagnucco, and George A. Lopez. 1998. Globalizing Human Rights: The Work of Transnational Human Rights NGOs in the 1990s. *Human Rights Quarterly* 20 (2):379–412.

Solingen, Etel. 1998. *Regional Orders at Century's Dawn: Global and Domestic Influences on Grand Strategy*. Princeton, NJ: Princeton University Press.

Starr, Harvey. 1991. Democratic Dominoes: Diffusion Approaches to the Spread of Democracy in the International System. *Journal of Conflict Resolution* 35 (2):356–81.

Starr, Harvey and Christina Lindborg. 2003. Democratic Dominoes Revisited: The Hazards of Governmental Transitions. *Journal of Conflict Resolution* 47 (4):490–519.

Thompson, William R. 1996. Democracy and Peace: Putting the Cart Before the Horse? *International Organization* 50 (1):141–74.

Vanhanen, Tatu. 1990. *The Process of Democratization: A Comparative Study of 147 States, 1980–88*. New York: Crane Russak.

Vanhanen, Tatu. 2000. A New Dataset for Measuring Democracy, 1810–1998. *Journal of Peace Research* 37 (2):251–65.

Wallerstein, Immanuel. 1979. *The Capitalist World-System*. New York: Cambridge University Press.

Watts, Duncan. 1999. *Small Worlds: The Dynamics of Networks Between Order and Randomness*. Princeton, NJ: Princeton University Press.

Weede, Erich. 1996. *Economic Development, Social Order, and World Politics: With Special Emphasis on War, Freedom, the Rise and Decline of the West, and the Future of East Asia*. Boulder, CO: Rienner.

Whitehead, Laurence. 1996. Three International Dimensions of Democratization. In *The International Dimensions of Democratization: Europe and the Americas*, edited by Laurence Whitehead, 3–26. Oxford: Oxford University Press.

Yamaguchi, Kazuo. 1991. *Event History Analysis*. Newbury Park, CA: Sage.

8 World society and human rights: an event history analysis of the Convention on the Elimination of All Forms of Discrimination against Women*

Christine Min Wotipka and Francisco O. Ramirez

A worldwide human rights regime has emerged, expanded, and intensified throughout the twentieth century, especially in the post-Second World War era. This regime involves a global system of expanding organizations, social movements, conferences, rules, and discourse promoting the human rights of individuals. This regime is universalistic in aspiration: all humans are expected to be covered by the regime. This universalism involves a discursive and organizational reframing of the more limited and more varying national citizenship emphasis; human rights in principle accrue to all individuals, regardless of their citizenship or residency. And, a growing number of types of individual persons can press for their human rights: women, children, ethnic minorities, indigenous peoples, gays and lesbians, the elderly, the disabled, and the imprisoned. The content of the human rights at stake also expands, from the rights of "abstract individuals" to the rights of individual members of a specific collectivity, e.g. from suffrage to reproduction rights for women. Also on the rise is both worldwide attention to human rights abuses and violations and national displays of commitment to human rights principles and policies. These unexpected developments have increasingly been highlighted by scholars working within both the disciplines of international relations (e.g. Donnelly 1986; Finnemore and Sikkink 1998; Keck and Sikkink 1998; Hathaway 2002;

* The authors contributed equally to this research. We are grateful for the feedback received from Frank Dobbin, Beth A. Simmons, Geoffrey Garrett, John W. Meyer, and the other participants in the International Diffusion of Democracy and Markets conference. We thank David Suarez and Jeong-Woo Koo for their assistance in data collection. For his assistance in data analysis we especially acknowledge Jeong-Woo Koo. We appreciate the suggestions related to this project received from the members of the Stanford Comparative Workshop and the Globalization Workshop in the Department of Sociology at the University of Minnesota.

Vreeland (forthcoming)) and macrosociology (Hafner-Burton and Tsutsui 2005; Tsutsui and Wotipka 2004; Smith 1995; Soysal 1994).

This chapter focuses on a specific national display of human rights commitment and that is the national ratification of the Convention on the Elimination of All Forms of Discrimination against Women (CEDAW). Women's rights increasingly constitute a central feature of the world human rights regime. At the international level, the United Nations system is replete with programs, specialized agencies, regional commissions, and international instruments aimed at addressing a plethora of women's issues. The first section of this chapter situates CEDAW within the broader context of the international development of women's rights, describing ratification trends and clarifying its content and the issues around ratification. We then address the basic question this chapter seeks to answer: why does a nation-state ratify this convention? Our starting point is a macrosociological world society perspective that asserts that the human rights regime and its theorization gives rise to a logic of appropriateness that leads nation-states to present themselves as entities affirming women's rights, especially in the international arena. The logic of appropriateness is a core premise in sociological neo-institutionalist arguments that seek to explain national policy adoptions or innovations as an international diffusion process involving mechanisms of emulation and enactment. A good nation-state identity is enacted by emulating policy that has been defined as integral to a good nation-state identity.

From a world society perspective, the ratification of CEDAW is a national policy decision conditioned by an international environment characterized by the triumph of political liberalism and democratic ideals and institutions. This has increasingly become the international environment within which nation-states have operated (on the increase of democracies, see Figure 1.1 in the Introduction to this book). Within this environment there are both exogenous shocks and diffusion mechanisms that account for both the growth in ratification behavior and the difference in the timing of ratification across space and time.

More concretely, a politically liberalizing and democratizing international environment should influence national ratification of CEDAW through the following mechanisms: (1) the establishment of conferences and organizations that promote women's rights; (2) the rise of expert theorizing on the value and rights of women; (3) the growth of "reference groups" of countries that ratify CEDAW; and (4) the increase of opportunities for national linkages to organizations and experience with treaties that emphasize human rights and/or women's rights in general. On the one hand, these mechanisms account for the overall growth of CEDAW ratifying countries. But to the extent that countries vary with respect to linkages and experiences and as regards their "reference groups," the world society perspective predicts differences in the timing of ratification.

The world society perspective and its implications are contrasted with the predictions of theories that emphasize the impact of economic, political, and cultural modernity as endogenous societal properties. The underlying premise of these arguments is that of independent governmental decision making. Countries with some economic, political, or cultural characteristics are more likely to ratify. We also consider the implications of power dependency arguments that focus on the influence of dominant actors in the international system and view developments therein as outcomes of power and interest. These arguments postulate exogenous sources of influence on national decision making but are more likely to emphasize coercive mechanisms. Policy adoption is mostly shaped by imposed "conditionalities," not primarily influenced by identity considerations. After setting forth the hypotheses these different theoretical perspectives imply, we describe the cross-national data and methods of data analysis we shall employ to test these hypotheses. Event history models are estimated to ascertain first, which variables predict ratifying CEDAW and then which predict ratifying CEDAW without reservations. We undertake these separate analyses to ascertain whether the more stringent criteria of ratification without reservations is influenced by factors different than those that shape the "softer" ratification outcome.

Lastly, we report our main findings and their implications for the world society perspective that motivated this research undertaking. We also reflect on the alternative perspectives whose implications are empirically examined as well. Our main findings show that there are both exogenous and endogenous processes at work. Ratification is influenced by some characteristics of countries as well as by some indicators of diffusion and of exogenous shocks. For the most part the same variables that influence ratification also increase the likelihood of ratification without reservations.

The "Women's Convention"

The United Nations Commission on the Status of Women (CSW), established in 1946 to monitor the situation of women and to promote women's rights, recommended to the General Assembly of the United Nations that 1975 be designated the International Women's Year. This event, along with the United Nations (UN) Decade for Women (1976–1985) touched off a new women's era in the United Nations and subsequently, a *global* women's movement (Chen 1996).

It was during the Decade for Women that the United Nations General Assembly adopted the Convention on the Elimination of All Forms of

Discrimination against Women.[1] Officially adopted in December 1979, it entered into force as an international treaty two years later.[2] Although a number of other international treaties have addressed the rights of women, such as the Convention on the Political Rights of Women (1953), the Convention on the Nationality of Married Women (1957), and the Convention on Consent to Marriage, Minimum Age for Marriage and Registration of Marriages (1962), CEDAW surpasses these other treaties in terms of its scope and in its monitoring capabilities. By ratifying CEDAW, states pledge to end discrimination against women in all forms. Article 1 defines discrimination as follows:

> any distinction, exclusion or restriction made on the basis of sex which has the effect or purpose of impairing or nullifying the recognition, enjoyment or exercise by women, irrespective of their marital status, on a basis of equality of men and women, of human rights and fundamental freedoms in the political, economic, social, cultural, civil or any other field.

Since its adoption in 1979 and up to 1989, the percentage of countries that ratified the Convention increased from less than 1 percent to about 60 percent. The ratification process continued in the following decade and by 1999 about 90 percent of the nation-states of the world had ratified this treaty. This pattern is evidenced in Figure 8.1. By June 2006, 187 countries had ratified the treaty, making it one of the most widely supported international human rights treaties (see Appendix 8.1). This descriptive finding is in and of itself surprising, given that all of these countries (save New Zealand) denied women the right to vote at the beginning of the twentieth century. That is, it would be surprising if one failed to recognize that CEDAW ratification is taking place within a broader international context favoring women's rights. Alternatively one could argue that this overall increase in ratification reflects the overall increase in the number of economically, politically, or culturally modern countries in the world. As noted earlier we will examine the implications of this perspective in contrast to the world society perspective.

Much of the success of CEDAW stems from the political and intellectual support it has received from women's national and international organizations (Fraser 1995). The Commission on the Status of Women, working in conjunction with these groups and female UN staff, was effective in persuading the Economic and Social Council (ECOSOC) and the General Assembly to accept CEDAW after many years of negotiations and compromise.

[1] See Fraser 1995 for a detailed history of the origins and progression of the Convention from a declaration.

[2] It entered into force thirty days following the ratification or accession by twenty states.

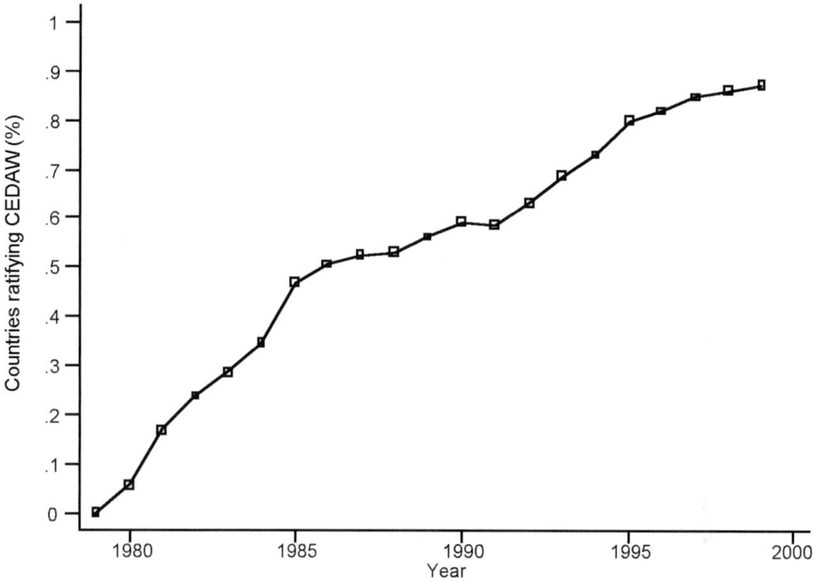

Figure 8.1 Cumulative percentage of ratifications of the Convention on the Elimination of All Forms of Discrimination against Women, 1979–1999

Figure 8.2 shows the hazard rate for all countries at risk of ratifying CEDAW. The hazard rate is derived as the probability that an event occurs at time *t*, conditional on the events not having occurred before time *t*. Figure 8.2 shows the hazard rate of nation-state ratifications of CEDAW from 1979 (the year in which it became open for ratification) to 1999. One of the widely used estimates of this hazard rate is called the Nelson–Aalen (NA) estimate (Cox and Oakes 1984).

Figure 8.2 reveals peaks around certain time points, notably around 1981, 1986, and lastly, 1996. These dates correspond with the timing of three United Nations-sponsored international women's conferences following the first conference in Mexico City in 1975. With each subsequent meeting, held in Copenhagen in 1980, Nairobi in 1985, and Beijing in 1995, a growing number of women participated in the conferences as representatives from an expanding number of non-governmental organizations (Clark *et al.* 1998). Among their demands was ratification of CEDAW by all countries.

Specific activities were also held at two of the conferences to promote ratification of the Convention. At the 1985 conference, the International

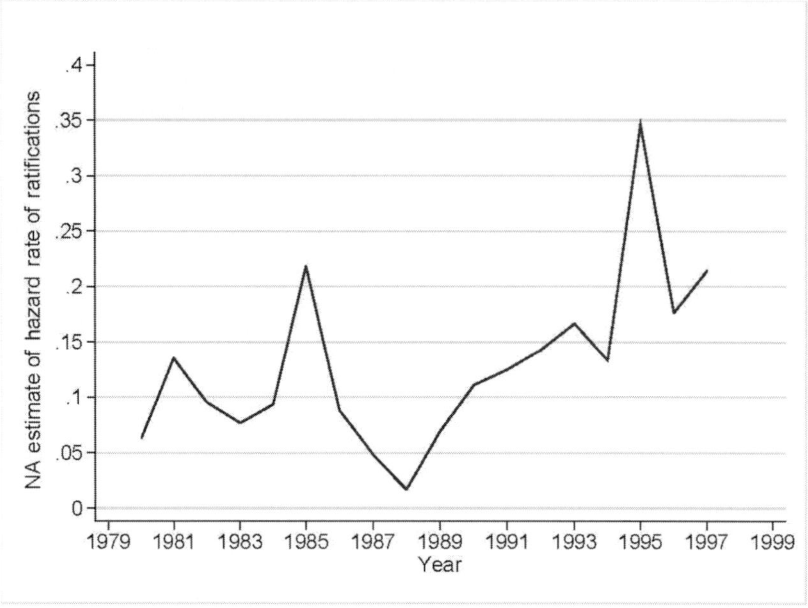

Figure 8.2 Hazard rates of ratifications of CEDAW, 1979–1999

Women's Rights Action Watch (IWRAW) was organized with the aim of promoting recognition of women's human rights under CEDAW. According to their website, IWRAW has since become "the primary international non-governmental organization that facilitates use of international human rights treaties to promote women's human rights and rights within families." Ten years later, participants at the Fourth World Conference on Women adopted a Platform for Action. Human rights was among the twelve main areas of concern in this conference. The first strategic objective under this heading called for the following:

> Promote and protect the human rights of women, through the full implementation of all human rights instruments, especially the Convention on the Elimination of All Forms of Discrimination against Women.

Governments were specifically encouraged to ratify and implement CEDAW and to limit reservations to the Convention.

The general pattern for ratifications tends to be early ratification. By 1985, over half of those countries that ratified the treaty had done so. Over the next five years, only about 13 percent of ratifications took place. Between 1991 and 1995, another 22 percent occurred. Since that time, the remaining 10 percent of ratifications transpired. Some differences emerge by region. Countries in Eastern Europe/Central Asia, the West, Latin America/Caribbean, and East Asia/Oceania tended to ratify within the first six years. Sub-Saharan African and South Asian countries lagged a bit further behind initially but not to the degree that Middle Eastern/North African countries did. In the case of the latter, in the first six years, less than 20 percent of ratifications occurred and none took place again until 1991. Most ratifications occurring in this region have taken place only since the mid-1990s. Of the 187 states that have ratified CEDAW, 86 ratified the Convention straightaway without first signing it. The remainder first signed then ratified it. In most instances, countries took from two to six years between the time of signing to the time of ratifying the Convention. In some instances it took as long as fifteen years. In the case of Afghanistan, nearly twenty-three years passed between signing and ratifying CEDAW. By and large, countries having the longest delays tended to be poorer countries that signed the Convention in 1980 but had more pressing issues on their agendas during the worldwide financial crisis of the ensuing decade.[3]

Only one country – the United States – has simply signed the treaty, thereby binding it "to do nothing in contravention of its terms" (United Nations 2003c).[4] After President Carter signed the treaty in 1980, the Senate Foreign Relations Committee not only failed to vote on CEDAW at that time, it did not even hold a hearing on it until 1990. In 1993, President Clinton was urged to support ratification of CEDAW in a letter signed by sixty-eight senators. Since then, the Senate Foreign Relations Committee has twice voted in favor of sending the treaty to the full senate for ratification. Before a senate vote takes place, the Committee must again vote in favor of sending it on. Human rights organizations contend that the international community as well as the US stands to benefit from US ratification of CEDAW. According to Human Rights Watch (2006),

> By ratifying CEDAW, the US would send a strong message that it is serious about the protection of women's human rights around the world. Ratification would also enable the US to nominate experts to the CEDAW Committee, and thereby be in a position to take part in interpreting CEDAW.

Furthermore, it's believed that rather than imposing requirements on the US to comply with laws it largely complies with anyway, CEDAW

[3] Nearly all of the countries having long delays between signing and ratifying first signed the Convention in 1980.

[4] See Plattner 1995–96 for more on why the US has yet to ratify CEDAW. We don't suspect the failure of the United States to ratify CEDAW has an impact on the remaining laggard countries. At the time of this writing, nearly half of the countries that had yet to ratify the Convention were Islamic countries. Instead of claiming reservations to many of the same articles found to be unacceptable by their Muslim brethren, these countries have simply chosen to neither sign nor ratify CEDAW.

ratification would provide a useful framework for examining the rights of women.

Despite the overall acceptance of CEDAW by a large number of nation-states, nearly a third of the state parties submitted reservations to CEDAW, invoking national law, tradition, religion, or culture as the source of its reservations (United Nations 2003a). A total of forty-nine countries have reservations against some articles in CEDAW. Countries from all regions of the world have submitted reservations but the number of Muslim countries ratifying CEDAW with reservations total 24, or 41 percent of all countries submitting reservations.

Across the board, the article having the most reservations is Article 29, paragraph 1, which declares that any dispute between two or more Parties concerning the interpretation or application of the Convention that is not settled by negotiation shall, at the request of one of them, be submitted to arbitration or to the International Court of Justice. Common areas of concern for Muslim countries include three articles, two of which are considered by the Committee on the Elimination of Discrimination against Women to be core provisions of the Convention. Article 2 is a broad statement in which States Parties agree to "condemn discrimination against women in all its forms, agree to pursue by all appropriate means and without delay a policy of eliminating discrimination against women" and to undertake seven specific actions to these ends. The second, Article 16, reads as follows: "States Parties shall take all appropriate measures to eliminate discrimination against women in all matters relating to marriage and family relations." In some instances, reservations are made against all eight paragraphs of Article 16; in others, specific paragraphs are deemed to run counter to Islamic law. The number and extent of reservations entered to these two articles is of particular concern to the Committee (United Nations 2003b). Lastly, Article 9, paragraph 2 is particularly unacceptable to Muslim countries. It states the following: "States Parties shall grant women equal rights with men with respect to the nationality of their children."

Furthermore, in some instances, Muslim countries have made overarching reservations against CEDAW such as the one submitted by Saudi Arabia, which states: "In case of contradiction between any term of the Convention and the norms of Islamic law, the Kingdom is not under obligation to observe the contradictory terms of the Convention." In response to such broad statements, a number of mostly Western European countries have submitted responses along the lines of the one made by Denmark to Saudi Arabia:

> The Government of Denmark finds that the general reservation with reference to the provisions of Islamic law are [sic] of unlimited scope and undefined character.

Consequently, the Government of Denmark considers the said reservations as being incompatible with the object and purpose of the Convention and accordingly inadmissible and without effect under international law.

Since its adoption, twenty-five countries have withdrawn all or some of their reservations to specific articles of CEDAW. Among them, over half are European countries. Although it is the most widely offensive article in the Convention as described above, Article 29, paragraph 1 has also seen ten countries withdraw their reservations against it, more than any other article. Still, the number and extent of the reservations is a concern for the monitoring Committee and for supporters and was a topic of discussion at the 1993 World Conference on Human Rights in Vienna (Stamatopoulou 1995). This concern leads us to undertake separate analyses of the variables that influence ratification and ratification without reservations.

By becoming party to the treaty in the form of ratification, states are legally bound to the provisions in the treaty and are monitored by the Committee on the Elimination of Discrimination against Women (also referred to as CEDAW). One year after its entry into force and every four years following, states must submit reports to the Secretary-General detailing the legislative, judicial, administrative, or other measures adopted toward implementation (Division for the Advancement of Women 2003).

While the debates continue as to the impact of international human rights treaties, female activists are quick to point out the benefits to ratifying CEDAW. With ratification, nearly all countries have had to implement policy changes including the incorporation of clauses providing equality of the sexes in national constitutions. Plattner (1995–96: 1260) contends that "a number of parties to CEDAW have incorporated the principles of the Convention into their national laws. The Convention has even influenced litigation in the field of discrimination." In their study of equal employment opportunity in Japan, Liu and Boyle (2001) argue that by providing normative and structural resources to activists, international treaties such as CEDAW have brought about positive change for women. The reporting mechanisms central to CEDAW and to other international human rights treaties work to shame negligent governments to act upon their agreements. Despite the challenges posed by implementation of the treaty, even traditional societies like Pakistan have succeeded in altering national laws to comply with CEDAW (Weiss 2003). We now turn to consider the world society perspective and its implications for CEDAW ratification.

World society, human rights, women's rights

Much of the literature on human rights in general and on women's rights in particular focuses on human rights abuses, violations, or at the very least, on the gaps between principles and policies on the one hand and practices on the other. Within this literature the triumph of human rights principles and even policies is not adequately problematized. Theories emphasizing power and interest as determinants of human rights outcomes do not square well with the history of the human rights regime. In varying degrees and for different reasons the Universal Declaration of Human Rights was initially opposed by dominant states such as the United States, Britain, and the Soviet Union (Lauren 1998). But in 1948 the General Assembly adopted the Universal Declaration of Human Rights as part of the International Bill of Rights. To be sure, debates between proponents of individual liberty versus those of communal need prevented agreement on more specific actions (Farer 1992). But a compromise resulted in the adoption of both the International Covenant on Civil and Political Rights and the International Covenant on Economic, Social, and Cultural Rights in 1966, which entered into force in 1976.

None of this makes much sense in a world in which nation-states are nothing more than fully autonomous hard-boiled calculating actors untouched by external environments or contexts. The first core assumption underlying the world society perspective is that nation-states are not bounded autonomous functioning systems. On the contrary, nation-states are increasingly constructed from and influenced by world models of progress and justice set forth as universalistic scripts for authentic nation-statehood (Meyer *et al.* 1997; Anderson 2006). These models operate as world standards that influence nation-states much as the broader organizational environment influences specific organizations (DiMaggio and Powell 1983). This common influence may operate through different mechanisms. When it is easier to establish that some desirable goals can be efficaciously achieved through some policy alternatives, policy diffusion may reflect a straightforward learning process. However, when there are no well-established technologies the spread of a common policy is more likely to reflect the triumph of a set of ideas and norms and involve emulative mechanisms. This common influence should result in greater nation-state isomorphism over time. This should be evident as more and more nation-states become attuned to the institutional sources of world standards as well as to their organizational carriers (Finnemore 1996).

A second core assumption is that collective progress and societal justice requires the development and activity of individual persons (see the papers in Thomas *et al.* 1987). The key idea is that national development is thought to be contingent on individual development. This assumption underlies the value of persons and their socialization, giving rise to the extraordinary faith in education that prevails throughout the world. To the celebration of education as human capital and sound investment is added a more diffuse emphasis on education as human right. Without a doubt this is the least controversial human right and even its extension to women is uncontested in most parts of the world. Within the European Union, for example, gender equality is linked to science policies and justified on both human capital and human rights grounds; efficiency and equity are invoked to justify dismantling obstacles to women's greater participation in science and technology (European Technology Assessment Network 2000). Thus, expert theorization links women's rights to the broader goals of collective progress via their enhanced human capital and productivity and to social justice via their enhanced political participation and contribution. Discrimination against women is denounced as both unjust and inefficient.

Lastly, it is assumed that the nation-state continues to bear much of the responsibility for enacting the proper commitments to progress and justice. Thus, as we have stated elsewhere:

> The proper nation-state has a proper human rights profile and that includes participating in the proper human rights organizations and conferences, signing the proper human rights treaties and conventions, developing proper human rights law and policy, and behaving as if adhering to the regime mattered. The enactment of the "human rights affirming regime" model is facilitated by the human rights regime and also fuels the expansion of the regime. That is, there are human rights treaties, organizations, and experts that influence nation-state enactment of human rights policies and this enactment adds to the taken for granted character of the regime (Ramirez *et al.* 2002).

The world human rights regime is activated in international conferences involving lawyers, scientists, and other professionals discussing human rights issues and in the work of transnational experts and organizations promoting human rights policies and the standards with which to evaluate their implementation. The regime is also evident whenever grassroots activists utilize world human rights discourse and tactics in pursuit of world legitimated agendas (Smith 1995; McAdam and Rucht 1993). A human rights literature, with human rights concepts and measures, reflects and contributes to the world human rights regime (Landman 2005; Bollen 1986; Donnelly 1986; Fraser 1994).

With the adoption of the aforementioned international covenants on civil and political as well as social, economic, and cultural rights, there emerged treaty bodies that monitored implementation both by clarifying the ways in which states could implement these rights and by obliging states to provide regular reports on their implementation efforts (United Nations 1995). As the number of treaties with monitoring bodies increased so did the number of states becoming party to them (Cole 2005; Tsutsui and Wotipka 2004; Hathaway 2002). The expansion and intensification of human rights protocols, and more broadly, human rights standards, increases the codification and identification of more practices as human rights abuses and violations. This is a special case of the more general sociological phenomena where increased egalitarian expectations facilitate the identification of a greater number of inequalities cum inequities.[5] More broadly, in the absence of agreed-upon egalitarian standards, all sorts of inequalities are less likely to be experienced as inequities.

Through what mechanisms are nation-states influenced by the broader world within which they are situated? From a world society perspective three general mechanisms are especially important. First, world standards are more likely to be activated at the nation-state level when there are world meetings or conferences, which function as focal points for the articulation of these standards (Lechner and Boli 2005). These conferences serve as opportunity structures for the professional delineation of these standards and their policy ramifications by diverse epistemic communities. These conferences also serve as moral revitalization sites for international norm entrepreneurs. Through processes of anticipatory, on-site, and subsequent socialization, these conferences influence nation-state enactment of world standards. The role of professionals and norm entrepreneurs as agents of change is well established in diverse literatures (DiMaggio and Powell 1983; Ikenberry 1990).

These conferences in part constitute an exogenous shock to which nation-states respond. We say in part because we recognize that some nation-states ratify earlier and may in fact push for conferences to further ratification. For other nation-states, though, the conferences that lead to further ratification are indeed occasions for anticipatory or on-site socialization.

A second general mechanism involves norm cascades or bandwagons (Finnemore and Sikkink 1998). The world society perspective stresses the degree to which the behavior of a nation-state is influenced by the behavior of other nation-states in general as well as by the behavior of nation-states within their region. The diffuse progress and justice goals nation-states are expected to pursue are not readily attained through efficacious

[5] See Cook and Hegvedt 1983 for a review of social psychological experimental data on this point; see also Stolte 1987.

technologies. Policy emulation under this condition is especially likely to be driven by external normative influence. The source of influence may be the world at large or regions and other "reference groups."

Lastly, the world society perspective assumes that nation-states vary with respect to how much access they have to the appropriate scripts and norms. The latter facilitate the sense making that paves the way for adherence to a given standard or norm. The more nation-states are embedded in the broader world the more they will learn how "to talk the talk" and maybe even how "to walk the walk." Embeddedness may take different forms but the general idea is to distinguish between countries that are better linked to and better integrated within the wider world versus those that are more isolated. Types of linkage to the wider world include memberships in international organizations in general or in issue specific ones (Berkovitch 1999; Boli and Thomas 1999; Tsutsui and Wotipka 2004) and national experience in international treaty ratification processes. Less embedded nation-states are less likely to figure out what constitutes appropriate nation-state identity and through what activities may such an identity be realized and broadcasted to other nation-states and international organizations. Or, alternatively, they may not be clueless but simply care less.

From a world society perspective the ratification of CEDAW is likely to be influenced by the availability of CEDAW promoting conferences, by the world and regional strength of CEDAW as a regime, and by the degree to which a nation-state is linked to the wider world that supports this regime. Alternative arguments emphasize the importance of societal modernization or of power dependency dynamics in the international system.

One set of alternative explanations emphasizes the economic, political, or cultural attributes of nation-states, contending that the more modern a nation-state is along each of these dimensions the more at risk it is of ratifying a very modern covenant, such as CEDAW. In all of these explanations the endogenous characteristics of nation-states are assigned greater weight in predicting the outcome. What these explanations share in common is a logic of development as emancipation from tradition. In economic terms the logic was often viewed as the emancipation that came with industrialization and the expansion of work-related opportunities. Though there was less consensus with respect to political modernization,[6] more recently political modernization is increasingly cast in political freedoms and rights terms. Lastly, cultural modernization is indeed a very contentious idea, as in the contrast between "The West" and "The

[6] For a classic discussion of political participation versus political institutionalization as distinctive modes of political modernization, see Huntington 1968.

Rest." But the underlying mechanism throughout these arguments is that internal changes in the direction of greater societal modernization is the driving force that leads to embracing a modern treaty. From this perspective it is less costly, and thus more likely, for a more modern society to ratify a treaty that expresses a point of view more consistent with its internal modern arrangements. From this perspective the worldwide increase in CEDAW ratifiers reflects a worldwide increase in societal modernization.

What may be called power dependency arguments share with the world society perspective the premise that exogenous forces are important. But these arguments are more likely to think of forces in a literal sense and to privilege coercive mechanisms. Some of these mechanisms may be straightforwardly coercive, such as those reflected in conditionality quid pro quo arguments. The uses of foreign aid or assistance to promote common policies favored by dominant actors illustrates this mechanism. For example, Dezalay and Garth (2002) contend that the development of human rights discourse and policy in Latin America was shaped by contacts with policy-making elites in the United States and reflected the interests and values of the latter. More subtle modes of coercion may follow from openness to trade if the dominant traders favor or engage in specific policies (Hafner-Burton 2005). So, if openness to trade indicates economic liberalization and if the latter is conducive to political liberalization, one might expect greater likelihood of CEDAW ratification among the more trade-open countries.

Hypotheses

From a world society perspective we examine three general hypotheses, emphasizing the positive influence on ratification of CEDAW of crucial time points, transnational developments, and linkages to the wider world. These hypotheses are:

Hypothesis 1: Countries are more likely to ratify CEDAW around the time of CEDAW promoting international conferences.

Hypothesis 2: Countries are more likely to ratify CEDAW if other countries throughout the world or throughout their region have already ratified it.

Hypothesis 3: Countries with stronger linkages to the wider world of international treaties and organizations are more likely to ratify CEDAW.

From a modernization perspective the general hypothesis of interest is:

Hypothesis 4: More developed, more democratic, and more westernized countries are more likely to ratify CEDAW.

And lastly, from a power dependency perspective one can examine the following hypothesis:

Hypothesis 5: Countries are more likely to ratify CEDAW if they are more dependent on powerful actors that favor CEDAW.

Methods of analysis

Methods and models of estimation

Event history analysis is an appropriate tool to explain events occurring to individuals (or in this case, countries) over a specified period of time (Allison 1984; Tuma and Hannan 1984; Strang 1994b). As the use of event history analysis becomes increasingly pervasive, more and more issues concerning phenomena at the national level have been examined using this method. There are, for example, event history analyses of environmentalism (Frank *et al.* 2000), of decolonization (Strang 1994a), of political leadership stability (Hanneman and Steinback 1990) and of the acquisition of women's suffrage rights (Ramirez *et al.* 1997).

Event history analysis offers a more dynamic method in that it provides coefficients demonstrating the influence of explanatory variables on the *rate* of treaty ratifications, a single, non-repeatable event involving discrete change. Event history analysis also allows for the possibility that some cases (countries) will not experience an event, as in the case of countries that have yet to ratify CEDAW, if ever. The data are "right-censored" in that we do not know if or when these countries will ratify the treaty in the future. The set of states at risk of becoming a party to CEDAW (the risk-set) is made up of all the countries in the world. Countries that gained their independence during this time period get inserted into the risk-set the year in which they become independent.

Assuming that changes in the hazard rate are a function of changing covariates, we used an exponential ("constant rate") model. In such models, the hazard rate is constant over time, following an exponential distribution. Accordingly, the change of the hazard rate over time in the exponential model only depends on the changes of values of the independent variables (Allison 1984). We do not believe that there is a clear theoretical reason for ratifications to be time dependent. The independent variables used in our models mostly capture why certain countries ratify CEDAW earlier than others.

Variables

We examine the rate at which states ratify the Convention on the Elimination of All Forms of Discrimination against Women from the time it was available for ratification (1979) to 1999. The data were coded from the United Nations (2003a). The event studied is whether a country ratifies CEDAW in a given year during the time period. When it does, it receives a value of 1 for that year. For those years in which a country does not become party to CEDAW or if it has already ratified CEDAW, the country receives a score of 0.[7]

In the analysis, we use several independent variables.[8] We begin with a set of endogenous variables. First, to test the modernization thesis, we use a measure of national economic development derived from a calculation of real gross domestic product (GDP) per capita in constant US$ (1995) (World Bank 2001). It is logged to correct for a skewed distribution. We include a measure of dominant religion of the population – a dummy variable for predominantly Islam (coded 1), derived from the CIA's World Factbook distinctions (2002)[9] – as well as a dummy variable for former or current Communist countries (coded 1) (CIA 2002; Perrett and Hogg 1989). To capture the influence of regime type, we used a dummy variable measuring a democratic regime versus a dictatorial one (coded 1) present in a country for every year in our analysis (Przeworski *et al.* 2000; Cheibub and Gandhi 2004).

We then test several measures to get at the notion of democracy and modernization. The first entail three measures of women's status. Two measures estimate the influence of women's seats in the national assembly and legislature (and its interaction with non-Eastern European/ Central Asian countries) and in part taps women's formal political clout. The variables are available from the United Nations (2000).

We then test measures of national political structure. We estimate the influence of British colonial heritage, the form of the national constitution, and leftist orientation of the chief executive's party. Constitutional imbalance of power traditions and a British colonial heritage, which assign greater weight to treaty ratification, are expected to negatively influence ratification.[10] Both are coded as dummy variables. Countries having one of the following constitutional forms are coded 1: chief executive or cabinet decision; rule or tradition of informing legislative body of signed treaties; or majority consent of one legislative body. The comparison categories include super-majority in one body or majority in two

7 When a country has already ratified CEDAW, it is eliminated from the risk-set.

8 Unless stated otherwise, all variables are measured continuously for the time period covered in this analysis, 1979–1999. Except for treaties variables, women's rights INGOs and dummy variables, the independent variables are lagged by one year.

9 A better variable would capture the state religion but such a measure produces enough inconsistencies that we have chosen not to use it in the analysis at this time; see Barrett *et al.* 2001.

10 Beth A. Simmons, personal communication.

legislative bodies or national plebiscite, which are assumed to render treaty ratification more difficult than the former forms. Former British colonies are coded 1. Finally, all other things being equal, leftist regimes are expected to favor CEDAW ratification. This variable is coded as a dummy variable with right, center, and other parties as comparison categories. Data are taken from the World Bank's governance data sets.

We then tried two variables aligned with dependency arguments. First, we included the amount of official development assistance and official aid (current US$) received by countries. Although it is unlikely that such aid would be conditional on ratification of CEDAW or other international human rights treaties for that matter, there may be normative pressures or attempts to appear legitimate within the human rights regime, which would motivate countries to ratify such treaties. Given that a major donor of such assistance and aid, the United States, has not ratified the Convention could, however, lessen the urgency to ratify this particular treaty. We also tried trade openness measured as imports plus exports divided by GDP. Both measures were derived from the World Bank (2001).

To assess the influence of international women's conferences on CEDAW ratification, we try a dummy variable for the years of the three conferences, which took place in 1980, 1985, and 1995. We expect that either in anticipation of the conferences or in response to pressures to ratify, countries were at greater risk of ratifying the Convention in the years around each conference.

Next, we try a range of variables that capture diffusion. To understand the influence of ratifications at the world and regional level, we first used a measure of world density, which quantifies the number of ratifications among all countries as of the previous year. We then tried two different measures of regional density. The first computes ratifications by region, also up to the previous year. The second set of diffusion variables interact regional density for each individual region. With these variables, we are able to ascertain whether or not countries within a particular region are influenced by ratifications within their own region. In all instances, we use a measure of seven distinct regions used by the World Bank and the Central Intelligence Agency: Sub-Saharan Africa, East Asia/Oceania, Eastern Europe/Central Asia, Latin America/Caribbean, Middle East/North Africa, South Asia, and the West (Western Europe, Australia, Canada, New Zealand, and the United States).

To get at density among countries of similar levels of development, we looked at the most developed and the least developed countries using separate measures. For one variable, we calculated ratifications among member states of the Organization for Economic Cooperation and

Development (OECD) as of the previous year interacted with a dummy variable for OECD member states.[11] We computed a similar interaction term for least developed countries (LDCs). Using these interaction terms, we are able to ascertain whether or not OECD member states (or LDCs) are influenced by ratifications among other OECD countries (or other LDCs). Thus, in addition to estimating the overall influence of regional density on ratification likelihood, we also estimate the influence of density among countries of similar levels of development.

Our indicators of national linkages to carriers of world models of human rights capture the strength of linkages to international human rights treaties and organizations. As for the former, we calculate states' ratifications of international human rights treaties other than CEDAW. More specifically, these include six multilateral treaties deposited with the Secretary-General that have treaty bodies to monitor their implementation (United Nations 1995; United Nations 2003a). The variable measures the total number of treaties available for ratification (other than CEDAW) that have been ratified by each country in a given year. We also use a measure of states' ratifications of other treaties concerning women – the Convention on the Political Rights of Women (1953), the Convention on the Nationality of Married Women (1957), and the Convention on Consent to Marriage, Minimum Age for Marriage and Registration of Marriages (1962). We coded the variable from 0–3, with 0 indicating that in that year, the country had not ratified any of these treaties, up to 3 meaning that all three treaties had been ratified by that year.

To capture organizational linkages, we use four variables. The first is a summation of memberships in international non-governmental organizations (INGOs) at the national level. Second, we count memberships in human rights international non-governmental organizations (HRINGOs) at the national level. The data were originally collected for three time points – 1978, 1988, and 1998. Using interpolation, we were able to fill in the years between these time points. The value for 1998 was used for 1999.[12] Next, we measured memberships in women's rights international non-governmental organizations (WINGOs) at the national level. The data through 1989 come from Berkovitch's (1999) study of women's rights and international organizations and then updated in the same manner up to 1999. So as to have uniquely independent values for

[11] OECD member states is computed as a dummy variable with 1 referring to those countries that ever were a member of OECD during the time period studied.

[12] A more detailed description of the coding scheme for this variable is described in Tsutsui and Wotipka 2004.

INGOs, we subtracted the number of HRINGOs and WINGOs from this variable. After adding one to each case (to address those cases having zeros), we then took the natural log to correct for skewed distributions. Finally, we include country memberships in intergovernmental organizations (IGOs) for each year. Data for all four variables were obtained from the *Yearbook of International Organizations* (Union of International Associations various years).

Descriptive statistics for and definitions of the independent variables are displayed in Table 8.1. The statistics are based on the complete twenty-year period during which time countries are at risk for ratification and thus represent typical values for our variables of interest. Addressing the issue of possible multicollinearity among independent variables, we found that correlations among most of the variables were modest (below .5).[13] The correlations between world density and density among both OECD countries (.81) and least developed countries (.79) were relatively high. Our two main analyses (ratifications and ratifications without reservations) provide us with two different samples with which to see if the effects of such density variables remain robust across analyses. Looking at the effects of world density, OECD density, and LDCs density, we see strikingly similar results between the models in Tables 8.2 and 8.3, thus indicating that multicollinearity is not a concern.

For the sake of this exploratory analysis, we attempted to include as many countries in the analysis as possible by filling in missing values whenever feasible, for example, by using interpolation to replace missing data. In those instances when a great deal of data was missing for too many years and/or too many explanatory variables, a country could not be included in the analysis. In most instances, the lost cases were small island countries that typically do not make it into cross-national analyses.

Results

The results from the event history analyses of the rate of becoming party to CEDAW are shown in Table 8.2. The final analysis includes 142 countries[14] having a total of 132 events (instances of ratification of

[13] In results not reported here, GDP per capita was highly correlated with female literacy and female life expectancy. In models using these measures of women's status, we removed GDP per capita.

[14] In 1979, the number of countries included in the analysis is 137 and in 1989, the number amounts to 140. The numbers fluctuate to reflect the changing number of independent countries in the world. See Appendix 8.1 for countries included in the analysis.

Table 8.1. *Definition and descriptive statistics for variables used in the analysis of ratifications of CEDAW, 1979–1999*

Variable	Definition	Mean	Standard deviation
National economic development	Measured by GDP per capita (constant 1995 US$)	5958.31	0.69
Democratization	Dummy variable of democratization (1-Democracy, 0-Autocracy)	.47	.50
Communist countries	Dummy variable of Communist countries (1-Communist, 0-non-Communist), time-varying	.05	.22
Islamic world	Dummy variable for primarily Muslim countries	.24	.43
Women's seats in assembly	Number of women's seats in the assembly or legislature	.10	.11
Women's seats*non-E. Europe	Interaction term of women's seats in assembly and non-Eastern European countries	.09	.11
Leftist regime	Dummy variable for leftist regime	.31	.46
Constitutional form	Dummy variable for chief executive or cabinet decision; rule or tradition of informing legislative body of signed treaties; or majority consent of one legislative body.	.85	.36
British colony	Dummy variable for countries that have ever been a British colony	.35	.48
Trade openness	Import plus export divided by GDP per capita	75.60	48.25
Official development assistance and aid	Official development assistance and official aid, current US$ (million)	241	426
UN women's conferences	Dummy variable of the years of UN women's conferences, 1980, 1985, 1995	.14	.35
World density	Cumulative number of countries that ratified CEDAW at the world level, one year lagged	77.92	42.02
Regional density	Cumulative number of countries that ratified CEDAW at the regional level, one year lagged	15.31	11.97
Regional density*Sub-Saharan Africa	Interaction term of regional density and Sub-Saharan Africa	6.06	11.78
Regional density*East Asia/Oceania	Interaction term of regional density and East Asia/Oceania	.96	3.1

Regional density*Eastern Europe/Central Asia	Interaction term of regional density and East Europe/Central Asia	.18	.95
Regional density*Latin America/Caribbean	Interaction term of regional density and Latin America/Caribbean	5.08	10.63
Regional density*Middle East/ North Africa	Interaction term of regional density and Middle East and North Africa	.3	1.21
Regional density*South Asia	Interaction term of regional density and South Asia	.18	.91
Regional density*West	Interaction term of regional density and West	2.54	6.58
OECD density*OECD countries	Interaction term of OECD density and OECD dummy variable (1-OECD countries, 0-otherwise)	2.73	6.87
OECD density	Cumulative number of OECD countries that ratified CEDAW, one year lagged	7.32	5.37
Least density*LDCs	Interaction term of density of least developed countries and LDCs dummy variable (1-LDCs, 0-otherwise)	3.37	7.8
Least density	Cumulative number of LDCs that ratified CEDAW, one year lagged	6.95	4.87
Human rights treaties	Propensity to ratify human rights treaties	3.14	1.87
Women's rights treaties	Propensity to ratify women's rights treaties	1.19	1.07
INGOs membership	Measured by memberships in international non-governmental organizations at the national level (add one)	596.45	629.67
HRINGOs memberships	Measured by memberships in human rights INGOs at the national level (add one)	24.74	19.61
WINGOs memberships	Measured by memberships in women's INGOs at the national level (add one)	38.15	30.89
IGO memberships	Measured by nation-state memberships in intergovernmental organizations	44.51	17.72
Total observations = 2952			

Table 8.2. *Exponential models of rate of ratification of CEDAW, 1979–1999*

	Model 1		Model 2		Model 3		Model 4		Model 5		Model 6		Model 7	
Independent variable[1]	Coef.	(S.E.)	Coef.	(S.E.)	Coef.	(S.E.)	Coef.	(S.E.)	Coef.	(S.E.)	Coef.	(S.E.)	Coef.	(S.E.)
Modernization														
GDP per capita (logged)	$-.37^{*}$	(.18)	.24	(.19)	$.61^{**}$	(.22)	.17	(.30)	.22	(.27)	.30	(.25)	$.56^{*}$	(.24)
Democratization	$.76^{**}$	(.24)	.37	(.24)	−.11	(.26)	$.46^{\dagger}$	(.25)	$.46^{*}$	(.25)	$.51^{\dagger}$	(.25)	.41	(.25)
Communist countries	−.51	(.49)	$.98^{\dagger}$	(.52)	$.95^{\dagger}$	(.52)	1.51^{*}	(.56)	1.69^{**}	(.57)	1.77^{**}	(.58)	1.49^{**}	(.56)
Islamic world	.08	(.24)	-1.74^{***}	(.35)	-1.41^{***}	(.37)	-1.50^{***}	(.35)	-1.42^{***}	(.36)	-1.50^{***}	(.35)	-1.57^{***}	(.35)
Women's status														
Women's seats in assembly	2.04	(1.73)	−2.06	(1.86)	$-3.32^{\dagger}$	(1.99)	−3.31	(2.11)	−2.44	(2.10)	−2.90	(2.08)	−3.11	(2.08)
Women's seats * non-Eastern Europe	.66	(1.65)	−2.42	(1.86)	.52	(2.01)	1.90	(1.99)	.95	(1.96)	1.48	(1.96)	1.37	(1.96)
National political structure														
Leftist party[2]	−.08	(.21)	$.87^{***}$	(.24)	$.77^{**}$	(.24)	$.42^{\dagger}$	(.25)	.39	(.25)	.38	(.25)	$.48^{\dagger}$	(.25)
Constitutional form[3]	.19	(.26)	1.93^{***}	(.41)	1.08^{*}	(.44)	$.70^{\dagger}$	(.38)	$.72^{\dagger}$	(.38)	$.71^{\dagger}$	(.38)	$.64^{\dagger}$	(.38)
British colony	−.12	(.21)	$-.54^{*}$	(.25)	$-.70^{**}$	(.26)	−.41	(.25)	$-.55^{*}$	(.26)	−.39	(.25)	$-.45^{\dagger}$	(.26)
Dependence														
Trade openness	−.001	(.002)	−.003	(.002)	$-.004^{\dagger}$	(.002)	.001	(.002)	.001	(.002)	.0003	(.002)	−.001	(.002)
Official development assistance and aid		$4.21e{-}10^{*}$		(.0001) 5.64e–1†		(.0001) 3.02e–10		(.0001) 3.06e–10		(.0001) 3.53e–10		(.0001) 5.92e–10*		(.0001)
Years														
UN women's conferences (1980, 1985, 1995)			1.59^{***}	(.24)	1.63^{***}	(.24)	1.70^{***}	(.25)	1.67^{***}	(.25)	1.72^{***}	(.25)	1.68^{***}	(.25)

Diffusion												
World density	.06***	(.004)	.06***	(.005)	.22***	(.03)	.22***	(.03)	.22***	(.03)	.22***	(.03)
Regional density	.03*	(.01)			.04*	(.01)	.03†	(.02)	.04*	(.02)	.04**	(.02)
Regional density* Sub-Saharan Africa			.07*	(.03)								
Regional density* East Asia/Oceania			.20***	(.05)								
Regional density* East Europe/Central Asia			.64***	(.16)								
Regional density* Latin America/ Caribbean			.13***	(.03)								
Regional density* Middle East/North Africa			.06	(.11)								
Regional density* South Asia			.29†	(.16)								
Regional density* West			–.03	(.04)								
OECD density					–.13***	(.03)	–.13***	(.03)	–.13***	(.03)	–.12***	(.03)
OECD density* OECD countries					–.49***	(.09)	–.50***	(.09)	–.50***	(.09)	–.47**	(.09)
Least density					–.08*	(.03)	–.08*	(.04)	–.08*	(.04)	–.08*	(.04)
Least density* least developed countries					–.18†	(.10)	–.19†	(.10)	–.20*	(.09)	–.19†	(.10)
Linkages – treaties and organizations												
Propensity to ratify: human rights treaties					.15†	(.08)	.15†	(.08)	.15†	(.08)	.18*	(.08)
Propensity to ratify: women's rights treaties					.01	(.11)	.03	(.11)	.01	(.11)	.06	(.12)

Table 8.2. (*cont.*)

	Model 1		Model 2		Model 3		Model 4		Model 5		Model 6		Model 7	
Independent variable[1]	Coef.	(S.E.)	Coef.	(S.E.)	Coef.	(S.E.)	Coef.	(S.E.)	Coef.	(S.E.)	Coef.	(S.E.)	Coef.	(S.E.)
INGOs (logged)							.69†	(.38)						
Women's rights INGOs (logged)									.87*	(.43)				
Human rights INGOs (logged)											.68†	(.39)		
IGOs (logged)													.01	(.22)
Constant	−7.05***	(.59)	−11.01***	(.88)	−11.16***	(.86)	−11.95***	(.87)	−11.40***	(.83)	−11.66***	(.82)	−11.55***	(.91)
Log likelihood	−133		240		261		267		267		267		265	
Number of ratifications	132		132		132		132		132		132		132	
Number of countries	142		142		142		142		142		142		142	
Yearly spells	1325		1325		1325		1325		1325		1325		1325	

Notes:

[1]Most of independent variables are one year lagged except for treaties, women's rights INGOs, and dummy variables

[2]A dummy variable: comparison categories include right, center, and other parties

[3]A dummy variable: main categories include individual chief executive or cabinet decision or rule or tradition of informing legislative body of signed treaties or majority consent of one legislative body

Comparision categories include super-majority in one body or majority in two legislative bodies or national plebiscite

$^{\dagger}p \leq .10$;

$^{*}p \leq .05$;

$^{**}p \leq .01$;

$^{***}p \leq .001$ (two-tailed tests)

CEDAW) over the time period 1979–1999. We report seven different models using differing combinations of the variables of interest.[15]

We begin by focusing on the effects of the endogenous variables in Model 1. These entail our measures of modernization, women's status, national political structure, and dependence. In Model 2, we then add years of UN women's conferences and the two main measures of diffusion. Model 3 also incorporates the effect of diffusion, this time with a focus on its effect within regions. The effect of diffusion among countries of similar levels of development gets tested in Models 4–7 as does the impact of our measures of treaty and organizational linkages.

The results are mostly stable from one model to the next and some clear patterns emerge. The results suggest inconsistent support for most of the endogenous variables when using just these variables. In Model 1, two variables impacting the risk of CEDAW ratification are economic development with a negative effect and democratization, which has a positive effect. In the other models, it appears that former or current Communist countries are more likely to be at risk for ratifying the treaty. The latter may be explained by the fact that the former Soviet-bloc countries quickly ratify nearly all international treaties, including CEDAW, soon after independence. On the other hand, being primarily Islamic strongly and negatively influences a country's risk of ratifying the Convention. Results for level of national economic development were not consistently significant.[16] We find no effect for the two measures of women's political power.[17]

We find some support that national political structure impacts a country's risk for CEDAW ratification. In two models, leftist regimes were significantly more likely to be at risk but these findings do not hold for the other models. The coefficients for constitutional form were positive and significant, suggesting that countries with lower hurdles to treaty ratification are more likely to ratify CEDAW. As was also expected given the

[15] In event history analysis, a simple observation of the coefficients is meaningless to compare the influence or magnitude of different independent variables. Given that the estimated models are non-linear, the coefficients have no direct linear interpretation, and the marginal effects of the variables differ depending on the values of other variables. The difficulties of interpreting the coefficients also stems from the fact that several independent variables (i.e. GDP, and organizational linkages variables) are power transformed by natural log. In this study, we are mainly concerned with signs and significance levels of variables. This interpretation method is consistent with other studies that use density variables as key covariates; see Baum and Oliver 1992; Carroll and Sevaminathan 2000; Carroll and Hannan 2000.

[16] We found similar results using a measure of urbanization from the World Bank 2001.

[17] We also tried other proxies for female incorporation, female literacy and life expectancy, which did not result in significant effects.

relative difficulty involved in the treaty ratification process, the effect of being a former British colony was negative throughout.

Dependency perspectives contend that dependence on powerful actors favoring CEDAW would increase the likelihood of its ratification by dependent countries. This argument was weakly supported by the findings. In some models, countries receiving more official development assistance and aid were more likely to ratify. In results not reported here but available from the authors, we first interacted aid with LDCs to see if it was the case that least developed countries receiving the most aid were also more prone to ratification. These results were not significant, thus suggesting that those most dependent on aid for their survival are not being coerced to ratify this treaty. As for trade openness, we found neither an effect for it alone nor when we interacted this variable with LDCs.

Turning to the exogenous variables, strong results were found for each model. In every case, the dummy variable representing the years of the last three UN international women's conferences is the strongest predictor of being at risk for ratifying CEDAW. It appears that the special attention given to CEDAW and to other human rights treaties protecting women at these conferences has been successful.[18]

The diffusion variables aligned with the norm cascade argument show significant results on CEDAW ratifications. As more countries as a whole ratify CEDAW, a country is much more likely to do so as well. Ratifications by other countries in the same region is also a consistent, though less strong, predictor of ratifications of CEDAW. This suggests an effect of external normative influences consistent with our second hypothesis. Furthermore, the influence of ratifications within each particular region significantly and positively impacted several regions – namely Sub-Saharan Africa, East Asia/Oceania, East Europe/Central Asia, and Latin America/Caribbean.[19] OECD countries (and LDCs) were significantly less likely to ratify the Convention had other OECD members (LDCs) already done so.

The linkage hypothesis is tested using different measures of connection to the relevant international treaties and organizations. The findings generally lend further support to the world society perspective. First,

[18] Similar results (not reported here) were found using a dummy variable for the years just prior to the conferences and (in separate analyses) a dummy variable for the years just after the conferences. This suggests that nation-states act upon the treaty as a form of anticipatory socialization as well as on-site socialization – keeping in mind that it may take up to a year or longer for nation-states to get treaties ratified.

[19] In order to further examine the effect of regional density in the West, we ran the model without the GDP per capita variable and again without the United States in the analysis, neither of which influenced the results.

the measure of a country's propensity to ratify human rights treaties other than CEDAW positively influenced ratifications of CEDAW. However, propensity to ratify earlier treaties concerning the rights of women did not have an impact on CEDAW ratifications. These findings suggest that perhaps ratification patterns are analogous for the major international human rights treaties with monitoring bodies similar to CEDAW (Wotipka and Tsutsui forthcoming).

The linkage hypothesis finds further support when we examine the effects of ties to international non-governmental organizations. We try each of the three variables in turn and find that having more memberships in INGOs weakly increases the rate of CEDAW ratifications. The same is true for memberships in human rights and women's rights INGOs. Memberships in intergovernmental organizations does not influence our dependent variable.

In order to ascertain whether the same variables impact ratifications without reservations, we try identical analyses using just those countries that ratified with CEDAW without reservations or had withdrawn all of their reservations by 1999. The sample includes 99 of the original 142 countries. Results may be found in Table 8.3.

The most striking finding is the stability of the strongest predictors of ratification found in the previous analysis. Years of the international women's conferences continue to exert a positive and significant influence as does diffusion of ratifications at the world level. Also, being Islamic again puts a country less at risk for ratifying CEDAW. Linkages in the form of human rights treaties and human rights organizations, now including IGOs, maintain their positive effect.

Some of the results for this more stringent test of CEDAW ratification differ in interesting ways. The impact of Communist countries (former and current) is no longer significant, suggesting that quite a few of these countries ratified but did so with reservations. Regional density of ratifications overall and by region lose their significance, which may mean that countries with a strong interest in CEDAW and no reservations against it did so regardless of their neighbors' actions. Finally, the impact of propensity to ratify early women's rights treaties becomes negative and significant in this analysis. These findings are difficult to interpret but may mean that the countries in this stricter sample do not take treaty ratification lightly and are not prone to ratifying women's treaties just for the sake of doing so. As indicated by the fact that CEDAW was found to be acceptable without reservations to certain articles, there is something about this treaty making it worthy among women's treaties of ratification.

In other analyses not reported here, we found no effect for a number of other variables. We tried two additional measures of modernization: a

Table 8.3. *Exponential models of rate of ratification of CEDAW with no reservations, 1979–1999*

	Model 1		Model 2		Model 3		Model 4		Model 5		Model 6		Model 7	
Independent variable[1]	Coef.	(S.E.)	Coef.	(S.E.)	Coef.	(S.E.)	Coef.	(S.E.)	Coef.	(S.E.)	Coef.	(S.E.)	Coef.	(S.E.)
Modernization														
GDP per capita (logged)	$-.66^{*}$	(.22)	$-.40^{\dagger}$	(.23)	−.30	(.24)	−.09	(.35)	−.12	(.34)	−.31	(.31)	−.05	(.29)
Democratization	$.99^{***}$	(.28)	.17	(.27)	.22	(.28)	.11	(.30)	.14	(.29)	.33	(.30)	.17	(.30)
Communist countries	$-1.23^{\dagger}$	(.65)	−.49	(.64)	−.54	(.64)	−.28	(.64)	−.16	(.64)	.16	(.65)	−.22	(.65)
Islamic world	−.41	(.32)	-1.56^{***}	(.39)	-1.50^{***}	(.43)	-1.70^{***}	(.41)	-1.61^{***}	(.42)	-1.50^{***}	(.40)	-1.81^{***}	(.41)
Women's status														
Women's seats in assembly	1.94	(2.88)	−.82	(3.06)	−.83	(3.13)	−2.08	(3.24)	−1.39	(3.24)	−1.16	(3.21)	−1.86	(3.25)
Women's seats * non-Eastern Europe	2.05	(2.77)	.99	(2.97)	1.54	(3.05)	3.20	(3.16)	2.55	(3.13)	2.62	(3.10)	3.04	(3.15)
National political structure														
Leftist party[2]	−.11	(.24)	$.45^{\dagger}$	(.24)	$.45^{\dagger}$	(.25)	$.86^{***}$	(.26)	$.83^{**}$	(.26)	$.73^{**}$	(.26)	$.85^{**}$	(.26)
Constitutional form[3]	.31	(.32)	1.46^{***}	(.41)	1.23^{**}	(.46)	$.89^{\dagger}$	(.49)	$.93^{\dagger}$	(.49)	1.06^{*}	(.50)	$.84^{\dagger}$	(.49)
British colony	−.19	(.24)	−.19	(.28)	−.25	(.29)	−.22	(.31)	−.33	(.32)	−.17	(.29)	−.14	(.31)
Dependence														
Trade openness	−.001	(.002)	−.003	(.003)	−.004	(.003)	−.002	(.003)	−.002	(.003)	.0002	(.003)	−.002	(.004)
Official development assistance		$-6.80e\text{-}10^{\dagger}$		(.0001)		$(.00017.68e\text{-}10^{\dagger})$		(.0001)		(.0001)		$(.00017.38e\text{-}10^{\dagger})$		(.0001)
and aid				$1.03e\text{-}09^{*}$				$8.45e\text{-}10^{\dagger}$		$1.08e\text{-}09^{*}$				
Years														
UN women's conferences (1980, 1985, 1995)			1.55^{***}	(.27)	1.54^{***}	(.28)	2.63^{***}	(.35)	2.65^{***}	(.36)	2.88^{***}	(.38)	2.82^{***}	(.39)
Diffusion														
World density			$.06^{***}$	(.005)	$.06^{***}$	(.007)	$.47^{***}$	(.07)	$.48^{***}$	(.07)	$.55^{***}$	(.07)	$.47^{***}$	(.07)
Regional density			$.05^{**}$	(.02)			.02	(.02)	.02	(.02)	.03	(.02)	.02	(.02)
Regional density * Sub-Saharan Africa					.05	(.04)								
Regional density * East Asia/Oceania					.12	(.07)								
Regional density * East Europe/ Central Asia					.19	(.41)								
Regional density * Latin America/ Caribbean					.02	(.03)								

Regional density* Middle East/ North Africa														
Regional density* South Asia					.34	(.32)								
Regional density* West					.02	(.04)								
OECD density							$-.60^{***}$	(.16)	$-.61^{***}$	(.16)	$-.73^{***}$	(.17)	$-.60^{***}$	(.16)
OECD density* OECD countries							$-.08^{*}$	(.03)	$-.08^{*}$	(.03)	$-.09^{*}$	(.04)	$-.08^{*}$	(.03)
Least density							-1.17^{***}	(.17)	-1.20^{***}	(.16)	-1.38^{***}	(.18)	-1.19^{***}	(.17)
Least density* least developed countries							$.07^{***}$	(.02)	$.07^{***}$	(.02)	$.06^{**}$	(.02)	$.07^{**}$	(.02)
Linkages – treaties and organizations														
Propensity to ratify: human rights treaties							$.18^{\dagger}$	(.08)	$.17^{\dagger}$	(.09)	.12	(.09)	$.18^{*}$	(.09)
Propensity to ratify: women's rights treaties							$-.32^{*}$	(.14)	$-.31^{*}$	(.14)	$-.37^{**}$	(.14)	$-.35^{*}$	(.14)
INGOs (logged)							.46	(.41)						
Women's INGOs (logged)									.72	(.50)				
Human rights INGOs (logged)											1.24^{**}	(.42)		
IGOs (logged)													$.46^{\dagger}$	(.27)
Constant	-6.61^{***}	(.69)	-8.58^{***}	(.93)	-8.59^{***}	(.91)	-10.70^{***}	(1.02)	-10.29^{***}	(1.01)	-10.70^{***}	(.99)	-11.43^{***}	(1.17)
Log likelihood	−118		123		126		168		168		172		169	
Number of ratifications	99		99		99		99		99		99		99	
Number of countries	142		142		142		142		142		142		142	
Yearly spells	1720		1720		1720		1720		1720		1720		1720	

Notes:

[1]Most of independent variables are one year lagged except for treaties, women's rights INGOs, and dummy variables

[2]A dummy variable: comparison categories include right, center, and other parties

[3]A dummy variable: main categories include individual chief executive or cabinet decision
or rule or tradition of informing legislative body of signed treaties or majority consent of one legislative body
Comparision categories include super-majority in one body or majority in two legislative bodies or national plebiscite

$^{\dagger}p \leq .10; ^{*}p \leq .05; ^{**}p \leq .01; ^{***}p \leq .001$ (two-tailed tests)

dummy variable for Protestant-dominant countries coded from the CIA (2002) and other measures related to democratization. The first was a combined index of civil liberties and political rights with scores ranging from a high of 14 down to 2, with higher scores indicating greater individual rights. The variable was derived from Freedom House (2001). The other was an eleven-point democracy index derived from the Polity IV data set (Marshall and Jaggers 2001). Neither measure of democratization produced significant results nor did the dummy variable for Protestant-dominant countries. We also tested a dummy variable for British legal heritage or common law.[20] Common law countries were no more likely to ratify CEDAW than other countries. Finally, we attempted a number of interactions, none of which yielded significant findings: INGOs with development; GDP with LDCs; and urbanization with LDCs.

We now turn to discussing our main findings in greater depth.

Discussion

Taken as a whole, what do these findings indicate about what influences countries to ratify CEDAW and CEDAW without reservations? The overriding implication of these findings is that there is support both for some of the mechanisms emphasized by the world society perspective and for some aspects of modernization and related explanations of policy choices. That is, there is evidence of interdependent decision making but also of some decision making reflecting nationally endogenous sources.

This discussion focuses on those indicators which behaved consistently across ratification of CEDAW and CEDAW without reservations analyses. In one sense these are the more robust findings because they hold even when the more stringent no reservations criteria is in place. From a world society perspective the key hypotheses emphasized the importance of the international women's conferences as socialization opportunities, of the world and regional strength of CEDAW as a regime, and of the degree of national linkages to the wider world which in principle increasingly privileges equality between women and men. Countries were indeed at greater risk of ratifying CEDAW in the years of international women's conferences. These conferences no doubt were shaped by a variety of democratizing forces favoring the equal treatment of women. But these

[20] Those countries such as England, the US, and most of the British Commonwealth countries using a legal system based on common law were coded 1 while all others were given a zero.

conferences were not only outcomes but also sites of norm entrepreneurship affirming the value of equality between women and men. These conferences were a commonality, some would argue, a common shock that all countries faced, and they significantly bumped up the number of ratifiers. Some of these ratifiers may have undergone "anticipatory socialization" in preparing for the conferences. Others may have been convinced in the give and take of the conference. And still others may have been swayed after the conference that there was some stigma associated with not ratifying. Interestingly enough, the idea that conferences would lead to "for show" ratifications, but not to perhaps more costly ratification without reservations, is not supported by the evidence.

Throughout these analyses, world and regional density measures were also a very important and positive influence. These measures capture the classical diffusion imagery of national decision making influenced by decisions made in other countries. The latter may be thought of as a "reference group," and perhaps surprisingly, this dynamic operates at the world level as well as at regionally specific ones. What other countries are ratifying is consequential; the national ratification of CEDAW is influenced by the international environment and the behavior of other nations is an important element of the international environment. The normative bandwagon idea is supported by the evidence.

But the international environment also consists of general and issue specific international governmental and non-governmental organizations. Enhanced membership in these organizations is increased exposure to the dominant scripts that emphasize the logic of appropriateness regarding national policy. Just as the founding father of Turkey once argued in favor of unveiling women so the West would take Turkey seriously, so too may a country today assume that world standards require a national profile opposed to discrimination against women. Countries vary with respect to how well they are linked to world standards via memberships in these organizations. Countries also vary with respect to how much experience they have ratifying treaties like CEDAW. Throughout these analyses experience with respect to ratifying human rights treaties increased the likelihood of ratifying CEDAW. And, ratification was also positively influenced by membership in international non-governmental organizations in general and in human rights and women's rights INGOS. These findings support the third main hypothesis informed by the world society perspective. Some (but not all) indicators of linkage behave as expected.

However, our analyses also offer some support for the premise that some national characteristics are important predictors of CEDAW and CEDAW without reservations ratification. Throughout these analyses

Islamic countries are less likely to ratify CEDAW while polities dominated by leftist parties are more likely to ratify the convention. Islamic countries are often imagined to be highly traditional in their cultures, especially with respect to family law and the political status of women. The sweeping character of a convention banning all forms of discrimination against women is apt to collide with the prevalent institutions and ideas in these countries. Quite the contrary, both the liberal and the socialist left are more likely to be receptive to equality between the sexes. So, while more general measures of economic development and political democracy do not fare well in analyses of CEDAW without reservations, these more specific indicators of the dominant religion and polity behave as expected. So, too does a measure of constitutional form that shows that ratification is more likely in regimes which facilitate treaty signing in general.

Conclusion

Though widely supported across the globe, the Convention on the Elimination of All Forms of Discrimination against Women has not been without its critics. Country-level evidence has demonstrated concrete changes in national laws to comply with articles found in the Convention. Yet none of the arguments presented in this chapter naively presuppose that ratification of CEDAW will have a one-to-one correspondence with implementation. In the neo-institutionalist spirit, world society theory emphasizes both the growing isomorphism among nation-states with respect to principles, policies, and even some organizational structures but also the extent of loose coupling between affirmed policy and actual practice.

However, it is also misleading to assume that the international field of human rights is inconsequential. Hathaway (2002) voices our overall assessment of the situation as follows:

> Treaties may lead to more aggressive enforcement by UN Charter-based bodies, which may take action against ratifiers and non-ratifiers alike. And human rights treaties and the process that surrounds their creation may have a widespread effect on the practices of *all* [author's italics] nations by changing the discourse about and expectations regarding those rights. The expressive functions of treaties, after all, has two aspects: it expresses the position of both the individual nation-state and of the community of nations with regard to the subject of the treaty. Although the individual expression need not be consistent with the intentions of the country to put the requirements of the treaty into place, the collective expression of a series of countries may have genuine effect . . . The treaty can thus influence individual countries' perceptions of what constitutes acceptable behavior (2002:2021).

Thus, a world of increased women's rights treaty ratifications may positively influence practice among both ratifiers and non-ratifiers. At the very least it is a world in which women's rights abuses and violations are likely to be perceived, exposed, and experienced as inequities. Through the twin emphases on women as human capital and women as human rights bearers all sorts of women's status issues are linked to national economic and political agendas. And, these in turn are legitimated by transnational conferences, which debunk and delegitimate all forms of discrimination against women.

What will it take for the remaining countries, including the United States, to finally ratify the Convention? While special sessions of the UN General Assembly and other meetings have reviewed and appraised implementation of the Beijing Platform for Action, plans to host a fifth international women's conference have yet to be made. It might just take another international women's conference to persuade the few remaining countries to ratify the Convention, thereby presenting themselves to the wider world as progress and justice seeking nation-states.

Appendix 8.1. *States parties to the Convention on the Elimination of All Forms of Discrimination against Women (CEDAW) and corresponding years of ratifications (98 signatories, 187 ratifiers, 59 countries having reservations; countries in bold are included in the analysis)*

Afghanistan	2003
Albania	1994
Algeria	1996*
Andorra	1997
Angola	1986
Antigua/Barbuda	1989
Argentina	1985*
Armenia	1993
Australia	1983*
Austria	1982*
Azerbaijan	1995
Bahamas	1993*
Bahrain	2002*
Bangladesh	1984*
Barbados	1980
Belarus	1981
Belgium	1985*
Belize	1990
Benin	1992
Bhutan	1981

Appendix 8.1. (*cont.*)

Bolivia	1990
Bosnia and Herz.	1993
Botswana	1996
Brunei Darussalam	2006*
Brazil	1984*
Bulgaria	1982
Burkina Faso	1987
Burundi	1992
Cambodia	1992
Cameroon	1994
Canada	1981
Cape Verde	1980
Central Afri. Rep.	1991
Chad	1995
Chile	1989*
China	1980*
Colombia	1982
Comoros	1994
Congo	1982
Congo, Dem. Rep.	1986
Costa Rica	1986
Côte d'Ivoire	1995
Croatia	1992
Cuba	1980*
Cyprus	1985*
Czech Republic	1993
Denmark	1983
Djibouti	1998
Dominica	1980
Dominican Rep.	1982
Ecuador	1981
Egypt	1981*
El Salvador	1981*
Equat. Guinea	1984
Eritrea	1995
Estonia	1991
Ethiopia	1981*
Fiji	1995*
Finland	1986
France	1983*
Gabon	1983
Gambia	1993
Georgia	1994
Germany	1985*
Ghana	1986
Greece	1983
Grenada	1990

Appendix 8.1. (*cont.*)

Guatemala	1982
Guinea	1982
Guinea-Bissau	1985
Guyana	1980
Haiti	1981
Honduras	1983
Hungary	1980
Iceland	1985
India	1993*
Indonesia	1984*
Iraq	1986*
Ireland	1985*
Israel	1991*
Italy	1985
Jamaica	1984*
Japan	1985
Jordan	1992*
Kazakhstan	1998
Kenya	1984
Kiribati	2004
Korea, PDR	2001
Korea, Rep.	1984*
Kuwait	1994*
Kyrgyzstan	1997
Laos	1981
Latvia	1992
Lebanon	1997*
Lesotho	1995*
Liberia	1984
Libya	1989*
Liechtenstein	1995*
Lithuania	1994
Luxembourg	1989*
Macedonia	1994
Madagascar	1989
Malawi	1987
Malaysia	1995*
Maldives	1993*
Mali	1985
Malta	1991*
Marshall Islands	2006
Mauritania	2001
Mauritius	1984*
Mexico	1981
Mauritania	2001
Mauritius	1984*
Mexico	1981

Appendix 8.1. (*cont.*)

Micronesia	2004*
Moldova	1994
Monaco	2005*
Mongolia	1981
Morocco	1993*
Mozambique	1997
Myanmar	1997*
Namibia	1992
Nepal	1991
Netherlands	1991*
New Zealand	1985*
Nicaragua	1981
Niger	1999
Nigeria	1985
Norway	1981
Oman	2006*
Pakistan	1996*
Panama	1981
Papua New Guinea	1995
Paraguay	1987
Peru	1982
Philippines	1981
Poland	1980*
Portugal	1980
Romania	1984*
Russian Federation	1981
Rwanda	1981
St. Kitts and Nevis	1985
St. Lucia	1982
St. Vincent	1981
Samoa	1992
San Marino	2003
São Tomé/Principe	2003
Saudi Arabia	2000*
Senegal	1985
Seychelles	1992
Sierra Leone	1988
Singapore	1995*
Slovakia	1993
Slovenia	1992
Solomon Islands	2002
South Africa	1995
Spain	1984*
Sri Lanka	1981
Suriname	1993
Swaziland	2004
Sweden	1980

Appendix 8.1. (*cont.*)

Switzerland	1997*
Syrian Arab Rep.	2003*
Tajikistan	1993
Tanzania	1985
Thailand	1985*
Timor-Leste	2003
Togo	1983
Trinidad/Tobago	1990*
Tunisia	1985*
Turkey	1985*
Turkmenistan	1997
Tuvalu	1999
Uganda	1985
Ukraine	1981
United Arab Emir.	2004*
United Kingdom	1986*
United States	1980[s]
Uruguay	1981
Uzbekistan	1995
Vanuatu	1995
Venezuela	1983*
Vietnam	1982*
Yemen	1984*
Yugoslavia	2001
Zambia	1985
Zimbabwe	1991

Notes: As of June 2006.
The following countries have neither signed nor ratified the treaty: Bermuda, **Iran**, Nauru, Qatar, Somalia, Sudan, Tonga.
*With reservations;
[s] Country signed but did not ratify the treaty.
Source: United Nations 2003a.

References

Allison, Paul David. 1984. *Event History Analysis: Regression for Longitudinal Event Data*. Beverly Hills, CA: Sage Publications.

Anderson, Benedict. 2006. *Imagined Communities: Reflections on the Origin and Spread of Nationalism,* new edition. London: Verso.

Barrett, David B., George Thomas Kurian, and Todd M. Johnson 2001. *World Christian Encyclopedia: A Comparative Survey of Churches and Religions in the Modern World,* 2nd ed. Oxford; New York: Oxford University Press.

Baum, Joel. A. and Christine Oliver. 1992. Institutional Embeddedness and the Dynamics of Organizational Populations. *American Sociological Review* 57: 540–59.

Berkovitch, Nitza. 1999. *From Motherhood to Citizenship: Women's Rights and International Organizations*. Baltimore: Johns Hopkins Press.

Boli, John and George M. Thomas, eds. 1999. *Constructing World Culture: International Nongovernmental Organizations Since 1875*. Stanford, CA: Stanford University Press.

Bollen, Kenneth A. 1986. Political Rights and Political Liberties in Nations: An Evaluation of Human Rights Measures, 1950 to 1984. *Human Rights Quarterly* 18: 567–91.

Carroll, Glenn R. and Michael T. Hannan. 2000. *The Demography of Corporations and Industries*. Princeton, NJ: Princeton University Press.

Carroll, Glenn R. and Anand Sevaminathan. 2000. Why the Microbrewery Movement? Organizational Dynamics of Resource Partitioning in the U.S. Brewing Industry. *American Journal of Sociology* 106 (3):715–62.

Central Intelligence Agency. 2002. *The World Factbook 2002*. Washington, DC: Central Intelligence Agency.

Cheibub, Jose and Jennifer Gandhi 2004. Classifying Political Regimes: A Six-Fold Classification of Democracies and Dictatorships. Presented at the Annual Meeting of the American Political Science Association.

Chen, Martha Alter. 1996. Engendering World Conferences: The International Women's Movement and the U.N. In *N.G.O.s, the U.N. and Global Governance*, edited by Thomas G. Weiss and Leon Gordenker, 139–53. Boulder, CO: Lynne Rienner Publishers.

Clark, Ann Marie, Elisabeth J. Friedman, and Kathryn Hochstetler. 1998. The Sovereign Limits of Global Civil Society: A Comparison of N.G.O. Participation in U.N. World Conferences on the Environment, Human Rights, and Women. *World Politics* 51: 1–35.

Cole, Wade M. 2005. Sovereignty Relinquished? Explaining Commitment to the International Human Rights Covenants, 1966–1999. *American Sociological Review* 70: 472–95.

Cook, Karen S. and Karen A. Hegtvedt. 1983. Distributive Justice, Equity, and Equality. *Annual Review of Sociology* 9: 217–41.

Cox, D. R. and David Oakes. 1984. *Analysis of Survival Data*. London: Chapman and Hall.

Dezalay, Yves and Bryant G. Garth. 2002. *The Internationalization of Palace Wars: Lawyers, Economists and the Contest to Transform Latin American States*. Chicago: University of Chicago Press.

DiMaggio, Paul J. and Walter W. Powell. 1983. The Iron Cage Revisited: Institutional Isomorphism and Collective Rationality in Organizational Fields. *American Sociological Review* 48: 147–60.

Division for the Advancement of Women. 2003. Convention on the Elimination of All Forms of Discrimination against Women. United Nations.

Donnelly, Jack. 1986. International Human Rights: A Regime Analysis. *International Organization* 40: 599–642.

European Technology Assessment Network. 2000. *Science Policies in the European Union: Promoting Excellence through Mainstreaming Gender Equality*. Brussels, Belgium: European Commission.

Farer, Tom J. 1992. The United Nations and Human Rights: More Than a Whimper, Less Than a Roar. In *Human Rights in the World Community: Issues and Action*, 2nd ed., edited by Richard Pierre Claude and Burns H. Weston, 227–43. Philadelphia: University of Pennsylvania Press.

Finnemore, Martha. 1996. Norms, Culture, and World Politics: Insights from Sociology's Institutionalism. *International Organization* 50: 325–47.

Finnemore, Martha and Kathryn Sikkink. 1998. International Norm Dynamics and Political Change. *International Organization* 52: 887–917.

Frank, David John, Ann Hironaka, and Evan Schofer. 2000. The Nation-State and the Natural Environment over the Twentieth Century. *American Sociological Review* 65: 96–116.

Fraser, Arvonne S. 1995. The Convention on the Elimination of All Forms of Discrimination Against Women (The Women's Convention). In *Women, Politics, and the United Nations*, edited by Anne Winslow, 77–94. Westport, CT: Greenwood Press.

Fraser, Elvis E. 1994. Reconciling Conceptual and Measurement Problems in the Comparative Study of Human Rights. *International Journal of Comparative Sociology* 35: 1–18.

Freedom House. 2001. Annual Survey of Freedom Country Scores 1972–73 to 2000–01. Available from http://www.freedomhouse.org/ratings/ [accessed July 15, 2001].

Hafner-Burton, Emilie Marie. 2005. Trading Human Rights: How Preferential Trade Agreements Influence Government Repression. *International Organization* 59: 593–629.

Hafner-Burton, Emilie Marie, and Kiyoteru Tsutsui. 2005. Human Rights in a Globalizing World: The Paradox of Empty Promises. *American Journal of Sociology* 110: 1373–411.

Hanneman, Robert A. and Robin L. Steinback. 1990. Military Involvement and Political Instability: An Event History Analysis 1940–1980. *Journal of Political and Military Sociology* 18: 1–23.

Hathaway, Oona A. 2002. Do Human Rights Treaties Make a Difference? *The Yale Law Journal* 111: 1935–2042.

Human Rights Watch. 2006. CEDAW: The Women's Treaty.

Huntington, Samuel P. 1968. *Political Order in Changing Societies*. New Haven, CT: Yale University Press.

Ikenberry, G. John. 1990. The International Spread of Privatization Policies: Inducements, Learning, and Policy Bandwagoning. In *The Political Economy of Public Sector Reform and Privatization*, edited by Ezra N. Suleiman and John Waterbury, 88–109. Boulder, CO: Westview Press.

Keck, Margaret E. and Kathryn Sikkink. 1998. *Activists beyond Borders: Advocacy Networks in International Politics*. Ithaca, NY: Cornell University Press.

Landman, Todd. 2005. *Protecting Human Rights: A Comparative Study*. Washington, DC: Georgetown University Press.

Lauren, Paul Gordon. 1998. *The Evolution of International Human Rights: Visions Seen*. Philadelphia: University of Pennsylvania Press.

Lechner, Frank J. and John Boli. 2005. *World Culture: Origins and Consequences*. Malden, MA: Blackwell Publishing.

Liu, Dongxiao and Elizabeth Heger Boyle. 2001. Making the Case: The Women's Convention and Equal Employment Opportunity in Japan. *International Journal of Comparative Sociology* 42: 389–404.

Marshall, Monty G. and Keith Jaggers. 2001. Polity IV Project: Political Regime Characteristics and Transitions, 1800–1999. Available at: www.cidcm.umd.edu/inscr/polity/ [accessed February 1, 2002].

McAdam, Doug and Dieter Rucht. 1993. The Cross-National Diffusion of Movement Ideas. *The Annals of the American Academy of Political and Social Science* 528: 56–74.

Meyer, John W., John Boli, George M. Thomas, and Francisco O. Ramirez. 1997. World Society and the Nation-State. *American Journal of Sociology* 103: 144–81.

Perrett, Bryan and Ian Hogg. 1989. *Encyclopedia of the Second World*. Harlow, UK: Longman.

Plattner, Margaret. 1995–96. The Status of Women under International Human Rights Law and the 1995 U.N. World Conference on Women, Beijing, China. *Kentucky Law Journal* 84: 1249–75.

Przeworski, Adam, Michael Alvarez, José Antonio Cheibub, and Fernando Limongi. 2000. *Democracy and Development: Political Regimes and Economic Well-being in the World, 1950–1990*. New York: Cambridge University Press.

Ramirez, Francisco O., John W. Meyer, Christine Min Wotipka, and Gili S. Drori. 2002. Expansion and Impact of the World Human Rights Regime: Longitudinal and Cross-national Analyses over the Twentieth Century. Funded National Science Foundation grant.

Ramirez, Francisco O., Yasemin Soysal, and Suzanne Shanahan. 1997. The Changing Logic of Political Citizenship: Cross-National Acquisition of Women's Suffrage Rights, 1890 to 1990. *American Sociological Review* 62: 735–45.

Smith, Jackie. 1995. Transnational Political Processes and the Human Rights Movement. *Research in Social Movements, Conflict and Change* 18: 185–219.

Soysal, Yasemin Nuhoglu. 1994. *Limits of Citizenship: Migrants and Postnational Membership in Europe*. Chicago: University of Chicago Press.

Stamatopoulou, Elissavet. 1995. Women's Rights and the United Nations. In *Women's Rights, Human Rights: International Feminist Perspectives*, edited by Julie Peters and Andrea Wolper, 36–50. New York: Routledge.

Stolte, John F. 1987. The Formation of Justice Norms. *American Sociological Review* 52: 774–84.

Strang, David. 1994a. British and French Political Institutions and the Patterning of Decolonization. In *The Comparative Political Economy of the Welfare State: New Methodologies and Approaches*, edited by T. Janoski and A. Hicks, 278–98. Cambridge: Cambridge University Press.

Strang, David. 1994b. Introduction to Event History Methods. In *The Comparative Political Economy of the Welfare State*, edited by Thomas Janoski and Alexander M. Hicks, 245–53. Cambridge: Cambridge University Press.

Thomas, George M., John W. Meyer, Francisco O. Ramirez and John Boli. 1987. *Institutional Structure: Constituting State, Society, and the Individual*. Beverly Hills, CA: Sage.

Tsutsui, Kiyoteru and Christine Min Wotipka. 2004. Global Civil Society and the International Human Rights Movement: Citizen Participation in International Human Rights Nongovernmental Organizations. *Social Forces* 83: 587–620.

Tuma, Nancy Brandon and Michael T. Hannan. 1984. *Social Dynamics: Models and Methods*. Orlando: Academic Press.

Union of International Associations. various years. *Yearbook of International Organizations*. Munich, Germany: K. G. Saur.

United Nations. 1995. *The United Nations and Human Rights, 1945–1995*. New York: United Nations.

United Nations. 2000. *Women's Indicators and Statistics Database Version 4, CD-ROM*. New York: United Nations.

United Nations. 2003a. *Chapter IV. Human Rights* (Multilateral treaties deposited with the Secretary-General). New York: United Nations.

United Nations. 2003b. *Reservations. Division for the Advancement of Women*. New York: United Nations.

United Nations. 2003c. *States Parties. Division for the Advancement of Women*. New York: United Nations.

Vreeland, James Raymond. Forthcoming. CAT Selection: Why Governments Enter into the UN Convention against Torture. *International Organization*.

Weiss, Anita M. 2003. Interpreting Islam and Women's Rights: Implementing CEDAW in Pakistan. *International Sociology* 18: 581–601.

World Bank. 2001. *World Development Indicators*. Washington, DC: World Bank.

Wotipka, Christine Min and Kiyoteru Tsutsui. Forthcoming. Global Human Rights and State Sovereignty: Nation-States' Ratifications of International Human Rights Treaties, 1965–1999. Paper presented at the Annual Meeting of the American Sociological Association, August 19, Anaheim, CA.

9 Conclusion

Geoffrey Garrett, Frank Dobbin, and Beth A. Simmons

The concurrent rise of liberal politics and free market economics around the world was a defining feature of the latter part of the twentieth century. The social sciences were not well positioned to explain this global phenomenon. Models of policymaking and political change had privileged domestic factors for at least half a century. From Lipset's view of democracy as the product of economic modernization within countries to Shonfield's division of the world into divergent national capitalisms, the underlying meta-model of political and policy change was one of unconnected domestic processes.[1]

As democracy and markets swept to the four corners of the globe, the limitations of purely domestic models became increasingly apparent. Countries democratized that Lipset would have considered too poor to do so. Chile and the United Kingdom, countries that Shonfield would surely never have associated as kindred capitalist spirits, led the world in privatization and deregulation. Phenomena such as these led pundits to propose common exogenous forces as the driver of global political and economic change. Globalization, fueled by technological innovations lowering costs to international exchange of goods, services, capital, and information, was seen as forcing governments to embrace the market and as undermining economically inefficient authoritarian regimes – leading to "the end of history," in Fukuyama's famous formulation.[2]

But the grandiose claims about the ubiquity of liberalism soon came to be challenged by events, notably anti-globalization protests and anti-modernity terrorist attacks. At the same time, social scientists have also moved toward a middle ground in terms of the balance between forces of change that are internal and external to countries. The "common stimulus, mediated response" model has been used to reconcile the broad trend toward liberal markets with substantial national variations in the speed and the end points of change. Big global forces, such as the faster,

[1] Lipset 1959; Shonfield 1965. [2] Fukuyama 1989.

freer, and cheaper movement of capital and goods, and information and ideas, are seen to create pressures for liberalization. But these pressures are channeled, modified, and sometimes blocked by conditions within countries such as government partisanship, public opinion, and socio-economic structures.[3]

The point of departure of this volume is our conviction that even the best expositions of the common stimulus, mediated response model still fail to capture important causal processes in the recent trend toward democracy and markets, as well as deviations from this trend. Broad common stimuli like globalization certainly do matter; so too do the domestic conditions that mediate their impact in different countries. But irrespective of how sophisticated in conception or well executed in practice, this model is inherently incapable of coming to grips with the interdependent decision making among countries that we consider to have been a central element in the spread of liberalization in recent decades.

The challenge the authors in this volume have faced has been to bring rigor both theoretically and empirically to the notion that markets and democracy have "diffused" among countries as a product of interdependent decision making, as well as to delineate the precise causal pathways through which this has happened.

With respect to theory, we have outlined four basic mechanisms of interdependent decision making: coercion, competition, learning, and emulation. These have then been tested empirically against different facets of liberalization – democratization, increasing the rights of women, cutting taxation, public sector downsizing, privatization, bilateral investment protections, and capital account liberalization – using cutting-edge statistical techniques analyzing data for large numbers of countries over several decades. Each chapter has been disciplined by the same protocols of inquiry by first taking into account all the non-diffusion causal processes that might plausibly have shaped the policy under analysis; and then by comparing the explanatory power of the different diffusion mechanisms political scientists, sociologists, and economists have proposed.

In this conclusion, we begin by assessing what we have learned from the empirical chapters about the likely drivers of the diffusion of liberal policies. There is ample evidence that each of the mechanisms has played some part in the trend to liberalism (and its limits). Rather than privileging any one of the contending meta-approaches to the world underpinning

[3] Keohane and Milner 1996.

our mechanisms – realism for coercion, materialism for competition, rationalism for learning, or constructivism for emulation – most of the studies in this volume underscore the great utility of incorporating insights from all these diverse analytic frameworks into models of interdependent policymaking.

We then move on to a broader discussion that places the recent wave of liberalism in historical context (both backward looking and forward looking). We also make some judgments about the likely power of diffusion processes outside the time period and policy areas on which this book has focused.

We do not have a naively teleological view of liberalism. The trends we have witnessed toward democracy and markets in recent decades have slowed down and there have been significant backlashes against them. We cannot rule out the possibility that the world may significantly reverse course against liberalism. However, as the world gets "smaller" with the shrinking of time and distance in all aspects of human endeavor, we believe that diffusion processes will likely become even more important than they have been in the recent past with respect to the spread of markets and democracy – and that the utility for social scientists of analyzing countries as interdependent rather than independent actors will only increase.

Four diffusion mechanisms

The chapters in this volume subject the four approaches to diffusion to close empirical scrutiny, and with explicit controls for the common stimulus, mediated response null hypothesis. We are thus confident in the results of these studies. They generate two principal findings. On the one hand, neither coercion nor learning has been particularly important to the spread of political and economic liberalism. Notwithstanding the appeal of traditional realist perspectives as well as Marxian notions of dependency, the studies in this volume do not adduce much support for the coercion hypothesis. The informational and inferential requirements are just too high for rational learning to play out in practice the way it is conceived in economics textbooks.

On the other hand, our chapters generate strong support for both competition and emulation. Countries that compete with each other for investment from footloose global capital must take seriously the policies of their competitor nations in those cases where investors can draw strong and direct connections between government policies and their rates of return – taxation, investor protections, and capital account policy. At the same time, the cause and effect of policies is not always so clear, even in cases such as public sector downsizing and privatization where economists have united behind the "more markets" position. In these cases, however, epistemic communities such as those among the fraternity of professional economists can have a marked impact on what governments do, by influencing what they consider the right thing to do in a world clouded by uncertainty. Thus, the logic of appropriateness highlighted by sociologists and constructivists with respect to "soft" issues such as human rights treaties are just as apparent in some issues of "hard" economics as well.

Coercion

Powerful countries have sometimes imposed political and economic liberalism on their vanquished foes. The United States' rebuilding of Germany and Japan largely in its own image after the Second World War is widely considered the paradigmatic – and essentially benign – example of such coercion. In the contemporary era, the US has often explicitly referred to these examples in its efforts to build democracy and markets in Afghanistan and Iraq.

Since Lenin's *Imperialism: The Highest Stage of Capitalism*, Marxian scholars have argued that interstate coercion is likely to take subtle forms in an interconnected world where economic power is at least as important as military might. According to this view, rich countries exert their will over poor countries through the use of economic carrots and sticks. Much attention has been focused on the International Monetary Fund (IMF) in recent years, in particular the attaching of specific conditions about economic policy (the "Washington Consensus" around liberalization, stabilization, privatization, and deregulation) to bailout packages for developing countries facing financial crises.

One can also argue, however, that the European Union practices a very soft form of coercion – and unlike IMF conditionality, one that tends to be lauded even in countries subject to it. Countries that wish to join the EU must first convince the existing members that they have stably democratic political systems and also must accept the EU's *acquis communitaire* of economic regulations as well as the right of the European Court of Justice to rule in economic disputes among member states.

Turning to the chapters in this volume, it should not be surprising that neither Gleditsch and Ward nor Wotipka and Ramirez adduced evidence of north–south coercion through IMF conditionality in the diffusion of democracy and human rights respectively. As they point out, though the IMF is probably supportive of liberal politics in a normative sense, it has shied away from attaching conditions regarding political reforms to its loan packages.

One would expect things to be different in the realm of economic policy. While IMF effects were moot in the Swank and Lee and Strang chapters that focused solely on Organization for Economic Cooperation and Development (OECD) countries, Elkins, Guzman, and Simmons and Kogut and Macpherson found evidence that countries subject to IMF loan programs were more likely to sign bilateral investment treaties and to privatize state-owned enterprises respectively. Given the emphasis the IMF attaches to the building of private capital markets as an essential element of creating robust market economies in developing countries, these effects should have been expected.

In both cases, however, the authors suggest that IMF linkages might not actually be evidence of coercion in the strict sense. Kogut and Macpherson contend that there is at least some volition involved in countries being under IMF programs, and that the resulting good housekeeping seal of approval has a positive impact on the value of privatized assets – creating incentives for countries to privatize. Elkins, Guzman, and Simmons suggest that the correlation between IMF obligations and bilateral investment treaties (BITs) may be more coincidental than causal. Countries that are willing to undertake IMF obligations are also more likely to be interested in investment treaties with developed economies, and there may be efficiencies involved in undertaking both simultaneously.

Quinn and Toyoda did not find any link between IMF lending and capital account liberalization. But the authors are quick to point out that the IMF has never formally embraced capital account liberalization as a necessary policy reform for developing countries, and indeed has backed off even further since the Asian financial crisis of 1997–1998. Instead, the IMF tends to view the development of strong private capital markets as a necessary precondition for capital account liberalization. But Quinn and Toyoda demonstrate a strong connection between accession to the European Union and the opening of capital accounts – since the EU in the late 1980s made capital account openness mandatory among existing and aspiring members.

Moving from the kinds of coercion associated with international organizations, some might have expected also to see that the US "imposed" its policy preferences for, or at least became a crucial focal point for coordination on, lower taxes and public sector downsizing among other OECD countries. But both Swank and Lee and Strang argue that this was not the case, focusing instead on competition and emulation as forces for policy diffusion in the economic policies of OECD countries.

Gleditsch and Ward do, however, make a compelling argument about the role of regional power resources in the development of democracy. They observe significant regional clustering of transitions to democracy, not only in the postwar period but since the third quarter of the nineteenth century. This effect shows up in the quantitative analyses even when domestic factors are controlled. Gleditsch and Ward's interpretation of this clustering is that backers of democracy need support from neighboring countries to effect change. Regional powers can thus retard democratization (as with the USSR in East Germany in the years before 1989) or the move to democracy (Brazil's role in Paraguay in the late 1980s). Their case studies provide suggestive evidence of the importance of regional power resources.

In sum, the evidence for the role of coercion in the diffusion of liberalism around the world in recent decades is at best mixed. Gleditsch and Ward make the novel argument that regional power resources play an important role in democratization. Elkins, Guzman, and Simmons and Kogut and Macpherson were able to isolate effects of IMF lending, but they were reticent to label these effects "conditionality" in the conventional sense. In marked contrast with the foreign policy of the G. W. Bush administration to try to generate markets and democracy in the Middle East via "the barrel of a gun," the studies in this volume suggest that the ability of the rich and powerful to impose their policies on the poor and the weak was not the primary engine of the diffusion of liberal policies in the past half century.

Competition

The hypothesis of diffusion by competition rests on the notion that countries liberalize to compete with each other for international market share and global investment. In the areas of taxation (Swank), investment protection treaties (Elkins, Guzman, and Simmons), and capital account openness (Quinn and Toyoda), our authors found clear evidence of this diffusion by economic competition mechanism.

Swank shows that after the US tax reform in 1986, other OECD countries moved in the direction of the new American model of "market-conforming" corporate taxation – in which the marginal rate of taxation on corporations was reduced while the tax base was broadened and loopholes were eliminated. He argues that countries followed the US lead for a very pragmatic reason: to attract investors with freedom to choose where and when to invest and interested in the higher rates of return that lower marginal corporate tax rates delivered. Swank's argument is similar to the argument about "go-it-alone" power originally developed by Gruber.[4] The OECD countries may not have wanted to change their

[4] Gruber 2001.

corporate tax systems, and they did not have to – so long as the US did not act. But once the US enacted their reforms, other countries had little choice but to follow suit.

Elkins, Guzman, and Simmons argue that when it comes to investment liberalization, countries signing bilateral investment treaties do not "follow the leader" but rather follow their economic competitors. They demonstrate that countries are more likely to sign BITs if others with similar trade partners have done so, because countries with similar trade partners tend to compete both in the same export markets and for foreign investment in similar sectors. But the underlying logic of competition is the same. BITs diffuse because of global competition among countries for mobile capital. Quinn and Toyoda find a similar game of follow-your-peers with respect to capital account liberalization, particularly among OECD countries. OECD countries do follow the lead taken by their major capital competitor, even if developing countries do not.

Corporate taxes, investment protection treaties, and capital account openness all have a direct impact on the bottom line of global firms and investors. Capitalists know what they like, and they can directly infer links between government policy and their rates of return. This is precisely the environment in which we would expect – and the studies in this volume find – diffusion by competition to be most powerful.

It might be tempting to think that this competitive dynamic would extend to all facets of economic policy in the contemporary global economy. But this is not the case, because the connection between policy and outcomes is not always direct or clear. This is the argument Lee and Strang and Kogut and Macpherson make in their studies of public sector downsizing and privatization. Notwithstanding the messianic "more market" rhetoric of some pundits, there is actually not much evidence that government downsizing and privatization increase rates of return in national economies. Hence it is not at all clear that governments need to engage in a competitive race to the bottom in these policy areas.

Ex ante, we had little reason to expect competition to be a powerful diffusion mechanism with respect to liberal political reforms, and this is borne out in the two studies of this phenomenon. The studies on democracy (Gleditsch and Ward) and on women's rights (Wotipka and Ramirez) find no evidence that political liberalization has spread by means of competition. One might have expected countries to compete for trade and foreign capital investment via political liberalization, if traders and investors had a strong preference for democracies over dictatorships. But for many years democracy and the promotion of human rights in developing nations was thought to put foreign capital at risk of various forms of expropriation and instability more generally. As a result, many believe that authoritarianism (and certainly its more benevolent strands) may be better for the economy at early stages of development.

Taken together these studies suggest that competition does stimulate countries to adopt policies that promise directly to influence rates of return and hence the investment and location decisions of mobile capital, notably policies governing capital taxes, investment, and capital accounts. Policies that might influence investment only indirectly and with uncertain effects – downsizing and privatization – were not noticeably shaped by competition. Democratization has been associated with the rise of free market competition, but investors have not routinely favored it.

As a result, political liberalization cannot readily be explained by the same competitive mechanisms that underlie policies to attract investment capital and increase product market share. This finding may help explain why economic liberalization does not lead in a lock-step fashion to political liberalization. A crucial bottom-line incentive – the policy moves of competitors – does not have the same power to pry open the doors of political liberalization as is the case with market-friendly innovations.

Learning

The notion of diffusion by learning has not been tested rigorously in previous studies. Proponents have often been content to demonstrate that some countries follow the lead of others, but there are plausible reasons for this (for example competition and emulation) that do not entail any learning from experiences, either direct or vicarious. In contrast, the chapters in this volume take a more stringent approach to testing for learning by examining whether the spread of a liberal policy to a new country was based on revealed evidence that it had the desired effects in other comparable nations.

With respect to domestic economic policy liberalization, both Swank and Kogut and Macpherson rule out learning effects in their policy domains. In the case of corporate tax reform, Swank shows that countries adopted the new American approach even though there was evidence that it *did not* work and *would not* work for them – because of overwhelming competitive pressures to curry favor with the markets. Kogut and Macpherson found that privatization was not undertaken as a tool for deficit reduction, and that there is little evidence that selling off state-owned assets has proved a successful strategy for stabilizing the state budget.

Lee and Strang do offer some evidence of learning with respect to public sector downsizing, but they do so in the context of a modified theoretical approach emphasizing the role of global communities of experts. They demonstrate that positive evidence that downsizing improved economic performance contributed to future downsizings in other countries. Interestingly, however, Lee and Strang also show that negative evidence did not discourage future downsizings. This implies that evidence-based learning is shaped by current economic thought. After the idea of government workforce reduction caught on as a liberal policy prescription, countries internalized positive but not negative evidence of its efficacy. This adds an interesting twist, suggesting that learning is conditioned on the presence of a theory that links cause to effect.

The two studies of foreign economic policies come to similar conclusions about the effects of learning on liberalization. Quinn and Toyoda show that "successful" capital account opening – defined as the growth record for countries within the region that have already liberalized – increased the probability that other countries in the region themselves subsequently liberalized. Elkins, Guzman, and Simmons similarly find evidence that governments emulate policies that "work." Using the beta coefficient for the effect of the number of BITs on capital inflows (controlling for growth), they found governments were more likely to sign BITs when evidence of their payoffs in terms of investment flows was strongest. It is likely in this case that the global policymaking environment, while noisy, allowed policymakers to draw at least tentative conclusions from existing natural experiments. One difference between these two studies, it should be noted, is that Quinn and Toyoda assumed lessons would be drawn from regional experiments, while Elkins, Guzman, and Simmons assumed lessons can be drawn from global experience.

With respect to political liberalization, Gleditsch and Ward demonstrate that countries are more likely to move toward democracy when their near neighbors have made the policy work. In the case of Paraguay, for instance, military leaders learned from their neighbors that the transition from military dictatorship to democracy need not result in a bloodbath and need not depose the existing party, and that free elections brought greater, not lesser, political stability. But in contrast, Wotipka and Ramirez did not find any evidence of learning in the signing of a key women's rights treaty, largely because they did not explicitly test for it. In the case of women's rights, learning models would be difficult to test as there are no clear predictions about measurable benefits, economic or otherwise. Where the policy in question is not a "well established technology" linked with clearly observable results, learning theory may not be directly applicable.

Our interpretation of the limited support presented in this volume for the strictly rational version of the diffusion by learning hypothesis is that its informational and inferential requirements are very high, much higher than theoretical economists tend to assume – and often too high to sway the behavior of governments in important policy areas. Consider the case of privatization. For many years economists considered Thatcher's initial privatizations a successful natural experiment from which other countries learned, updated their priors about the efficacy of nationalized versus privatized industries, and sold off their state-owned enterprises. In fact, it has proved very hard to demonstrate that privatization "works," either in terms of making an individual firm more profitable, or a national economy more productive. Rational learning is highly compatible with game-theoretic approaches to social change, but this volume suggests that its utility in explaining national policy change may be limited.

Emulation

Diffusion by emulation suggests that policies and practices spread through a process of socially informed mimicry. The "world polity" approach suggests that new policy approaches are constructed as "appropriate" at the global level based on the histories and theories of leading nations. Constructivists argue that epistemic communities of experts may act as missionaries facilitating the transfer of policy ideas among countries. Most previous research on emulation has focused on areas like human rights and the building of state bureaucracies rather than on economic reforms or broader political reforms like democratization.

In keeping with this prior work, Wotipka and Ramirez find strong evidence of emulation in the spread of women's rights treaties around the world. Though domestic factors have clearly had an impact on this indicator of political liberalization, the popularity of women's rights treaties abroad as well as national membership in international organizations had marked effects on the likelihood that a country would ratify the world's most comprehensive women's rights treaty. They interpret these effects in a world polity framework in which countries are motivated by the desire to act "appropriately." Skeptics of course may argue that this kind of diffusion is not very consequential, because the tangible costs of violating human rights are low, and hence the threshold for signing them is not high.

What is perhaps most surprising in this volume, however, is the strength of emulation-style mechanisms in several policy areas, including economic policies, that traditionally are analyzed in strictly rationalist and materialist terms. Three studies in the economic policy arena provide powerful evidence of the impact of diffusion by emulation in the global spread of market-oriented policies.

Kogut and Macpherson highlight the role of epistemic communities of experts dispersed around the world but bound together by a common world view regarding policy in their area of expertise. They argue that it was the global dispersion of American-trained economists – initially from the University of Chicago but then from all leading economics departments as the Chicago School became more dominant in the profession – that resulted in the spread of privatization to all corners of the globe. The more American-trained economics Ph.Ds. in a country, the more likely it was that their countries enacted privatization programs. Kogut and Macpherson are careful to show that this effect was exogenous, that is, that it was not simply the case that countries that wanted to privatize hired pro-privatization American economists. They also make a strong case that local conditions and conflicts also shaped the embrace of privatization – mediating the process of social construction that occurs with each and every adoption.

Lee and Strang also focused on the global epistemic community of economists in their study of public sector downsizing. They demonstrate, however, that the power of the epistemic community supporting downsizing worked principally through how governments interpreted developments in other countries. Governments were more likely to reduce their own public sector employment not only when countries they viewed as peers downsized, but also when it seemed that such policies worked in terms of improving macroeconomic performance. In marked contrast, however, governments tended to ignore evidence that increasing public sectors were good for the economy. The epistemic community in favor of downsizing served to frame how governments viewed developments in other countries – it was not a process of rational and objective learning.

Quinn and Toyoda also argue for the impact of epistemic communities with respect to the spread of capital account liberalization. But the community they identify is very different from the pro-market elite of the economics profession in the privatization and downsizing cases. They argue that global anti-capitalist sentiments expressed by political elites, and reflected in global support for Communist parties, has had a strong negative effect on capital account openness. As the epistemic community of economists promoted capital account openness, the community of anti-capitalist political elites countered that trend. The stronger this anti-capitalist sentiment in other countries, the less likely a given nation was to open its capital account.

Perhaps the most important feature of this argument is that, contra the broad sweep of "world polity" arguments about the propagation of Western/liberal policies around the world, Quinn and Toyoda demonstrate the impact of contrary anti-capitalist and anti-Western sentiments on developing countries in particular. They thereby counter the prevailing imagery of a world in which new ideas flow seamlessly from core to periphery.

All in all, international organizations and policy elites appear to have strong effects on policy liberalization, both economic and political. It may be that policy elites prepare the ground for learning in the economic arena, causing national leaders to recognize evidence consistent with theory and to neglect evidence that is inconsistent. It also seems that the same processes of the articulation of appropriate policies by central figures and promotion by international organizations that promote political liberalization also promote economic liberalization. In the case of political reform, the experts are human rights advocates and lawyers and the international organizations that orbit around the United Nations. In the case of market reform the experts are economists who gravitate to the international financial institutions.

The future of liberalism

If we had been writing this book a decade ago, we would probably have concluded that the processes driving more markets and more democracy around the world would continue into the indefinite future. Today there is good reason to be more circumspect. We strongly believe, however, that this says more about political and economic liberalism as an outcome than it does about diffusion as a process. We are agnostic on the future of liberalization. But we are convinced that the processes of international diffusion we have chronicled in this volume will be of increasing importance to economic, political, and social change around the world – regardless of whether these lead to the further propagation of liberalism, a backlash against it, or unrelated waves of global change.

When the history is written, the mid-1990s might come to appear the high point of the spread of economic and political liberalism around the world. The post-Communist countries of Eastern and Central Europe were in the midst of pro-market economic revolutions with strong public support in their fledgling democracies. China was joined by India on the path to liberal economic reform, making markets an increasing reality for two-fifths of the world's population. Latin American leaders finally decided to take their Washington Consensus medicine, sometimes with considerable enthusiasm. The World Trade Organization (WTO) was created to entrench and preside over a global economy founded on strongly liberal principles.

Indeed, the Washington Consensus was all the rage not only in developing countries but in the developed world as well. Europe moved toward the creation of the euro on the backs of fiscal discipline and tight monetary policy, coupled with privatization and deregulation within member states. Australia and New Zealand took the baton from Thatcher in the marketizing vanguard, under nominally leftist governments. The Clinton administration's core economic goals were to balance the budget and "to end welfare as we know it." The focus on the market economy was so powerful that it replaced international security at the top of the foreign policy agenda, as President Clinton's administration bailed out Mexico and Russia to defend their efforts simultaneously to create democracy and markets.

But cracks soon appeared to slow down the marketization and democratization juggernauts. Large-scale and rolling protests against the global economy occurred with increasing intensity wherever and whenever leaders gathered at major G8, IMF, World Bank, and WTO meetings from Paris to Seattle to Genoa. Citizens in former Communist countries and in Latin America grew disenchanted by the mismatch between what they had been promised democracy and markets would bring and what seemed to be a far less appealing reality of gaping chasms between globalization's winners and losers. Europe's leading continental economies remained happy to talk the talk of more markets, but their governments were unwilling to walk the walk amid widespread popular resistance and resentment.

Just six weeks after the bloody and violent Genoa protests against the G8, Islamic jihadis crashed two planes into the twin towers of the World Trade Center in New York, expanding the backlash against markets and democracy into a backlash against modernity writ large. The six years since September 11 have witnessed a pitched battle between the West and the rest, not only in the war on terrorism but also in economics and politics. Populist politicians promising to protect their citizens against the vagaries of the market have flourished in Eastern and Central Europe and in Latin America. Citizen support for democracy in these countries has waned dramatically. Deep regional divides between those who have benefited from globalization and those who have not pervade countries as different as China, India, Mexico, and the United States. The ironically named Doha "development round" of WTO talks stalled because of insuperable divisions over agriculture. Western governments steadfastly committed to protecting their tiny farming sectors are charged with the height of hypocrisy by developing countries with massive populations supported by subsistence agriculture.

Sober analysis with the benefit of hindsight will show that this slowdown in the march of liberalism was probably inevitable. The spread of markets and democracy exhibited a strong S-curve dynamic. At some point in the late 1990s or early 2000s, the process was bound to slow down simply because most countries had liberalized most facets of their economies and polities. In addition to this numerical logic, the spread of markets exacerbated the divide between haves and have-nots both within and among countries, causing citizens to question the merits of the democratic institutions associated with turning this gap into a gulf.

Moreover, it was likely that increasing interconnections among countries would generate the need for increasing public sector interventions in economic affairs. Issues as diverse as environmental degradation and the piracy of intellectual property are global in scope and cannot simply be addressed by more markets without the careful construction of international agreements among governments to regulate them.

But while all these considerations suggest that a slowdown in marketization and democratization was to be expected, they do not necessarily suggest that a complete reversal of direction is imminent. The question is a live one of whether the slowdown in the penetration of economic and political liberalism into all facets of life in all countries will ultimately be followed by an illiberal epoch.

Economic historians are quick to point out that the last great era of international economic openness collapsed into a spiral of depression, protectionism, and fascism in the first half of the twentieth century, with the implication that it could easily happen again because the same troubling preconditions are evident today. The counter view is that the contemporary forces of globalization – above all technologies that shrink time and space – are a genie that cannot be put back in the bottle. On this view, the world of the market is here to stay, and for some this is a good thing for democracy as well. The first half of the last century can even be seen through rose-colored glasses as an unfortunate blip – albeit a long and devastating one – on Fukuyama's path to the end of history.

We choose to remain agnostic on the question of whether the course of the twenty-first century will repeat the last hundred years. But this is orthogonal to the principal focus of this volume: on the process of international diffusion itself. We have analyzed the spread of markets and democracy because of their global preeminence in the last decades of the twentieth century. The question for us is whether the diffusion processes we have analyzed in this book will continue to be of great consequence for economic, political, and social change, irrespective of the directions and manifestations of that change. Our answer to this question is an unequivocal "yes."

The future of international diffusion

At its core, the process of globalization concerns the more widespread and more rapid movement across national boundaries not of only capital, goods, and services but also of ideas, information, and people. In recent decades, the tendency has been to associate this free movement with liberalization. But it is clear that free movement can fuel anti-liberalism as well. The increasingly global phenomena of protests against the international economic institutions as well as international terrorism have been made possible by cell phones, the Internet, and the freer movement of people – the other face of the globalization the protesters and terrorists have been mobilized against.

Irrespective of whether one considers the trend toward ever freer global movement an unalloyed good or not, it is increasingly clear that it is very difficult, if not impossible, for governments to reverse it – and in particular to counteract through policy the technological innovations that have shrunk time and space. Government regulations on different types of capital flows tend only to stimulate more creativity in the markets regarding how to use derivatives and other innovative transactions to circumvent them. Efforts by China to close off access to the Internet, much like American efforts to curb offshore gambling and pornography, tend to be more symbolic than effective. Smuggling of people and products lessen the effects of formal barriers to migration and trade.

The result is a smaller and more connected world in which the two diffusion mechanisms that this volume has shown to be most prominent in the recent past – economic competition and social emulation – will likely become more powerful, not less. The greater the opportunities executives have to shop around the globe for investment and production venues, the more national governments will have to pay attention to what others are doing in the competition for business. The denser person-to-person networks of communication become, not only face-to-face but using the dizzying array of new communications technologies, the more likely it is that policy ideas – liberal, illiberal, or having nothing to do with liberalism – will flow across political boundaries.

Notwithstanding post-9/11 US foreign policy in Afghanistan and Iran, we do not expect coercion to become a more prominent mechanism for diffusion because it seems out of step with our world, characterized by a mosaic of decentralized networks beyond the control of public officials. In contrast, hegemonic ideas may continue to flow via experts and advocates around the world. But ideas are theorized, touted, and legitimated; they are not well enforced at gunpoint. They seem not even to be enforceable at loan-point by the IMF. Indeed, coercive efforts tend to spawn effective resistance, much as we have seen since the mid-1990s with respect to the rise of both anti-globalization and Islamic extremism.

There is also little reason to believe that well-informed learning will become more widespread. The studies in this volume have shown that it was very difficult for governments clearly to discern cause and effect from liberal policy experiments in other countries in the last decades of the twentieth century. The task will only become more complicated in the future as the world in which policies operate becomes ever more complex and multidimensional. This raises the danger that undesirable trends will spread in the future by processes of more or less "unreasoned" mimicry without a real performance check, either in response to what economic competitors are doing or because of the practices among self-identified peer nations.

Even if the world deviates from its liberal trajectory and into trends such as nationalism, expropriation, protection, and authoritarianism, diffusion would likely play a pivotal role. Coercion might be more prominent in any such wave than was the case for liberalism because overt uses of force have historically been more common in establishing authoritarian regimes than democratic ones. Protection provides short-term "competitive" advantages for some producers. Governments might learn that certain forms of expropriation are tolerated by investors, and retreat from their increasingly liberal treatment of foreign direct investment.

Certainly, illiberal policies can and may diffuse in the future, as they have in the past. Many people believe that the nature of humanity's interconnectedness is inherently biased in favor of liberalism. While we hope from a normative standpoint that this is the case at least for political liberalism, from the positive perspective as social scientists we cannot rule out the possibility of resurgent illiberalism. Either way, we believe that the diffusion mechanisms we have identified in this volume will play critical roles in the future of global policy and political change.

Conclusion

Let us conclude by underlining two lessons learned from this volume regarding core issues in the contemporary social sciences. First, a theoretical duality that sets up an exclusive juxtaposition of material and ideational explanations is largely passé. Almost all of the studies in this volume have emphasized that material incentives can and do coexist with less rational, more subjective influences on decision making. Governments may decide to sign a women's rights treaty because of the social pressures emanating from UN conferences *and* to access development assistance; they may privatize to realize competitive advantages over their trade partners *and* because Chicago-trained economists influence policymaking; they may liberalize the capital account because "it works" *and* to curry favor with investors by accelerating the pace of liberalization. Governments clearly respond to multiple stimuli and for different reasions, both material and otherwise.

Second, national governments do not operate in splendid isolation from each other. It is much easier to do social science research assuming governments are independent actors reacting to exogenous "constraints" inside and outside their borders. But this volume has shown that this independence assumption is violated over and over again, and that only by building models of interdependent decision making among governments can we understand some of the most important phenomena of our time.

Domestic explanations are only a part – and in some cases, a small part – of the explanation for the spread of liberal policies this past half century. Closed-polity models that focus exclusively on domestic institutions, coalitions, and interests are therefore missing much of the action, even if they consider these variables as filters on an external environment characterized by common exogenous shocks. Statistically, proceeding on the basis of domestic politics alone or "common stimulus, mediated response" models risks introducing massive omitted variable bias into our understandings of policy. The risk is that by making the apparently innocuous simplifying assumption of countries as independent actors, we will greatly misunderstand how the world really works. By examining the diffusion mechanisms that have facilitated the spread of liberalization in the twentieth century, these chapters have contributed to a more comprehensive understanding not only of the policies that have contributed to our more thoroughly globalized world but also to the underlying interdependence of the international system.

References

Fukuyama, Francis. 1992. *The End of History and the Last Man*. New York: Free Press.

Gruber, Lloyd. 2001. *Ruling the World*. Princeton: Princeton University Press.

Keohane, Robert M. and Helen V. Milner, eds. 1996. *Internationalization and Domestic Politics*. New York: Cambridge University Press.

Lipset, Seymour M. 1959. *Political Man*. Garden City: Doubleday.

Shonfield, Andrew. 1965. *Modern Capitalism*. London: Oxford University Press.

Index

Note: Page numbers in *italics* refer to figures and tables.